MCAT

SCIENCE
REVIEW

MCAT

SCIENCE REVIEW

**Total Science Preparation
for the Medical College Admission Test**

IRVIN W. KATZ, M.Ed.
with
JOSE P. IRIARTE, M.A.T.

ARCO
New York   London   Toronto
Sydney   Tokyo   Singapore

ARCO

Simon & Schuster, Inc.
15 Columbus Circle
New York, NY 10023

DISTRIBUTED BY PRENTICE HALL TRADE SALES

Manufactured in the United States of America
4   5   6   7   8   9   10

Library of Congress Cataloging in Publication Data

Katz, Irvin W.
    MCAT science review.

    1. Medical colleges—United States—Entrance exami-
nations—Study guides. I. Iriarte, Jose P. II. Title.
[DNLM: 1. Medicine—Examination questions. W 18 K19m]
R838.5.K37   1983   610'.76   83-11948
ISBN 0-668-05745-9 (pbk.)

Printed in the United States of America

Contents

Acknowledgments

The authors acknowledge with deep gratitude the contributions made to this volume by Dr. Anthony J. Pappas, Dr. Robert L. Pope, Dr. Mary Powell, Dr. Bill Bordeaux, Mr. Joe Ackner, Mr. Mel Silver, Mr. Roy Elkin, and Mrs. Esther Shrago.

MCAT
SCIENCE
REVIEW

Introduction

The new MCAT was designed to evaluate the prospective medical student's knowledge and problem-solving skills in biology, chemistry, and physics, and to assess the student's reading comprehension and quantitative skills. The new MCAT was developed under the direction of the Association of American Medical Colleges (AAMC) in an attempt to measure the knowledge and skills identified as particularly relevant to the content of medical school curricula and the practice of medicine. The new MCAT was first administered in the spring of 1977.

The test consists of 4 sections:

1. *Science Knowledge section*. This section is divided into three subsections (biology, chemistry, and physics) with a total of 125 multiple-choice questions.

2. *Science Problems section*. This section consists of 22 sets. Each set consists of a problem which represents a medically relevant situation and three related multiple-choice questions. Each problem in this section is developed around two or more scientific concepts or principles and may involve more than one of the three scientific disciplines.

3. *Skills Analysis: Reading section*. This section consists of sets, each containing a passage with information in a prose format followed by several questions based upon the information given. This section contains a total of 68 questions.

4. *Skills Analysis: Quantitative section*. This section is similar to the Reading section, but the information is presented in a quantitative format.

The following schedule should give you an idea of the time devoted to each area of the new MCAT.

			questions	time
MORNING	Science Knowledge		125	135 min.
	Biology	consecutive subsections	(38)	(25 min.)
	Chemistry		(49)	(60 min.)
	Physics		(38)	(50 min.)
	Break			10 min.
	Science Problems		66	85 min.
	Lunch break			60 min.
AFTERNOON	Skills Analysis: Reading		68	85 min.
	Break			10 min.
	Skills Analysis: Quantitative		68	85 min.

1

This book has been written to help students to prepare to take the new MCAT. Chapters Four through Seven review the topics covered in the new MCAT: biology, inorganic chemistry, organic chemistry, and physics. Each of the four chapters also contains practice questions in each area of study. The last chapter (Chapter Eight) is a sample MCAT. In order to prepare yourself to take the new MCAT, you should not only take the practice tests and the sample exam but should also become thoroughly familiar with the topics covered in the science reviews, referring to textbooks for coverage of topics considered especially difficult.

There are six separate scores reported for this test:

1. Biology Knowledge + Biology Problems = Biology Score
2. Chemistry Knowledge + Chemistry Problems = Chemistry Score
3. Physics Knowledge + Physics Problems = Physics Score
4. Science Problems Score = Biology Problems + Chemistry Problems + Physics Problems
5. Skills Analysis: Reading
6. Skills Analysis: Quantitative

Each score is reported on a scale from 1 (lowest) to 15 (highest). The mean score tends to be about 8.0 with an approximate standard deviation of 2.5. A table for interpreting standard scores is provided with each score report from the American College Testing Program.

While each medical school sets its own requirements, a standard score of 10 to 12 is considered quite acceptable, while a standard score lower than 8 indicates that additional preparation is needed in that area. If additional preparation is needed in a particular area, the questions missed in the practice tests can be used as a guide to those areas which most need review.

The complete contents of a one-year course in each of the disciplines involved cannot be covered in a work of this scope. What we have done in this book is to present subject reviews and practice questions to help you familiarize yourself with the topics covered in the new MCAT and with the question format. Hopefully, this will enable you to obtain the best possible score on the new MCAT.

CHAPTER ONE

The New MCAT

Purpose of This Book

This *MCAT Science Review* has a very specific purpose and serves a very distinct population. Certain assumptions have been made by the authors, and some difficult choices have been made so that this book will be more useful to our targeted population.

We have assumed that a person using this book contemplates taking the MCAT in the foreseeable future. This volume will serve to channel your review. It also can be useful in the early stages of your undergraduate premed curriculum by pointing out those areas which will be covered in the MCAT. Thus, the premed student will have an overview of those areas of current course work necessary for the new MCAT.

The book concentrates on those areas in the sciences which are covered by the new MCAT. A complete listing of these areas can be found in the *New MCAT Student Manual*, which is published by the Association of American Medical Colleges and is available from them. It is also available in most college book-stores. Our coverage of topics follows the outline indicated in that publication, although the lettering has been changed for increased clarity.

Since this volume does not attempt to review the entire biology, chemistry, and physics curricula, it cannot and should not be used as a review book for your courses. For this purpose, one of the standard review books would be far more useful. Moreover, it would be impossible for the authors in a single volume to completely cover any topic in the sciences in the depth required by a college-level course. Therefore, it is not the purpose of this book to serve as a substitute for the completion of courses in the various disciplines required for a thorough premedical preparation.

It should also be noted that this volume does not attempt to review the Skills Analysis sections of the MCAT. That review can be better accomplished by using a standard test preparation review book. However, the sample MCAT offered in this book is a complete exam, including the Math and Verbal Skills Analysis sections.

Structure and Use of This Volume

The structure of this book follows a very simple format. After several introductory sections covering some pertinent information about the new MCAT, medical school admissions, and test-taking strategy and tactics, four chapters of review in biology, inorganic chemistry, organic chemistry, and physics are presented. Each chapter has a practice test following the review, with an answer key appended. Finally, a sample MCAT is presented with an answer key.

While the authors recognize that every student follows his or her individual pattern in preparing for an exam, this book is designed in a specific manner to obtain maximum benefits from its use. This can be done in one of two ways.

Perhaps the most useful way to use this volume is to review one topic at a time. As you review each topic, ask yourself the following questions: Do I completely understand what this topic covers? Do I know the meaning of every word used in this section? Can I work out quantitative questions concerning this topic? If you are able to answer all of the above questions affirmatively, you probably don't need to supplement your review with additional work. However, if you cannot answer "yes" to all the above questions, then you need a more intensive review of the topic. For this purpose, a standard review book of the discipline involved would be helpful, or reference to the original textbook you used in college. Many students find it effective to study for the MCAT in small groups. If you use this method, then a member of the group who is particularly knowledgeable in one area of study can help you to refresh your knowledge in that area. You, in turn, can be helpful to the others in the group when they encounter areas in which they are weak.

Once you have completed a review of one discipline in the above manner, then you are ready to take the practice test at the end of that chapter. Your results on this test will indicate which areas of knowledge still need to be reviewed. These weak areas should be gone over meticulously, since they present problems to you. If you find that some specific areas are completely unfamiliar to you, then on the actual MCAT itself you should make an educated guess on questions in those specific areas and not spend much time trying to puzzle through such questions.

A second method of review (less desirable, in our opinion) is to attempt the practice test offered at the end of each chapter *before* studying the material. It is important that you *do not guess* at any of the answers in using this method. Answer only those questions about which you are sure. Then check your answers with the answer key. Those answers which are correct represent areas about which you know enough, so they should have a lower priority in your review schedule. Those questions which you have omitted or which you have answered incorrectly represent areas which need further review. You then have an idea of those sections of our review book which need the most emphasis. If, after reviewing those sections, you are still having difficulty, then you should use one or more of the methods described above to reinforce your knowledge. This type of review might be necessary in situations where not enough time is available for complete review of all areas covered on the MCAT.

While it is not always possible to plan and execute an ideal review schedule, a haphazard approach will seldom yield satisfactory results. Therefore, we offer the following suggestions in helping you to plan your study approach to this important examination.

1. Select a suitable location for your study sessions. It is important that you be psychologically and emotionally prepared when you study. You should select a quiet, uncluttered place where you will be undisturbed. If possible, this should be a place that you do not use for any other purpose. If you usually work in your room, find another quiet spot for this review. You must be aware that when you are in your "study place," you are there to study for the MCAT and *only* for the MCAT.

2. Select a time of day for your study sessions. We each work on our own individual biological clock. You should know by this time in your educational career when you obtain the maximum effectiveness from your study time.

3. Determine the length of time for each study session. Here, too, you should know yourself well enough to decide just how long you can obtain fruitful results for the time invested. Do not lengthen your sessions beyond this

optimum period. It is far more rewarding to start your review earlier and use more sessions than to feel, mistakenly, that more time per session will yield proportional results.

4. Set a reasonable goal for each review session. Do not alter this goal. If you really understand the subject before the allotted time has expired, either terminate your study or review the area in more detail, but do not begin another area. If you find that you have not allotted enough time to review a particular subject area, do not extend the time of the session, except for a minute or two. Rather, schedule an additional session in this area. In making up your master study schedule, it is, therefore, important that you leave some sessions unscheduled in order to provide time for these extra sessions.

5. It is important that you devise a master study schedule prior to beginning your review. This can be done by surveying the material to be covered and deciding approximately how much time you need for each review area. Then, by adding up these allocations, obtain the total time needed for study. If you then divide this total time by your optimum session time, you will have a rough idea of how many review sessions you will need. For example, if you determine that you will need 100 hours to review, and you know that your optimum review time per session is two hours, then you can estimate that you will need 50 review sessions. Targets should be established for each session as indicated above, with a few extra sessions to cover unforeseen problems. You will then need to determine how often you wish to study. If you plan three study sessions per week of two hours each, you are going to study six hours per week. If a total of 100 hours is required, then you should start your review at least four months before the exam.

What Is the New MCAT?

The new MCAT is an examination offered by the Association of American Medical Colleges. It replaces the old MCAT, which had been offered prior to April 1977. Both examinations were designed to help medical schools in deciding which applicants should be offered admission. Research determined that the old exam had not effectively predicted which students would be successful in pursuing their studies in medical school and had not been a satisfactory tool for admissions committees. The ineffectiveness of the old MCAT stemmed from its failure to emphasize the science skills areas. Since these areas form the greater part of the first and second year curricula in medical schools, otherwise bright students were failing their courses because of a lack of preparation in the basic sciences. To remedy this deficiency, the new MCAT was developed. Although definitive studies have not yet been completed, preliminary evidence indicates that the new MCAT is doing a much better job in discriminating between successful and unsuccessful medical school students than did the old exam.

When Is the New MCAT Offered?

The new MCAT is offered both in the fall and spring on a Saturday, usually in early April and late September or early October. (Dates and sites are available on Sundays for those applicants whose religious convictions preclude their taking the test on Saturday, or who have other valid reasons for not being able to take the exam on Saturday.) There are no make-up tests available. Special testing accommodations are possible for handicapped or disabled candidates. These arrangements must be made with the test administrator, the American College Testing Program (ACT).

All students must register with ACT in order to sit for the MCAT. Registration forms are available on your college campus, or can be obtained by writing directly to ACT at the following address:

> MCAT Registration
> The American College Testing Program
> P.O. Box 414
> Iowa City, Iowa 52243

At this writing, the fee for registration is $45.00. There is an extra fee of $5.00 for Sunday or foreign registration. The MCAT is offered in many cities in Canada and in at least 50 foreign countries. Registration deadlines are usually five weeks prior to the exam, and may be longer for special or foreign registrations.

When Should Applicants Take the New MCAT?

There are many considerations involved in the decision as to when and how often to take the MCAT. First, let us examine what might be called the typical student.

This student is pursuing a four-year undergraduate program as a premedical student. He or she may or may not be majoring in one of the sciences, but will have taken a number of courses in various science and math areas. Normally, this student should first take the MCAT in the spring of junior year, and then repeat the exam (if necessary) in the fall of senior year. This course of action is recommended only if the student has already completed basic courses in physics, chemistry, organic chemistry, and biology, and has a current and thorough knowledge of precalculus mathematics. Students not thoroughly grounded in the basic sciences and math might do well to defer taking the MCAT until they have acquired such knowledge. It does not help an applicant's chances for admission if he obtains a very low score on the MCAT, even if he manages to improve that score subsequently. Whether you are ready to take the exam will become evident after you have completed the review course offered in this volume and have taken the sample MCAT at the end of the book. As a bench mark, you should be able to obtain a score of at least 50% on the exam *exclusive* of any answers that might have been guesses. It may well be that you will do extremely well on your first attempt at the MCAT. It would then seem inappropriate to take the exam again, with the ever-present chance that your score may decrease.

Students involved in a three-year baccalaureate program and seeking medical school admission must necessarily take their MCAT one year in advance of other students. This means taking the exam for the first time in the spring of their second college year, a formidable prospect in view of the demanding level of science knowledge required.

Other applicants who are not now in school or who are enrolled in foreign schools as undergraduates, have special considerations in deciding when to take the exam. As a general rule, these students should take the exam in the spring approximately 18 months prior to their preferred medical school admission. This may seem to be very early, but since the normal application deadline for medical schools is about November 1 of the year prior to admission, the spring date is the last one which will give medical school admissions committees sufficient time to make a considered judgment of an application. Submission of exam results from the September administration might be delayed, lost, or invalidated, and thus might not be available for consideration before the deadline.

What Is the Cost of the New MCAT?

The fee for the new MCAT, at present, is $45.00 for candidates in the United States, Canada, and Puerto Rico, and $50.00 for administrations in foreign countries or on Sundays. At present, there is no waiver of fees for any reason.

Many of the medical schools in the United States and Canada are members of the American Medical College Application Service (AMCAS). When you apply to any of these schools, you must use a standard application form. These forms are available in your premedical advisor's office. Results of the MCAT are *automatically* sent to these schools, and score reports should not be sent to any of the schools which are members of AMCAS.

Other medical schools are not members of AMCAS. These schools must be listed on the application form in order for a score report to be forwarded to them. Up to six of these non-AMCAS school reports may be ordered without an additional charge. If you need more than six, there is an additional charge. A copy is also sent to the test-taker.

In addition, there are separate instructions in the new MCAT application booklet for special situations such as applications to schools of podiatry and osteopathy. You must read this booklet thoroughly and follow its instructions to the letter. Following directions properly is a prerequisite for success in medicine, and improper procedure in the early stages of the application process can prejudice your chances for admission.

How Does AMCAS Operate?

The Association of American Medical Colleges cooperates with admission offices of various medical schools in order to simplify the application process. The result of this cooperation is AMCAS. AMCAS does not make admission decisions. It merely collects, collates, and organizes pertinent admissions material and forwards this material to its member medical schools. Thus, initially you must complete only *one* application for *all* AMCAS schools to which you apply. AMCAS does all the rest and submits a copy of the completed application and transcripts to *each* AMCAS school on your list. This service is available only to beginning medical students who apply on a regular basis. The earliest one may submit a completed application to AMCAS is June 15 of the year prior to requested admission. The latest date varies from school to school. After this first stage of the application process, if a medical school which has received and reviewed your AMCAS application is interested in having you continue the application process, it will send its own additional application for you to complete.

What Does AMCAS Cost?

AMCAS charges a fee for the service it renders. The fee for AMCAS service to one school is $30, plus $12 for each additional school. There is also a $12 fee for service to a school after the original request has been submitted to AMCAS. Applicants who are financially unable to pay the above fees may request a fee waiver from AMCAS.

You should survey the list of medical schools in the MCAT application materials to see which schools are members of AMCAS and which are not. Membership in AMCAS is unrelated to the quality of a medical school. Every medical school not in AMCAS has its own application process and you must complete a separate application and submit a separate transcript to each non-AMCAS school.

CHAPTER TWO

Some Thoughts on Medical School Admissions

The writers of this book have been involved in medical school admissions counseling since 1962. During this period, we have developed certain definite impressions which may be of use. It must be emphasized that the admission process is not a computerized, mechanical process. Thus, any guidelines that we offer must be considered in the light of common sense, which will apply in every individual case. Fashions come and go in medical school admissions just as in other fields, and what might be true today may not be true tomorrow. However, we must proceed with the best information that is available to us at the present time. With the above caveats in mind, let us proceed to some generalized statements.

The first general statement that must be made is that gaining admission to medical school is a long shot. That is, more applicants to medical schools are rejected than accepted. During the past ten years, the percentage of accepted applicants has *never* been over 50%. Of course, within certain categories the percentages have been higher. That is, students with A averages and scores of 12 or better on the MCAT have an acceptance above 50%. Conversely students with C averages and scores below 7 on the MCAT have an acceptance ratio of almost zero.

What does this mean for *average* medical school applicants? It means that they must consider alternative courses of activity at the same time that they are pursuing medical school admission. They must plan what they intend to do "if" they are not accepted into medical school. This might involve application to an alternative graduate level school, a decision to attend a foreign medical school, or an apprenticeship in the family business. Whatever it might be, the alternative solution should be pursued at the same time that you are applying to medical school. It should not be delayed until you learn whether you have been accepted into medical school. Not waiting has a double purpose. It allows you to proceed with your career or education without a lapse of time, and it cushions the psychological trauma which often accompanies rejection by several medical schools.

What about reapplying? Statistics show that your chances of being accepted after having been rejected are quite small unless there is a major change in your record. Of course, one of the major changes that can be made is to improve your MCAT score. So, reapplication is one of the alternatives that should be considered. If you are still in school, you should devote your time to improving your grade point average, especially in the sciences and math; and you should start preparing to take the MCAT a second time.

If you are out of school, how you use your time is very important. Medical school admissions committees might reconsider an application if your recent work experience indicates some unusual accomplishment or talent.

If you intend to reapply, you should not register in another graduate program. Medical schools, as a general rule, consider these students not dedicated enough to medicine to persevere in the face of adversity.

If the above generalizations seem somewhat contradictory, they might well be. How can you pursue alternative courses of action if by so doing you reduce the chance of acceptance into medical school? There is, of course, an ultimate day of reckoning. However, by pursuing alternative choices, you can postpone the final decision until the latest possible moment, at which time, hopefully, you will have more data on which to base your decision. Without such alternate choices, you are left with feelings of defeat and hopelessness (which can ruin subsequent career choices in terms of satisfaction and internal psychological stability).

The next thought that should be considered in the process of medical school admission is the relevance of undergraduate preparation. For many students, this preparation is more or less mandated if their undergraduate institution has a premedical program. This planned program reduces the number of options that a student has and turns out a group of premed majors who differ very little in their undergraduate preparations. This will be good for those students who do very well in this program, since they will rank high in the group and should be favored by medical school admissions committees, all other factors being equal.

However, for those students whose colleges do not have a formal premed program, or for those students who feel that they will not emerge in a superior position in a formal premed program, there are several factors which should be considered in their choice of majors and courses.

The first factor is that the *quality* of undergraduate preparation is more important than the *quantity*. Thus, if we examine the number of courses that *most* medical schools *require* for admissions, we come up with a very small list: biology, inorganic chemistry, organic chemistry, physics, and English. However, fewer than 5% of applicants with C averages are admitted to medical schools, regardless of the difficulty and depth of their preparation. Furthermore, if we attempt to relate medical school admissions to undergraduate majors, we find that the second highest percentage of acceptances belongs to majors in religion, followed by majors in biochemistry and exceeded only by majors in biomedical engineering (which, at the moment, is a "hot" program in premedical education).

Therefore, provided that you receive good grades in the basic science courses, and have taken enough of them to do well on the MCAT, the rest of the undergraduate curriculum should be widely diversified. Medical schools know that budding physicians will have little opportunity to broaden their cultural horizons once they begin their medical education. They are also aware of the increasing need for physicians to be more than just storehouses of medical information: they must relate to their patients on a human basis and they must have ample cultural and physical pursuits in nonmedical areas so that they can refresh and preserve themselves for the rigorous demands which will be made upon them during their medical careers.

The next factor that is important in determining medical school admissions is that of *motivation*. Medical admissions committees know that medicine is one of the professions to which the largest number of undergraduate students aspire. They are also aware that the motivations for becoming a physician come from many sources. These include parental pride, monetary rewards, scholastic excellence, desire to please parents, and many other sources which do not represent the main motivational factors considered important by medical school admissions committees.

Perhaps the primary motivational factors considered by medical school admissions committees are the answers to certain questions: Why do you want to work with sick people as your life work? How have you demonstrated your desire to be a physician during the last few years? In what manner will you demonstrate a desire to help humanity once you have become a physician? Are you willing to devote the next six to seven years to your medical preparation, putting aside all other considerations? The key factor in answering such motivational questions is the record you have established in the years prior to your medical school application. Admissions committees know that applicants are aware of the "correct" answers to their questions. Therefore, they are mainly concerned with demonstrated examples of motivation such as your experience in a health care facility during summers; research projects you have completed in the medical or science areas; volunteer work in your local hospital or health care facility; community involvement in fund raising for medically oriented purposes such as the Heart Fund, Cancer Fund, etc.; participation in drug, alcohol, or antismoking education programs, etc. It is hardly an exaggeration to say that applicants with fine academic records and good MCAT scores will find medical school admission difficult if they do not offer evidence of some type of involvement with others in a helping capacity. An informative discussion of all aspects of medical school admissions is offered in a publication of the Association of American Medical Colleges called "Medical School Admission Requirements," which is available from the Association, and should also be available in your college bookstore.

It should be re-emphasized that admission to medical school is not a mechanical process. Recommendations, age, sex, minority status, and a host of other factors influence the final decision. Every year, students are admitted to a wide range of medical schools with an equally wide range of undergraduate records, MCAT scores, and recommendations. The bottom line is to do the best you can, and not to prejudge yourself. If you want to be a physician, then make your best effort. Perhaps the worst thing that could happen is for you to look back later in life and wonder whether you really could have made it if you had given it your best shot.

CHAPTER THREE

Strategy and Tactics in Taking the MCAT

We would like to be able to say that a thorough review of the material in this volume will guarantee an excellent result on the MCAT. However, we recognize that, in addition to the intellectual ability of the student to absorb the facts and concepts presented, the strategy and tactics involved in the actual test-taking process have much to do with the final results. That is, once you have learned all the material you can, there are other factors which will influence the results. In this chapter we discuss some of these factors and indicate some approaches that have produced excellent results for an entire generation of test-takers.

Some Thoughts on Test Taking

Most people do not realize that taking a test really involves taking *two* tests. The first evaluates the test taker's knowledge of the material on the test. Thus, a test of mathematics requires knowledge of the subject and also might require application of that knowledge to new situations.

The second test, which is much less understood, evaluates the individual's knowledge of test-taking skills. Every test involves a certain rationale or logic in its planning: the nature of the questions involved, the objectives of the test, the scoring, and a host of other variables that the test maker uses, either consciously or unconsciously (intuitively), in constructing the test. Most people are not aware of, or choose to ignore, these factors, and, consequently, do not perform as well on this second test as they may on the first. In this section we will discuss test-taking skills (the "second test") in order to help you obtain maximum results.

MENTAL APPROACH

Since the test maker is usually not a psychologist or psychiatrist, he is not concerned with the mental attitude of the test taker. He assumes that the test taker comes to the test with the knowledge required *and* the ability to demonstrate it on the examination. He also assumes that the test taker is prepared in both respects.

What is the desired attitude toward a test? While acknowledging that it differs from person to person, we have found that some general observations apply to everyone.

1. If you have prepared to the best of your ability, you must bring a positive attitude to the test. That does not mean that you inflate your expectations unrealistically. It means that you recognize you have done all that you can to prepare, and that you will accept whatever results may follow from that preparation.

2. You should recognize that you are not perfect and are going to miss some questions. No one can ascertain in advance just which questions they are. It is important that you do not dwell on these questions, but that you concentrate on the areas of the test where you have a reasonable chance of being successful.

3. Learn how to deal with test anxiety. Much study has been devoted to test anxiety, and to its relationship with anxiety in general. Test anxiety can be divided into two areas—pretest and during-test.

A. *Pretest anxiety* is usually proportional to the importance of the test and the amount and quality of test preparation. The more important the test, the higher the level of anxiety. The better the preparation, the lower the level of anxiety. Thus we see that there are two ways to control pretest anxiety.

1. Since anxiety is proportional to test importance, an effort must be made to arrive at a *realistic* evaluation of the test's significance. There is no doubt that the MCAT is important, but is it *that* important? Can you not retake it? Can you not apply to a less competitive school if your scores are not high enough? Do you really want to "psych" yourself out of doing well by exaggerating the effect of the test on your life? Perhaps a career in medicine is not for you after all? Does that mean your life will be over? Is there no other way you could be a happy and productive member of society?

2. Since anxiety is inversely proportional to the amount and quality of test preparation, its reduction must involve a good program of preparation. If you know you are ready for the exam, you will help to keep your anxiety at a reasonable level. This book is designed to help accomplish this task.

Recognize that a *reasonable* amount of test anxiety is important. "Reasonable" means enough to get all the juices flowing but not enough to paralyze the brain.

B. *During-test anxiety* usually stems from an inability to answer questions successfully, or from a recognition that questions are not being answered rapidly enough to complete the test. This type of anxiety can usually be handled by using one or more of the following techniques.

1. Answer the easy questions first. This relieves both causes of during-test anxiety.

2. If you encounter a series of questions that are foreign to you, or you feel yourself getting tired or foggy, take a break—a timed break—for exactly one minute. Try to relax during this period, and eat a piece of candy or some other high-carbohydrate food. Think of something pleasant and relaxing. You will be surprised at the better attitude you have when you return to the test.

3. Don't be afraid to guess, and then don't second-guess yourself. Self-doubt encourages anxiety and vice-versa. Once you have made your best effort at a question, forget about it unless you remember some important item of information or learn the answer from another question.

4. However you do it, learn to relax during the rest periods between sections of the exam. Whether it be through deep breathing, isometrics, or bio-feedback, use this time to get yourself back on track. Forget about the previous sections and concentrate on what lies ahead. What is done is done. Now on to the next challenge!

PHYSICAL APPROACH

"A sound mind in a sound body." This dictum has been with us since the ancient Greeks. While preparing for exams certainly requires preparing the mind, students too often neglect the requirement of a healthy body for proper test preparation.

A well-prepared body (of which the brain is an essential part) requires a number of steps.

1. Treat your body kindly as you prepare for an exam. Do not overtire it by keeping late hours or not getting enough sleep. Get enough exercise during your study regimen.

2. Get to know the length of your optimum study period. This varies from person to person, but everyone has a point at which the return on added preparation is quite minor compared with the additional expenditure of time and effort. Your study schedule should reflect your optimum study time. Thus, some people can study for two or more hours continuously, while others learn more if they schedule several half-hour sessions with breaks in between.

3. When you begin your study session, start with the most difficult areas. You will learn more when you are fresh. Do not yield to the natural tendency to put off the most difficult subjects until last. Chances are that you will not give these areas the necessary attention.

4. Conversely, do not use up an excessive amount of your study time on one item or area. If, after a reasonable effort, you still do not understand, go to someone else for help or recognize that you are going to be deficient in this area and write it off.

5. The night before a test should be devoted to relaxation. This is especially true if you have devoted days or weeks to preparing for the exam. That is not to say that you should stay up all night having fun; it means doing something that takes your mind off the exam.

6. Get a good night's sleep before the exam. Wake up early and give yourself plenty of time to get to the exam site. Lay out all the materials you will need the night before so you will not have to think about them the morning of the exam. Eat a good breakfast with some fruit juice and some protein. Take some snacks or candy with you to the exam to use when you need them.

7. This may be a good time (just before leaving) to review a *few* key terms such as formulas or definitions that you have had difficulty remembering. No heavy reviewing will pay off, since it will tend to confuse you.

8. When you arrive at the test site, pick out the best seat possible and try to relax. This is *not* a good time to discuss the exam with your friends. Doing so will only raise your anxiety level and dilute your concentration.

DURING THE EXAM

1. Make sure that you listen carefully to all directions given by the proctor. Make equally certain that you read the directions on the test carefully.

2. If you have any questions about the directions or the test questions themselves, do not be afraid to ask for help. You may not have your question answered, but you should ask anyway.

3. You should have developed a test strategy before starting the exam. Do not change it unless the exam differs radically from the format you expected. We offer some suggestions in this volume for a test strategy. Your strategy may differ. The important point is to have *some* well-thought-out strategy and to stay with it throughout the exam.

4. You should have a method for gauging your use of time. By using your watch properly, you can see if you are ahead of your optimum pace, right on it, or behind. According to your pace, you may have to make decisions about which questions to guess on, and which questions you are able to devote time to answering.

5. Don't forget to use the techniques described in the section on during-test anxiety if you feel the test getting away from you. The time spent in regrouping in this manner will pay off in final results.

Let us examine the various sections of the MCAT to see how much time should be allotted to each question.

Biology	38 questions	25 minutes
Chemistry	49 questions	60 minutes
Physics	38 questions	50 minutes
Science Problems	66 questions	85 minutes
Reading	68 questions	85 minutes
Quantitative	68 questions	85 minutes

We can see that, with the exception of the Biology section, all the sections can be covered at a pace of about one question per minute, which leaves an ample allowance for checking over answers at the end to see that they are in the right place, and to discover any omissions or miscalculations you may have made. The pace for the Biology section, with the same allowance for checking answers, is about two questions per minute. This suggests that there will be very little calculation in the Biology section.

SCIENCE KNOWLEDGE

This section includes, for the most part, multiple-choice questions that require the application of a principle or point of knowledge included in the required topics outlined in the *New MCAT Student Manual*. Since there is no penalty for guessing, these questions should all be answered. We suggest that you answer the questions in order the first time through, and indicate to yourself those questions to which you wish to return after you have completed the section. That is, you will encounter three types of questions in this section: those you immediately know; those which you think you know, or at least have some idea about; and those about which you have no idea at all. Of course, you will answer the first type immediately. And you should *guess* at the third type immediately (using the hints about guessing that we will give you later) since you are not likely to get any good ideas about the correct answer no matter how many times you go over the question (and you would be taking away time from the remaining type of question). Those that remain are the ones that should be marked in the test booklet so that you can return to them after the first time through. Perhaps you will remember some fact that will help you choose an answer. Remember, since the MCAT is a multiple-choice test, you can reduce the odds against you if you can eliminate one or more of the wrong answers, even if you are not completely sure about the correct one. Again we emphasize that *there is no penalty for guessing*. If you omit any answers, you are penalizing yourself vis-a-vis the other test-takers, for they will surely get correct answers on some of their guesses, and thus wind up with a relatively better score than you will.

Going through the questions this way will almost certainly put you ahead of the pace required for completion of the section, and give you the feeling of leisurely pursuing the borderline questions without any feeling of urgency.

SCIENCE PROBLEMS

This section includes, for most of the questions, a short descriptive paragraph or reading passage, followed by several questions. These questions are complex and require a full understanding of the scientific principles involved as well as an ability to synthesize knowledge from one or more areas into a new paradigm or configuration.

We suggest handling this material in the following fashion.

1. Since all questions within each section have the same value, it is important to tackle first those areas which are your strong points. If, after reading the descriptive material, you realize that you know very little about the topic, go on to the next set of questions. Continue this process until you find a set that looks as if you will have little difficulty. Then, answer *all* the questions in that section, making certain that they are entered in the proper portion of the answer sheet.

2. After you have gone through the section for the first time, return to those sets which you omitted. It is now imperative that you handle these. Look at the answers to see if you can eliminate any of them. Some of the things to look for are:

    ● Two answers that are more or less contradictory will indicate that one of them is probably incorrect. To find out which one, study the rest of the answers. They will generally be grouped on one side of the two opposing answers. This side probably contains the correct answer, since test-makers do not usually indicate several answers that are way off target.

    ● Study the answers to see whether several of them differ mainly in the *degree* of response that they offer, rather than in the content. This should indicate that one of those answers is the correct choice. Words such as "always," "never," "largest," "quickest," and other superlatives usually indicate incorrect answers.

    ● Study the other questions in the set to see if they hint at the correct answer to the question you are considering. Often, a follow-up question does not make any sense unless a particular answer to a previous question is the correct one.

3. After you have done all you can to handle these questions, and have marked your choices in the proper portion of the answer sheet, answer those questions that still remain. We have no particular advice on how best to do this. Most test-makers now recognize that test-taking tactics often involve selection of later choices rather than earlier ones, and have adjusted their answer keys accordingly. In other words, whenever a choice is reduced to two or more possible answers, the latter answer is a better choice than the earlier one (e.g., between A and C, C is a better guess). Perhaps the safest method is to indicate the same letter on all the guesses you make. In this way, you are almost certain to obtain the average number of correct answers on your guesses. Other methods could achieve better results if you are lucky, but could be equally disastrous if you are not.

READING

This section contains a number of short reading passages, concerned mainly with science-related material, followed by a number of multiple-choice questions. Many students who feel fairly confident about their ability to be successful with antonym or synonym identification questions, analogies, or sentence completions often feel less confident about reading comprehension questions on standardized tests. The time factor is often mentioned as the test-taker's greatest worry. "There are so many passages," is a typical complaint; "and I have to read them over and over again." Other test-takers feel anxious about the unfamiliarity of the material or about how to answer some of the usual questions which consistently appear in this section of the examination. One student moans, "Even though I read the paragraph three times and was sure I understood it, I still kept feeling unsure of which answer to select as the best title."

Suggestions are offered here to help you read more efficiently. While it is certainly true that there is no substitute for plenty of daily reading practice to increase your skills in understanding what you read, even the less ambitious reader may profit from following some of the general guidelines suggested below.

1. *Skim the passage* to learn the general subject being discussed. A science paragraph, for example, will generally be followed by factual questions, so references to tone, style, or point of view usually will not appear in connection with technical material.

2. *Then review the questions briefly* to alert yourself to any key words or phrases to be kept in mind when rereading the passage. At this time you may also be able to eliminate some of the choices which seem too broad (ones that use expressions like "always," "must," "without exception," etc.) or too narrow ("never," etc.).

3. *Then read the passage quickly but carefully*, keeping the questions in mind. When you find the appropriate phrase or sentence which answers one of the questions, read through the choices for that question and select the correct response. If you are unable to locate the answer immediately, proceed to another point. Remember, all questions on the MCAT are of equal value, so try to do the easiest questions first, in order to use your time most efficiently. You can return to the more difficult questions later if you have extra time.

Types of reading questions on the MCAT

While this volume cannot possibly cover every kind of reading question, there are certain types of questions which seem to be favored on the MCAT. Following is an analysis of each of these types with suggestions for coping with them. The ability to recognize each type of question will aid you in deciding how to proceed in order to arrive at the answer in the least possible time with the least possible chance of error.

1. *The Title Question.* This question may be expressed in a variety of ways, but it involves an overall understanding of the topic of the reading passage. *Read the first few sentences carefully.* Often the topic sentence, which will summarize the main idea, is placed at the beginning of the reading selection. Your job is to pinpoint the topic sentence without being distracted by supporting examples or by other digressions from the main idea. *You also should consider the conclusion of the passage.* Occasionally, an author will prefer to list supporting examples at the start of the passage, and then to summarize the topic at the conclusion. Rarely will you find the

summarizing sentence within the body of a passage. Avoid choosing an answer that is either too specific or too general. All the material in the selection should be covered in the title, but nothing beyond the selection.

2. *General Implication Question.* The implication question, which also can be phrased in a variety of ways, requires the test-taker to interpret or extrapolate the information contained in the passage, or to apply such information to a hypothetical situation or set of circumstances, and to determine the correct response. Such questions require you to use your own judgment in finding the answer. You will not find the answer to this type of question in the passage. Do not waste time looking for it. Reason through the information given in the passage and the question, and draw conclusions about what the author means and his orientation and direction. Then, answer the question from the point of view of the author of the passage, and *do not go beyond the implications of the passage.* Do not invent facts that are not mentioned in the passage to support an implication. Any projections that you make must be based on information mentioned in the selection. *Do not be misled by statements in the passage taken out of context or used inappropriately.* Just because one of the implication responses contains a quote from the passage does not necessarily make it correct. Such responses are often used to decoy the test-taker.

3. *Definition in Context Question.* This type of question requires you to know the definition of the word being used, as well as how it is used in the context of the selection. Often, its use in the passage differs from normal usage. This requires you to try to *substitute a word of your own* for the one used in the selection. Failing this, ask yourself whether the word in question has a positive or negative meaning. If this does not give the correct answer, it should at least eliminate some of the wrong responses, which is almost as good. *Look through the other questions.* Often, you will find that other questions will help you answer the definition in context question because they use the given word in a way that reveals the answer. *Read adjoining sentences in the passage.* These may help you define the given word by giving examples or synonyms of it. *Look for synonyms and antonyms in the response choices.* These are usually included as traps for the unwary. However, you can be reasonably sure that the answer is within *the group of sentences containing the antonyms or synonyms* and therefore can eliminate *other* answers.

4. *The Factual Question.* This type of question is a favorite on the MCAT. *It usually contains the phrase, "According to the passage . . ."* Do not be misled by a response choice that seems to be correct or one that you know is factually correct if it does not appear in the paragraph. The passage may, in fact, be a recitation of an author's belief that has been disproven or is at odds with the facts. Again, the answer to this type of question *must* appear in the passage or *must* be a synonymous rephrasing of information given in the paragraph. In order to work most efficiently on this type of question, first *zero in on the part of the passage to which the question refers.* This will usually be one or two sentences. *Check to make certain that the fact included in this portion of the passage is the fact that is called for by the question.* Carefully examine the form of the question. It may call for a fact that is *not* mentioned in the passage. This requires finding three or four facts that *are* mentioned. We suggest that you do this by process of elimination, starting from the last answer choice and working backward. As soon as you find that one of the facts requested is not in the paragraph, do not waste any more time on the question looking for the other facts. We suggest starting from the last response since the test-makers know that

you will have to proceed by process of elimination, and thus will try to make you use as much time as possible.

5. *The Specific Implication Question.* There are two types of specific implication questions on the MCAT. The first type asks you to decide whether certain statements are assumptions, confirmed conclusions, suggested conclusions, or conclusions without a basis in the selection. The second type asks whether the statement *is* or *is not* supported or contradicted by information in the paragraph.

   You should use a similar approach for both types of questions. First, the reading selection should be examined to determine whether the statement has a definite basis in the paragraph. If such a basis can be found, then you can assume that the conclusion is confirmed or the statement is supported. If this confirmation or support cannot be found, then the methods used for the general implication question should be employed. This should yield an answer as to whether the statement is a suggested conclusion, an assumption, or a contradiction. Remember, there must be some basis in the paragraph for drawing such suggested conclusions or assumptions. If there is no material in the selection that can support any of the above contentions, then we must assume that the conclusion in the statement is without basis or is neither supported nor contradicted by material in the reading selection. Thus, by following a logical process of elimination you are able to save considerable time and increase your chances for a correct answer. Remember, *there is no penalty for guessing.* There is a penalty, however, for taking too much time on one question. Therefore, if you cannot find support for a statement or any material that allows you to make a logical inference, then indicate the response which states that there is no relation to the paragraph, and go on to the next selection.

QUANTITATIVE

This section, for the most part, requires the test-taker to interpret a graph or chart. This interpretation includes categories similar to those found on the specific implication questions in the Reading section. After the chart or graph is presented, you must determine whether each of a series of questions is supported, contradicted, or neither supported nor contradicted by the information given in the chart or graph.

Generally, these questions do not involve any greater knowledge of math than simple arithmetic. They do, however, require a clear head and a logical pursuit of the correct answer. Here are some suggestions as to how to proceed with maximum effectiveness.

1. Determine the categories measured by the vertical and horizontal axes of the graph or chart. You cannot begin to answer the questions until these axes are recognized and understood.

2. Read the questions carefully. Be certain that you are attempting to *answer the question being asked.* These are very carefully phrased so that the careless or unwitting reader may be trapped into the wrong answer.

3. Do all your calculations on paper. You may save a few seconds, but estimates or calculation done in your head will often lead to incorrect answers. When you make your calculations on paper, you also give yourself the opportunity to check for incorrect answers if you have time at the end of the section.

4. Pace yourself. Check your rate of speed after 20 minutes. You should have completed 17 questions. Check again after another 20 minutes to see if you are maintaining your pace. Do not give more than the allotted time to any one question unless you are very close to getting the answer.

5. Some questions will seem deceptively simple. If you find a question that seems easy enough for a fourth-grader, you probably have overlooked some aspect of the question. Reread the question for subtleties and check to make sure that you are trying to answer the proper question.

CHAPTER FOUR

Biology Review

Molecular Biology

ENZYMES

An enzyme is a globular protein which acts as a catalyst (a substance which regulates the rate of a chemical reaction and itself remains unchanged). Enzymes are effective in very small quantities and a single enzyme molecule is able to catalyze thousands of reactions per second. Through their catalytic action, enzymes enable cells to carry out reactions that would otherwise require higher temperatures.

Enzyme activity is temperature- and pH-dependent. Generally speaking, increasing temperature increases the rate of enzyme activity. However, at high temperatures—over 60°C—the enzyme may be denatured by an irreversible alteration of its tertiary structure. There is an optimum pH for the activity of each enzyme and a significant deviation from that pH usually results in the inactivation of the enzyme (e.g., pepsin in the duodenum).

Enzymes work by providing a place (the *active site*) to which the reacting chemicals may adhere and on which the reaction may take place. The reacting chemicals are known as *substrate*.

Enzyme and substrate show a *lock-and-key* fit. The specific structure is due to the precise folding of the protein chain into a highly specific tertiary globular structure.

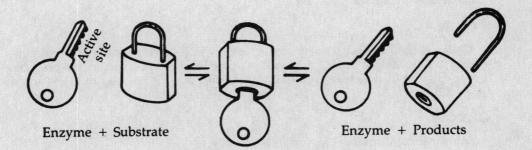

Enzyme + Substrate   Enzyme + Products

Enzyme-Substrate Complex

Enzymes characteristically work in sequence in a multistep process, with each step catalyzed by a different enzyme. One method of stopping the sequence by feedback inhibition is allosteric interaction, when one of the products in the series (usually the final product) combines with one of the enzymes (usually the first) at a site other than the active site. When the product, the effector, and the enzyme interact, the shape of the active site has been altered so that it is no longer functional, and the sequence stops. The effector fits in its site as precisely as the substrate fits the active site.

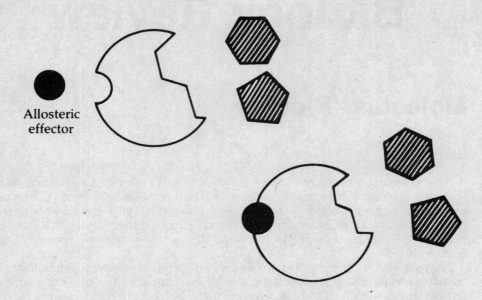

Allosteric effector

Many enzymes work in conjunction with other compounds known as *coenzymes*. Most coenzymes are vitamins, contain vitamins, or have vitamins as their precursors. Coenzymes function as carrier or acceptor molecules for substrates.

There is a generally accepted view that genes act by influencing enzyme production: *"one gene—one enzyme."* Since not all proteins are enzymes (i.e., structural proteins), this hypothesis has been expanded to *"one gene—one polypeptide chain."*

BIOENERGETICS

Energy

Cells get their energy from oxidizing energy-rich carbon-containing molecules (sugars, fats, amino acids, nucleotides) to energy-poorer molecules plus free energy, some of which is used to convert ADP to ATP (see figure at the top of page 23).

Glucose

The most common fuel molecule is glucose:

$$C_6H_{12}O_6 + 6O_2 \rightarrow 6CO_2 + 6H_2O + 686 \text{ kcal.}$$

Obtaining energy from glucose takes place in two steps:

1. Glycolysis (also called fermentation): This is an anaerobic process and can be used by some organisms as their only energy-yielding mechanism. For most cells, however, it is the first step.

2. Krebs Cycle and Electron Transport Chain: In most cells, the pyruvate initially produced by glycolysis yields further energy via the Krebs cycle (also known as the citric acid cycle or the tricarboxylic acid cycle) and

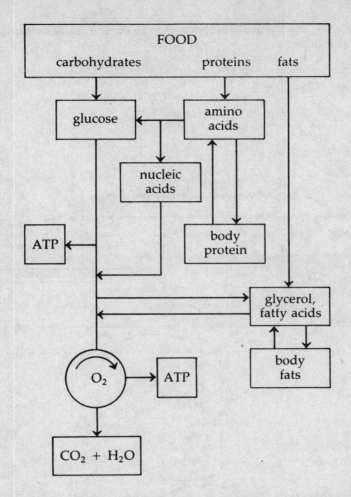

electron transport chain. These energy-yielding equations constitute what is called "cellular respiration" and require oxygen. In eucaryotes they take place in the mitochondrion. Within the inner compartment of the mitochondrion there is a solution containing Krebs cycle enzymes. The electron transport chain enzymes are built into the surfaces of the cristae or inner folded membrane of the mitochondrion.

Glycolysis and cellular respiration are summarized in the chart on the following page.

In glycolysis it is necessary to have 2 ATP's per glucose molecule to start the reaction. Through the process 4 ATP's plus 2 NADred are generated, making the entire process's net yield 2 ATP plus 2 NADred.

The overall reaction is:

Glucose + 2ATP + 4ADP + 2NADox →
$$2C_3H_4O_3 + 2ADP + 4ATP + 2NADred$$

In anaerobic organisms the pyruvate is decarboxylated to acetaldehyde which is then reduced to ethanol:

$$CH_3\overset{O}{\overset{\|}{C}}-\overset{O}{\overset{\|}{C}}-OH \searrow CH_3\overset{O}{\overset{\|}{C}}-H \to CH_3CH_2OH$$
$$\searrow CO_2$$

In muscle cells, the pyruvate is reduced to lactic acid, which results in muscle soreness and fatigue:

$$CH_3\overset{\displaystyle O}{\overset{\|}{C}}-\overset{\displaystyle O}{\overset{\|}{C}}-OH \rightarrow CH_3\overset{\displaystyle H}{\overset{|}{C}}-\overset{\displaystyle O}{\overset{\|}{C}}-OH$$
$$\underset{\displaystyle OH}{}$$

GLYCOLYSIS:

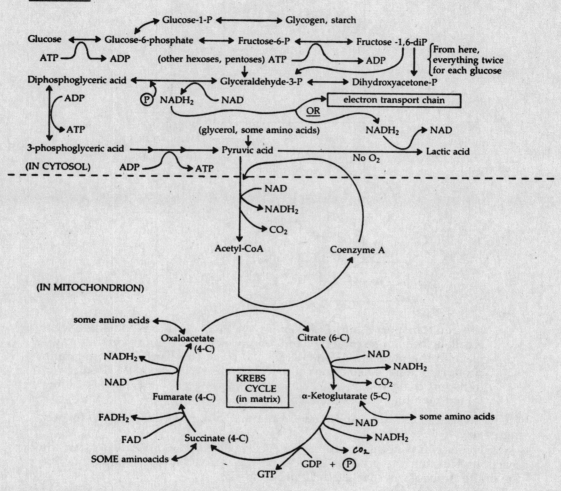

ELECTRON TRANSPORT SYSTEM:
(inner membrane)

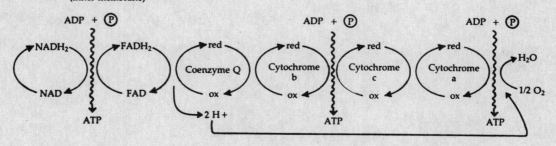

In the Krebs cycle, for each acetyl group, the yield is: 1 ATP, 3 NADred and 1 FPred. From 1 glucose molecule, 2 acetyl groups go through the cycle, yielding 2 ATP, 6 NADred and 2 FPred.

NADred and FPred are electron carriers of high energy. In electron transport they are passed downhill and energy is released to form ATP through a process called oxidative phosphorylation.

From each pair of electrons passed from NADred to oxygen, 3ATP's are formed. From each FPred, 2 ATP's are formed.

In summary, from 1 glucose molecule that passes through glycolysis and cellular respiration, we get:

glycolysis ––––––––––––––	2ATP + 2NADred	=	8ATP
pyruvate to acetyl-co-A ––––––	2NADred	=	6ATP
Krebs cycle –––––––––––––	2ATP + 6NADred		
	2FPred	=	24ATP
		(total)	38ATP

Other Sources

Lipids and proteins can also be utilized as sources of energy. Fats (triglycerides) are broken down into glycerol and fatty acids. The fatty acids undergo beta-oxidation in the liver and can be converted into acetyl-co-A which then enters the Krebs cycle. Proteins can be utilized for energy if their amino acids are converted into certain of the Krebs cycle intermediates. The chart on page 26 illustrates the metabolism occurring in the cell.

NUCLEIC ACIDS

Nucleotides

Nucleic acids are polymers of nucleotides. A nucleotide is composed of a sugar, phosphate, and a base which may be either a purine or a pyrimidine. The sugar is a 5-carbon sugar: in RNA it is ribose; in DNA it is deoxyribose.

$$PO_4—SUGAR—BASE$$

The purines are *adenine* and *guanine*.
The pyrimidines are thymine, cytosine, and *uracil*.
A nucleotide:

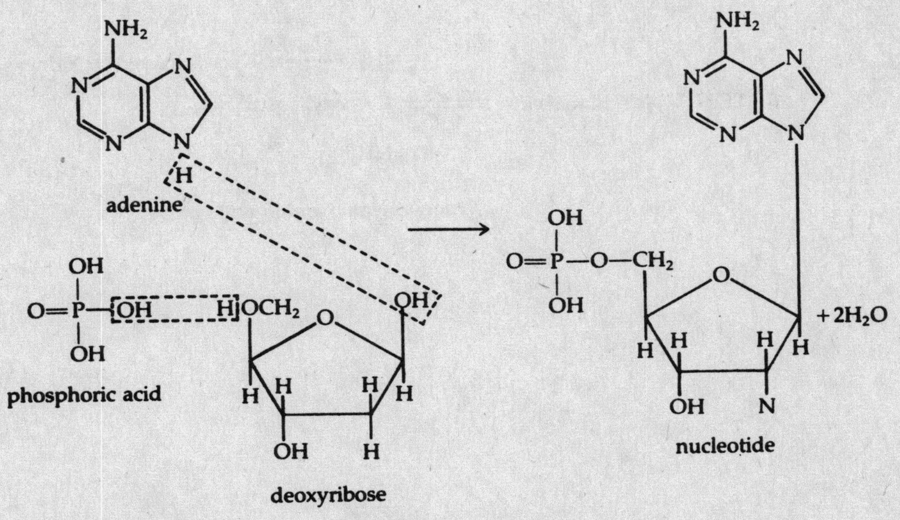

phosphoric acid

deoxyribose

nucleotide

+2H$_2$O

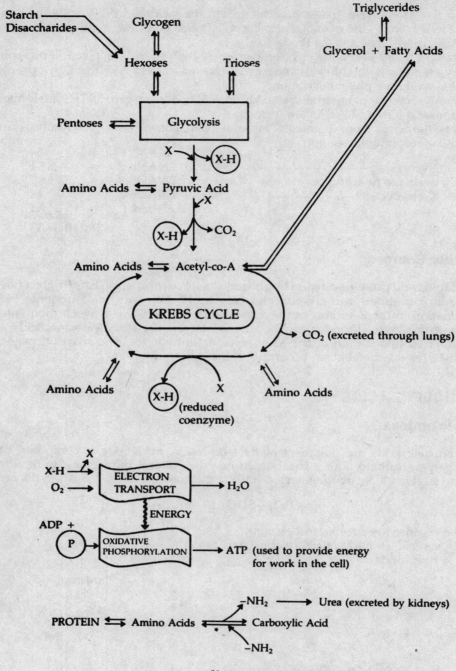

Watson-Crick Model of DNA

Two strands of sugar-PO$_4$-sugar-etc., form the framework of a double helix. The bases, held together by a hydrogen bond, form the rungs.

Adenine will only pair up with thymine and guanine with cytosine (in RNA, uracil takes the place of thymine). This is summarized as follows:

A–T
C–G

Information is carried in the sequence of the bases. There are 20 amino acids to be coded. If 1 nucleotide coded 1 amino acid, only 4 amino acids could be coded. If two nucleotides were responsible for the coding, 16 amino acids could be coded. With 3 nucleotides determining an amino acid, 64 can be indicated. In conclusion, a "triplet" code is sufficient for all amino acids, duplicates, and "stop" messages.

Replication of DNA

Implicit in the double and complimentary structure of the DNA helix is the method by which it reproduces itself. The DNA molecule "unzips" down the middle (the bases break apart at the hydrogen bonds), the strands separate and two strands form, one alongside each old one. Each strand acts as a template for the new: If a thymine is in the old strand, only an adenine will fit; etc., this is known as *semi-conservative replication*.

Semi-conservative replication was confirmed by the experiments of Meselson and Stahl with *E. coli* grown on N^{15}: All DNA was labeled with heavy N. DNA from parent, F_1 and F_2 generations were extracted and ultracentrifuged. The results showed all heavy DNA in parent, all midweight DNA in F_1, and half midweight DNA and half normal DNA in F_2.

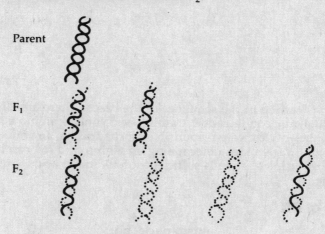

This has also been confirmed with radioactive isotopes.

DNA replication is an enzymatic reaction that requires DNA polymerase.

Similarities and Differences Between DNA and RNA

RNA	DNA
● Found in cytoplasm	● Found in nucleus
● Sugar: Ribose	● Sugar: deoxyribose
● Bases: Adenine Guanine Uracil Cytosine	● Bases: Adenine Guanine Thymine Cytosine
● Does not possess regular helical structure	● Helical
● Usually single-stranded	● Double-stranded
● Major function: Transcribe genetic message of DNA and translate it into proteins	● Major function: carry genetic code

BIOSYNTHESIS

Types of RNA

Messenger RNA. Long single strand forms along DNA using 1 strand of DNA as template. This process is called *transcription*. The sequence of 3 nucleotides is a codon for a specific amino acid.

Transfer RNA. Small molecules formed in the nucleus. They have a cloverleaf form. There are more than 20 tRNA's, and they serve as a link or adaptor between amino acids and mRNA. The amino acid is bonded at ACC end, then attaches to mRNA at anticodon—assuring that only one amino acid can be brought in at any one point.

UAA   mRNA

Each type of tRNA is specific for one of the amino acids.

Ribosomal RNA. Ribosomes are small bodies that are found free in the cytoplasm or attached to the membranes of the endoplasmic reticulum. They are half protein and half RNA and are formed in the DNA of the nucleolus. Each is composed of 2 subunits. Ribosomes attach to mRNA as it is formed and move along the RNA strand; tRNA attachment occurs at the point where mRNA is attached to the ribosome and amino acids are assembled into proteins. The synthesis of proteins using the information coded in mRNA is called *translation*.

Mechanism of Protein Synthesis

| (I) exposed DNA strand | (II) formation of mRNA | (III) completed mRNA | (IV) tRNA with amino acids move into position on mRNA | (V) completed protein chain |

Cellular Biology

THE EUCARYOTIC CELL

In eucaryotic cells the hereditary material is separated from the cytoplasm by a nuclear envelope which contains pores through which materials can pass to the cytoplasm.

Structure and Function of Cell Organelles in the Eucaryotic Cell

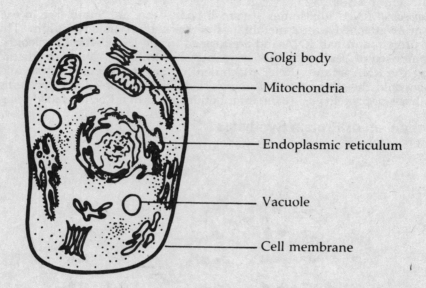

Golgi body

Mitochondria

Endoplasmic reticulum

Vacuole

Cell membrane

Cell Membrane. Consists of phospholipid and cholesterol molecules arranged so their hydrophobic tails are pointed inward. Globular proteins are embedded at intervals. In plant cells, a cell wall lies outside of the cell membrane.

Nucleus. Contains the chromosomes; is composed of DNA and protein. The nucleolus, visible within the nucleus, is the site of formation of ribosomal RNA.

In the cytoplasm are found:

Endoplasmic reticulum. A network of membranes subdividing the cytoplasm, continuous with the outer membrane of the nuclear envelope. Contains many of the cell enzymes lined up in order on the surface, allowing biochemical activities to be performed in sequence.

Ribosomes. Site of protein synthesis. In cells synthesizing protein "for export," most of the ribosomes are attached to the endoplasmic reticulum (known as *rough endoplasmic reticulum*).

Golgi bodies. These function as packaging centers. Each consists of a group of loosely stacked, flattened sacs. Evidence suggests that proteins produced for export are channeled into Golgi bodies and packaged in vesicles in which they travel to the outer cell membrane and are discharged. Animal cells usually contain only one, while plant cells may have many. A cell's total set of Golgi bodies is called the *Golgi complex*.

Lysosomes. These are a product of the Golgi bodies. They are bags of hydrolytic enzymes kept separate from the rest of the cell by membranes. They digest bacteria and other food particles taken up by the cell. They are also involved in the breakdown of worn-out cell organelles. Sometimes they may destroy entire cells (as in the resorption of the tadpole tail).

Mitochondria. This is the place where cellular respiration takes place. They are surrounded by 2 outer membranes and have a complex inner membrane structure called *cristae*. Mitochondria are found in both plant and animal cells.

Plastids. These are found only in plant cells and are bound by 2 outer membranes. There are three types:

- leucoplasts—colorless, site of starch production and storage of lipids and proteins
- chromoplasts—synthesize and retain pigments, responsible for colors of fruits, vegetables, and flowers
- chloroplasts—organelles in which photosynthesis takes place

Vacuoles. These are spaces in the cytoplasm filled with water and solutes, surrounded by a single membrane.

Microfilaments. Threadlike fibrils about 60 Å in diameter. These are believed to be actin—associated with movement of the cytoplasm.

Microtubules. These are tiny tubes about 0.02 micron in diameter, assembled from globular protein subunits. They function as internal skeletons and are the major components of cilia, flagella, and spindle fibers.

Cilia and flagella. These are long, thin (.2-micron) structures extending from the surface of eucaryotic cells, associated with movement. Flagella are the longer of the two structures. They consist of 9 pairs of microtubules surrounding 2 additional solitary microtubules in the center. Underlying each cilium is a basal body consisting of 9 triplets with no microtubules in the center.

Centrioles. These are structurally similar to basal bodies, typically occur in pairs at right angles to each other, and are small cylinders about .2 microns in diameter. Centrioles are found only in cells that have cilia or flagella and may also be involved in forming the spindle (although cells without centrioles can also form spindles).

Chromosomes. These are composed of protein and DNA and are found within the nucleus. When the cell is not dividing, the chromosomes are visible only as a tangle of fine threads (called *chromatin*).

Nucleolus. the nucleolus, like the chromosomes, is composed of protein and DNA. It is the most conspicuous body in the nucleus and is formed from a portion of a chromosome. The nucleolus is the site at which rRNA (ribosomal RNA) is formed.

Mitosis in the Eucaryotic Cell

Cell division includes mitosis or nuclear division and cytokinesis or division of the cytoplasm. The process of mitosis is divided into 4 phases:

Prophase. Chromatin condenses. Chromosomes become visible—each consists of two duplicate chromatids connected at the kinetochore. The centriole pairs move apart forming spindle fibers. The nucleolus disperses, and the nuclear envelope breaks down.

Metaphase. Chromosomes move back and forth along the spindle and become arranged at the midplane of the cell.

Anaphase. Each kinetochore divides and the chromatids (now chromosomes) separate, being drawn to opposite poles of the spindle.

Telophase. The chromosomes have reached opposite poles and cytokinesis has begun. The spindle disperses. A new daughter centriole arises from each mature centriole so that each cell has 2 centriole pairs. The nuclear envelope re-forms and the chromosomes become diffuse.

When a cell is not dividing it is spoken of as being in interphase. Chromosomes are duplicated during interphase if mitosis is to occur.

In the cell cycle, a cell goes through G_1, S, G_2 and the mitotic phases. Interphase is equal to the G_1, S, and G_2 stages combined. During the S phase, RNA production in the nucleus ceases and DNA duplication occurs.

Characteristics and Life Cycle of Fungi

There are many classification schemes, but true fungi are usually placed in kingdom Plantae (subkingdom Thallophyta, phylum Fungi (division Eumycophyta), and there are five classes:

1. Oomycetes: aquatic water molds, produce male and female gametes.
2. Zygomycetes: terrestrial habitat, have zygospores.
3. Ascomycetes: sexual spores in sacs called asci.
4. Basidiomycetes: sexual spores in club-shaped structures called basidia.
5. Fungi imperfecti: sexual stages unknown.

Life cycle. In general, fungi exist as haploid multinucleate mycelia, capable of reproducing asexually by fragmentation of mycelium or the production of spores in sporangia. Sexual reproduction is initiated by the coming together of hyphae of different mating strains. Gametangia form. Then nuclei unite, forming diploid zygotes, and meiosis occurs, forming haploid sexual spores. Germination of these spores gives rise to haploid mycelia (see the figure at the top of page 33).

Most fungi have cell walls composed of chitin. Lichens are a symbiotic combination of a fungus and an alga.

PROCARYOTES (VIRUSES AND BACTERIA)

Procaryotes differ from eucaryotes in the following ways:

- simpler cell
- no nuclear membrane
- no complex chromosomes
- no endoplasmic reticulum
- no mitochondria
- no chloroplasts or other plastids
- no 9 + 2 flagella
- do not reproduce sexually (there are mechanisms in bacteria for genetic recombination)
- have rigid cell walls containing amino acids

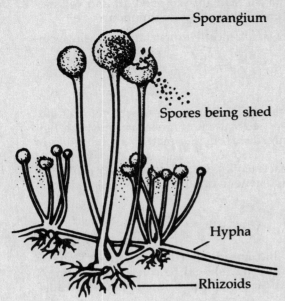

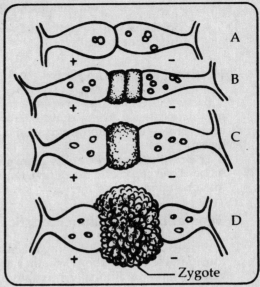

General Defining Characteristics of Bacteria

Bacteria are the smallest cellular organisms and are the oldest and most abundant organisms on earth. They have a rapid rate of cell division and great metabolic versatility. They can survive in many environments that support no other life form. Bacteria are ecologically important as decomposers; some bacteria fix nitrogen (no eucaryotes are able to use nitrogen in gaseous form). Many bacteria are economically valuable in the production of cheese, vinegar, yogurt, and antibiotics. Some bacteria cause disease in plants, animals, and man.

Bacteria reproduce by fission. The bacterial chromosome is a circular molecule of double-stranded DNA. Each cell characteristically contains more than one DNA molecule although a single molecule contains the full complement of genetic material. The DNA molecules attach to special areas in the cell membrane, which separate as the cell grows (this strategem ensures that each new cell receives a chromosome.

Fertilization and meiosis do not occur in bacteria. There are three mechanisms in bacteria that serve the function of providing genetic recombination:

1. Transformation: Genetic material is passed from one cell to another by means of isolated DNA.

2. Conjugation: Some or all of the chromosome from a donor cell is passed to a recipient.

3. Transduction: A portion of bacterial chromosome is carried to another cell by a virus.

Classes of Bacteria

1. Eubacteria: are distinguished mainly by their shapes.
   - bacilli—straight rods
   - cocci—spherical (1) in pairs: diplococci
     (2) in clusters: staphylococci
     (3) in chains: streptococci
   - spirilli—long spiral rods
   - vibrios—short curved rods

2. Myxobacteria: slime bacteria.

3. Spirochetes: very long, with an axial filament wrapped around cell in a double helix; contractions of filament cause whirling motion.

4. Rickettsia and Mycoplasma: very small, mostly intracellular parasites; cultured with difficulty.

Nutrition and Metabolism

Bacteria are extremely versatile metabolically. Some are capable of an autotrophic existence (chemosynthetic or photosynthetic); however, most are heterotrophs—either saprophytes utilizing dead organic matter, or parasites in living organisms.

Their nutritional versatility allows bacteria to occupy almost every ecological niche. Their rapid rate of cell division and genetic variability allow a fast selection in a changing environment.

General Defining Characteristics of Viruses

Viruses are not cellular organisms and are difficult to categorize. There is considerable doubt about whether or not they should be considered "living." Viruses have traditionally been studied with bacteria because they also cause diseases in plants and animals.

Viruses are composed of nucleic acid, either RNA or DNA, enclosed in a protein coat. The protein coat determines the specificity of the virus: a cell can be infected by a virus only if it has a receptor site for the virus protein.

In some viral infections the protein coat is left outside the cell; in others the entire virus enters the cell but once inside, the protein is destroyed by enzymes. The DNA serves as a template for more viral DNA and for mRNA. The virus uses the ribosomes, tRNA, amino acids, and nucleotides of the host cell to replicate itself. In the case of RNA viruses, the viral RNA serves as template for more RNA and acts directly as mRNA. Viral particles are assembled within the host cell; then they leave the cell, often lysing the membrane.

Viruses often cause an infected cell to produce *interferon*, a protein, which interferes with viral replication.

Bacterial viruses or bacteriophages consist of DNA and protein. Phage particles have a hexagonal head and a complex tail. They attach to bacterial cell walls at specific receptor sites by the tails and only the DNA enters the cell. A complete cycle of virus infection takes only about 20 minutes, and at the end, hundreds of new virus particles are released as the cell lyses.

Developmental and Organismal Biology

EMBRYOLOGY

Fertilization occurs after egg has completed the first meiotic division. The egg nucleus completes its second meiotic division only if fertilized. Then it and the sperm nucleus move to center of cell and fuse to form a zygote. This activates the egg-initiating development.

Development takes place in three stages:

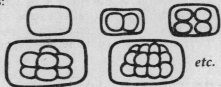

1. Cleavage: The original egg cell is divided with little or no change in volume. When cleavage is complete, the embryo will consist of a hollow sphere of cells called a *blastula*.

2. Gastrulation: This involves movement of cells into new relative positions and establishes the axes of the embryo and the three body layers (endoderm, mesoderm, and ectoderm). An opening called the *blastopore* forms, and cells from the outer surface move through the blastopore. When the movement of cells is complete, the central part of the dorsal surface of the gastrula flattens becoming the neural plate, which folds to form the neural tube. The cells underlying the neural plate become the notochord (mesodermal). The small segment of tissue on the dorsal lip of the blastopore is known as the "organizer" because it induces the cells overlying it to form the neural tube.

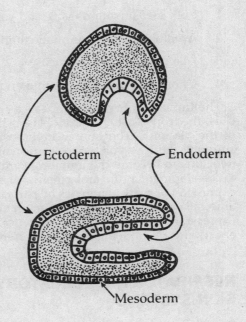

3. Organogenesis: Organ systems begin to develop by this process of embryonic induction, in which one tissue induces changes in an adjacent tissue with which it comes in contact (either by growth or by cell migration).

Each of the three primary germ layers established at gastrulation gives rise to particular tissues and organs.

1. Ectoderm: epidermis, central nervous system, and senses.

2. Mesoderm: notochord, muscles, bones and cartilage, heart, blood and blood vessels, excretory organs, gonads, inner lining of skin, and outer linings of digestive and respiratory tracks and of body cavities.

3. Endoderm: inner linings of digestive and respiratory tracks, and digestive glands.

In gastrulation, the three layers of cells begin to differentiate, or form the different tissues and organs, as stated above. The organs of the body are developed from tissues derived from one or more of these germ layers. All organs originate in two or more of the layers.

Chemicals called *organizers* in the embryo appear to direct the development of tissues and organs. The actions of organizers are part of the process of *embryonic induction*. This process takes place when two different tissues come in contact with one another or close enough to exchange chemical materials.

Differentiation is the process by which cells become different from each other and from their parent cells in structure and function. Differentiation takes place by the mechanisms previously described and brings about *morphogenesis*, or the appearance of the characteristic form of organs and organisms.

Extraembryonic Membranes

In amniotic eggs (reptiles, birds, and mammals) the embryo is surrounded by four protective membranes.

1. Yolk sac: surrounds yolk and connects embryo to it.

2. Amnion: encloses amniotic fluid in which embryo floats.

3. Allantois: collects wastes.

4. Chorion: surrounds embryo and all its membranes.

The human embryo develops as a cell mass surrounded by an outer layer of cells, the tropoblast. The tropoblast becomes the chorion and later, the fetal part of the placenta. The human embryo is surrounded by an amnion filled with amniotic fluid. A yolk sac with no yolk is present. The allantropic membrane develops to become the umbilical cord.

Development at the molecular level may be visualized as a gradual, sequential expression of particular genes by particular cells with a repression of other genes. Since all cells of an organism contain all the genetic information, this sequential expression is under both the influence of the cytoplasm as formed during oogenesis and of inducing substances transmitted by other cells.

RESPIRATORY, CIRCULATORY, LYMPHATIC, RENAL, AND SKIN SYSTEMS

Respiratory System

Air enters through the *nostrils* where it is warmed, humidified, and filtered. It passes to the *pharynx*, then to the *larynx* (site of the vocal cords), to the *trachea*, to the two *bronchi*, and through smaller and smaller passageways to the *bronchioles*. All these are lined with ciliated mucus-producing epithelial cells.

Gas exchange occurs between the air in the *alveoli* and the blood in the capillaries by diffusion. A pair of lungs has about 300 million alveoli, providing a respiratory surface approximately 40 times the surface area of the body.

The lungs are surrounded by a thin membrane and the thoracic cavity is lined with a similar membrane. These are shown as the *pleura*. They secrete a small amount of fluid which lubricates them.

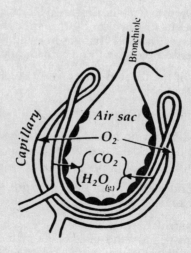

GAS EXCHANGE IN ALVEOLUS (AIR SAC)

Lungs empty and fill as a result of changes in the thoracic capacity produced by intercostal muscles and the diaphragm. Although these are voluntary muscles, they are under involuntary control of nerves in the respiratory center in the *medulla oblongata* which respond to slight changes in the H^+ and HCO_3^- concentration in the blood.

Transport of Oxygen

Hemoglobin has 4 globin-heme units per molecule and thus can carry 4 atoms of oxygen. The partial pressure of O_2 in the blood as it leaves the lungs is 100 mm Hg, at which pressure the hemoglobin is saturated with oxygen. The partial pressure of oxygen of the blood in the capillaries is about 40 mm Hg and oxygen is given up to the tissues. At this pressure, the hemoglobin is still about 70% saturated, keeping an emergency supply in case the demand should increase as a result of exercise.

Myoglobin is found in skeletal muscle. It resembles a single unit of the hemoglobin molecule and has a greater affinity for oxygen than hemoglobin. (It begins to release significant amounts of oxygen only when the PO_2 falls below 20 mm Hg.) Thus, during strenuous exercise, myoglobin provides an additional reserve of oxygen for active muscles.

Transport of Carbon Dioxide

A small amount of CO_2 is carried in the blood as dissolved CO_2, some is bound to amino acid groups of the hemoglobin molecule, but the greatest part is carried in the blood as bicarbonate,

$$CO_2 + H_2O \underset{\text{anhydrase}}{\overset{\text{carbonic}}{\rightleftharpoons}} H_2CO_3 \rightleftharpoons H^+ + HCO_3^-$$

The enzyme carbonic anhydrase is found in red blood cells. As CO_2 is taken up, the blood becomes more acid and at higher acidity, hemoglobin releases oxygen more readily.

Control of Respiration

The medulla oblongata receives messages from monitoring cells in aorta and carotid arteries. These signal when oxygen concentration in blood decreases. CO_2 concentrations are monitored directly by centers in the brain as well as by the monitor cells in the arteries. The control of PCO_2 is of great importance. If the concentration of CO_2 increases only slightly, breathing immediately becomes deeper and faster, permitting more CO_2 to leave the blood. If you deliberately hyperventilate, you feel faint and dizzy because of the blood's increased alkalinity.

Circulatory System

Man and other vertebrates have a closed circulatory system consisting of the blood, the vessels, and the heart (which provides the force that moves the blood through the vessels). The heart, arteries, and veins are the means for getting the blood to and from the capillaries, where the actual function of the circulatory system is carried out.

Blood returning from the systemic circulation through the superior and inferior venae cavae enters the right atrium and is pumped to the right ventricle. From there it is then pumped out through the pulmonary arteries to the lungs where it is oxygenated. Blood from the lungs enters the left atrium through the pulmonary veins, is pumped to the left ventricle, and then out through the aorta to the body tissues.

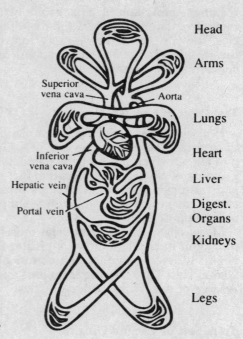

The beat of the mammalian heart is controlled by a region of specialized muscle tissue in the right atrium—the sinoatrial node—which functions as the heart's pacemaker. Excitation spreads from the pacemaker through the atrial muscles, causing both atria to contract simultaneously. When the wave of excitation reaches the atrioventricular node, its conducting fibers pass the stimulation to the bundle of His, which triggers simultaneous contraction of the ventricles. Because the fibers of the atrioventricular node conduct electrical impulses slowly, the ventricles do not contract until the atrial beat has been completed. The fibers of the bundle of His conduct the impulse approximately six times as fast as the rate of regular cardiac muscle fibers, thus insuring that the fibers of the ventricle contract as a unit.

Blood

The average person has about 5 liters of blood. About 55% of the blood is plasma. Plasma is 90% water and carries a number of ions and molecules such as glucose, fats, amino acids, fibrinogen, antibodies, hormones, enzymes, and waste materials such as urea and uric acid. The remaining 45% of the blood is made up of erythrocytes, leucocytes, and platelets.

Red Blood Cells

Red blood cells are used to transport oxygen. There are some 25×10^{12} of these in the entire body or about 5 million per cubic millimeter of blood. An individual cell has a life span of 120 to 130 days. New ones are produced within the bone marrow at the rate of about 1½ million per second.

Red blood cells are called *erythrocytes*. During development in bone marrow the nucleus is extruded and all other cellular structures, including mitochondria, dissolve, leaving almost the entire volume of the cell filled with hemoglobin. A small percentage of immature RBC's in which not all the organelles have dissolved may be released in circulation. These cells are called *reticulocytes* and take their name from the remnants of organelles still present.

Erythrocytes are biconcave in shape and are usually stained with Wright's blood stain in methanol. They carry oxygen in the form of oxyHb or carboxyHb. Most RBC's are recycled in the liver: the globin and the iron of the heme are salvaged. The remainder of the heme is converted to *bilirubin* and excreted in the bile.

Each RBC carries antigenic blood type chemicals (antigens) on its surface. The two most important blood groupings are the A-B-O system and the Rh system.

A-B-O System

The possible proteins present are A and B; type O lacks both proteins

Blood Type	Compatible with:	
A	A, O	
B	B, O	
AB	A, B, AB, O	(universal recipient)
O	O	(universal donor)

Rh System

If Rh protein is present, it is Rh-positive; if the protein is absent, it is Rh-negative. An Rh-positive baby may be incompatible with its Rh-negative mother (erythroblastosis fetalis).

White Blood Cells

There are 6,000 to 9,000 white blood cells per cubic millimeter of blood. White blood cells are colorless, have nuclei, move by means of pseudopodia, and many are phagocytic. They are of the following types:

1. Neutrophils: produced in bone marrow; active in phagocytosis.

2. Lymphocytes: produced in lymphatic tissue.
   - B-cells—produced in lymph cells; synthesize antibodies
   - T-cells—produced by cells originating in the thymus gland; involved in graft rejection and other immune phenomena.

3. Eosinophils: produced in bone marrow; active in phagocytosis, have a high histamine content and cause reaction to allergies.

4. Basophils: produced in bone marrow; high granularity in cytoplasm obscures nucleus; phagocytic.

5. Monocytes: produced in bone marrow; have clear cytoplasm; are phagocytic; common in tonsils and other lymphatics.

Notes: 1. The majority of leukocytes are multinucleated.
2. The majority of leucocytes carry agglutinogens (antibodies).
3. Many leukocytes can facilitate *diapedisis* (migration out of capillaries or blood vessels).

Platelets

Platelets are cytoplasmic fragments of large cells in bone marrow (called megakaryocytes). These play a role in clot formation since they contain a protein (called thromboplastin) essential to blood clotting. The mechanism of blood clotting is as follows:

- Thrombocytes (platelets) release thromboplastin.

  ↓

- Thromboplastin, along with Ca^{++}, vitamin K, and other factors in the blood, catalyzes the conversion of prothrombin (in blood plasma) to thrombin.

  ↓

- Thrombin enzymatically catalyzes the conversion of fibrinogen (in plasma) to polymerized threads of fibrin (scab).

Lymphatic System

This is another circulatory system, which routes the fluid forced out of the capillaries back to the blood.

Lymph capillaries end blindly in tissue. Lymph travels through **progressively larger vessels** and empties into the vena cava by way of two ducts (the thoracic duct and the right lymphatic duct). Lymph moves by contractions of **body muscles**, and valves prevent backflow. Lymphatic fluid transports some foods, particularly fats.

Nodes

The two functions of the lymph nodes are (1) manufacture of lymphocytes (B-cells); and (2) removal of foreign particles (dead cells, dust, cancer cells, etc.).

Spleen

The spleen manufactures lymphocytes, breaks down aged and defective red blood cells, and recycles iron.

Thymus

This is the original site of production of T-cell lymphocytes. All T-cells **are** derived from cells that originate in the thymus and then leave to colonize blood, lymph nodes, and bone marrow.

Tonsils and Adenoids

These are lymphoid tissues concerned with lymphocyte production.

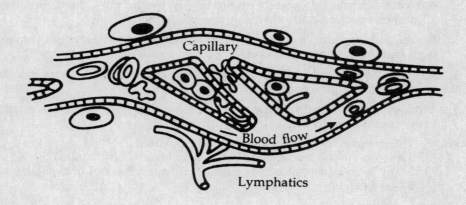

Renal System

The organ chiefly responsible for regulating the chemical environment of the body is the *kidney.* The functional unit of the kidney is the *nephron,* which consists of a long tubule with a closed end called *Bowman's capsule.* The other end of the tubule is called the collecting duct and drains into the *ureter* through a funnel, the *renal pelvis.* Each of man's kidneys contains about a million nephrons. Each Bowman's capsule contains a cluster of capillaries, the *glomerulus.* Blood is pumped into the glomerulus under sufficient pressure to force the plasma (not the larger proteins) through the capillary walls. Other molecules are secreted from the peritubular capillaries into the renal tubules. As the fluid travels through the tubules, almost all the water and useful substances are reabsorbed into the blood stream through capillaries surrounding the tubules. Waste materials and some water pass into the ureter and are excreted from the body.

The means by which water is conserved and a hypertonic urine is excreted is the *loop of Henle.* Approximately 20% of man's nephrons (much greater percentages in other animals such as the kangaroo and rat) have long loops of

Henle. Sodium (or perhaps Cl) is actively transported out of the ascending loop into the interstitial fluid. This sodium diffuses back into the descending loop and recirculates to the ascending loop where it is pumped out again. The results of this recirculation of sodium are that (1) as urine passes through the loop of Henle, much salt but little water is removed; and (2) the lower part of the loop is bathed in a fluid containing a much higher salt concentration than the blood. As the urine descends through the collecting duct which traverses the zone of high salt concentration, water pours out by osmosis if antidiuretic hormone (ADH) is present and a hypertonic urine is excreted. (ADH causes the membrane of the collecting duct to be permeable to water.)

Principal regulation of kidney function is due to ADH. If ADH is not present, the collection tubes remain relatively impermeable to water, little passes back to the blood, and more water is excreted in the less-concentrated urine.

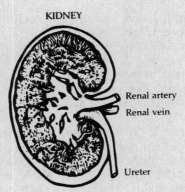

KIDNEY

Renal artery
Renal vein
Ureter

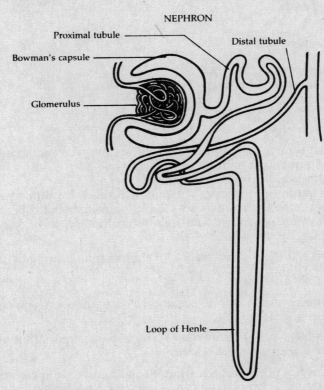

NEPHRON

Proximal tubule
Distal tubule
Bowman's capsule
Glomerulus
Loop of Henle

ADH is a neurohormone secreted by the hypothalamus and stored in the posterior pituitary gland. Osmotic receptors located in the hypothalamus monitor solute concentration in the blood. Presure detectors in walls of heart, aorta, and carotid arteries detect changes in blood volume. Low blood pressure or high dilute concentration stimulate ADH and the conservation of body water.

A second control is aldosterone, a steroid hormone from the adrenal cortex which increases the reabsorption of sodium.

By these mechanisms of osmoregulation, the body maintains its fluid content within ±1%.

The Skin System: Thermoregulation

In homeotherms, 80–90% of the oxidative energy is expended maintaining thermal homeostasis.

Temperature of the blood is monitored in the hypothalamus (hot and cold receptors of the skin are *not* involved in regulation). Fever is due to a resetting of the "thermostat" primarily caused by a protein released by neutrophils, and is part of the inflammatory response.

As the external temperature rises, blood vessels near the skin surface dilate and the blood supply to the skin increases. Perspiration begins. Since evaporation requires heat energy, the blood beneath the skin surface cools. Sweating is the principal route of water loss.

At low external temperatures the cutaneous vessels constrict, limiting the heat loss from the skin surface. Shivering is a means of increasing heat production by mobilizing glucose and ATP and releasing their energy as motion and heat. More thyroid hormone is produced (increasing metabolic rate). A drastic drop in temperature stimulates the release of adrenalin (which also increases metabolic rate).

Functions of the skin system are:

- temperature regulation
- protection
- sensory
- vitamin D synthesis

Epidermis

1. Stratified squamous epithelium

    - stratum cornium (not present on mucous membranes)—keratinized; desquamation; dead
    - stratum licidium—clear; dead layer
    - stratum granulosum—pigmented; cell lysis; thin layer
    - stratum spinosum—prickle-cells; alive; almost cuboidal
    - stratum germinativum—almost columnar; alive; pigmented; melanoblasts interspersed

2. Hair follicles—continuation of the stratum germinativum.

Dermis

1. Basement membrane: cementlike substance between epithelium and underlying dermis.

2. Collagen fibers: proteinous fibers; areolar, dense, fibrous, etc; responsible for fingerprints; run in bundles.

3. Arrector pili muscles: myoepithelial contractile fibers suspended between stratum germinativum and base of hair follicles; produces "goosepimples" when contracted.

4. Sebaceous glands: oil glands; empty contents in shaft of hair follicles.

5. Sweat glands: coiled tubules ending in acini, reach surface via pores.

6. Lymph nodes: connective tissue packets of reticular connective tissue in dermis; lymphocytes present.

7. Fat cells: adipose deposits.

8. Capillaries: subcutaneous networks.

9. Sensory nerve endings: specialized endings of PNS.

10. Neutrophils: diapeditic WBC's; phagocytes.

11. Venules and arterioles: ramifications of systemic and venous systems.

12. Scar tissue: dense connective tissue (may be due to acne or injury).

THE DIGESTIVE SYSTEM

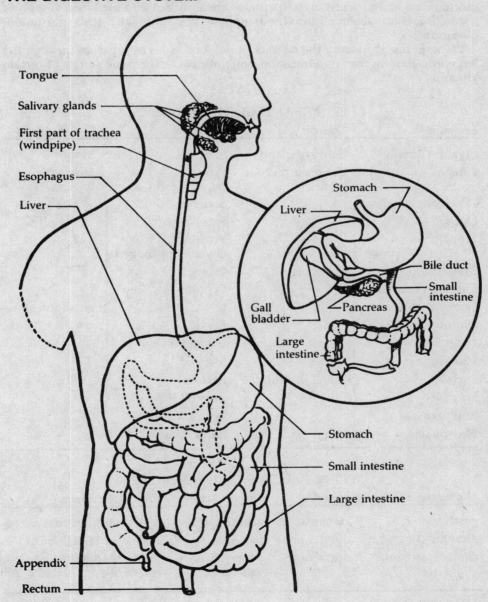

Digestion is the process by which food is broken down into molecules that can be taken into the blood stream and distributed to the cells. Food is processed initially in the *mouth*, where the breakdown of starch begins; and then in the *stomach*, where highly acidic gastric juices begin to break down proteins. Most of the digestion occurs in the small intestine; digestive hormones are secreted by intestinal cells and these, in turn, stimulate the functions of the pancreas and liver. The *pancreas* synthesizes and secretes a number of digestive enzymes and an alkalizing fluid which neutralizes the HCl of the gastric juice. The pancreas is also the source of insulin and glucagon, hormones secreted into the blood stream and involved in the other metabolic activities. The *liver* produces bile salts which emulsify fats and performs a wide variety of functions. It is the source of plasma proteins involved in blood clotting; breaks down a variety of toxic substances; activates a number of hormones; converts nitrogenous waste into urea; stores vitamins and minerals; and regulates blood glucose.

Absorption of food molecules takes place largely in the small intestine. Monosaccharides, amino acids, and dipeptides are absorbed into the blood vessels of the villi; fats are absorbed into the lymphatic vessels as fatty acids and monoglycerides.

Water is resorbed from the residue of the food mass as it passes through the large intestine. In the large intestine symbiotic bacteria are the source of certain vitamins.

PRINCIPAL DIGESTIVE ENZYMES

Enzyme	Source	Substrate	Site of action
Ptyalin (Amylase)	Salivary glands	Starches	Mouth
Pepsin	Stomach mucosa	Proteins, pepsinogen	Stomach
Pancreatic amylase	Pancreas	Starches	Small intestine
Lipase		Fats	
Trypsin		Proteins, chymotrypsinogen	
Chymotrypsin		Proteins	
Carboxypeptidase		Peptides	
Deoxyribonuclease		DNA	
Aminopeptidase	Small intestine	Peptides	
Dipeptidase		Dipeptides	
Maltase		Maltose	
Lactase		Lactose	
Sucrase		Sucrose	
Enterokinase		Trypsinogen	
Phosphatases		Nucleotides	

PRINCIPAL DIGESTIVE HORMONES

Hormone	Source	Site of Action	Effect (stimulates)
gastrin	stomach	gastric glands	release of intestinal juices
secretin	duodenum	pancreas	release of HOH, HCO_3^-
choleocystokinin	duodenum	pancreas, gallbladder	prod. of enzymes rel. of bile

All blood from the digestive tract flows into the hepatic portal vein and passes through the liver before entering the systemic circulation.

Functions of the Liver (partial list)

- glycogenesis
- glyconeogenesis
- storage of fat-soluble vitamins
- deamination and transamination of amino acids
- secretion of bile salts and bile pigment
- β-oxidation of fats
- production of many plasma proteins
- destruction of old red blood cells

Vitamins

The table below lists the major fat-soluble and some water-soluble vitamins, their sources and the effect of a deficiency of each vitamin.

Water-soluble vitamins (B complex)		
Vitamin	Sources	Deficiency effects
B_1 (thiamine)	whole cereal grains, legumes, nuts, milk, pork	beriberi, diseases of nervous system
B_2 (riboflavin)	milk, lean meat, liver, fish, egg whites	dermatitis, glossitis, inflammation of mouth and tongue
B_3 (pantothenic acid)	yeast, egg, liver, kidney, milk	retarded growth, emotional instability, gastrointestinal discomfort
B_4 (choline)	egg yolk, fats	hepatosis, alcoholic cirrhosis of liver, dermatosis, anemia
B_5 (niacine; nicotinic acid)	liver, coffee, lean meats	pellagra, stunted growth
B_6 (pyridoxine)	meat, fish, egg yolk, whole cereal grains	convulsion in infants, retarded growth
B_7 (biotin)	yeast, liver	dermatitis, scaly and greasy skin
B_9 (folic acid)	yeast, soybean, wheat, liver, kidney, eggs	mitosis, inhibition of cell division
B_{12} (cyanocobalamin)	liver, meats, eggs, seafood	pernicious anemia

Fat-soluble vitamins		
Vitamin	Sources	Deficiency effects
A	fish, liver, eggs, butter, cheese, precursor in carrots and other vegetables	night blindness; excessive light sensitivity

Fat-soluble vitamins (continued)

Vitamin	Sources	Deficiency effects
D (calciferol)	irradiated milk; produced in body by ultraviolet irradiation of skin	abnormal growth of bones and teeth, rickets
E (α-tocopherol)	vegetable oils, leafy vegetables, wheat germ oil	sterility
K	green leaves, alfalfa leaves	hemorrhage, slow clotting of blood

THE SKELETAL AND SKELETAL MUSCLE SYSTEMS

Skeletal System

Cartilage is the primary component of the skeletons of embryos of all vertebrates. It is progressively replaced by bone as development proceeds. In adults of higher vertebrates cartilage is retained where firmness and flexibility are needed (ends of ribs, articulating surfaces of joints, walls of larynx and trachea, external ear, and nose). It is a vascular tissue and, therefore, slow to repair after damage.

Compact bone is composed of structural units called Haversian systems. Each such unit is irregularly cylindrical and composed of concentrically arranged layers of hard inorganic matrix ($CaCO_2$ and $Ca_3(PO_4)_2$) surrounding a microscopic central Haversian canal. Blood vessels and nerves pass through this canal. The scattered, irregular-shaped bone cells lie in small cavities, called *lacunae*, located along the interfaces between adjoining concentric layers of the hard matrix. Exchange of materials between the bone cells and blood vessels in the Haversian canals is by way of radiating canalicules that penetrate and cross the layers of matrix.

Some bones are partly spongy, consisting of a network of hardened bars with the spaces between them filled with marrow. Other bones are more compact, with their hard parts an almost continuous mass and having only microscopic cavities. The shafts of typical long bones consist of compact bone surrounding a large central marrow cavity.

Some bones are joined together by immovable joints or sutures, as the skull; others are held together at movable joints by ligaments.

Muscles

Skeletal muscles act by contracting. They are typically attached to two or more bones directly, or by means of tendons. When the muscle contracts, the bones move around a joint. Most skeletal muscles work in antagonistic pairs; one slowly relaxes as the other one contracts (e.g., biceps and triceps of the arm).

Some muscles are never completely relaxed, but are kept in a state of partial contraction called *muscle tone* or *tonus*. This tone is maintained by alternate contraction of different groups of muscle fibers, so that no single fiber has a chance to fatigue.

During violent muscular activity the energy demands may be greater than can be met by complete respiration alone (after the oxyhemoglobin has been used up insufficient oxygen reaches the tissues). The muscles obtain the extra oxygen they need from lactic acid fermentation, an anaerobic process, and incur an *oxygen debt*. When the violent activity is over, you continue to breathe hard, supplying the liver with the large quantities of oxygen required to convert lactic acid to pyruvic acid and to oxidize the pyruvic acid for the energy needed to resynthesize glucogen from the rest of the lactic acid.

Skeletal muscles respond only to neurons from the somatic system and although many somatic reflexes exist, in general these muscles are under voluntary control (unlike smooth and cardiac muscles, which are innervated by the autonomic system).

A muscle consists of bundles of muscle fibers held together by connective tissue. Each fiber is a single cell with many nuclei, arising from the fusion of a large number of embryonic muscle precursor cells. These fibers are large cells 50 to 100 microns in diameter and often several centimeters long. They are surrounded by an outer cell membrane called *sarcolemma*. Each fiber is made up of many cylindrical *myofibrils*, which are rods of contractile proteins). The fibril is divided into segments (*sarcomeres*) by thin dark partitions called *Z-lines* which run from myofibril to myofibril across the fiber, giving the muscle cell its striated appearance. Each sarcomere is composed of thick and thin protein filaments. Contraction involves the sliding of the thin filaments between the thick ones. The thick filaments are myosin, the thin ones are F-actin.

A SARCOMERE

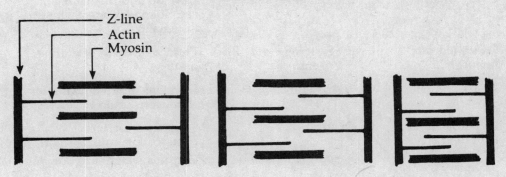

— Z-line
— Actin
— Myosin

Note: For contraction to occur, myosin, actin, Ca^{++}, and ATP must be present.

THE ENDOCRINE AND NERVOUS SYSTEMS

The Endocrine System

The endocrine glands secrete their products into the blood stream. The products of endocrine glands are hormones which act as messengers by altering the metabolism of particular cells. The principal endocrine glands, the hormones they secrete, and the effects on target tissues are summarized below.

GLAND	HORMONE	PRINCIPAL EFFECT
Pituitary, anterior lobe	Thyrotropic hormone (TSH)	Stimulates thyroid gland.
	Follicle-stimulating hormone (FSH)	Stimulates ovarian follicle, spermatogenesis.
	Luteinizing hormone (LH)	Stimulates interstitial cells in male, corpus luteum in female.
	Adrenocorticotropic hormone (ACTH)	Stimulates adrenal cortex.

GLAND	HORMONE	PRINCIPAL EFFECT
	Growth hormone	Stimulates bone and muscle growth, inhibits oxidation of glucose, promotes breakdown of fatty acids.
	Prolactin (LTH)	Stimulates milk production and secretion in "prepared" gland.
Thyroid	Thyroxine and other similar hormones	Stimulate and maintain metabolic activities.
	Calcitonin	Inhibits calcium release from bone.
Parathyroid	Parathormone	Maintains normal calcium level and bone growth.
Ovary (follicle)	Estrogens	Develop and maintain secondary sex characteristics in females.
Ovary (corpus luteum)	Progesterone and estrogens	Promote growth of uterine tissue.
Testis	Testosterone	Develops and maintains sex characteristics in males.
Hypothalamus (stored and released by the posterior pituitary)	Oxytocin	Stimulates uterine contractions, milk ejection.
	Vasopressin (ADH)	Controls water excretion.
Adrenal cortex	Aldosterone, cortisol, and other hormones similar to cortisol	Control carbohydrate, protein, and lipid metabolism, salt and water balance.
Adrenal medulla	Adrenaline (epinephrine, norepinephrine)	Increases blood sugar and heart beat, dilates blood vessels.
Pancreas	Insulin	Lowers blood sugar, increases storage of glycogen.
	Glucagon	Stimulates breakdown of glycogen to glucose in liver.
Pineal	?	Function in man is unknown.

The Nervous System

The nervous system, like the endocrine system, provides a means of communication between different parts of the organism and with the outside world.

The functional unit of the nervous system is the *neuron*. It consists of a *cell body* which contains the nucleus and thin extensions protruding from the cell body. One type of extension is the *dendrite*. These are highly branched reception areas for signals coming to the neuron. They usually carry impulses toward the cell body, and there may be more than one per neuron. The other type of extension, the *axon*, usually carries impulses away from the neuron and generally neurons have only one (which may be branched). Axons are often enveloped in a myelin sheath formed by *Schwann cells*. This sheath provides electrical insulation, thus speeding up the transmission of impulses. The *nodes of Ranvier* are gaps in the axon sheath that occur at the junction of adjacent Schwann cells.

There are three types of neurons:

1. Motor neurons (efferent): carry impulses outward to the effectors (muscles or glands).

2. Sensory neurons (afferent): transmit impulses received by sensory receptors to CNS

3. Interneurons (association): receive messages from sensory neurons and send out impulses to other interneurons or to motor neurons.

The Nerve Impulse

The cell membrane of the axon is relatively impermeable to Na^+ and by an active transport mechanism pumps Na^+ out and pumps K^+ in. As a consequence the concentration of K^+ is higher inside and the Na^+ concentration is higher outside the cell membrane; thus an electrical potential (called the *resting potential*) exists across the membrane of about 70 millivolts.

A stimulus affects the axon by causing a small section to become permeable to sodium ions: they rush in and the electrical potential across the membrane drops. This is called depolarization and has a duration of approximately 1.5 milliseconds. The electrical potential switches from -70 millivolts to $+50$ millivolts or a total of approximately 120 millivolts. This abrupt, transitory change is called the *action potential*. The membrane then regains its previous impermeability to sodium ions, which are pumped out; potassium ions are pumped in, and the original resting potential is restored.

The impulse travels the length of the axon as a self-regenerating chain reaction in which the action potential in one segment sets off another action potential in the adjacent segment. This way the axon, which would be a poor electrical conductor, is capable of transmitting a nerve impulse with undiminished intensity. This is an all-or-nothing reaction and can only vary in the frequency of the transmission (about 1,000 impulses per second is the limit because there is a brief refractory period between impulses).

The Synapse

The junction across which a nerve impulse travels from one cell to another is known as a synapse. Transmission is by chemical means: the impulse causes the vesicles of the synaptic knobs to empty their contents into the synaptic gap. The transmitter substance crosses the gap and combines with receptor molecules in the membrane of the postsynaptic cell. Synapses are one-way junctions. Among the chemical transmitters are serotonin, acetylcholine, adrenalin, noradrenalin, etc. These substances are rapidly destroyed by specific enzymes after their release.

The Central Nervous System and the Peripheral Nervous System

The brain and spinal cord constitute the central nervous system (CNS). The remainder, lying outside the CNS, is termed the peripheral nervous system (PNS) and can be subdivided into *somatic* and *autonomic*. Somatic includes both motor and sensing neurons; the autonomic is entirely a motor system controlling heart muscle, glands, and smooth muscle.

Somatic Nervous System. In a single reflex action the stimulus is received by a receptor cell and transmitted to the spinal cord. The sensory neuron synapses with an interneuron which, in turn, relays the signal to a motor neuron. The motor neuron causes the appropriate muscle to contract. This is termed a "reflex arc" and allows an "automatic" response before the brain has had time to process the information. The brain, however, is informed.

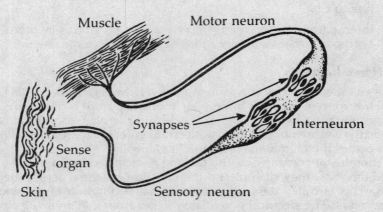

Muscle   Motor neuron

Synapses   Interneuron

Sense organ

Skin   Sensory neuron

Autonomic Nervous System. The autonomic system is divided into the sympathetic and the parasympathetic systems. Most of the major organs are innervated by neurons from both systems. The effects of these systems are often antagonistic to one another. In general the sympathetic system produces the effect of exciting organs involved in fight-or-flight reactions while the parasympathetic system stimulates those organs involved in more tranquil functions. Each system also inhibits most organs stimulated by the other.

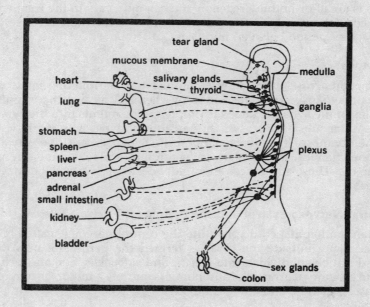

	SYMPATHETIC	PARASYMPATHETIC
Location	Thoraxolumbar	Cranio-sacral
Anatomy	Synapse close to the central nervous system	Synapse close to organ innervated
Example of transmitter compound	Epinephrine	Acetylcholine
Effect	Preparation for physical activity	Promotes vegetative functions (i.e., digestion)

THE REPRODUCTIVE SYSTEM

Gametogenesis in the male occurs in the seminiferous tubules of the testes. The tubules contain two types of cells—Sertoli cells (which nourish the developing cells) and the spermatogenic cells. The series of changes resulting in the formation of sperm cells begins with the growth of spermatogonia into large cells known as primary spermatocytes. At the first meiotic division each primary spermatocyte divides into 2 haploid secondary spermatocytes. The second meiotic division results in the formation of 4 haploid spermatids. The spermatids differentiate into functional sperm cells.

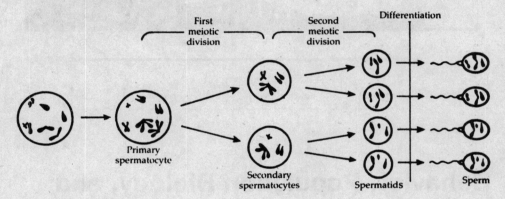

The ovaries are the gamete-producing organs in the female. The primary oocytes develop within nests of cells called follicles. The oocytes (from which the egg develops) are in the outer layer of the ovary. A primary oocyte undergoes

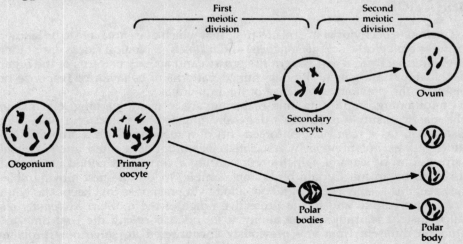

a meiotic division to produce a secondary oocyte and a polar body. This first meiotic division begins within the human fetus during the third month of fetal development and ends at ovulation (this may take place 50 or more years later, at menopause). The second meiotic division, which produces the egg cell and a polar body, does not take place until after fertilization. The first polar body may also divide.

MENSTRUAL CYCLE

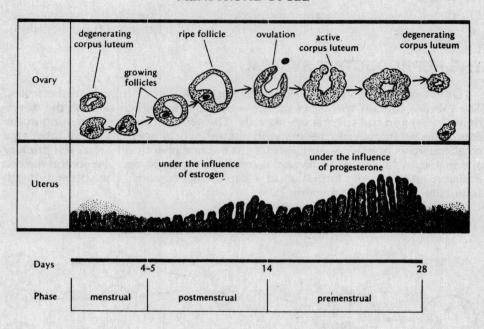

Behavior, Population Biology, and Evolution

BEHAVIOR

The innate behavior of organisms (i.e., that which does not have to be learned) includes biological clocks (*biorhythms*) and *instincts*. Biological clocks are unidentified internal factors that govern the growth and activity patterns of the organism. Instincts are genetically determined patterns of behavior or response not based on the previous experience of the individual.

Conditioning, imprinting, and reasoning are forms of learning. *Conditioning* (the classic example is Pavlov's dog salivating to the sound of a bell) is the association (as a result of reinforcement) of a response with a stimulus with which it was not previously associated. *Imprinting* is a rapid and extremely narrow form of learning which occurs during a very short period in the early life of an organism. Certain birds, for example, follow the first moving object they see; this is an act of recognition, a following response that keeps the young birds close behind and in the protective range of the mother. *Reasoning*, also called insight learning, is the ability to respond correctly the first time to a situation different from any previously encountered; to solve new problems mentally without the necessity of trial and error. Reasoning is the type of learning most prevalent in higher primates, particularly man.

A population is a group of organisms of the same species occupying a particular area at the same time. A community consists of all the populations in a particular area. The role of a population within a community is called the ecological *niche*. The kinds and numbers of organisms in a community are determined by factors in the environment and interactions among the various populations. Among the types of interactions are *competition*, which may result in the elimination of one species or its relegation to a noncompetitive position, and *symbiosis*. Symbiosis is the close association between organisms of different species that live together; the association may be beneficial to both (mutualism), beneficial to one and harmless to the other (commensalism), or beneficial to one and harmful to the other (parasitism).

Dominance is a term used to indicate that not all species in a community are present in equal numbers. It is usual to find a few species that are dominant, i.e., that account for most of the biomass. It is also a term used for describing social hierarchies where dominance/subordination relationships (e.g., pecking order among chickens) tend to give order and stability to the relationships within the group.

A *predator* is an organism that is free-living and feeds on other living organisms. The various trophic (feeding) levels in a system are linked by predator/prey relationships. These relationships tend to regulate the number of organisms but, unlike competition, seldom result in the elimination of a species; they have profound evolutionary effects on the various species.

GENETICS

General Discussion

Chromosomes (colored bodies) are thin, threadlike structures composed of DNA and protein, found in the nucleus of cells and on which genes are located. A *gene* is the unit of heredity, the sequence of nucleotides in DNA that dictates the amino acid sequence of proteins. The position of a gene on a chromosome is known as its *locus*. In diploid organisms a characteristic is determined by a gene pair located on homologous chromosomes, one from each parent. These paired genes are called *alleles*. If an allele is expressed in the phenotype to the exclusion of the other it is *dominant*. If both alleles must be present to be expressed, then they are *recessive*. The *phenotype* is the appearance or outward characteristics of an organism, while the *genotype* is the genetic make-up of an organism. When both genes are alike, the organism is *homozygous* for that trait; if the genes are different it is *heterozygous*. The phenotype characteristic of the vast majority of individuals of a species in a natural environment is called the *wild type*. A *hybrid* is a cross between two genetic types.

Mendel stated the *Principle of Segregation* in his first law: Hereditary traits are determined by discrete factors which occur in offspring as pairs—one factor from each parent. The pairs are separated in sex cells resulting in two kinds of gametes, one gene of the pair in each. Mendel's second law, the *Principle of Independent Assortment*, states that in a cross involving two traits, they behave as if they were entirely independent of one another. (All the traits Mendel studied were on different chromosomes.) If the traits are carried on the same chromosome, they do not assort independently but are linked or are in linkage groups. If the traits are carried on the sex chromosomes they are said to be *sex-linked*. Any chromosomes other than the sex chromosomes are called *autosomes*. Autosomes are alike within pairs. The pair of sex chromosomes is dissimilar in one sex, usually the male.

Near the beginning of meiosis (but not mitosis) the chromosomes arrange themselves in homologous pairs. Each chromosome consists at this stage of 2 identical chromatids attached to each other at the kinetochore. Thus, the pairing process involves 4 chromatids; the resulting complex is known as a *tetrad*. At the time of pairing some genetic material is generally exchanged between homologues. This process is known as *crossing over* and increases the number of different genetic combinations that any given cross can produce, and therefore contributes to *variability* in the population.

CROSSING OVER

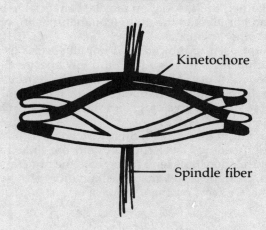

Other sources of genetic variability are *mutations*, which are abrupt changes in genotype. On a molecular basis, a mutation is any change in the sequence of nucleotides in a DNA molecule. These mutations, together with the genetic recombinations that occur at fertilization and meiosis, are the source of variations necessary for biological evolution.

Evolution can be thought of as a change in genetic make-up of populations in successive generations. The *gene pool* is the sum of all the genes possessed by all the individuals in the population. In populations there may be many different alleles although each diploid individual may only possess a maximum of two. The prevalence of an allele in a population is expressed as its gene frequency. The Hardy-Weinberg Law was an attempt to explain why both dominant and recessive genes remained in a population and said, in effect, that sexual recombination does not by itself change the composition of the gene pool. This equilibrium applies only to large populations. In smaller populations the changes in the gene pool which occur as a result of chance are called *genetic drift*.

Extrachromosomal inheritance has been observed in some plants where some characteristics of plastids are inherited exclusively from the maternal plant. The F-factor in *E. coli* is an episome or cytoplasmic factor that is transferred from donor to recipient during conjugation.

Genetic Crosses

Simple dominant homozygous monogenetic cross:

Key: Let "T" stand for tallness (dominant)
 Let "t" stand for shortness (recessive)

1. diploid cells: male   ×   female

2. haploid cells:

3. box cross:

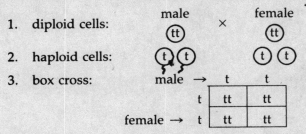

4. phenotype ratio: 4 tall/none short (100% dominance)

5. genotype ratio: 4 Tt / 0 Tt / 0 tt

Simple recessive homozygous monogenetic cross:

1. diploid cells:

2. haploid cells:

3. box cross:

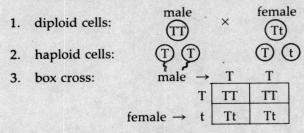

4. phenotype ratio: 4 short / none tall (100% recessive)

5. genotype ratio: 4 tt / 0 TT / 0 Tt

Dominant homozygous-heterozygous monogenetic cross:

1. diploid cells:

2. haploid cells:

3. box cross:

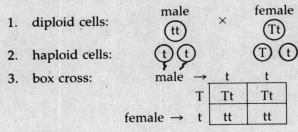

4. phenotype ratio: 4 tall / none short

5. genotype ratio: 2 TT / 2 Tt

Recessive homozygous-heterozygous monogenetic cross:

1. diploid cells:

2. haploid cells:

3. box cross:

4. phenotype ratio: 2 tall / 2 short

5. genotype ratio: 2 Tt / 2 tt

Heterozygous-heterozygous monogenetic cross:

1. diploid cells:

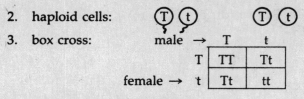

2. haploid cells:

3. box cross: male → T   t

	T	t
T	TT	Tt
t	Tt	tt

female →

4. **phenotype ratio: 3 tall / 1 short**

5. **genotype ratio: 1 TT / 2 Tt / 1 tt**

Dominant homozygous-recessive homozygous monogenetic cross:

1. diploid cells:

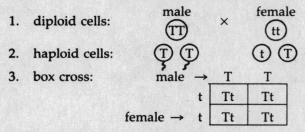

2. haploid cells:

3. box cross: male → T   T

	T	T
t	Tt	Tt
t	Tt	Tt

female →

4. **phenotype ratio: 4 tall / none short**

5. **genotype ratio: 4 Tt / 0 TT / 0 tt**

Blending-intermediate inheritance; heterozygous monogenetic cross:

1. diploid cells:

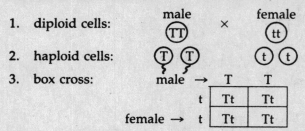

2. haploid cells:

3. box cross: male → T   T

	T	T
t	Tt	Tt
t	Tt	Tt

female →

4. **phenotype ratio: 4 medium / none tall / none short**

5. **genotype ratio: 4 Tt**

Blending-intermediate inheritance; heterozygous monogenetic cross:

1. diploid cells:

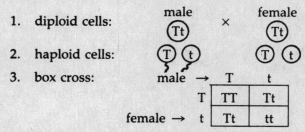

2. haploid cells:

3. box cross: male → T   t

	T	t
T	TT	Tt
t	Tt	tt

female →

4. **phenotype ratio: 1 tall / 2 medium / 1 short**

5. **genotype ratio: 1 TT / 2 Tt / 1 tt**

Heterozygous (dihybrid) digenetic cross:

1. diploid cells: male   ×   female
                     TtBb   TtBb

Key: Let "T" stand for tallness (dominant)
 Let "t" stand for shortness (recessive)
 Let "B" stand for black (dominant)
 Let "b" stand for white (recessive)

2. haploid cells (4 types):

    male
   (TB) (Tb) (tB) (tb)

    female
   (TB) (Tb) (tB) (tb)

3. box cross:

male →	TB	Tb	tB	tb
female → TB	TTBB	TTBb	TtBB	TtBb
Tb	TTBb	TTbb	TtBb	Ttbb
tB	TtBB	TtBb	ttBB	ttBb
tb	TtBb	Ttbb	ttBb	ttbb

4. phenotype ratio: 9 tall, black / 3 tall, white / 3 short, black / 1 short, white

5. genotype ratio: unnecessary

Heterozygous (trihybrid) trigenetic cross:

Key: Let "T" stand for tallness (dominant)
 Let "t" stand for shortness (recessive)
 Let "B" stand for black (dominant)
 Let "b" stand for white (recessive)
 Let "A" stand for skinnyness (dominant)
 Let "a" stand for fatness (recessive)

1. diploid cells:

   male   ×   female
   (TtBbAa)   (TtBbAa)

2. haploid cells (8 types):

      male
 (TBA) (TBa) (TbA) (Tba) (tBA) (tBa) (tbA) (tba)

      female
 (TBA) (TBa) (TbA) (Tba) (tBA) (tBa) (tbA) (tba)

3. box cross:

	TBA	TBa	TbA	Tba	tBA	tBa	tbA	tba
TBA	TTBBAA	TTBBAa	TTBbAA	TTBbAa	TtBBAA	TtBBAa	TtBbAA	TtBbAa
TBa	TTBBAa	TTBBaa	TTBbAa	TTBbaa	TtBBAa	TtBBaa	TtBbAa	TtBbaa
TbA	TTBbAA	TTBbAa	TTbbAA	TTbbAa	TtBbAA	TtBbAa	TtbbAA	TtbbAa
Tba	TTBbAa	TTBbaa	TTbbAa	TTbbaa	TtBbAa	TtBbaa	TtbbAa	Ttbbaa
tBA	TtBBAA	TtBBAa	TtBbAA	TtBbAa	ttBBAA	ttBBAa	ttBbAA	ttBbAa
tBa	TtBBAa	TtBBaa	TtBbAa	TtBbaa	ttBBAa	ttBBaa	ttBbAa	ttBbaa
tbA	TtBbAA	TtBbAa	TtbbAA	TtbbAa	ttBbAA	ttBbAa	ttbbAA	ttbbAa
tba	TtBbAa	TtBbaa	TtbbAa	Ttbbaa	ttBbAa	ttBbaa	ttbbAa	ttbbaa

male

female

4. phenotype ratio: 27 tall, black, skinny
9 tall, black, fat
9 tall, white, skinny
3 tall, white, fat
10 short, black, skinny
2 short, black, fat
3 short, white, skinny
1 short, white, fat

5. genotype ratio: unnecessary

EVOLUTION AND COMPARATIVE ANATOMY

The inheritable variations among individuals in populations occur by chance; all the factors in the environment acting upon these variations is what Darwin called natural selection. For natural selection to occur three things are required:

1. The organisms must be capable of reproduction.

2. Heritable differences among these organisms must exist.

3. The organisms must be tested in the environment.

Three general types of selection operate within populations:

1. Stabilizing selection: the continual elimination of extremes.

2. Disruptive selection: the two extreme types increase at the expense of intermediate forms.

3. Directional selection: selects from the most extreme phenotypic characteristics. Directional selection in nature results in genotypic and phenotypic changes in populations.

Speciation is the formation of one or more new species. The three most important factors involved are:

1. Genetic isolation of a population.

2. Availability of a new ecological niche.

3. Time.

Genetic isolation can occur on remote islands or by other types of geographical or behavioral barriers. Diversification of a group of organisms to fill all the ecological space available is called *adaptive radiation* and is believed to be the major pattern of evolution. Darwin's finches are an example.

Taxonomic Relationships

Living things are classified in a hierarchy of categories on the basis of phylogenetic relationships:

Kingdom
    Phylum
        Class
            Order
                Family
                    Genus
                        Species

Each category is a collective unit containing one or more groups from the next-lower level in the hierarchy.

Biology Review Practice Test

ANSWER SHEET

1 Ⓐ Ⓑ Ⓒ Ⓓ Ⓔ	17 Ⓐ Ⓑ Ⓒ Ⓓ Ⓔ	33 Ⓐ Ⓑ Ⓒ Ⓓ Ⓔ	49 Ⓐ Ⓑ Ⓒ Ⓓ Ⓔ	65 Ⓐ Ⓑ Ⓒ Ⓓ Ⓔ
2 Ⓐ Ⓑ Ⓒ Ⓓ Ⓔ	18 Ⓐ Ⓑ Ⓒ Ⓓ Ⓔ	34 Ⓐ Ⓑ Ⓒ Ⓓ Ⓔ	50 Ⓐ Ⓑ Ⓒ Ⓓ Ⓔ	66 Ⓐ Ⓑ Ⓒ Ⓓ Ⓔ
3 Ⓐ Ⓑ Ⓒ Ⓓ Ⓔ	19 Ⓐ Ⓑ Ⓒ Ⓓ Ⓔ	35 Ⓐ Ⓑ Ⓒ Ⓓ Ⓔ	51 Ⓐ Ⓑ Ⓒ Ⓓ Ⓔ	67 Ⓐ Ⓑ Ⓒ Ⓓ Ⓔ
4 Ⓐ Ⓑ Ⓒ Ⓓ Ⓔ	20 Ⓐ Ⓑ Ⓒ Ⓓ Ⓔ	36 Ⓐ Ⓑ Ⓒ Ⓓ Ⓔ	52 Ⓐ Ⓑ Ⓒ Ⓓ Ⓔ	68 Ⓐ Ⓑ Ⓒ Ⓓ Ⓔ
5 Ⓐ Ⓑ Ⓒ Ⓓ Ⓔ	21 Ⓐ Ⓑ Ⓒ Ⓓ Ⓔ	37 Ⓐ Ⓑ Ⓒ Ⓓ Ⓔ	53 Ⓐ Ⓑ Ⓒ Ⓓ Ⓔ	69 Ⓐ Ⓑ Ⓒ Ⓓ Ⓔ
6 Ⓐ Ⓑ Ⓒ Ⓓ Ⓔ	22 Ⓐ Ⓑ Ⓒ Ⓓ Ⓔ	38 Ⓐ Ⓑ Ⓒ Ⓓ Ⓔ	54 Ⓐ Ⓑ Ⓒ Ⓓ Ⓔ	70 Ⓐ Ⓑ Ⓒ Ⓓ Ⓔ
7 Ⓐ Ⓑ Ⓒ Ⓓ Ⓔ	23 Ⓐ Ⓑ Ⓒ Ⓓ Ⓔ	39 Ⓐ Ⓑ Ⓒ Ⓓ Ⓔ	55 Ⓐ Ⓑ Ⓒ Ⓓ Ⓔ	71 Ⓐ Ⓑ Ⓒ Ⓓ Ⓔ
8 Ⓐ Ⓑ Ⓒ Ⓓ Ⓔ	24 Ⓐ Ⓑ Ⓒ Ⓓ Ⓔ	40 Ⓐ Ⓑ Ⓒ Ⓓ Ⓔ	56 Ⓐ Ⓑ Ⓒ Ⓓ Ⓔ	72 Ⓐ Ⓑ Ⓒ Ⓓ Ⓔ
9 Ⓐ Ⓑ Ⓒ Ⓓ Ⓔ	25 Ⓐ Ⓑ Ⓒ Ⓓ Ⓔ	41 Ⓐ Ⓑ Ⓒ Ⓓ Ⓔ	57 Ⓐ Ⓑ Ⓒ Ⓓ Ⓔ	73 Ⓐ Ⓑ Ⓒ Ⓓ Ⓔ
10 Ⓐ Ⓑ Ⓒ Ⓓ Ⓔ	26 Ⓐ Ⓑ Ⓒ Ⓓ Ⓔ	42 Ⓐ Ⓑ Ⓒ Ⓓ Ⓔ	58 Ⓐ Ⓑ Ⓒ Ⓓ Ⓔ	74 Ⓐ Ⓑ Ⓒ Ⓓ Ⓔ
11 Ⓐ Ⓑ Ⓒ Ⓓ Ⓔ	27 Ⓐ Ⓑ Ⓒ Ⓓ Ⓔ	43 Ⓐ Ⓑ Ⓒ Ⓓ Ⓔ	59 Ⓐ Ⓑ Ⓒ Ⓓ Ⓔ	75 Ⓐ Ⓑ Ⓒ Ⓓ Ⓔ
12 Ⓐ Ⓑ Ⓒ Ⓓ Ⓔ	28 Ⓐ Ⓑ Ⓒ Ⓓ Ⓔ	44 Ⓐ Ⓑ Ⓒ Ⓓ Ⓔ	60 Ⓐ Ⓑ Ⓒ Ⓓ Ⓔ	76 Ⓐ Ⓑ Ⓒ Ⓓ Ⓔ
13 Ⓐ Ⓑ Ⓒ Ⓓ Ⓔ	29 Ⓐ Ⓑ Ⓒ Ⓓ Ⓔ	45 Ⓐ Ⓑ Ⓒ Ⓓ Ⓔ	61 Ⓐ Ⓑ Ⓒ Ⓓ Ⓔ	77 Ⓐ Ⓑ Ⓒ Ⓓ Ⓔ
14 Ⓐ Ⓑ Ⓒ Ⓓ Ⓔ	30 Ⓐ Ⓑ Ⓒ Ⓓ Ⓔ	46 Ⓐ Ⓑ Ⓒ Ⓓ Ⓔ	62 Ⓐ Ⓑ Ⓒ Ⓓ Ⓔ	78 Ⓐ Ⓑ Ⓒ Ⓓ Ⓔ
15 Ⓐ Ⓑ Ⓒ Ⓓ Ⓔ	31 Ⓐ Ⓑ Ⓒ Ⓓ Ⓔ	47 Ⓐ Ⓑ Ⓒ Ⓓ Ⓔ	63 Ⓐ Ⓑ Ⓒ Ⓓ Ⓔ	79 Ⓐ Ⓑ Ⓒ Ⓓ Ⓔ
16 Ⓐ Ⓑ Ⓒ Ⓓ Ⓔ	32 Ⓐ Ⓑ Ⓒ Ⓓ Ⓔ	48 Ⓐ Ⓑ Ⓒ Ⓓ Ⓔ	64 Ⓐ Ⓑ Ⓒ Ⓓ Ⓔ	80 Ⓐ Ⓑ Ⓒ Ⓓ Ⓔ

BIOLOGY PRACTICE TEST

1. With each ventricular systole
   A) the cardiac output decreases   C) ventricles fill with blood
   B) blood pressure decreases   D) blood pressure increases

2. Which of the following cell division stages is unique to meiosis?
   A) prophase   B) interkinesis   C) telophase   D) none of these

3. Which of the following is derived from mesoderm?
   A) liver   B) epidermis   C) lung   D) dermis

4. A structure linked to aging within the cell is called
   A) vacuole   B) ribosome   C) lysosome   D) Golgi apparatus

5. A deficiency in vitamin C would result in
   A) poor blood clotting   B) scurvy   C) rickets   D) anemia

6. The nutrient with the highest caloric value per gram is
   A) starch   B) protein   C) glucose   D) fat

7. The growth of an organism is most likely controlled by
   A) fats   B) sugars   C) minerals   D) proteins   E) carbohydrates

8. The type of RNA found in the nucleus is
   A) messenger RNA   B) ribosomal RNA   C) transfer RNA   D) none of these

9. Which of the following vitamins is water-soluble?
   A) A   B) B   C) D   D) E

10. To be alleles, genes must be
    A) similar in position, but not necessarily on homologous chromosomes
    B) both homozygous, on homologous chromosomes
    C) hybrids, in the same place on homologous chromosomes
    D) similar in position, controlling for the same trait, and on homologous chromosomes

11. The center for control of normal respiration is located in the
    A) cerebellum   B) medulla   C) cerebrum   D) lungs

12. Materials cannot be transported into a cell against a concentration gradient by
    A) osmosis   B) phagocytosis   C) active transport   D) pinocytosis

13. The retinal image is
    A) reversed   B) inverted   C) upright   D) both A and B

14. The centromere is found in the
    A) chromosome   B) spindle   C) nucleolus   D) centrosome

15. Which circulatory pathway is absent in mammals?
    A) renal portal   B) hepatic portal   C) lymphatic   D) dorsal aorta

16. An organism has genotype AaBbCc. What part of its gametes will be Abc?
    A) 1/2   B) 1/3   C) 1/8   D) 1/9

17. A cell would shrivel in
    A) a hypertonic medium   C) an isotonic medium
    B) a hypotonic medium   D) Ringer's solution

18. Which of the following enzymes is specific to carbohydrate metabolism?
    A) lipase   B) pepsin   C) amylase   D) chymotrypsin

19. Intercostal cartilages are found in the
    A) ribs   B) skull   C) pelvis   D) knee

20. The stage in cell division marked by chromosome separation is
    A) interphase   B) telophase   C) prophase   D) anaphase

21. Chromosomes that are similar in size and shape are called
    A) homozygous   B) heterozygous   C) homologous   D) hermaphrodites

22. Visual sensations are identified in the brain at the
    A) parietal lobe   B) frontal lobe   C) occipital lobe   D) fissure of Rolando

23. Air which moves freely through the human respiratory system with each breath is
    A) complemental air   B) tidal air   C) residual air   D) supplemental air

24. The vein joining two beds of capillaries is
    A) superior vena cava   B) inferior vena cava   C) subclavian   D) portal

25. The myelin sheath of a nerve axon is derived from a
    A) dendrite   B) Schwann cell   C) Meissner corpuscle   D) Purkinje cell

26. The tongue does not have specific taste buds for
    A) sweet   B) sour   C) alkaline   D) salty

27. People with blood group O can receive blood from people with blood type
    A) O, A, AB   B) O only   C) O, A, B   D) AB only

28. Which of the following bases is not found in RNA?
    A) cytosine   B) guanine   C) uracil   D) thymine

29. Which is a liquid form of connective tissue?
    A) sweat   B) urine   C) water   D) blood   E) none of these

30. Bipolar neurons would most likely be found
    A) innervating a sense organ (sensory-afferent)   C) in a ganglion
    B) in the cerebrum   D) as a hypophyseal organ

31. Which of the following is derived from the ectoderm?
    A) gonads   B) pituitary   C) pancreas   D) mesentery

32. The energy for resynthesis of ATP in muscle is provided by
    A) lactic acid   B) ATP   C) creatine phosphate   D) glycine

33. Which of the following is most directly active in protein synthesis?
    A) nuclear membrane   B) Golgi bodies   C) mitochondria   D) ribosome

34. In cyclic phosphorilation, what is the electron carrier?
    A) cytochrome   B) ATP   C) ferredoxin   D) NADP

35. In mammals, the embryonic allantois becomes the
    A) ovary   B) urinary bladder   C) large intestine   D) kidney

36. The liver does not
    A) destroy red blood cells   C) secrete hormones
    B) manufacture cholesterol   D) produce nitrogenous wastes

37. An example of an undifferentiated cell is the
    A) hepatic cell   B) cardiac cell   C) neuronal cell   D) fibroblast cell   E) alveolar cell

38. A common aid in the treatment of goiterism is
    A) the scintillation counter   C) the tranplantation technique
    B) the radioisotope   D) the amino acid analyzer

39. Which of the following relationships always aid both species?
    A) competition   B) symbiosis   C) mutualism   D) parasitism

40. Which of the following is derived from the endoderm?
    A) bladder   B) blood   C) skeletal muscle   D) visceral muscle

41. The transmission of impulses between nerve cells and muscle cells is produced by
    A) cholinesterase   B) electricity   C) neostigmine   D) acetylcholine

42. An organism has genotype AABb. What percent of its gametes will be Ab?
    A) 100%   B) 75%   C) 50%   D) 25%

43. Blood entering the kidney nephron first flows through
    A) Henle's loop   B) Bowman's capsule   C) proximal convoluted tubule   D) glomerulus

44. Which of the following is not a vitamin?
    A) biotin   B) folic acid   C) ACTH   D) tocopherol

45. One of the distinguishing taxonomical characteristics in man is his
    A) notochord   B) backbone   C) spleen   D) heart   E) brain

46. The period in life during which the manufacturing of blood cells is transferred from the long to flat bones is
    A) childhood   B) adolescence   C) adulthood   D) old age

47. Which of the following is absent in procaryotic cells?
    A) chlorophyll   B) cell wall   C) endoplasmic reticulum   D) flagella

48. The hormone inhibiting ovarian follicular growth is
    A) FSH   B) testosterone   C) luteinizing hormone   D) progesterone

49. The sickle cell trait can be advantageous
    A) never   B) in America   C) in Africa   D) always

50. What blood type is possible in a child whose father is O, Rh-negative and whose mother is B, Rh-negative
    A) B, Rh-positive   B) A, Rh-negative   C) O, Rh-negative
    D) all the above types are possible

51. Polar bodies are produced in
    A) mitosis   B) spermatogenesis   C) somatic cells   D) fertilization (oogenesis)

52. If brown eyes are dominant and blue eyes are recessive, what percentage of offspring can be expected to have blue eyes if one parent has brown eyes and the other has blue eyes?
    A) 0%   B) 25%   C) 50%   D) cannot be determined from information given

53. According to the modern interpretation of Hackel's principle "Ontogeny recapitulates phylogeny,"
    A) Darwin's Theory of Evolution is incorrect
    B) the ontogeny of a new species will be only slightly different from that of the parent species
    C) mammalian embryos develop into fish embryos, then amphibian embryos, followed by reptilian embryos, etc.
    D) the more closely related two species are, the more divergent their earlier stages of embryonic development

54. Coenzymes are present in which of the following?
A) vitamins B) fats C) carbohydrates D) amino acids

55. A deficiency in vitamin B_1 would result in
A) poor blood clotting B) beriberi C) night blindness D) pellagra

56. A hormone produced by the posterior lobe of the pituitary is
A) vasopressin B) prolactin C) somatotrophic hormone D) ACTH

57. Which of the following is a derivative of the mesencephalon?
A) pineal B) pons C) optic lobes D) cerebellum

58. When pieces of undifferentiated salivary mesoderm and ectoderm are cultivated together, they develop into secretion pockets and ducts characteristic of normal salivary glands. This is an example of
A) differentiation by interaction C) evolution
B) independent development D) chemical modulation

59. Brittle bones may be caused by all of the following except
A) advanced age B) lack of vitamin D C) parathyroid disorders D) acromegaly

60. Which of the following secretions is active in the digestion of both carbohydrates and proteins?
A) ptyalin B) pepsin C) gastric juice D) pancreatic juice

61. Which of the following statements about white blood cells is not true?
A) manufactured in bone marrow C) lack a nucleus
B) manufactured in lymph glands D) move by means of pseudopods

62. Which of the following processes takes place within the cell?
A) peristalsis B) recapitulation C) cyclosis D) cessation

63. Which of the following is a hydrogen pair acceptor in the Krebs cycle?
A) NAD B) ADP C) citric acid D) acetyl-co-A

64. Where does digestion start?
A) stomach B) intestine C) esophagus D) mouth

65. How are hormones distributed throughout the body?
A) by ducts B) by ductless glands C) by blood D) by dendrites

66. Which of the following structures is present in plant cells but not in animal cells?
A) cell membrane B) nuclear membrane C) cell wall D) centrosome

67. Where is oxyhemoglobin produced?
A) spleen B) lungs C) liver D) heart

68. The covering of a virus is composed of
A) DNA B) RNA C) protein D) lipid

69. Classification of organisms is not based on which of the following characteristics?
A) structure B) ancestry C) size D) development

70. The head of a sperm is made up mostly of
A) nucleus B) food C) yolk D) flagellum

71. Rearrange the following in proper sequence in order of occurrence.

1—blastula
2—zygote

3—two-celled stage
4—gastrula

A) 3-2-1-4   B) 2-3-1-4   C) 2-1-3-4   D) 2-3-4-1

72. Which of the following hormones assists the cell in utilizing glucose?
A) cortisone   B) ACTH   C) insulin   D) prolactin

73. Excessive production of a hormone from the _____ results in gigantism.
A) pituitary   B) thymus   C) pineal   D) thyroid

74. Consider that yellow is dominant over green in garden peas. Which of the following crosses would serve to illustrate the Law of Dominance?
A) homozygous yellow × heterozygous yellow
B) heterozygous yellow × heterozygous yellow
C) homozygous yellow × homozygous yellow
D) homozygous yellow × homozygous green

75. In the above problem, suppose Y represents yellow and y represents green. Which of the following crosses would be expected to result in 75% yellow offspring?
A) Yy × YY   B) Yy × Yy   C) YY × yy   D) Yy × yy

76. Which of the following is not a component of the reflex arc?
A) medulla oblongata   B) dendrite   C) synapse   D) ventral horn cell

77. Which of the following is derived from endoderm?
A) lining of the respiratory tract   B) muscle   C) pituitary gland   D) all of these

78. Which of the structures at right would be most severely affected if the cell were to experience a decrease of oxygen?
A) 1   B) 2   C) 3   D) 4

79. In the diagram at right, which structure is responsible for the synthesis of enzymes?
A) 1   B) 2   C) 3   D) 4

80. Breakdown of nutrients into carbon dioxide and water takes place in structure
A) 1   B) 2   C) 3   D) 4

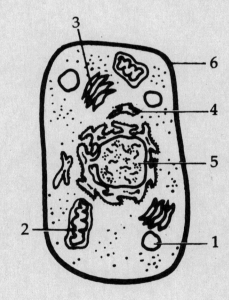

BIOLOGY ANSWER KEY

1. D	21. C	41. B	61. C
2. B	22. C	42. C	62. C
3. D	23. B	43. D	63. A
4. C	24. D	44. C	64. D
5. B	25. B	45. A	65. C
6. D	26. C	46. B	66. C
7. D	27. B	47. C	67. B
8. A	28. D	48. D	68. C
9. B	29. D	49. C	69. C
10. D	30. A	50. C	70. A
11. B	31. B	51. D	71. B
12. A	32. C	52. D	72. C
13. D	33. D	53. B	73. A
14. A	34. A	54. A	74. D
15. A	35. B	55. B	75. B
16. C	36. C	56. A	76. A
17. A	37. D	57. C	77. A
18. C	38. B	58. A	78. B
19. A	39. C	59. D	79. D
20. D	40. A	60. D	80. B

CHAPTER FIVE

Inorganic Chemistry Review

Chemical Properties of the Elements

ATOMIC STRUCTURE

Bohr Structure of the Hydrogen Atom

In 1913 Niels Bohr combined several earlier developments with his interpretation of the line spectrum of hydrogen and proposed a model for the hydrogen atom consisting of a proton at its nucleus and an electron in orbital motion about the nucleus. The structure he proposed was a departure from classical physics and provided the basis for understanding why atoms absorb and emit only certain light frequencies. This model does not work for any atom other than hydrogen but it led to the more general concepts of Quantum Theory. Some of the features of this model are:

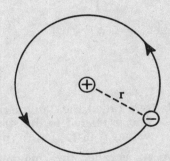

BOHR-RUTHERFORD MODEL FOR THE HYDROGEN ATOM

1. The electron moves around the proton in a circular orbit.

2. Only certain orbital radii are permitted (those radii for which the angular momentum of the electron is an integral multiple of $h/2\pi$).

3. There is no tendency for the electron to gain or lose energy while in orbit.

4. Energy is absorbed or emitted when the electron changes orbits. This energy is either lost or gained in discrete "packets" whose magnitudes equal the energy difference between the two orbits.

Quantum Numbers

Quantum numbers arise naturally from Quantum Theory and are obtained by Schrodinger's Equation. Based on a wave description of the electron, each of the four quantum numbers describes a different physical property.

n n ("principal quantum number") is related to the probability per unit volume of finding the electron in a given volume element at various distances from the nucleus (orbits). n can take all interger values from 1 to ∞. The energy of the electron is given by $E = -K/n^2$.

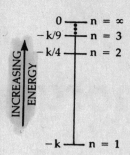

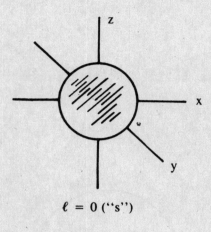

$\ell = 0$ ("s")

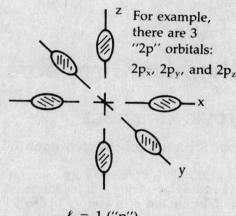

For example, there are 3 "2p" orbitals: $2p_x$, $2p_y$, and $2p_z$

$\ell = 1$ ("p")
for $n \geq 2$

ℓ ℓ is called the "angular momentum" or "azimuthal" quantum number and is related to the shape of the orbital (electron cloud). The range of values is 0, 1, . . ., to $(n-1)$ for each value of n.

m_ℓ m_ℓ is called the "magnetic moment" quantum number and is related to the orientation of the orbital in space. m_ℓ takes all integer values from $-\ell$ to $+\ell$, including zero.

m_s m_s is called the "spin" quantum number. m_s is related to the spin of the electron on its axis (clockwise or counterclockwise) and can take values $+1/2$ and $-1/2$.

All of these may be combined into various representations:

- level ----------- n
- sublevel -------- n and ℓ
- orbital --------- n, ℓ and m_ℓ
- wave function----- n, ℓ, m_ℓ and m_s

Ground and Excited States

Ground state—All electrons are in lowest possible energy levels.
Excited state—Some electrons are in energy levels other than the lowest possible ones.

Absorption and Emission Spectra of Atoms

A spectrum is the result of the resolution of light into its components. It may be classified as one of two types: *continuous* (if all wavelengths are observed) and *line spectrum* (if only some wavelengths of light are visible).

Atoms display line (not continuous) spectra. This is best explained by the existence of discrete orbitals within which each electron must move.

Absorption—Radiant energy (light) is absorbed and the system gains energy. The absorption spectrum looks like a continuous spectrum with some "blacked-out" lines. The black lines appearing in the absorption spectrum correspond to those wavelengths of light which were absorbed by the system to excite electrons out of their ground state.

Emission—Radiant energy (light) is emitted and the system loses energy. The emission spectrum consists of a series of lines each corresponding to a wavelength of emitted light.

Electronic Structure of Atoms

Electrons are placed in their positions following three rules:

1. Aufbau Principle: Electrons occupy the lowest available energy level.

2. Pauli Exclusion Principle: No two electrons in an atom may have identical values for their sets of four quantum numbers (i.e., if two electrons are in the same orbital, then they must have opposite spins).

3. Hund's Rule: Electrons occupy orbitals equivalent in energy, one in each orbital, with parallel spins, until all such orbitals are filled up.

$1S_1$																	$1S_2$
$2S_1$	$2S_2$											$2P_1$	$2P_2$	$2P_3$	$2P_4$	$2P_5$	$2P_6$
$3S_1$	$3S_2$											$3P_1$	$3P_2$	$3P_3$	$3P_4$	$3P_5$	$3P_6$
$4S_1$	$4S_2$	$3D_1$	$3D_2$	$3D_3$	$3D_4$	$3D_5$	$3D_6$	$3D_7$	$3D_8$	$3D_9$	$3D_{10}$	$4P_1$	$4P_2$	$4P_3$	$4P_4$	$4P_5$	$4P_6$
$5S_1$	$5S_2$	$4D_1$	$4D_2$	$4D_3$	$4D_4$	$4D_5$	$4D_6$	$4D_7$	$4D_8$	$4D_9$	$4D_{10}$	$5P_1$	$5P_2$	$5P_3$	$5P_4$	$5P_5$	$5P_6$
$6S_1$	$6S_2$	$5D_1$	$5D_2$	$5D_3$	$5D_4$	$5D_5$	$5D_6$	$5D_7$	$5D_8$	$5D_9$	$5D_{10}$	$6P_1$	$6P_2$	$6P_3$	$6P_4$	$6P_5$	$6P_6$
$7S_1$	$7S_2$	$6D_1$	$6D_2$	$6D_3$													

$4F_2$	$4F_3$	$4F_4$	$4F_5$	$4F_6$	$4F_7$	$4F_8$	$4F_9$	$4F_{10}$	$4F_{11}$	$4F_{12}$	$4F_{13}$	$4F_{14}$	$5D_1$
$5F_2$	$5F_3$	$5F_4$	$5F_5$	$5F_6$	$5F_7$	$5F_8$	$5F_9$	$5F_{10}$	$5F_{11}$	$5F_{12}$	$5F_{13}$	$5F_{14}$	$6D_1$

The $5D_1$ and $6D_1$ "drop" to the 4F and 5F while these sublevels are being filled and do not reappear until their completion.

The order of adding electrons is left-to-right along each row. When a row is completed, the next row is started. This results in adding electrons in order of increasing energy, as required by the Aufbau Principle.

The following mnemonic device should help you remember the order in which sublevels are filled.

Maximum number of electrons in each sublevel:
S ------------- 2 electrons
P ------------- 6 electrons
D ------------- 10 electrons
F ------------- 14 electrons

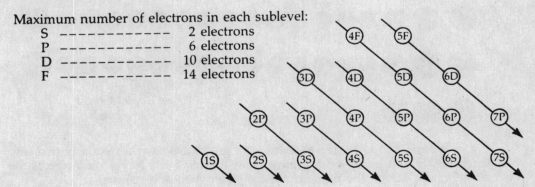

PERIODIC TABLE

Classification of Elements

The classification of elements into groups was originally and independently done by Meyer and Mendeleev on the basis of similarities between their chemical and physical properties. Based on the fact that properties repeat (periodicity), elements were grouped so that those in the same group (column) display similar properties.

The classification of elements into groups is now done by their electronic structure: elements in the same group have the same outer electronic configuration, that is, the same number of valence electrons.

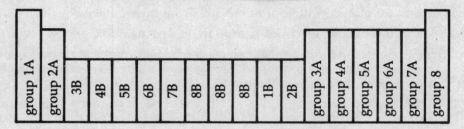

The number of valence electrons for an element in an A group equals the group number. For example:

Nitrogen—$1S_2, 2S_2, 2P_3$

(group 5A)   5 valence electrons (outer shell)

Relative Atomic Sizes

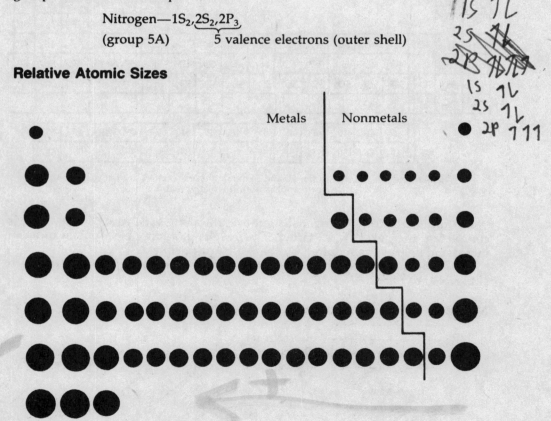

Metals   Nonmetals

The atomic diameter decreases as you go to the right across a period and increases as you go down a group. Note the relatively larger diameter of the noble gases, due to the filling up of the outer shell of electrons.

Comparison of Physical and Chemical Properties

METALS		NONMETALS

• Good electrical conductors
• Good heat conductors
• Lustrous
• malleable
• ductile
• States at room temp. and 1-atm pressure: all solid except Hg (liquid)
	PHYSICAL PROPERTIES	• Poor electrical conductors
		• Poor heat conductors
		• Not lustrous
		
		• States at room temp. and 1-atm pressure:
		  11 gases (H_2, O_2, Cl_2, F_2, N_2, and all the noble gases)
		   1 liquid (bromine)
		  10 solids (the rest)

• Form basic oxides • Form cations in solution • Have low ionization potential and readily form cations • Good reducing agents • Usually found in nature in the form of ores (combined with a nonmetal such as oxygen or sulfur)	**CHEMICAL PROPERTIES**	• Form acidic oxides • Form anions in solution (often with oxygen attached to nonmetal) • Have high electron affinities and readily form anions • Good oxidizing agents

Where A metals are representative and B metals are transition metals, chemical bonding can be generalized as follows:

A metal + nonmetal → ionic compound

nonmetal + nonmetal → covalent compound

B metal + nonmetal → (varies)

Variation of Chemical Properties (Excluding the Noble Gases)

The effect of position on the atomic table upon various properties is illustrated below.

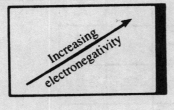

Increasing electronegativity

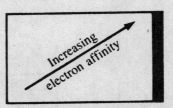

Increasing electron affinity

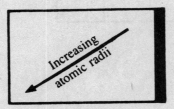

Increasing atomic radii

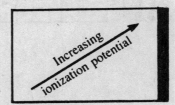

Increasing ionization potential

PERIODIC TABLE OF THE ELEMENTS

Representative elements (s block)

Representative elements (p block)

Transition elements (d block)

Inner transition elements (f block)

1A	2A	3B	4B	5B	6B	7B	8B	8B	8B	1B	2B	3A	4A	5A	6A	7A	8A
1 H 1.0080																	2 He 4.0026
3 Li 6.941	4 Be 9.0122											5 B 10.81	6 C 12.011	7 N 14.007	8 O 15.9994	9 F 19.00	10 Ne 20.183
11 Na 22.9898	12 Mg 24.305											13 Al 26.98	14 Si 28.09	15 P 30.974	16 S 32.064	17 Cl 35.453	18 Ar 39.95
19 K 39.102	20 Ca 40.08	21 Sc 44.96	22 Ti 47.90	23 V 50.94	24 Cr 51.996	25 Mn 54.94	26 Fe 55.85	27 Co 58.93	28 Ni 58.71	29 Cu 63.55	30 Zn 65.37	31 Ga 69.72	32 Ge 72.59	33 As 74.92	34 Se 78.96	35 Br 79.9	36 Kr 83.8
37 Rb 85.468	38 Sr 87.62	39 Y 88.91	40 Zr 91.22	41 Nb 92.91	42 Mo 95.94	43 Tc 98.91	44 Ru 101.07	45 Rh 102.91	46 Pd 106.4	47 Ag 107.87	48 Cd 112.4	49 In 114.82	50 Sn 118.69	51 Sb 121.75	52 Te 127.6	53 I 126.9	54 Xe 131.3
55 Cs 132.91	56 Ba 137.34	57 La 138.91	72 Hf 178.49	73 Ta 180.95	74 W 183.85	75 Re 186.2	76 Os 190.2	77 Ir 192.2	78 Pt 195.1	79 Au 196.97	80 Hg 200.59	81 Tl 204.37	82 Pb 207.2	83 Bi 208.98	84 Po (210)	85 At (210)	86 Rn (222)
87 Fr (223)	88 Ra (226)	89 Ac (227)															

58 Ce 140.12	59 Pr 140.91	60 Nd 144.24	61 Pm (147)	62 Sm 150.4	63 Eu 151.96	64 Gd 157.25	65 Tb 158.93	66 Dy 162.5	67 Ho 164.93	68 Er 167.26	69 Tm 168.93	70 Yb 173.04	71 Lu 174.97
90 Th 232.04	91 Pa 231.04	92 U 238.03	93 Np 237.05	94 Pu (242)	95 Am (243)	96 Cm (247)	97 Bk (247)	98 Cf (247)	99 Es (254)	100 Fm (253)	101 Md (256)	102 No (254)	103 Lw (257)

States of Matter

GAS PHASE

Characteristics of Gases

1. Gases expand to fill any container.
2. Gases change shape to fit the container.
3. Gases are easily compressible.
4. Gases diffuse rapidly.
5. 1 mole of an *ideal gas* occupies 22.4 liters at STP (standard temperature and pressure: 0°C and 760 mmHg)

Units Used with the Gas Phase

Temperature ------------------ °C, °K, °F
Pressure -------- force/area ----- dyne/cm
                                    torr = mmHg, atmospheres
Quantity ------------------- grams (mass), moles
Volume ------------------- ml, l, cm^3, etc.

Ideal Gas Law

The Ideal Gas Law summarizes the following relationships:

Gay-Lussac's Law: $P = kT$ (V is constant). (The pressure of a gas at constant volume is directly proportional to its absolute temperature.)

Boyle's Law: $P = k/V$ (T is constant). (The volume of a gas at constant temperature is inversely proportional to the applied pressure.)

Charles' Law: $V = kT$ (P is constant). (The volume of a gas at constant pressure is directly proportional to its absolute temperature.)

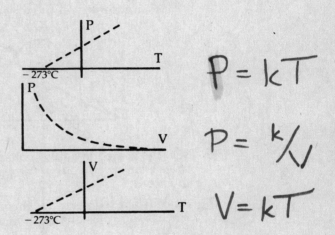

$$P = kT$$

$$P = k/V$$

$$V = kT$$

The density of a gas is proportional to the pressure at a given temperature and to the molecular weight at a given temperature and pressure.

IDEAL GAS LAW

$$PV = nRT \quad \text{or} \quad mw = \frac{gRT}{PV} \quad \text{or} \quad d = \frac{mwP}{RT}$$

P = pressure, V = volume, T = temperature in °K, d = density, R = ideal gas constant, g = mass in grams, mw = molecular weight, n = number of moles

Kinetic Molecular Theory of Gases

Postulates

1. Gases consist of molecules in continuous, random motion.
2. A gas occupies a very large volume in comparison to the volume of all its molecules.

3. Collisions between molecules are elastic (no attractive forces exist between the molecules).

4. The average kinetic energy is proportional to the absolute temperature of the gas.

Deductions

1. Pressure is caused by collisions on the walls (the more collisions, the higher the pressure).

2. The volume of the gas molecules themselves is negligible compared to the volume of the container.

3. The average velocity of particles in a gas is directly proportional to the absolute temperature of the gas. Thus, when the velocity is zero so is the temperature; and the velocity increases with increasing temperature.

4. The average molecular velocity is inversely proportional to the square root of the molecular weight of the gas.

5. Not all particles have the same velocity; rather, there is a distribution centered about the average velocity (see the Maxwell-Boltzman distribution curves below).

   (At higher temperatures the mean is higher, but the frequencies are lower and the distribution range wider.)

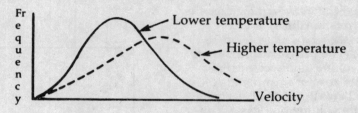

6. If gas is heated in a fixed volume, then pressure increases because higher molecular speed causes the particles to collide with the walls more frequently.

7. At constant temperature, the pressure decreases as the volume increases since fewer collisions per unit area occur as the walls move farther apart.

Deviations of Real Gas Behavior from Ideal Gas Law

Because real gases have attractive forces between particles and because these particles do occupy volume, deviations occur from the behavior predicted by the Ideal Gas Law. These deviations are most predominant at high pressures (low relative volumes, where the volume of the container is not so large compared to the volume of the gas molecules) and at low temperatures (when the kinetic energy of the particles is low and the forces between the particles become relatively more important).

Mixtures of Gases

Gases form homogeneous mixture (solutions) in all proportions. Their properties are:

$$n_t = n_1 + n_2 + n_3 + \ldots$$
$$V_t = V_1 + V_2 + V_3 + \ldots$$
$$T_t = T_1 + T_2 + T_3 + \ldots$$
$$P_t = P_1 + P_2 + P_3 + \ldots$$

The several quantities P_i are called the partial pressures and may be calculated by

$$P_iV = n_iRT \quad \text{or} \quad P_i = X_iP_t \text{ (where } X_i = \text{ the mole component \#i)}$$

CONDENSED PHASES

Properties of Liquids and Solids

LIQUIDS		SOLIDS
• Flow to fit container shape. • Do not expand to fit container. • Not easily compressible.	CHARACTERISTICS	• Do not flow. • Do not expand to fit container. • Not compressible. Crystalline Solids • Melt at one temperature. • Tend to break with smooth surfaces.
• Vapor pressure (pressure exerted by that portion of the liquid which vaporizes at a given temperature in a closed container). "Volatility" decreases when nonvolatile solute is added (or when attractive forces between particles increase). • Boiling point (the temperature at which the vapor pressure of the liquid equals the external pressure) increases as the vapor pressure decreases. • Viscosity (resistance to flow) generally decreases as temperature increases and increases as the attractive forces between the particles increase. • Surface tension (the energy required to increase the surface area by a unit amount) increases as the attractive forces between particles increase. This is a measure of the inward pull on the surface and causes the meniscus. • Heat of vaporization (heat required to cause a given amount of liquid to vaporize) increases as the attractive forces between particles increase.	PHYSICAL PROPERTIES	• Heat of fusion (heat required to cause a given amount of solid to melt) increases as the attractive forces between particles increase. Heat of fusion is equal to the negative heat of crystallization. • Melting point (the temperature at which the substance changes phase from solid to liquid or vice versa) increases as the attractive forces between particles increase. *Crystalline solids* are often confused with *amorphous solids* which are not really solids but supercooled liquids (particles are still random but the flow is extremely slow). Amorphous solids get soft over a temperature range and break with jagged edges. Examples include glass, plastics, and rubber.

Qualitative Explanation

In liquids, the particles are random and close together. There is enough space for particles to move past one another.

In solids, the particles are highly ordered, held rigidly in place and close together. There is no translational motion of particles but they may vibrate.

Quantitative Treatment

Liquids are very difficult to deal with quantitatively since both kinetic energy and attractive forces between particles are involved.

Solids are treated as orderly 3-dimensional crystal lattices which can be reproduced by displacement of the fundamental unit cell. There are three general types of unit cells: *simple* cubic, *body-centered* cubic and *face-centered* cubic. Cells are sometimes characterized by the number of nearest neighbors or "coordination number" which is often 4 (tetrahedral) or 6 (hexahedral arrangement).

Crystal Classification

CRYSTAL CLASSIFICATION	UNIT PARTICLES	FORCES BETWEEN PARTICLES	PROPERTIES	EXAMPLES
Atomic	atoms	London Dispersion	soft, very low melting point, poor electrical and thermal conductors	rare gases: Ar,Kr
Molecular	polar and nonpolar molecules	Van der Waals forces: London Dispersion, dipole-dipole, hydrogen bonds	soft, low to moderately high melting point, poor electrical and thermal conductors	methane, sugar, dry ice
Ionic	positive and negative ions	electrostatic attraction	hard and brittle, high melting point, poor electrical and thermal conductors in solid state	salts
Network	atoms (a single molecule)	covalent bonds	very hard, very high melting point, poor thermal and electrical conductors	SiC, quartz, diamond
Metallic	cations in electron cloud	metallic bonds	soft to very hard, low to very high melting points, excellent electrical and thermal conductors, ductile and malleable	all metallic elements

FORCES BETWEEN PARTICLES

1. Interionic
   - very strong
   - operate in ionic substances (between A metals and nonmetals)
   - determine the properties of ionic substances.

2. Covalent
   - very strong
   - operate between two nonmetals and sometimes between B metals and nonmetals
   - determine the chemical properties of network compounds
   - determine the physical properties of network compounds
   - do not determine the chemical properties of molecular compounds
   - determine the physical properties of molecular compounds

3. Intermolecular
   - relatively weak
   - determine the physical properties only of atomic and molecular compounds
   - known collectively as "Van der Waals" forces:

WEAKER ↑

Dipole-dipole—(between polar molecules)

London Dispersion—(instantaneous induced dipole attractions)

STRONGER ↓

Hydrogen bonding—(hydrogen atom on one molecule to a small electronegative atom on another molecule or another part of the same molecule)

PHASE EQUILIBRIA

Phase Changes

The changes from one phase to another are illustrated in the figure below:

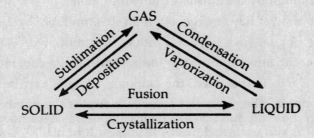

Phase Diagram

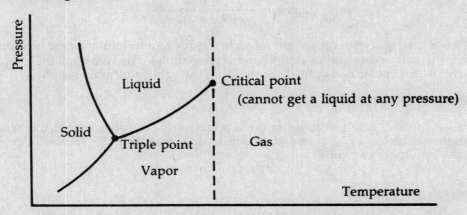

A phase diagram such as the one above can be used to obtain the following information:

- boiling point at a given pressure
- melting point at a given pressure
- conditions for equilibrium between various phases
- conditions for existence of various phases
- triple point
- critical temperature
- critical pressure
- behavior upon heating or cooling at constant pressure
- behavior upon compression or expansion at constant temperature

Chemical Reactions

CHEMICAL COMPOUNDS

Description of Composition

$$\% \text{ weight:} \quad \%A = \frac{(\text{grams of A})(100)}{\text{total grams}}$$

empirical formula: simplest formula, C_6H_6 = CH

Procedure for calculating the empirical formula from either the percent or mass composition:

1. Determine the number of moles of each component.
2. Divide through by the smallest number of moles.
3. If you do not yet have integers (within .05), multiply by 2.
4. If you do not yet have integers (within .05), multiply by 3.
5. Continue with integers until only integers are obtained for mole quantities.
6. When integers are obtained, the empirical formula may be set up.

Molecular formula: The molecular formula indicates the number of atoms of each element in the compound. While ionic compounds have no molecules, the term "formula" is still used and means "simplest formula."

Mole: Can be converted to grams and vice versa by using

$$\text{moles} = \frac{\text{grams}}{\text{molecular weight}}$$

Atomic weight: Atomic weight refers to the average weight of a type of atoms and is usually expressed in amu's (atomic mass units). The sum of all the atomic weights in a molecule is called the molecular weight or formula weight.

Avogadro's Number

One mole of any substance is the amount of the substance with the same number of atoms as 12 grams of carbon-12, that is, 6.02×10^{23} atoms or Avogadro's number of atoms.

MASS CHANGES

Stoichiometry

Stoichiometry is that branch of chemistry that deals with the quantitative relationships that exist between substances undergoing chemical change, such as how much of one substance will react with or be produced by a given quantity of another. Two methods are suggested for solving stoichiometric problems, the mole method and the proportion method.

MOLE METHOD

What weight of HCl in grams may be obtained by heating 234 g of NaCl with excess H_2SO_4? The balanced reaction is:

$$2NaCl + H_2SO_4 \rightarrow Na_2SO_4 + 2HCl$$

Solution:

$$234 \text{ g NaCl} = \frac{234 \text{ g}}{58.5 \text{ g/g mole}} = 4 \text{ g moles NaCl}$$

From the balanced equation we see that 2 g moles NaCl produce 2 g moles HCl, so 4 g moles NaCl will produce 4 g moles HCl.

$$4 \times 36.5 \text{ g} = 146 \text{ g}$$

PROPORTION METHOD
(same problem)

Place the formula weights multiplied by the correct coefficients below the formulas in the equation and the amounts (given and unknown) above.

$$\overset{234\ g}{2NaCl} + H_2SO_4 \rightarrow Na_2SO_4 + \underset{2(36.5\ g)}{\overset{X\ g}{2HCl}}$$
$$\underset{2(58.5\ g)}{}$$

and then set up and solve the proportion.

Solution:

$$\frac{234}{117} = \frac{X}{73}$$

or   X = 146

Law of Conservation of Mass

The mass before a chemical reaction is the same as after, and is expressed in the balancing of the equation.

Chemical Equations

Components: reactants $\xrightarrow[\text{(yield)}]{\text{produce}}$ products

Descriptions:

$$1N_2 + 3H_2 \rightarrow 2NH_3$$

1. In terms of *molecules*: 1 molecule of nitrogen reacts with 3 molecules of hydrogen to form 2 molecules of ammonia.

2. In terms of *moles*: 1 mole of nitrogen reacts with 3 moles of hydrogen to form 2 moles of ammonia.

General types:

1. *Precipitation:* Two ions in solution combine to form a product which precipitates.

$$X^{+m} + Y^{-n} \rightarrow X_nY_m \text{ (S)}$$

2. *Oxidation-Reduction:* Oxidizing agent oxidizes reducing agent (or, reducing agent reduces oxidizing agent).

    Mnemonic device, LEO says GER, can be useful: *Loss* of *Electrons* is *Oxidation*; *Gain* of *Electrons* is *Reduction*.

oxidizing agent + reducing agent $\leftrightharpoons$ reduced subst. + oxidized subst.

    Redox equations may be balanced like algebraic systems of equations by first balancing the electrons lost or gained in each half-reaction.

Example:

$$MnO_4^- + Fe^{+2} \rightarrow Mn^{+2} + Fe^{+3}$$

oxidation: $Fe^{+2} \leftrightharpoons Fe^{+3} + 1e^-$

reduction: $Mn^{+7} + 5e^- \leftrightharpoons Mn^{+2}$

Multiplying the top equation by 5 and adding it to the bottom equation we get .

$$5Fe^{+2} + Mn^{+7} \rightarrow 5Fe^{+3} + Mn^{+2}$$

One special redox case is *disproportionation*, or self oxidation-reduction. *Example:*

$$Cl_2 + Cl_2 \rightleftharpoons Cl^- + ClO^- \text{ (in basic solution)}$$
(Equation not balanced)

3. *Acid-Base*

Acid: • yields H_3O^+ in solution (Arrhenius)
     • yields a proton (Brönsted-Lowry)
     • accepts an electron pair (Lewis)
Base: • yields OH^- in solution (Arrhenius)
     • accepts protons (H^+) (Brönsted-Lowry)
     • yields an electron pair (Lewis)

Reaction:

Arrhenius   An acid reacts with a base to produce a salt and water.

$$acid + base \rightarrow salt + H_2O$$

Brönsted-Lowry An acid transfers a proton to its conjugate base.

$$acid_1 + base_2 \rightarrow base_1 + acid_2$$

Example:

$$H_2O + NH_3 \rightarrow OH^- + NH_4^+$$

Lewis   Base donates a pair of electrons to an acid.

$$base + acid \rightarrow adduct$$

ENERGY CHANGES IN REACTIONS

Energy

Energy is the ability to do work or transfer heat. There are two main kinds of energy: *kinetic energy* or energy due to motion ($KE = \frac{1}{2}mv^2$) and *potential energy* or energy due to position or state.

Forms of energy: heat (measured in calories), light, chemical energy, mechanical energy, electrical energy.

Enthalpy

The thermodynamic function *enthalpy* is defined by

$$H = E + PV \text{ (at constant pressure)}$$

where E is the internal energy, P is the pressure and V is the volume.

Enthalpy is often called the "heat content." The change in enthalpy,

$H_{prod.} - H_{react.} = \Delta H$, is the heat absorbed by a process at constant pressure. The change in enthalpy is related to the internal energy of the system by the expression

$$\Delta H = \Delta E + P\Delta V$$

Enthalpy, like internal energy, pressure, volume, and temperature, is a function of the state of the system alone, independent of the manner in which that state was achieved.

A reaction is *exothermic* if heat is given up,

$$A + B \rightarrow C + D + n \text{ cal } (\Delta H = -n \text{ cal})$$

or *endothermic* if heat is absorbed

$$m \text{ cal } + E + F \rightarrow G + K (\Delta H = m \text{ cal})$$

Special Cases of Enthalpy Change

- Heat of vaporization ‒‒‒‒‒‒‒‒‒‒ ΔH(vap)
- Heat of condensation ‒‒‒‒‒‒‒‒‒‒ ΔH(cond)
- Heat of sublimation ‒‒‒‒‒‒‒‒‒‒ ΔH(sub)
- Heat of deposition ‒‒‒‒‒‒‒‒‒‒ ΔH(dep)
- Heat of fusion ‒‒‒‒‒‒‒‒‒‒‒‒ ΔH(fus)
- Heat of crystallization ‒‒‒‒‒‒‒‒ ΔH(cryst)
- Heat of formation ‒‒‒‒‒‒‒‒‒‒‒ ΔH(formation)
  (The enthalpy change when 1 mole of a compound is formed from its constituent elements. If formation takes place at 1 atm and 25°C and all reactants and products are in their most stable forms, then it is called the "standard heat of formation." The heat of formation of an element is taken as zero.)
- Energy of bond formation ‒‒‒‒‒‒‒ ΔH(bond formation)
  (The energy released (at constant pressure) when two very distant atoms come together to form a bond.)
- Bond dissociation energy: (the opposite of the energy of bond formation.)

General Rules

1. The energy change is proportional to the amount of substance involved.

2. The energy change for the reverse reaction has the same magnitude, but opposite sign, as the forward reaction.

3. In a step reaction, the energy change for the reaction is the summation of the energy changes for each step (ΔH, ΔS and ΔG are additive).

4. In an overall process, the energy change for the reaction is independent of the pathway followed.

Hess's Law of Constant Heat Summation

The change in enthalpy for any chemical reaction is constant, regardless of whether the reaction occurs in one or several steps.

Hess's Law allows us to treat thermochemical equations algebraically.

Spontaneity

The spontaneity of a reaction refers to its tendency to proceed (or happen by itself).

1. Enthalpy and spontaneity: At first it was thought that exothermic reactions were spontaneous. While this is generally true, exceptions do exist. For example:

$$H_2O \text{ (liq.)} \rightarrow H_2O \text{ (s)}$$

is an exothermic change, but not spontaneous at any temperature above freezing.

2. Entropy and spontaneity: Entropy is a measure of the randomness of the system (the symbol is S). Its changes obey the same general rules as changes in enthalpy.

$$\Delta S = S_{prod.} - S_{react.}$$

$$\Delta S = \frac{1}{T} \int dQ = \frac{Q}{T}$$

A positive value for ΔS means the system is becoming more random:
- from solid to liquid
- from liquid to gas
- number of moles of gas increasing as reaction proceeds
- etc.

Entropy, like enthalpy, is related to spontaneity. The spontaneity of a chemical reaction depends on the balance of these two quantities, minimum enthalpy change versus maximum entropy change.

3. Free energy and spontaneity: A third thermodynamic function, the free energy (symbol G), is related to the enthalpy and entropy of a system by the equation

$$\Delta G = H - T\Delta S$$

Changes in free energy obey the same general rules as the other two functions. The change may be obtained by

$$\Delta G_{reaction} = \Delta G_{products} - \Delta G_{reactants}$$

ΔG is directly related to spontaneity.
- If negative, the process is spontaneous as written.
- If zero, the process is in equilibrium.
- If positive, the process is not spontaneous as written. Rather, it is spontaneous in the opposite direction.

Observations

1. Contrary to many "conservation" principles, entropy can be created at will and tends to increase in natural processes if everything else is equal. No process is possible in which entropy decreases.

2. Often (not always), at relatively low temperatures H determines the sign on G, while at high temperatures T S determines the sign on G.

RATE PROCESSES: KINETICS

Rate

Kinetics is that area of chemistry dealing with the rates at which chemical reactions occur.

The following factors affect the rate:

- the nature of the reactants
- the temperature (a temperature increase of about 10°C causes the rate to double)
- the concentration (directly related to the rate)
- the presence of a catalyst

The rate is not determined by thermodynamics but by individual steps called mechanisms. It is often assumed that the slowest step is the most important one (the rate-determining step). The net equation represents the sum of the equations for the steps.

A potential energy diagram for the hypothetical reaction $X_2 + Y_2 \leftrightharpoons X_2Y_2 \leftrightharpoons 2XY$ is shown in the figure below.

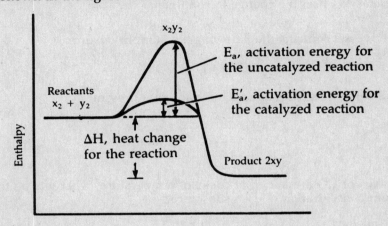

Rate Expression

If $aA + bB + \ldots \rightarrow$ products, then rate $= k[A]^a[B]^b \ldots$ where k is the rate constant and a, b, ... are the orders of their respective reactants. $a + b + \ldots$ is the overall order.

The rate is dependent on the activation energy and not on the energies of either the reactants or the products.

Equilibrium

At equilibrium, the forward reaction rate is equal to the reverse reaction rate. While equilibrium is an overall dynamic situation, there appears to be no overall reaction in either direction.

Quantitatively, equilibrium is dealt with as follows: Given the balanced equation

$$aA + bB \rightleftarrows cC + dD$$

the equilibrium constant, K, is found by

$$K = \frac{[C]^c[D]^d}{[A]^a[B]^b}$$

(If $K \gg 1$, then there are mainly products in the equilibrium; if $K \ll 1$, then there are mainly reactants in the equilibrium).

K is affected only by changes in temperature, not by adding a catalyst or by changes in concentrations.

Concentrations of reactants and products present in solution are expressed in (moles solute)/(liters solution), i.e, molarities. If products and/or reactants are gaseous, partial pressures measured in atmospheres may be used instead of molar concentrations.

$$K = \frac{(P_C)^c \cdot (P_D)^d}{(P_A)^a \cdot (P_B)^b}$$

In this case, liquids and solids are not included in the equilibrium expression (their concentration is taken to be [1]).

Le Chatelier's Principle

If a system at equilibrium is subjected to a change of conditions which disturbs the equilibrium, the system will shift towards a new equilibrium state in such a direction as to offset the change in conditions.

Example:
A 1-liter vessel contains the following equilibrium mixture:

$$CO + Cl_2 \rightleftharpoons COCl_2$$

The following quantities of each substance are present:

$$COCl_2 \ ------- \ .4 \text{ moles}$$
$$CO \ --------- \ .1 \text{ moles}$$
$$Cl_2 \ -------- \ .5 \text{ moles}$$

If .3 moles of CO are added at constant temperature, what will be the new equilibrium concentration of each substance?

$$K = \frac{[COCl_2]}{[CO][Cl_2]} = \frac{(.4)}{(.1)(.5)} = 8$$

$$K = \frac{(.4 + x)}{(.1 + .3 - x)(.5 - x)} \leftarrow \text{new concentrations}$$

$$8 = \frac{(.4 + x)}{(.2 - .9x + x^2)}$$

Solving the quadratic equation (and ignoring the negative root):

$$x \approx .177$$
$$[COCl_2] = .577$$
$$[CO] = .223$$
$$[Cl_2] = .323$$

Aqueous Solutions

GENERAL PROPERTIES

Solutions

Solute: That which is being dissolved, usually the substance present in smaller quantity.
Solvent: That which does the dissolving, usually the substance present in greater quantity.

There are three qualitative ways of distinguishing concentration:

1.   dilute—concentrated
2.   unsaturated—saturated—supersaturated
3.   real—analytical

There are two quantitative ways of distinguishing concentration:

1.   amount of solute/total amount
     M   = molarity (moles of solute/liter of solution)
     X_A = mole fraction (moles of A/total moles)
     N   = normality (equivalents of solute/liter of solution)
     % by weight = (grams of solute) (100)/(total grams)

2.   amount of solute/amount of solvent
     m   = molality (moles of solute/kg of solvent)

Colligative Properties of Solutions

Colligative properties are those that depend on the number of solute particles in the solution, but not on the kind of solute.

Vapor pressure depression: The vapor pressure of the solvent decreases as non-volatile solute is added.

Boiling point elevation: The boiling point of the solvent increases as nonvolatile solute is added.

Freezing point depression: The freezing point of the solvent decreases as non-volatile solute is added.

These properties are illustrated in the following phase diagram.

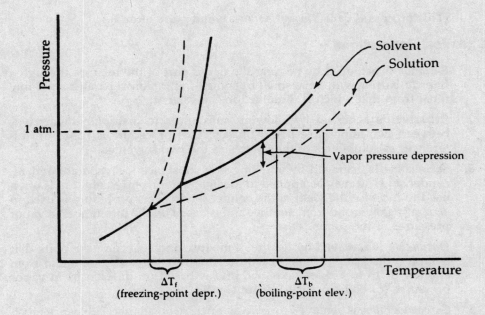

Osmosis: This is a special case of diffusion and is concerned with the flow of solvent from a region of low concentration of solute to a region of high concentration *across a semipermeable membrane.* Tendency to occur is measured in terms of osmotic pressure (the pressure that must be applied to stop osmosis); at constant temperatures the osmotic pressure is proportional to the concentration of the solution.

Freezing Point Depression Boiling Point Elevation

$$\Delta T = -i \cdot K_f \cdot m \qquad \Delta T = +i \cdot K_b \cdot m$$

where i = number of particles per molecule, m = molality, K_f = 1.86 for water, K_b = .52 for water and ΔT is in °C or °K.

Colloids

Colloids are homogeneous solutions that contain particles larger than ions or molecules but small enough to be generally invisible under a microscope. Colloidal matter (solute) is considered the dispersed phase suspended in the dispersal medium (solvent). Colloidal systems include aerosols, foams, emulsions, and gels. Colloidal systems scatter light (Tyndall effect) and can be used to show Brownian motion. True solute particles, such as salts, can be removed from colloidal systems by dialysis or ultrafiltration.

SOLUBILITY

Ions in Aqueous Solution

Ions may come from:

1. Weak electrolytes if solute only partially ionizes (NH_3, CH_3COOH, etc.).

2. Strong electrolytes if solute ionizes to a large extent (HCl, HNO_3, H_2SO_4, NaCl, etc.)
    The equation for the product of ions (solvation) is

$$M_uX_v + (u \cdot p + v \cdot q)H_2O = uM(H_2O)_p + vX(H_2O)_q$$

(This process is called *hydration* and p and q are often 6.)

Chemical Separations

1. *Filtration* is achieved by passing the liquid part of the mixture through a filter (a barrier with very small openings). Filtration separates solid material from that which is dissolved in the solvent.

2. *Extraction* is achieved by allowing substances to distribute themselves between two immiscible liquid phases. This procedure is based on differences in solubilities of the solutes in the two solvents.

3. *Sublimation* is achieved by allowing one substance to evaporate and recondense. Heat may be applied to the evaporation and a cold trap is often used to increase the yield of the condensation. This procedure is used in separating one solid from another and is based on the differences in vapor pressures of the solids.

4. *Distillation* is achieved by heating a mixture and collecting the parts that boil off ("distillate"). This procedure is used to separate one liquid from another or from a dissolved solid and is based on differences in vapor pressures (or boiling points) of substances.

5. *Chromatography* is achieved by placing mixture on an inert substance (such as paper) and allowing solvent to slowly move the mixture on the substance. Different components move at different speeds and thus can be separated.

6. *Dialysis* is the separation of dissolved particles from a colloidal system and is based on the fact that colloidal particles are much larger than molecules or ions. A semipermeable membrane is used as shown on page 87.

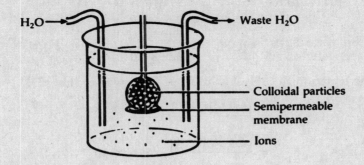

$H_2O \rightarrow$ Waste H_2O

Colloidal particles
Semipermeable membrane
Ions

Solubility Product

The solubility product is only used when discussing slightly soluble substances or precipitation reactions. For the chemical reaction.

$$M_pX_q \rightleftharpoons pM^+ + qX^-$$

the Law of Mass Action gives us

$$K = \frac{[M]^p [X]^q}{[M_pX_q]}$$

Since the term in the denominator is nearly constant, it may be incorporated into the constant giving us the *solubility product constant*, K_{sp}.

$$K_{sp} = [M]^p [X]^q$$

Common Ion Effect

When an ion is present in both the substance being dissolved and in the solvent, a depression in the solubility of the substance may occur based on the Le Chatelier's Principle.

Example:
What is the H^+ concentration in a .1 M solution of HAc that has been made .15 M in NaAc? ($K_{HAc} = 1.8 \times 10^{-5}$)

$$HAc \rightleftharpoons H^+ + Ac^-$$

$$1.8 \times 10^{-5} = \frac{[H^+][Ac^-]}{[HAc]}$$

$$= \frac{X (.15)}{(.1)}$$

$$X = 1.2 \times 10^{-5}M$$

pH

pH is defined as the negative logarithm of the activity of the hydronium ion concentration. Since it is experimentally impossible to determine the activities of single ions and since the activities of $H^+(aq)$ approximate the concentrations of $H^+(aq)$ in dilute solutions, we use pH based on activities and concentrations interchangeably.

Example:
A .1 M solution of a weak base has pH 10.6. What is its ionization constant?

$$pH = 10.6 \rightarrow log[H^+] = -10.6 = .4 - 11$$
$$[H^+] = 2.5 \times 10^{-11}$$
$$[OH^-] = \frac{1.0 \times 10^{-14}}{2.5 \times 10^{-11}} = 4.0 \times 10^{-4}$$

From the equation $B + H_2O \rightleftharpoons BH^+ + OH^-$ we see that $[BH^+] = [OH^-]$

$$K = \frac{[BH^+][OH^-]}{[B]}$$
$$= \frac{(4.0 \times 10^{-4})^2}{(.1)} = 1.6 \times 10^{-6}$$

ACIDS AND BASES

Equilibrium Constants for Acids and Bases

Acid dissociation constant:

$$HA + H_2O \rightleftharpoons H_3O^+ + A^-$$
$$K_A = \frac{[H_3O^+][A^-]}{[HA]}$$

Base dissociation constant:

$$\dot{B} + H_2O \rightleftharpoons BH^+ + OH^-$$
$$K_B = \frac{[BH^+][OH^-]}{[B]}$$

Ion product of water:

$$K_w = [H_3O^+][OH^-] = 1.0 \times 10^{-14}$$

K_A and K_B for conjugate acids and bases are related by the equation

$$K_w = K_A \cdot K_B$$

Equilibrium constants are often discussed in terms of pK_A and pK_B where pH $= -log X$.

General Ways of Discussing the Acidity or Basicity of a Solution (at 25°C)

	$[H^+]$ or $[H_3O^+]$	pH $= -log [H^+]$
acid	greater than 10^{-7}	less than 7
neutral	10^{-7}	7
basic	less than 10^{-7}	greater than 7

	$[OH^-]$	pOH $= -log [OH^-]$
acid	less than 10^{-7}	greater than 7
neutral	10^{-7}	7
basic	greater than 10^{-7}	less than 7

pH and pOH are related in the following way.

$$pH + pOH = 14 \ (25°C)$$

Buffers

A buffer solution is one capable of maintaining its pH at some fairly constant value even when small amounts of acid or base are added. A buffer may be prepared from a weak acid or a weak base and a salt of the weak electrolyte.

The action of a buffer may be described in terms of the Bronsted concept. For example, an acetic acid-acetate buffer

$$HAc \ + \ H_2O. \ \leftrightharpoons \ H_3O^+ \ + \ Ac^-$$

ACID 1   BASE 2   ACID 2   BASE 1

neutralizes the effect of small additions of hydronium ion because of the large concentration of the base Ac^- present. Small additions of OH^- ion are also neutralized by the HAc which is present in relatively large concentration.

Example:

A buffer solution contains 1 M concentrations of HAc and NaAc and has a pH of 4.74. The ionization constant for HAc is 1.8×10^{-5}. What is the pH of the solution after .01 M HCl is added to 1 liter of the solution?

$$HAc \leftrightharpoons H^+ + Ac^-$$

$$K = \frac{[H^+][Ac^-]}{[HAc]}$$

$$1.8 \times 10^{-5} = \frac{X \ (.99)}{(1.01)}$$

$$X = 1.85 \times 10^{-5} M$$

$$pH = 4.73$$

Neutralization

Acid species and base species react to yield a product lacking the distinctive properties of either species. This type of reaction is called a neutralization and in order to be complete it is necessary that the total acid added to the system be equal to the total base initially present (or vice versa). The amouint of acid or base is determined by the number of molecules multiplied by the number of acid or base functions per molecule (by equivalents).

The addition of an acid to a base solution (or vice versa) to determine the point of complete neutralization is called a *titration*. The point of complete neutralization or endpoint is determined by use of an indicator. An indicator is usually a weak acid or a weak base whose acid form is colored differently than its conjugate base.

ELECTROCHEMISTRY

Electrochemistry is based on electron-transfer (oxidation-reduction) reactions. The flow of electrons in an electrical circuit is often compared to the flow of liquid in a pipe. A comparison of terms follows:

Amount	gallons, quarts, etc.	= = coulombs
Rate	gallons/min	= = amperes
Driving force	pressure	= = voltage

Electrolytic Cell

The electrolytic cell uses electron flow to cause a nonspontaneous chemical reaction to occur $(E < 0)$. An electrolytic cell is a driven cell, electricity causes the chemical reaction to occur. Oxidation occurs at the anode; reduction occurs at the cathode.

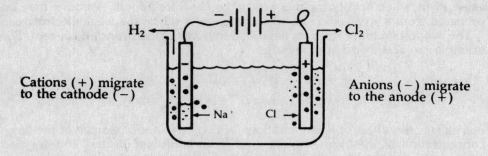

Cations (+) migrate to the cathode (−)

Anions (−) migrate to the anode (+)

Cathode reaction:

$$Na^+ + 1e^- \rightarrow Na$$

Anode reaction:

$$2Cl^- \rightarrow Cl_2(g) + 2e^-$$

The product appearing at the cathode cannot be sodium because it would then react immediately with water. The reaction sequence is

$$2Na^+ + 2e^- \rightarrow 2Na$$
$$2Na + 2 H_2O \rightarrow 2Na^+ + 2OH^- + H_2(g)$$

The end result at the cathode is the reduction of water. In concentrated brine solution the two half-reactions and the overall cell reaction are

$$2Cl^- \rightarrow Cl_2(g) + 2e^-$$
$$2H_2O + 2e^- \rightarrow 2OH^- + H_2(g)$$
$$\overline{2H_2O + 2Cl^- \rightarrow Cl_2(g) + 2OH^- + H_2(g)}$$

Galvanic Cell

A galvanic cell uses a spontaneous chemical reaction to cause electrons to flow in the circuit (E > 0). This cell is also called a "voltaic cell" or a "battery." The anode (oxidation) and the cathode (reduction) must be separated or heat change will be produced instead of electron flow. An electrical contact is necessary.

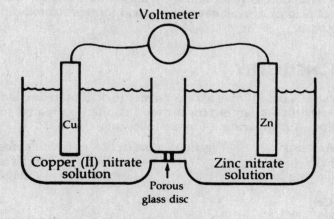

The overall chemical reaction can be written as the sum of the two half-reactions:

$$Cu^{+2}(aq) + 2e^- \rightarrow Cu$$
$$Zn \rightarrow Zn^{+2}(aq) + 2e^-$$
$$\overline{Cu^{+2}(aq) + Zn \rightarrow Cu + Zn^{+2}(aq)}$$

Electrons are released at the zinc electrode and taken up at the copper electrode, making the electron flow in the external circuit from right to left.

Concentration Cell

A concentration cell is a special type of galvanic cell. One half-reaction is the reverse of the other; they only differ in that the reactants and products are at different concentrations.

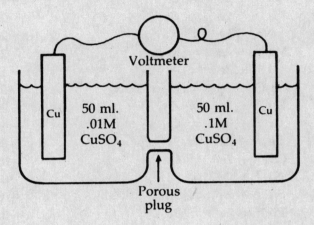

Voltmeter

Cu | 50 ml. .01M CuSO$_4$ | 50 ml. .1M CuSO$_4$ | Cu

Porous plug

Faraday's Law

There is a quantitative relationship between the amount of electricity passing through a cell and the extent of chemical reaction that occurs.

$$1 \text{ Faraday} = 96,500 \text{ coulombs}$$
$$= \text{the charge of 1 mole of electrons}$$

Cell Potential

Separation of the overall equation into components leads to the idea that total voltage (cell potential) can also be separated into components, one associated with each half-reaction.

Voltages associated with half-reactions are generally organized into a table showing *reductions only*. Oxidation half-reactions are obtained by reversing the reduction half-reactions and the voltages are obtained by reversing the sign on the reduction potential ($E°$). To determine whether a particular combination of half-reactions will spontaneously occur, add the respective voltages algebraically: if the sum is positive, the cell is galvanic; if the sum is negative, the cell is electrolytic.

Example:
Consider the reaction

$$Cu^{+2} + Zn \rightarrow Cu + Zn^{+2}$$

used for illustration of the galvanic cell.

$$Cu^{+2} + 2e^- \rightarrow Cu \qquad (+ .337 \text{ v})$$
$$\underline{Zn \rightarrow Zn^{+2} + 2e^- (+ .7628\text{v})}$$
$$Cu^{+2} + Zn \rightarrow Cu + Zn^{+2} \ (1.10 \text{ v}) \text{ approx.}$$

SOME STANDARD ELECTRODE POTENTIALS AT 25°C

Half-reactions	Reduction Potentials E°(volts)
$Li^+ + e^- \leftrightharpoons Li$	-3.045
$K^+ + e^- \leftrightharpoons K$	-2.925
$Ba^{+2} + 2e^- \leftrightharpoons Ba$	-2.906
$Ca^{+2} + 2e^- \leftrightharpoons Ca$	-2.866
$Na^+ + e^- \leftrightharpoons Na$	-2.714
$Mg^{+2} + 2e^- \leftrightharpoons Mg$	-2.363
$Al^{+3} + 3e^- \leftrightharpoons Al$	-1.662
$2H_2O + 2e^- \leftrightharpoons H_2 + 2OH^-$	-0.828
$Zn^{+2} + 2e^- \leftrightharpoons Zn$	-0.7628
$Cr^{+3} + 3e^- \leftrightharpoons Cr$	-0.744
$Fe^{+2} + 2e^- \leftrightharpoons Fe$	-0.4402
$Cd^{+2} + 2e^- \leftrightharpoons Cd$	-0.403
$Ni^{+2} + 2e^- \leftrightharpoons Ni$	-0.250
$Sn^{+2} + 2e^- \leftrightharpoons Sn$	-0.136
$Pb^{+2} + 2e^- \leftrightharpoons Pb$	-0.126
$2H^+ + 2e^- \leftrightharpoons H_2$	0
$Cu^{+2} + 2e^- \leftrightharpoons Cu$	0.337
$Cu^+ + e^- \leftrightharpoons Cu$	0.521
$I_2 + 2e^- \leftrightharpoons 2I^-$	0.5355
$Fe^{+3} + e^- \leftrightharpoons Fe^{+2}$	0.771
$Ag^+ + e^- \leftrightharpoons Ag$	0.799
$Br_2 + 2e^- \leftrightharpoons 2Br^-$	1.0652
$O_2 + 4H^+ + 4e^- \leftrightharpoons 2H_2O$	1.229
$Cr_2O_7^{-2} + 14H^+ + 6e^- \leftrightharpoons 2Cr^{+3} + 7H_2O$	1.33
$Cl_2 + 2e^- \leftrightharpoons 2Cl^-$	1.3595
$MnO_4^- + 8H^+ + 5e^- \leftrightharpoons Mn^{+2} + 4H_2O$	1.51
$F_2 + 2e^- \leftrightharpoons 2F^-$	2.87

Inorganic Chemistry Review Practice Test

ANSWER SHEET

1 Ⓐ Ⓑ Ⓒ Ⓓ	17 Ⓐ Ⓑ Ⓒ Ⓓ	33 Ⓐ Ⓑ Ⓒ Ⓓ	49 Ⓐ Ⓑ Ⓒ Ⓓ	65 Ⓐ Ⓑ Ⓒ Ⓓ
2 Ⓐ Ⓑ Ⓒ Ⓓ	18 Ⓐ Ⓑ Ⓒ Ⓓ	34 Ⓐ Ⓑ Ⓒ Ⓓ	50 Ⓐ Ⓑ Ⓒ Ⓓ	66 Ⓐ Ⓑ Ⓒ Ⓓ
3 Ⓐ Ⓑ Ⓒ Ⓓ	19 Ⓐ Ⓑ Ⓒ Ⓓ	35 Ⓐ Ⓑ Ⓒ Ⓓ	51 Ⓐ Ⓑ Ⓒ Ⓓ	67 Ⓐ Ⓑ Ⓒ Ⓓ
4 Ⓐ Ⓑ Ⓒ Ⓓ	20 Ⓐ Ⓑ Ⓒ Ⓓ	36 Ⓐ Ⓑ Ⓒ Ⓓ	52 Ⓐ Ⓑ Ⓒ Ⓓ	68 Ⓐ Ⓑ Ⓒ Ⓓ
5 Ⓐ Ⓑ Ⓒ Ⓓ	21 Ⓐ Ⓑ Ⓒ Ⓓ	37 Ⓐ Ⓑ Ⓒ Ⓓ	53 Ⓐ Ⓑ Ⓒ Ⓓ	69 Ⓐ Ⓑ Ⓒ Ⓓ
6 Ⓐ Ⓑ Ⓒ Ⓓ	22 Ⓐ Ⓑ Ⓒ Ⓓ	38 Ⓐ Ⓑ Ⓒ Ⓓ	54 Ⓐ Ⓑ Ⓒ Ⓓ	70 Ⓐ Ⓑ Ⓒ Ⓓ
7 Ⓐ Ⓑ Ⓒ Ⓓ	23 Ⓐ Ⓑ Ⓒ Ⓓ	39 Ⓐ Ⓑ Ⓒ Ⓓ	55 Ⓐ Ⓑ Ⓒ Ⓓ	71 Ⓐ Ⓑ Ⓒ Ⓓ
8 Ⓐ Ⓑ Ⓒ Ⓓ	24 Ⓐ Ⓑ Ⓒ Ⓓ	40 Ⓐ Ⓑ Ⓒ Ⓓ	56 Ⓐ Ⓑ Ⓒ Ⓓ	72 Ⓐ Ⓑ Ⓒ Ⓓ
9 Ⓐ Ⓑ Ⓒ Ⓓ	25 Ⓐ Ⓑ Ⓒ Ⓓ	41 Ⓐ Ⓑ Ⓒ Ⓓ	57 Ⓐ Ⓑ Ⓒ Ⓓ	73 Ⓐ Ⓑ Ⓒ Ⓓ
10 Ⓐ Ⓑ Ⓒ Ⓓ	26 Ⓐ Ⓑ Ⓒ Ⓓ	42 Ⓐ Ⓑ Ⓒ Ⓓ	58 Ⓐ Ⓑ Ⓒ Ⓓ	74 Ⓐ Ⓑ Ⓒ Ⓓ
11 Ⓐ Ⓑ Ⓒ Ⓓ	27 Ⓐ Ⓑ Ⓒ Ⓓ	43 Ⓐ Ⓑ Ⓒ Ⓓ	59 Ⓐ Ⓑ Ⓒ Ⓓ	75 Ⓐ Ⓑ Ⓒ Ⓓ
12 Ⓐ Ⓑ Ⓒ Ⓓ	28 Ⓐ Ⓑ Ⓒ Ⓓ	44 Ⓐ Ⓑ Ⓒ Ⓓ	60 Ⓐ Ⓑ Ⓒ Ⓓ	76 Ⓐ Ⓑ Ⓒ Ⓓ
13 Ⓐ Ⓑ Ⓒ Ⓓ	29 Ⓐ Ⓑ Ⓒ Ⓓ	45 Ⓐ Ⓑ Ⓒ Ⓓ	61 Ⓐ Ⓑ Ⓒ Ⓓ	77 Ⓐ Ⓑ Ⓒ Ⓓ
14 Ⓐ Ⓑ Ⓒ Ⓓ	30 Ⓐ Ⓑ Ⓒ Ⓓ	46 Ⓐ Ⓑ Ⓒ Ⓓ	62 Ⓐ Ⓑ Ⓒ Ⓓ	78 Ⓐ Ⓑ Ⓒ Ⓓ
15 Ⓐ Ⓑ Ⓒ Ⓓ	31 Ⓐ Ⓑ Ⓒ Ⓓ	47 Ⓐ Ⓑ Ⓒ Ⓓ	63 Ⓐ Ⓑ Ⓒ Ⓓ	79 Ⓐ Ⓑ Ⓒ Ⓓ
16 Ⓐ Ⓑ Ⓒ Ⓓ	32 Ⓐ Ⓑ Ⓒ Ⓓ	48 Ⓐ Ⓑ Ⓒ Ⓓ	64 Ⓐ Ⓑ Ⓒ Ⓓ	80 Ⓐ Ⓑ Ⓒ Ⓓ

INORGANIC CHEMISTRY PRACTICE TEST

1. All neutral atoms have
   A) the same number of protons as neutrons
   B) the same number of neutrons as electrons
   C) the same number of electrons as protons
   D) the same number of protons, neutrons, and electrons

2. Which of the following pairs of elements is most likely to form an ionic compound?
   A) Na and F   B) C and Si   C) Al and O   D) Li and I

3. The oxidation number of Mn in $KMnO_4$ is
   A) +1   B) +3   C) +5   D) +7

4. What does the secondary quantum number, ℓ, describe?
   A) energy of an electron   C) orientation of an orbital in space
   B) shape of an orbital   D) spin of an electron

5. Which of the following has the highest melting point?
   A) NaI   B) I_2 C) ICl   D) HI

6. The percent of hydrogen in $C_6H_5NH_2$ is
   A) .075   B) .75   C) 7.5   D) none of these

7. What is the number of moles of hydrogen required to product 4 moles of ammonia prepared according to the following equation?

$$N_2 + 3H_2 = 2NH_3$$

   A) 4   B) 6   C) 9   D) 18

8. Covalent bonding
   A) is characterized by electron transfer from one atom to another
   B) occurs between two atoms of greatly different electron affinities
   C) is characteristic of water-soluble substances
   D) is characterized by the mutual sharing of an electron pair between two substances

9. Which of the following increases the rate of reaction between two substances?
   A) increased temperature   C) presence of a catalyst
   B) increased concentrations of reactants   D) all of these

10. Measurements in an experiment show the pH of a .1 molar solution of an acid HX to be 2.876 at 25°C. Determine the numerical value of Ka for HX at 25°C.
    A) 1×10^{-4} B) 2.4×10^{-4} C) 1.8×10^{-5} D) 5×10^{-6}

11. The most electronegative elements are found among the
    A) metals   B) transition metals   C) nonmetals   D) lanthanides and actinides

12. Which of the following is a necessary characteristic of a good reducing agent?
    A) reacts violently   C) tends to gain electrons
    B) has negative oxidation potential   D) is readily oxidized

13. Five liters of a gas at STP weigh 6.25 grams. What is its molecular weight?
    A) 1.25 g   B) 14 g   C) 28 g   D) 56 g

14. What volume will 6.02×10^{23} atoms of chlorine occupy as a gas at STP?
    A) 11.2 ℓ B) 22.4 ℓ C) 33.6 ℓ D) 44.8 ℓ

15. If more reactant is added to a reaction at equilibrium, initially
    A) the equilibrium will remain unchanged
    B) the forward reaction rate will increase
    C) the forward and the reverse reaction rates will increase
    D) the forward reaction rate will increase while the reverse reaction rate will decrease

16. What is the best method for separating starch and salt in water?
    A) filtration B) extraction C) dialysis D) distillation

17. Which of the following has an ionic bond?
    A) HCl B) C_6H_6 C) H_2O D) CsF

18. If the oxide of element A is correctly written in formula form as AO, which of the following formulas is also correct?
    A) ACl B) AS C) AF_4 D) A_2Cl_3

19. A solution has $[H^+] = 2 \times 10^{-2}$. Therefore it has
    A) pH = 2 B) $[O_4^-] = 5 \times 10^{-11}$ C) $[OH^-] = 5 \times 10^{-13}$ D) pH = 10.3

20. The solubility of CaF_2 at 25°C is 2.2×10^{-4} moles/liter and the equilibrium equation for a saturated solution of CaF_2 is

$$CaF_2 \leftrightharpoons Ca^{+2} + 2F^-$$

Find the solubility product constant, K_{sp}, for CaF_2.
    A) 1×10^{-5} B) 4.2×10^{-11} C) 2.5×10^{-4} D) 5×10^{-14}

21. Which of the following shows the greatest affinity for an additional electron?
    A) F B) Ce C) Hg D) Na

22. A small piece of gold foil is placed in a solution containing zinc ions. What would the reaction potential be?

$$Zn^\circ = Zn^{++} + 2e^- \qquad E^\circ = +.76 \text{ v}$$
$$Au^\circ = Au^{+++} + 3e^- \qquad E^\circ = -1.42 \text{ v}$$

    A) -1.34 v B) 2.18 v C) -2.18 v D) -5.02 v

23. What fraction is needed to correct the volume of a gas to STP if the gas is at 100°C and 800 mm Hg pressure?
    A) $\dfrac{0 \times 800}{100 \times 770}$ B) $\dfrac{273 \times 800}{373 \times 760}$ C) $\dfrac{273 \times 760}{373 \times 800}$ D) none of these

24. The accompanying figure approximates the angular distribution curve for the orbital of what azimuthal quantum number $\ell = $ _____ ?
    A) 0 B) 1 C) 2 D) 3

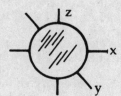

25. An atom exhibits paramagnetic properties when it has unpaired electrons. Carbon has 6 outer electrons but still exhibits paramagnetism. The theory which best explains this occurrence is
    A) Hund's Rule   C) Aufbau Principle
    B) Pauli Exclusion Principle D) quantum mechanics

26. Which of the following properties decreases as the atomic number increases in a group of the periodic table?
    A) atomic radius   C) number of valence electrons
    B) electronegativity   D) none of these

27. .78 moles of a particular gas have been found to occupy 578 ml at a temperature of 260°K. What pressure does this gas exert?
    A) 578 mm Hg   B) 219 mm Hg   C) 2,190 mm Hg   D) 21,900 mm Hg

28. The type of bonding in NCl_3 is best described as
    A) ionic   B) covalent   C) metallic   D) none of these

29. Which of the following is an appropriate definition for oxidation?
    A) the process of losing electrons
    B) the process of gaining electrons
    C) the process of interchanging electrons between two species
    D) the process of decreasing the oxidation number of a species

30. What is the maximum number of electrons that could occupy the $n = 3$ energy level?
    A) 2   B) 8   C) 18   D) 32

31. When the equation:

$$aCA_3 (PO_4)_2 + bH_3PO_4 \rightarrow cCa(H_2PO4)_2$$

    is correctly balanced, the sum of the coefficients $a + b + c$ will be
    A) 5   B) 8   C) 10   D) 14   E) 16

32. Which of the following is a statement of the Pauli Exclusion Principle?
    A) electrons in equivalent orbitals have parallel spins
    B) electrons occupy the lowest possible energy levels
    C) no two electrons in the same atom may have the same identical set of quantum numbers
    D) none of these

33. Which of the following is the correct electron configuration for Mn^{2+}?
    A) $1S^2\ 2S^2\ 3S^2\ 4S^2$ C) $1S^2\ 2S^2\ 2p^6\ 3S^2\ 3p^6\ 3d^5$
    B) $1S^2\ 2S^2\ 2p^6\ 3S^2$ D) $1S^2\ 2S^2\ 2p^6\ 3S^2\ 3p^6\ 4S^2\ 3d^5$

34. Which of the following has the smallest radius?
    A) Ba^- B) Ba C) Ba^+ D) Ba^{++}

35. The anode is
    A) the electrode at which reduction takes place
    B) the electrode towards which cations move in a cell
    C) always the positive electrode
    D) none of these

36. Which of the following equations correctly gives the relationship between the changes in enthalpy, entropy, and free energy?
    A) $\Delta G = \Delta H - T\Delta S$ B) $\Delta H = \Delta G - T\Delta S$ C) $\Delta S = \Delta H - T\Delta G$ D) none of these

37. For Ag_2CrO_4, $K_{sp} =$
    A) $[Ag^+]^2[CrO_4^{--}]$ B) $[2Ag^+][CrO_4^{--}]$ C) $[2Ag^+]^2[CrO_4^{--}]$ D) none of these

38. The acid dissociation constant for HCN is 4.0×10^{-10}. What is the hydrolysis constant for CN^-?
    A) 1×10^{-14} B) 4×10^{-10} C) 2.5×10^{-5} D) 1.69×10^{-24}

39. The weight, in grams, of one hydrogen atom is
    A) 1.0 B) 2.0 C) 6.02×10^{23} D) 1.69×10^{24} E) none of these

40. Which could represent the range of quantum number m_ℓ?
    A) $+\frac{1}{2}, -\frac{1}{2}$ B) 1, 2, 3, ... C) $-1, -1+1, ..., 1-1, 1$ D) $0, 1, 2, ..., n-1$

41. A sample of benzene (C_6H_6) vapor is at 110°C and 1 atm pressure. Find its density (in g/l):
    A) 2.11 B) .047 C) .753 D) .0002

42. Comparing the *average speed* of He and Ne atoms, at the same temperature and pressure
    A) He atoms would move faster
    B) Ne atoms would move faster
    C) both He and Ne atoms would move with the same speed
    D) cannot be determined from the information given

43. Which of the following oxides is acidic?
    A) BaO B) CaO C) Na_2O D) SO_3

44. 50 ml of a base are needed to neutralize 25 ml of a .2 N solution of an acid. The normality of the base is
    A) .1 B) .2 C) .3 D) .4

45. What would be the effect on the pH of an acetic acid solution of adding some solid sodium acetate to the solution?
    A) increase   C) no effect
    B) decrease   D) first increase and then decrease

46. When an electron in hydrogen gas is excited from its ground state to the fourth energy level, the maximum number of spectral lines emitted as it returns to its ground state would be
    A) 1 B) 4 C) 5 D) 6

47. The phase diagram for a certain substance is shown in the figure at right. What is the normal boiling point for this substance?
    A) 25°C   C) 50°C
    B) 40°C   D) 100°C

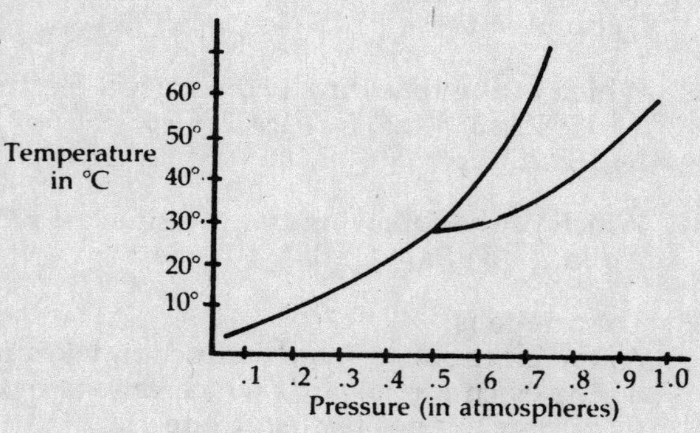

48. The substance represented in the phase diagram at right sublimes in what pressure range?
    A) below .5 atm
    B) at .5 atm
    C) between .5 and 1.4 atm
    D) above 1.4 atm

49. Once a catalyzed reaction has reached equilibrium, the addition of more catalyst will result in
    A) more product   C) an increased forward reaction rate
    B) more reactant   D) no change

50. Assuming the reaction $2H_2 + O_2 \rightarrow 2H_2O$ is single-step, the forward rate is given by
    A) $k[H_2]^2[O_2]$ B) $\dfrac{k[H_2]^2[O_2]}{[H_2O]^2}$ C) $k[2H_2][O_2]$ D) $k[2H_2][O_2] - k[2H_2O]$

51. 3×10^{22} atoms of element X weigh 12 g. The atomic weight of element X is approximately
    A) 6 B) 12 C) 24 D) 240

52. Which of the following molecules shows both covalent and ionic bonds?
    A) CH_4 B) C_6H_6 C) NH_4Cl D) HOH

53. Find the simplest formula of a compound which contains, by weight, 85.6% carbon and 14.4% hydrogen.
    A) CH B) CH_2 C) CH_3 D) CH_4

54. The critical temperature of water is higher than that of oxygen, (O_2). This can best be explained by the fact that
    A) H_2O has fewer electrons than O_2 C) H_2O has a dipole moment
    B) H_2O has two covalent bonds   D) H_2O has a linear shape

55. Sodium chloride is an alternating array of Na^+ ions and Cl^- ions in a face-centered cubic lattice crystal. How many nearest neighbors would a Na^+ ion have in this crystal structure?
    A) 2 B) 4 C) 6 D) 8

56. Which of the following would be expected to have a low molar heat of fusion?
    A) a molecular solid   C) a covalent solid
    B) an ionic solid   D) a metallic solid

57. In water, which of the following will exhibit ionic bonding?
    A) O_2 B) H_2 C) HCl D) ClF E) N_2

58. What volume will a gas occupy at 20°C and 770 mm Hg, if it occupies 600 ml at STP?
    A) 600 ml B) 652.4 ml C) 635.6 ml D) 551.8 ml

59. Determine the ΔH for the reaction

$$3CH_4 + 3CO_2 = C_6H_{12}O_6$$

given that

$$Ch_4 + 2O_2 = CO_2 + 2H_2O + 14.8 \text{ kcal}$$
$$6CO_2 + 6H_2O = C_6H_{12}O_6 + 6O_2 + 18.9 \text{ kcal}$$

A) -33.7 kcal B) 33.7 kcal C) 63.3 kcal D) -63.3 kcal

60. Which of the following corresponds to the symbol and definition for entropy?
    A) E—measure of the work obtainable from the system
    B) N—measure of the polarity of a substance
    C) S—measure of the randomness of the system
    D) H—measure of the heat content of the system

Questions 61–66 refer to the following equilibrium

$$2SO_2(g) + O_2(g) \rightleftharpoons 2SO_3(g) + 45 \text{ kcal}$$

61. The concentration of O_2 at equilibrium will increase if
    A) the pressure is increased   C) SO_2 is added to the system
    B) the system is cooled   D) SO_3 is added to the system

62. Addition of heat to the system will
    A) increase the concentration of SO_3 C) leave the equilibrium unchanged
    B) increase the concentration of SO_2 D) decrease the concentration of O_2

63. Increasing the pressure on the system will cause
    A) the concentration of SO_2 to decrease   C) the concentration of SO_3 to increase
    B) the concentration of O_2 to decrease   D) all of these

64. Which of the following changes will cause additional heat to be released?
    A) an increase in the concentration of SO_3
    B) an increase in the pressure
    C) removal of O_2
    D) none of these changes can cause additional heat to be released

65. The number of moles of oxygen at equilibrium will increase if
    A) an inert gas is added to the system   C) SO_3 is added to the system
    B) SO_2 is added to the system   D) the pressure is increased

66. The concentration of SO_3 at equilibrium will increase if
    A) the temperature of the system is lowered
    B) the volume of the container is increased
    C) O_2 is removed from the system
    D) the pressure is lowered

67. Find the voltage of the cell employing the reaction

$$Sn° + 2H_3O^+(1 \text{ m}) \rightarrow Sn^{++}(1 \text{ m}) + H_2 (1 \text{ atm}) + 2H_2O$$

    A) +.14 v   B) −.2 v   C) +.28 v   D) none of these

68. Which statement best reflects Le Chatelier's Principle?
    A) in a system which is reaching equilibrium, the addition of more reactant will cause equilibrium to be reached faster
    B) if a system in equilibrium is changed in any way, the system will shift so as to offset the effect of the change
    C) both reactants and products stop reacting when equilibrium is reached
    D) a system originally not in equilibrium will shift so as to approach equilibrium

69. How are the solubility of a substance in water and its K_{sp} related?
    A) as solubility increases so does K_{sp}
    B) as solubility increases, K_{sp} decreases
    C) as solubility increases, K_{sp} remains constant
    D) the relationship between solubility and K_{sp} is much too complex to predict

70. What is the pH of a .15 m solution of HCl?
    A) .824   B) 1.00   C) 1.50   D) 1.15

71. According to the Lewis Acid-Base Theory, ammonia is:
    A) an acid   B) a base   C) neutral   D) amphoteric

72. Which of the following would lower the pH in water solution?
    A) KCl   B) NaCl   C) $CuSO_4$ D) Na_3PO_4

73. 20 ml of .01 M $BaCl_2$ solution are mixed with 20 ml of .005 M Na_2SO_4 solution. The K_{sp} for $BaSO_4$ is 1.1×10^{-10}. Will $BaSO_4$ precipitate?
    A) yes   B) no   C) not enough information given

74. What is the product formed at the anode during the electrolysis of NaCl?
    A) Na   B) H^+ C) Cl_2 D) OH^-

75. Find the pH of a .2 M solution of acetic acid $HC_2H_3O_2$. The dissociation constant for $HC_2H_3O_2$ is 1.8×10^{-5}.
    A) 4.74   B) 2.37   C) 9.05   D) 2.72

76. Which of the following K's indicates the reaction goes farthest towards completion?
    A) K = 100   B) K = 10   C) K = 1   D) K = .01

77. In a neutralization of sulfuric acid by sodium hydroxide, 49 g of H_2SO_4 and 80 g of NaOH are present. After the reaction is completed, how much left-over reactant will there be?
   A) none, they will both be used up   C) 24.5 g H_2SO_4
   B) 40 g NaHO   D) none of these

78. What volume of H_2SO_4 (1 m) will be needed to neutralize 50 ml of 1 m NaOH?
   A) 12.5 ml   B) 25 ml   C) 50 ml   D) 100 ml

79. Which of the following equations best illustrates hydrolysis?
   A) $H^+ + OH^- = H_2O$

                                          C) $HCl + H_2O = H_3O^+ + Cl^-$
   B) $H^+ + NH_3 = NH_4^+ + H_2O$ D) $CH_3COO^- + H_2O = CH_3COOH + OH^-$

80. In the equation $HCO_3^- + H_3O = H_2CO_3 + H_2O$, according to the Brönsted-Lowry definition
   A) HCO_3^- is an acid
   B) H_3O^+ is an acid and H_2O is its conjugate base
   C) HCO_3^- and H_2CO_3 are conjugate bases
   D) H_3O^+ is an acid and HCO_3^- is its conjugate base

INORGANIC CHEMISTRY ANSWER KEY

1. C	21. A	41. A	61. D
2. A	22. B	42. A	62. B
3. D	23. B	43. D	63. D
4. B	24. A	44. A	64. B
5. A	25. A	45. A	65. C
6. C	26. B	46. D	66. A
7. B	27. D	47. B	67. A
8. D	28. B	48. A	68. B
9. D	29. A	49. D	69. A
10. C	30. C	50. A	70. A
11. C	31. B	51. D	71. B
12. D	32. C	52. C	72. C
13. C	33. C	53. B	73. A
14. A	34. D	54. C	74. C
15. B	35. D	55. C	75. D
16. C	36. A	56. A	76. A
17. D	37. A	57. C	77. B
18. B	38. C	58. C	78. B
19. C	39. D	59. D	79. D
20. B	40. C	60. C	80. B

CHAPTER SIX

Organic Chemistry Review

Structure and Stereochemistry of Covalently Bonded Molecules

COVALENT BONDING

Bonding

In covalent bonding, an atom acquires a stable electron structure by sharing electrons with another atom (in ionic bonding there is a transfer of electrons from one atom to another, forming charged atoms called ions). Covalent compounds, in contrast with ionic compounds, tend to have low boiling points and are not electrical conductors. Most bonds found in organic compounds are of the covalent type.

In the normal covalent bond, each atom contributes one electron to the bond pair. In a *coordinate* covalent bond one atom contributes both electrons to the bond pair. It is possible to have double and even triple covalent bonds between two atoms.

When two atoms approach each other and form a chemical bond, the electron shells of the two atoms repel each other (and so do the atoms' positive kernels); an attractive force exists, however, between the nucleus of one atom and the electron shell of the other. These attractive and repulsive forces between the two atoms result in a net attractive force between them, forming a bond with a fairly definite distance between the atoms.

ATOMIC COVALENT RADII IN Å UNITS

Bond	H	C	N	O	F	Cl	I
single	.30	.77	.70	.66	.64	1.14	1.33
double		.67	.61	.66			
triple		.60	.55				

Lewis Dot Structure

By this method, covalent bonds are shown as part of the total electron structure.

103

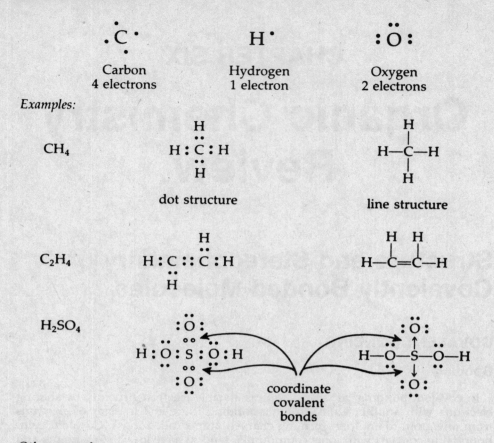

Examples:

Other examples:

Resonance

Resonance exists in molecules of polyatomic ions which may be represented by two or more structural formulas having approximately equal energies and differing only in the position of the electrons. The properties of the compound will not be those expected of any one of the formulas, but rather a hybrid of all of them.

When the contributing structures are of about the same stability, then *resonance* is important. The resonance hybrid is more stable than any of the contributing structures. The increase in stability is called the *resonance energy*: the more nearly equal the stabilities of the contributing structures, the greater the resonance energy.

Examples:

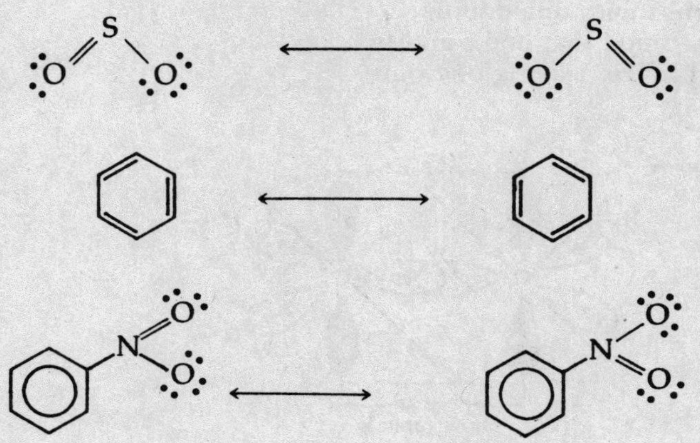

In general, molecules in resonance such as the ones above do not contain one single bond and one double bond, but two *identical* bonds, each one intermediate between a single and a double bond. This *hybrid bond* possesses half of the double bond character and half of the single bond character and has been described as a one-and-one-half bond.

$$X::Y \longleftrightarrow {}^{+}X \quad :\ddot{Y}^{-}$$

$${}^{+}X \overset{---}{=} Y^{-} \qquad \text{(resonance hybrid)}$$

Bonding in Hydrocarbons

Pi and sigma bonds are two types of bonds formed by carbon atoms. Bonds between hybrids (s-sp-sp^2 or sp^3) are called σ (sigma) bonds).

Single bonds: A single bond is formed between two carbons by the overlap of two sp^3 orbitals.

Example: Ethane (C_2H_6)

Methane (CH_4) has a tetrahedral structure as a result of the hybridization of one s and three p orbitals in one carbon atom. Ethane, with two carbon atoms, is pictured below. In it two tetrahedra are joined by an overlap of two of the sp^3 orbitals.

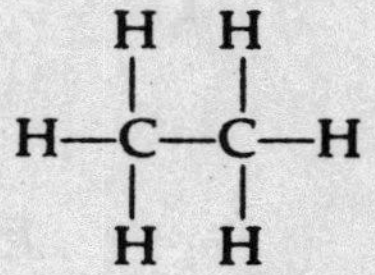

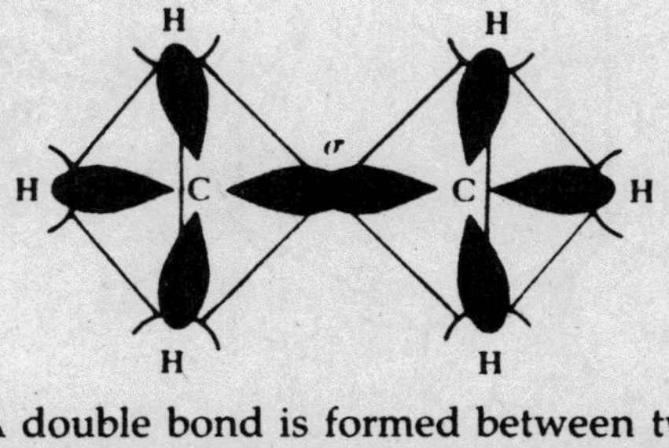

Double bonds: A double bond is formed between two carbons by the overlap of two sp^2 orbitals (sigma) and the overlap of two pure p orbitals (pi bond).

Example: Ethene (C_2H_4)

In the alkenes with one double bond, it is assumed that one s and two p orbitals hybridize, leaving one pure p orbital.

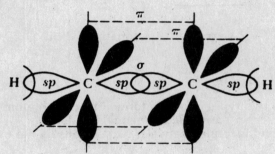

Pure *p* orbitals

Triple bonds: A triple bond is formed between two carbons by the overlap of two sp orbitals and four pure p orbitals (pi bonds).

Example: Ethyne (C_2H_2)

In the alkynes with one triple bond, it is assumed that one s and one p orbital hybridize, leaving two pure p orbitals.

H—C≡C—N

Benzene: The carbon and hydrogen atoms of benzene lie on a plane, with the 6 carbon atoms of benzene forming a regular hexagon with corner angles of 120°. Although the structure is usually represented with alternating single and

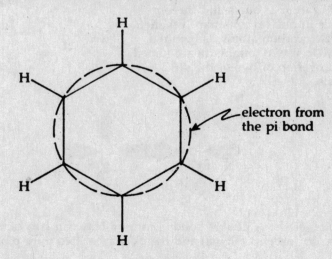

electron from the pi bond

double bonds, the structure is actually a resonance hybrid with 6 identical one-and-one-half bonds. Each carbon atom forms 3 sp^2 hybrid orbitals and leaves 1 pure p orbital. The sp^2 orbitals for each carbon atom lie in a plane with the p orbital at right angles with the plane of the sp^2's.

The types of bonds are summarized in the following table:

TYPE	ANGLE	C——C BOND LENGTH	BOND ENERGY
single	109.5°	1.54 Å	83 kcal/mole
double	120°	1.34 A°	146 kcal/mole
triple	180°	1.20 Å	199 kcal/mole
benzene	120°	1.40 Å	

Electron Properties

Electronegativity and Charge Distribution

The electronegativity of an element is the ability of an atom of the element to attract electrons to itself. Fluorine is the most electronegative of all elements and cesium is the least (most electropositive). The following elements are of the greatest concern to the organic chemist:

$$F = 4.0 \qquad I = 2.5$$
$$O = 3.5 \qquad S = 2.5$$
$$N = 3.0 \qquad C = 2.5$$
$$Cl = 3.0 \qquad H = 2.1$$
$$Br = 2.8 \qquad P = 2.1$$

Polar Bonds

When elements of different electronegativities form a bond, there is polarization of the bond. If the electronegativity of A is less than that of B, the polarization is from A to B:

$$A \rightarrow B$$
$$+ \qquad -$$

We can indicate polarity with the symbols δ_+ and δ_-, indicating partial positive and negative charges. The greater the difference in electronegativities between two atoms, the more polar the bond will be.

Examples:

$$\overset{\delta_+ \quad \delta_-}{H—F} \qquad \overset{\delta_-}{O} \qquad \overset{\delta_-}{N}$$

Partial Ionic Character

Every covalent bond between two unlike atoms (or two like atoms each having different bonding) has some extremely small degree of ionic character due to the greater attraction of electrons by one of the atoms. The electronegativity scale may be used to make predictions.

$$\underset{+ \quad -}{H \rightarrow C} \qquad \underset{+ \quad -}{C \rightarrow Cl} \qquad H \!-\! \overset{\displaystyle H}{\underset{\displaystyle H}{C}} \!\rightarrow\! \overset{\displaystyle Cl}{\underset{\displaystyle Cl}{C}} \!\rightarrow\! Cl$$

Dipole Moment

Molecules that have an *uneven* distribution of electron charges will orient themselves in an electric field. The dipole moment of a molecule is the product of the positive and negative charges on the molecules (they must be equal) multiplied by the distance between them.

The following molecules have zero dipole moment ($\mu = 0$).

$$O\!=\!C\!=\!O \qquad Cl\!-\!\overset{\displaystyle Cl}{\underset{\displaystyle Cl}{C}}\!-\!Cl \qquad \overset{\displaystyle Cl}{\underset{\displaystyle Cl}{\diagdown}}B\!-\!Cl$$

Lewis Acids and Lewis Bases

A Lewis acid is a substance that can accept pairs of electrons; a Lewis base is one which can donate pairs of electrons.

Examples:

$AlCl_3$ is a Lewis acid because it can accept an electron pair.

NH_3 is a Lewis base because it is capable of donating an electron pair.

$$Cl\!-\!\overset{\displaystyle Cl}{\underset{\displaystyle Cl}{Al}}\!\leftarrow\!:\!\overset{\displaystyle H}{\underset{\displaystyle H}{N}}\!-\!H$$

$$\text{(Lewis acid)}H^+ \leftarrow :\!\underset{\displaystyle \cdot\cdot}{\overset{\displaystyle H}{O}}\!-\!CH_3 \text{ (Lewis base)}$$

STEREOCHEMISTRY

Polarization of Light: Specific Rotation

An ordinary ray of light vibrates in all directions perpendicular to its line of propagation. Light that vibrates in only one plane (by passing through a crystal, etc.) is called *plane-polarized light*. When plane-polarized light is passed through certain solutions, the plane of polarization can either be rotated left (l, levo) or right (d, dextro); the degree of rotation can be easily measured in the laboratory. Optical activity is a property of the molecules themselves. It has been established that molecules which have the ability to rotate light are *chiral* (asymetric)—that

mirror

$$\begin{array}{cc} \underset{|}{\overset{\displaystyle H}{}} & \underset{|}{\overset{\displaystyle H}{}} \\ I\!-\!\bigcirc\!-\!Cl & Cl\!-\!\bigcirc\!-\!I \\ \overset{|}{SO_3H} & \overset{|}{SO_3H} \end{array}$$

is, they contain at least one chiral (asymetric) carbon (having four different groups attached to it).

A geometric figure is called chiral if its image in a plane mirror cannot be brought to coincide with itself.

The two figures at the bottom of page 108 are not superimposable so the molecule is chiral.

Isomerism

The existence of two or more compounds having the same numbers and kinds of atoms and same molecular weights is called *isomerism*. Structural isomers are those that result from the different orders in which carbon or other atoms may be attached to each other.

SKELETON ISOMERS

$$
\begin{array}{c}
\overset{\displaystyle H}{\underset{\displaystyle H}{\overset{|}{\underset{|}{H-C}}}} - \overset{\displaystyle H}{\underset{\displaystyle H}{\overset{|}{\underset{|}{C}}}} - \overset{\displaystyle H}{\underset{\displaystyle H}{\overset{|}{\underset{|}{C}}}} - \overset{\displaystyle H}{\underset{\displaystyle H}{\overset{|}{\underset{|}{C}}}} - H
\end{array}
$$

$$
\begin{array}{c}
\overset{\displaystyle H}{\underset{\displaystyle H}{\overset{|}{\underset{|}{H-C}}}} - \overset{\displaystyle CH_3}{\underset{\displaystyle H}{\overset{|}{\underset{|}{C}}}} - \overset{\displaystyle H}{\underset{\displaystyle H}{\overset{|}{\underset{|}{C}}}} - H
\end{array}
$$

POSITION ISOMERS

$$
\begin{array}{c}
CH_3 - \overset{\displaystyle Cl}{\underset{\displaystyle H}{\overset{|}{\underset{|}{C}}}} - CH_3
\end{array}
$$

$$
\begin{array}{c}
CH_3 - \overset{\displaystyle H}{\underset{\displaystyle H}{\overset{|}{\underset{|}{C}}}} - \overset{\displaystyle H}{\underset{\displaystyle H}{\overset{|}{\underset{|}{C}}}} - Cl
\end{array}
$$

FUNCTION ISOMERS

$$CH_3 - O - CH_3$$

$$CH_3 - CH_2 - OH$$

Stereoisomerism

Steroisomerism occurs when isomers have the same structural formula. Stereoisomerism is caused by the different possible orientations of atoms in space. The two types of stereoisomers are:

1. Geometric cis-trans isomers: These do not rotate plane-polarized light (see alkenes).

2. Optical isomers: These are members of a set of stereoisomers of which at least two are optically active—that is, they have the ability to rotate the plane of polarized light. Those that rotate to the left are called levorotatory (l form) and those that rotate to the right are called dextrorotatory (d form). Two isomers that are mirror images of each other (not superim-

posable) are called optical antipodes, active compounds, or *enantiomers*. Enantiomers rotate polarized light by equal angles but in opposite directions. Such isomers differ markedly in biological activity but are very similar in physical and chemical properties.

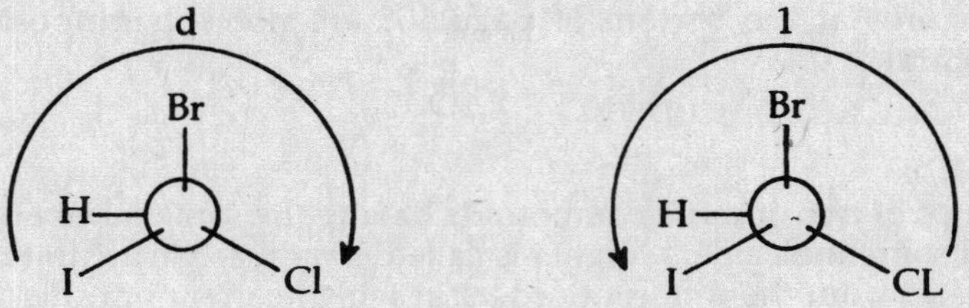

$$\text{ROTATION} = \alpha_{D}^{20°C} \, [M]$$

(Specific rotation
"D"-line of sodium,
20°C, M = molarity)

A *racemic mixture* is one which contains equal amounts of the two optically active forms, resulting in zero rotation. A racemic mixture can be separated into the optically active forms. Biological means of separating racemic mixtures were discovered by Pasteur (many microorganisms will destroy one optical isomer, leaving the other untouched).

Hydrocarbons

CLASSIFICATION

Hydrocarbons are organic compounds containing *only* the elements *carbon* and *hydrogen*. The hydrocarbons can be classified into two broad categories.

1. Aliphatic: open-chain compounds and those cyclic compounds which resemble open-chain compounds.

2. Aromatic: Benzene and the compounds which resemble benzene in chemical behavior.

ALIPHATIC COMPOUNDS

Alkanes

Alkanes (paraffins) are the simplest of the aliphatic hydrocarbons and have the following characteristics:

1. They are saturated, with no double or triple bonds.

2. The general formula is C_nH_{2n+2}.

3. Each member of this homologous series differs from the preceding member by a CH_2 group.

4. The simplest member of the series is methane, CH_4.

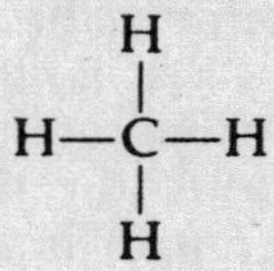

$$H-\overset{\displaystyle H}{\underset{\displaystyle H}{C}}-H$$

Nomenclature of Alkanes

CH_4 ------	methane		C_7H_{16} -----	heptane
C_2H_6 -----	ethane		C_8H_{18} -----	octane
C_3H_8 -----	propane		C_9H_{20} -----	nonane
C_4H_{10} ----	butane		$C_{10}H_{22}$ ----	decane
C_5H_{12} ----	pentane			
C_6H_{14} ----	hexane		etc.	

All alkanes end in *-ane*.

In naming aliphatic compounds under the Geneva (IUPAC) system, the following rules are used.

1. The names listed are used for all straight-chain hydrocarbons (normal).

2. Branched-chain hydrocarbons are considered as *derivatives* of a straight-chain hydrocarbon with one or more hydrogen atoms replaced by alkyl radicals. The longest straight chain in the molecule is considered the parent hydrocarbon. The carbon atoms of the parent hydrocarbon are numbered from the end that gives the branched hydrocarbon atoms the lowest number.

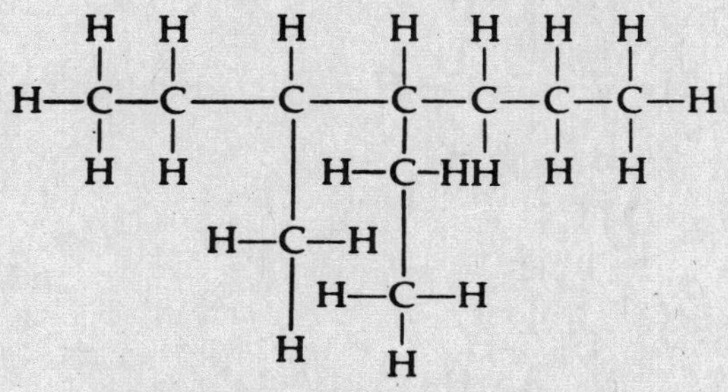

(3-methyl-4-ethylheptane)

3. The names of the side chains (branches) are added as *prefixes* to the parent compound. Their position is indicated by adding the number of the carbon atom to which they are attached. If two branches are on the same carbon atom, the number is repeated. The numbers precede the names of the groups and are separated from them by hyphens. If the same group repeats on several carbons or on the same carbon, this may be indicated by the use of the prefixes *di-*, *tri-*, etc. Consecutive numbers are separated from each other by commas.

4. Side chains are considered alkyl groups (alkane radicals), that is, alkanes lacking one hydrogen atom. Radicals cannot exist on their own for any length of time and so must be bonded to another unit.

Examples:

methyl:

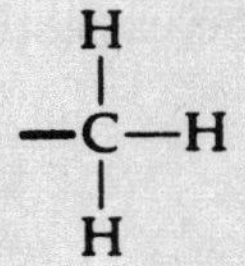

ethyl:

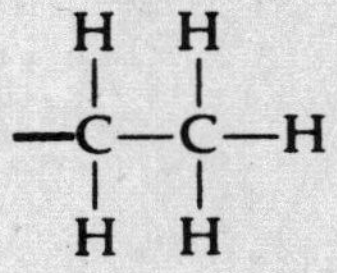

$$\text{propyl:}$$

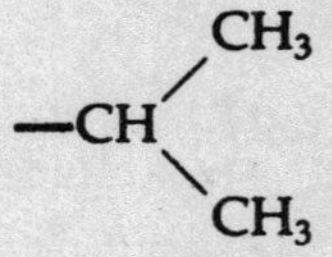

$$\begin{array}{c} & CH_3 \\ & | \\ -CH & \\ & | \\ & CH_3 \end{array} \qquad -CH_2-CH_2-CH_3$$

isopropyl   n-propyl

butyl: $-CH_2-CH_2-CH_2-CH_3$ n-butyl

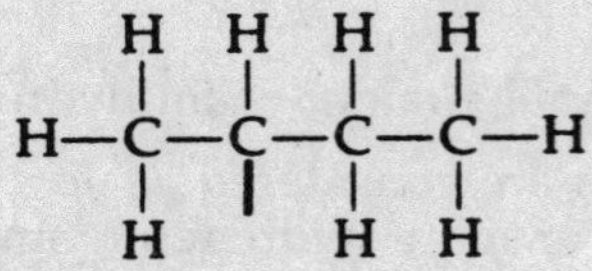

$$\begin{array}{ccccccc} & H & H & H & H \\ & | & | & | & | \\ H- & C- & C- & C- & C- & H \\ & | & | & | & | \\ & H & & H & H \end{array}$$

sec-butyl

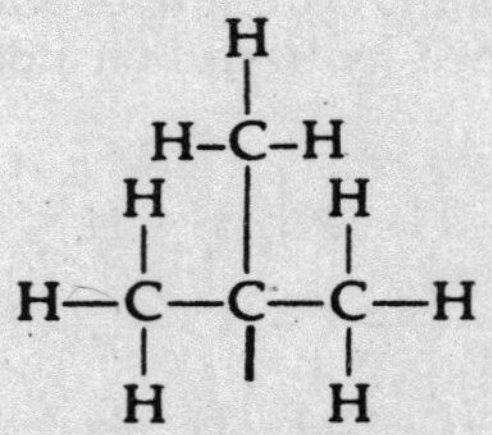

$$\begin{array}{c} H \\ | \\ H-C-H \\ \end{array}$$
$$\begin{array}{ccccc} H & & H \\ | & & | \\ H-C- & C- & C-H \\ | & | & | \\ H & & H \end{array}$$

tert-butyl

$$\begin{array}{c} H \\ | \\ H-C-H \\ \end{array}$$
$$\begin{array}{ccccc} H & & H \\ | & & | \\ H-C- & C- & C-H \\ | & | & | \\ H & H \end{array}$$

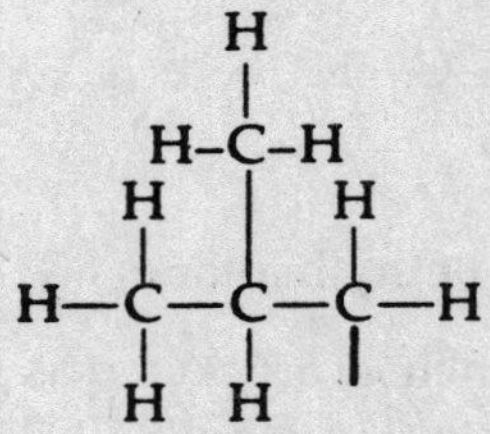

isobutyl

Examples of nomenclature:

The longest chain (numbered) has six carbons—compound is a hexane

(3,4-dimethylhexane)

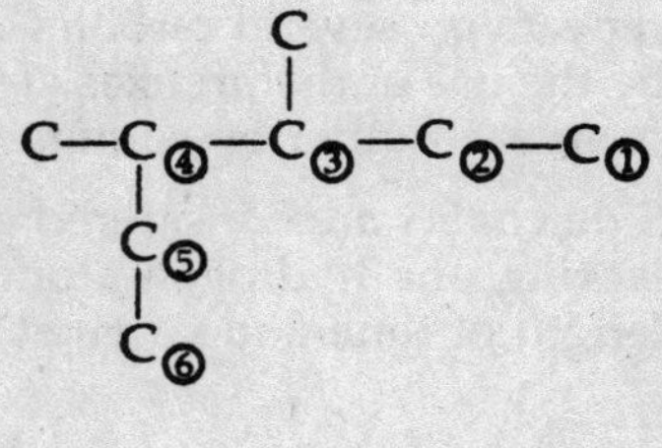

We try to name the longest chain that will leave the easiest-to-name side chains.

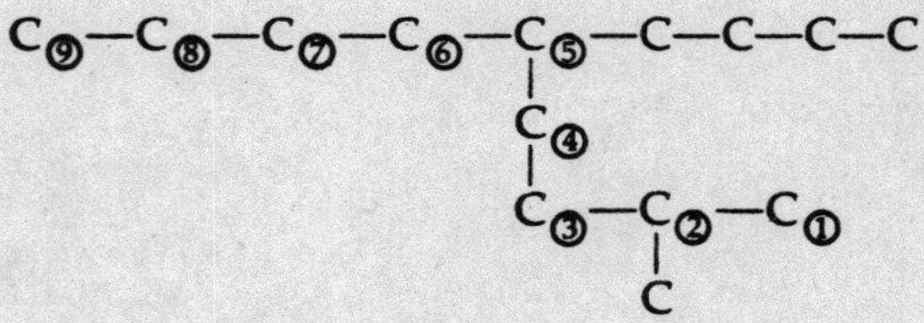

(2,4-dimethyl-5-butylnonane)

Physical Properties of Alkanes

As in all organic compounds, the physical properties of the alkanes depend in general upon the number and kinds of atoms in the molecule and the way in which these atoms are attached to each other.

1. *Physical state:* At 25°C and 760 torr pressure, the normal hydrocarbons are gaseous from C_1 to C_4, liquid from C_5 to C_{17}, and solids from C_{18} on up.

2. *Boiling point:* The boiling point of normal alkanes increases with increased molecular weight. This increase in boiling point is due to larger attraction between the molecules (Van der Waals forces). Branching of the chains *always* results in lowering the boiling point, since branching reduces the Van der Waals forces.

3. *Melting Point:* Melting points of normal alkanes do not follow a smooth curve relationship with increased molecular weights. There is one curve for molecules with an even number of carbon atoms and another for those with odd numbers. In general, the more symmetric and compact the molecule, the higher its melting point will be.

4. *Density:* Density in normal alkanes increases with increased molecular weight. From .63 g/cm³ at 20°C for pentane to .77 g/cm³ for pentadecane. This increase is due to the increased attraction between the molecules (as evidenced by the increase in boiling points).

5. *Solubility:* Alkanes are almost completely insoluble in water since they have a very small attraction for water molecules (which, on the other hand, have a very high attraction for each other). Alkanes have a very high miscibility with many other nonpolar organic compounds.

6. *Viscosity:* The viscosity of alkanes increases with chain length due to greater attraction between molecules.

Combustion, Substitution and Other Properties of Alkanes

1. *Inertness to most reagents:* Alkanes are not affected by acids, bases, oxidizing agents, or most other reagents.

2. *Oxidation at high temperatures (combustion):* In the presence of oxygen or strong oxidizing agents at high temperatures alkanes burn to CO_2 and H_2O.

Example:

$$C_3H_8 + 5 O_2 \rightarrow 3CO_2 + 4H_2O$$

(kcal/g *decrease slightly* as molecular weight increases)

3. *Decomposition at high temperatures (pyrolysis):* At sufficiently high temperatures, hydrocarbons decompose in the absence of oxygen—this reaction is known as cracking or pyrolysis. Cracking is used to produce a great variety of saturated and unsaturated hydrocarbons of lower molecular weight than the parent form.

4. *Isomerization:* In the presence of certain catalysts (and, usually, elevated temperatures) it is possible to convert isomers into other isomers.

5. *Substitution reactions:* Substitution reactions with alkanes are possible; alkanes do not undergo addition reactions. Direct substitution of alkanes has limited use since the alkane molecule is not very selective of which hydrogen is replaced. One of the most common substitution reactions of alkanes is halogenation at 300+°C in the presence of light and/or ultraviolet radiation.

Example:

$$CH_4 + Cl_2 \rightarrow CH_3Cl + HCl$$

This reaction is considered a *free radical reaction*. The light splits the chlorine molecule into two chlorine radicals, each with an unpaired electron.

$$:\overset{\cdot\cdot}{\underset{\cdot\cdot}{Cl}}\cdot \qquad\qquad \cdot\overset{\cdot\cdot}{\underset{\cdot\cdot}{Cl}}:$$

One of the radicals reacts with the methane, forming HCl and a methyl radical. The other chlorine radical reacts with the methyl radical to form CH_3Cl.

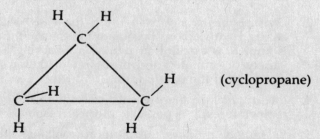

The reaction above continues, resulting in a mixture containing CH_3Cl, CH_2Cl_2, $CHCl_3$, CCl_4, and CH_4 in various amounts.

The relative rates at which the primary, secondary, tertiary, etc., hydrogens are replaced is 1:3.25:4.43:etc. at 300°C and approaches 1:1:1:etc. at higher temperatures. With Br_2, the process is more selective, with rates 1:80:1600 for the 1°, 2°, 3° free radicals.

6. *Free radical stability:* None of the conditions favoring the formation of stable free radicals is present to any great degree and hence, alkanes are relatively inert. In general, free radical stabilities are 3° > 2° > 1°.

7. *Ring formation:* Saturated hydrocarbons with a cyclic structure (alicyclic compounds) also occur. These compounds have the general formula of alkenes, C_nH_{2n}, but show all the chemical properties of alkanes.

Example:

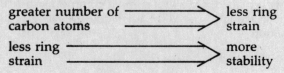

(cyclopropane)

The geometry of cyclopropane in relation to the carbon-carbon bond angle (109° 28') leads to "ring strain."

greater number of carbon atoms ⟶ less ring strain

less ring strain ⟶ more stability

Cyclopentane most closely approaches the correct carbon-carbon bond angle with 108°, but the higher cycloalkanes "pucker" the rings in order to cut down their measures closer to 109$\frac{1}{2}$°.

Alkenes

Alkenes form the second homologous series of aliphatic hydrocarbons. Alkenes with one double bond have the general formula C_nH_{2n}. Alkenes are considered "unsaturated" due to the presence of a double bond. It is the presence of double bonds that makes the alkenes far more reactive than their corresponding alkanes, with many addition reactions possible at the double bond position. The double bond also brings the two carbon nuclei closer together, resulting in a stronger bond.

Nomenclature of Alkenes

The Geneva (IUPAC) rule for naming alkenes resembles the rule for naming alkanes, except that the ending of the compounds is *-ene*. The parent compound is considered the longest chain containing the double bond. Atoms are numbered from the end closest to the double bond. The double bond is indicated by a number preceding the parent name. Side chains are named and their positions indicated as in the alkanes.

Examples:

(ethene)

$$H-\overset{\overset{\displaystyle H}{|}}{C}=\overset{\overset{\displaystyle H}{|}}{C}-H$$

(2-methyl-3-ethyl-1-hexene)

(3-chloro-1-propene) $Cl-CH_2CH=CH_2$

Physical Properties of Alkenes

The physical properties of alkenes are very similar to those of their corresponding alkanes. The solubility of the lower-molecular-weight alkenes in water, although slight, is considerably greater than that of the alkanes. This is due to the double bond attraction to the positive end of the water molecule.

Cis-Trans Isomerism

Cis-trans isomerism is a type of geometric isomerism associated with double bond structure in organic molecules; it is also known as *stereoisomerism*. Cis-trans isomers are *not optically active*. Cis-trans isomers result because the two double-bonded carbons and the four atoms or groups joined to them lie in a plane and free rotation is not possible about the double bond. If the two groups on each carbon atom are different, two stereoisomers can result. If the two groups are alike, then only one isomer is possible. If like groups are on the same side, we get the cis-isomer, if they are on opposite sides, we get the trans-isomer.

H Cl   Cl Cl
| | | |
C=C   C=C
| | | |
Cl H   H H

trans dichloroethane   **cis dichloroethane**

Cis-trans isomers differ in both physical and chemical properties. Trans-isomers should have zero dipole moment, whereas cis-isomers should have a moment. The trans-isomer usually has the higher melting point. The stability of geometric isomers varies with their constitution—some isomers convert on heating, but the conversion is more frequently catalyzed by light or free radicals. In general, the trans-isomer is more stable than the cis-isomer.

Intermediate Carbonium Ion (Carbocation) Stability in Reactions

Carbocations are incapable of more than a momentary existence. These are ions that contain a carbon atom with only six shared electrons in the outer shell.

$$
\left[\begin{array}{c} H \quad\; H \\ | \qquad | \\ H-C-:\overset{..}{C}:-H \\ | \\ Br \end{array} \right]^{+}
$$

Carbocations are, despite their short life span, extremely useful in the theory of chemical transformations. Carbocations are formed when an acid is brought into the vicinity of a molecule that can furnish an unshared electron pair (Lewis base) or a multiple bond that can be moved into an unshared pair at the demand of the reagent.

Carbocation formation theory can be used to "explain" addition reactions in alkenes.

1. In the presence of the reagent, the double bond "opens up".

C—C
..   +

2. Positive ion of solvent adds to negative carbon, forming carbocation.

3. Negative ion adds to carbocation forming new compound.

$$
\begin{array}{c} H \;\; H \\ | \;\;\; | \\ C=C \\ | \;\;\; | \\ H \;\; H \end{array} \underset{\substack{(HBr)\\ or\,(HCl)\\ or\,(HI)\\ etc.}}{\longleftrightarrow} \begin{array}{c} H \;\; H \\ | \;\;\; | \\ H-C-C-H \\ + \;\; .. \end{array} \longrightarrow \left[\begin{array}{c} H \;\; H \\ | \;\;\; | \\ H-C-C-H \\ + \;\;\; | \\ H \end{array} \right]^{+} \xrightarrow{Br^{-}} \begin{array}{c} H \;\; H \\ | \;\;\; | \\ H-C-C-H \\ | \;\;\; | \\ Br \;\; H \end{array}
$$

The more stable the carbocation, the more likely it is that the reaction will take place. In the addition of acids to asymmetrical alkenes, the H^{+} will add to the carbon having the most hydrogens, while the negative member will add to the carbon with the fewest hydrogens.

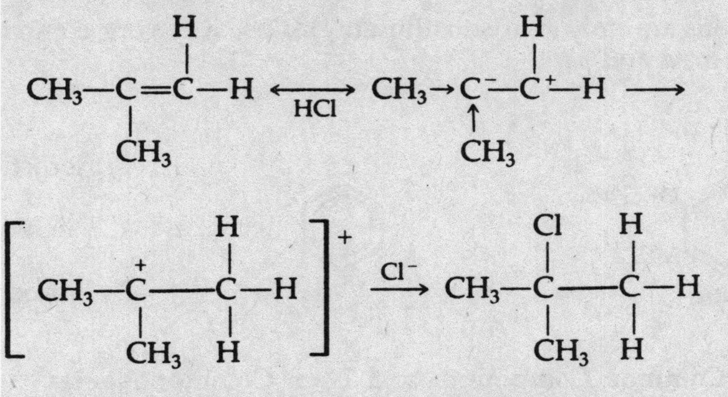

$$CH_3-\overset{\underset{\displaystyle CH_3}{|}}{\overset{\displaystyle H}{C}}=\overset{\displaystyle}{C}-H \underset{HCl}{\longleftrightarrow} CH_3\rightarrow\overset{\underset{\displaystyle CH_3}{|}}{\overset{\displaystyle H}{C}}-\overset{\uparrow}{C}{}^{+}-H \longrightarrow$$

$$\left[CH_3-\overset{\underset{\displaystyle CH_3}{|}}{\overset{+}{C}}-\overset{\underset{\displaystyle H}{|}}{\overset{\displaystyle H}{C}}-H \right]^{+} \overset{Cl^-}{\longrightarrow} CH_3-\overset{\underset{\displaystyle CH_3}{|}}{\overset{\displaystyle Cl}{C}}-\overset{\underset{\displaystyle H}{|}}{\overset{\displaystyle H}{C}}-H$$

The above is known as Markovkinoff's Rule and can be used to predict the most likely product to be formed. When oxygen is present in the presence of HBr, peroxides are formed and these produce exceptions to the rule.

AROMATIC COMPOUNDS: BENZENE AND ITS DERIVATIVES

Benzene (C_6H_6) is considered the compound from which all aromatic compounds are derived. In aromatic compounds, the benzene nucleus remains intact during many types of reactions. The benzene nucleus is extremely resistant to addition reactions but readily lends itself to single or multiple substitution reactions.

Nomenclature of Substituted Benzenes

The benzene molecule can be represented as:

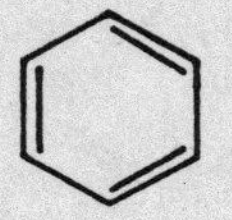

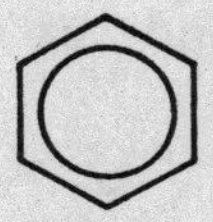

Each corner of the benzene diagram represents one carbon atom. The carbon atoms can be numbered from 1 to 6 and the substituted groups named and numbered. There is only one isomer of a monosubstituted benzene since all carbons are equivalent.

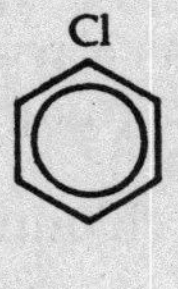

(chlorobenzene) 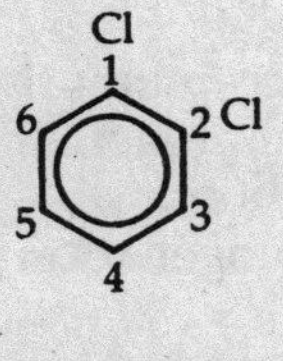   (1,2-dichlorobenzene) 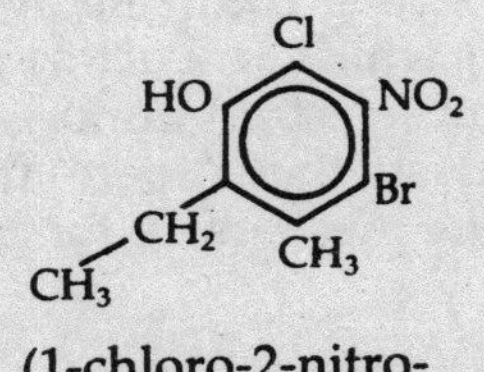   (1-chloro-2-nitro-
3-bromo-4-methyl-
5-ethyl-6-
hydroxybenzene)

It is also possible to name the parent compound as the benzene derivative in position 1.

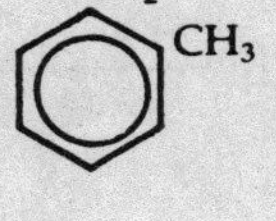

(2-methylnitrobenzene)

Where there are only two substituted groups, it is very common to use the terms *ortho, meta* and *para*.

Example:

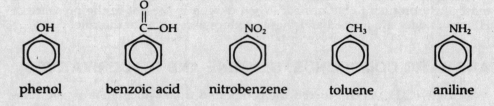

orthodichlorobenzene
or
1,2-dichlorobenzene
or
2-chlorochlorobenzene

Some Very Common Compounds and Their Common Names

OH	$\overset{\overset{O}{\|\|}}{C-OH}$	NO₂	CH₃	NH₂
phenol	benzoic acid	nitrobenzene	toluene	aniline

Resonance of Benzene Nucleus

Resonance is the ability of a compound to exist in two or more structures, differing only in their electron distributions. The properties of the compound will not be those of any of the structures, but rather a hybrid of all of them. *An ion or molecule in which resonance can occur will always be more stable than one in which it cannot.* The benzene nucleus is very stable because it has resonance states. This also accounts for the existence of only one isomer for chlorobenzene, etc., since the double bonds are not fixed (as is the case in alkenes).

Delocalization of Electrons

The most common reactions of benzene are substitutions. The reagents used are strong oxidizing agents (Cl_2, Br_2, Fe, $AlCl_3$, $FeBr_3$, HNO_3, fuming H_2SO_4, etc.) which will act as electron acceptors; the benzene ring acts as a reducing agent (electron donor). It is the approach of strongly electrophilic groups plus catalysts that "open" the double bonds.

The mechanism for aromatic halogenation is illustrated here for chlorination.

1. $Cl_2 + FeCl_3 \rightleftharpoons Cl_3Fe\overset{\ominus}{-}Cl\overset{\oplus}{-}Cl$

2. $Cl_3\overset{\ominus}{Fe}-\overset{\oplus}{Cl}-Cl + C_6H_6 \longrightarrow C_6H_5\overset{\overset{\displaystyle H}{\diagup}}{\underset{\underset{\displaystyle Cl}{\diagdown}}{{}^{\oplus}}} + FeCl_4^-$

3. $C_6H_5\overset{\overset{\displaystyle H}{\diagup}}{\underset{\underset{\displaystyle Cl}{\diagdown}}{{}^{\oplus}}} + FeCl_4^- \longrightarrow C_6H_5Cl + HCl + FeCl_3$

Oxidizing Agents	Ions
Cl_2, $AlCl_3$	Cl^+
Br_2, $FeBr_3$, Fe	Br^+
R-Cl, $AlCl_3$	R^+
HNO_3, H_2SO_4	NO_2^+
fuming H_2SO_4	$-SO_3H$

Orientation in Benzene Derivatives

If a second substitute, Y, is to be introduced in C_6H_5X, the position taken by Y (ortho, meta, or para), depends on the electron orientation of X.
Ortho-para orienting groups are electron donors.

very strong:
$$-\overset{\underset{|}{CH_3}}{N}-CH_3 \qquad -\overset{\underset{|}{H}}{N}-H \qquad -OH$$

intermediate:
$$-\overset{\underset{|}{H}}{N}-\overset{\underset{||}{O}}{C}-CH_3 \qquad -O-\overset{\underset{||}{O}}{C}-CH_3 \qquad -O-CH_3$$

weak:
$$\underbrace{-Cl \qquad -Br \qquad -I}_{\text{(deactivate weakly)}}, \quad -CH_3$$

Meta orienting groups deactivate.

$$N(CH_3)_3{}^+ > NO_2 > SO_3H > CN > COOH > CHO$$

Example:

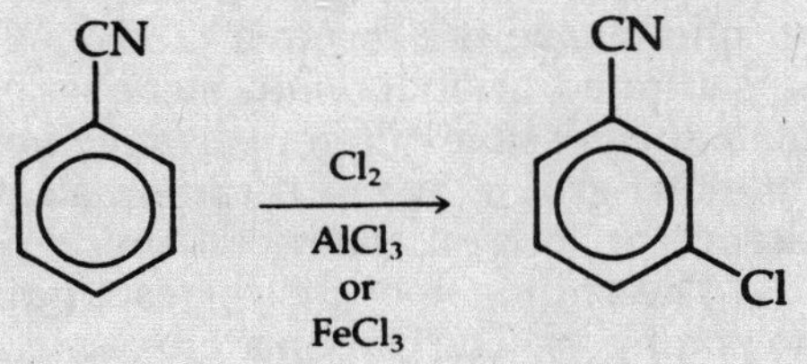

Common Aromatic Properties

1. Special type of unsaturation (no addition).
2. Stable 6-carbon nucleus.
3. Formed with ease.
4. Ease of substitution.

Molecular Geometry

All 6 carbon atoms of benzene lie in a plane and the hydrogen atoms or substituent groups radiate from them in the same plane. The carbon atoms are at the corners of a regular hexagon.

BENZENE GEOMETRY

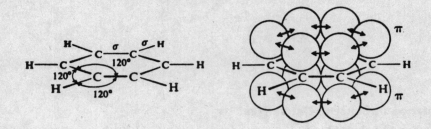

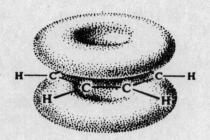

Organic Compounds That Contain Oxygen

ALCOHOLS

Nomenclature

Alcohols are aliphatic compounds containing the $-OH$ (hydroxyl) group. The simplest saturated alcohols have the formula $C_nH_{2n+2}O$. There are also poly-hydroxy alcohols, unsaturated alcohols, and alcohols having other functional groups attached. Due to the possible different arrangements of the carbon atoms and the position of the OH group, even a 4-carbon alcohol has four isomers.

In the IUPAC system, the longest chain containing the hydroxyl group determines the surname. The ending *-e* of the corresponding saturated hydrocarbon is changed to the ending *-ol*. The carbon atoms are numbered in the manner which will give the hydroxyl-bearing carbons the lowest possible numbers. Side chains are named and numbered as before.

(2-methyl-1-propanol)

CH$_3$OH—methanol or methyl alcohol (wood alcohol)
CH$_3$CH$_2$OH—ethanol or ethyl alcohol (grain alcohol)

TYPES OF ALCOHOLS

$$C—C—OH \qquad C—\overset{\overset{\displaystyle C}{|}}{C}—OH \qquad C—\overset{\overset{\displaystyle C}{|}}{\underset{\underset{\displaystyle C}{|}}{C}}—OH$$

Primary   Secondary   Tertiary

Properties of Alcohols

Acidity

Alcohols are weak acids (with the possible exception of methanol, they are weaker acids than water) in the sense that they can lose a hydrogen ion and form the alkoxide ion, RO^-.

It is the hydrogen attached to the oxygen of the OH group that gives alcohols their acid properties. When sodium is slowly added to an alcohol, hydrogen gas is released. The relative strengths of alcohols as acids are $1° > 2° > 3°$.

This difference in relative strengths is due to the greater electron density around a tertiary carbon than about a secondary carbon, and greater density around a secondary carbon than about a primary carbon.

$$C{\rightarrow}\overset{\overset{\displaystyle H}{|}}{\underset{\underset{\displaystyle H}{|}}{C}}{-}OH \qquad C{\rightarrow}\overset{\overset{\displaystyle H}{|}}{\underset{\underset{\displaystyle C}{\uparrow}}{C}}{-}OH \qquad C{\rightarrow}\overset{\overset{\displaystyle C}{\downarrow}}{\underset{\underset{\displaystyle C}{\uparrow}}{C}}{-}OH$$

A greater negative charge on the carbon holds the hydrogen with greater force.

Physical Properties

1. *Boiling point:* Alcohols have higher boiling points than their corresponding hydrocarbons, due to hydrogen bonding. Boiling points of normal alcohols increase with increasing molecular weight. Chain branching lowers boiling point, as in hydrocarbons.

2. *State:* Alcohols change from liquids to solids as their molecular weights increase.

3. *Solubility:* Alcohols follow the rule "like dissolves like." Alcohols containing three or fewer carbons are miscible with water at 20°C, but butyl alcohol is soluble to the extent of less than 10%. Higher molecular weight alcohols are completely immiscible.

Reactions of Alcohols

Dehydration

Dehydration is an acid-catalyzed process. A molecule of water is removed from each alcohol molecule.

Examples:

$$H—\overset{\overset{\displaystyle H}{|}}{\underset{\underset{\displaystyle H}{|}}{C}}—\overset{\overset{\displaystyle H}{|}}{\underset{\underset{\displaystyle H}{|}}{C}}—OH \quad \xrightarrow[\substack{\text{(acid)}\\ \text{85\% } H_3PO_4 \\ \text{conc. } H_2SO_4 \\ \text{etc.}}]{\text{dehydrating agent}} \quad \overset{\overset{\displaystyle H}{|}}{\underset{\underset{\displaystyle H}{|}}{C}}{=}\overset{\overset{\displaystyle H}{|}}{\underset{\underset{\displaystyle H}{|}}{C}}$$

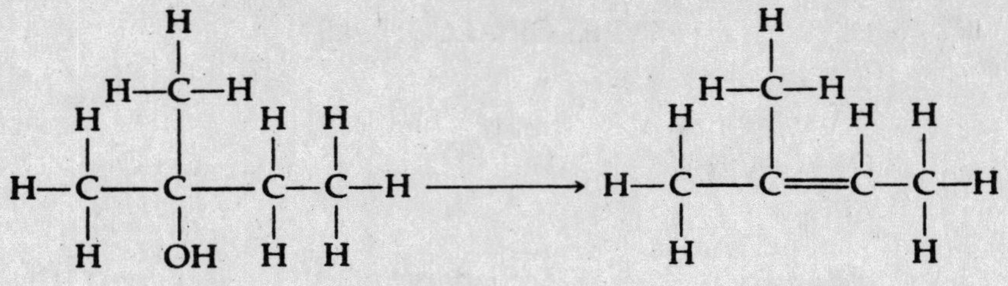

$$\underset{\substack{H \\ | \\ H-C-H \\ | \\ H \quad \quad H \; H \\ | \quad \quad | \; | \\ H-C-C-\!\!-C-C-H \\ | \quad | \quad | \; | \\ H \quad OH \; H \; H}}{} \longrightarrow \underset{\substack{H \\ | \\ H-C-H \\ | \\ H \quad \quad H \; H \\ | \quad \quad | \; | \\ H-C-C=\!\!C-C-H \\ | \quad \quad \quad | \\ H \quad \quad \quad H}}{}$$

The general direction for dehydration is:

$$\text{alcohol} \rightarrow \text{alkene}$$

Oxidation

Primary alcohol → through aldehyde to carboxylic acid with the same number of carbons.

Secondary alcohol → to ketone with the same number of carbons.

Tertiary alcohol → resists oxidation with mild oxidizing agents; strong agents will take them to ketones with a lesser carbon content.

Oxidizing Agents:

$$\xrightarrow{\;OH^-, KMnO_4\;}$$
$$\xrightarrow{\;H_3O^+\;}$$
$$\xrightarrow{\;H_3O^+, K_2Cr_2O_7\;} (CrO_3)$$

Examples:

(primary alcohol) ⟶ (aldehyde) ⟶ (carboxylic acid)

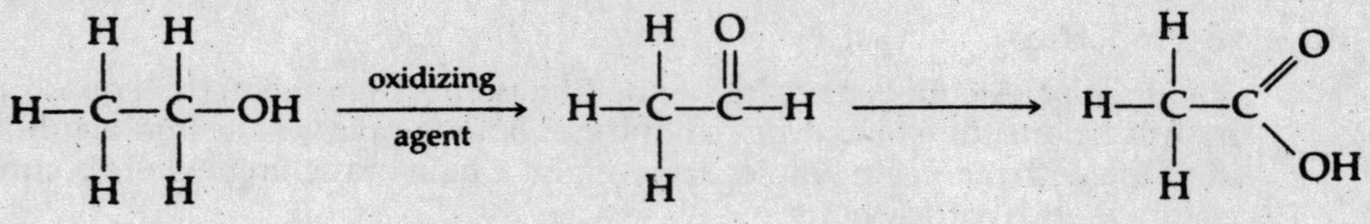

$$\underset{\substack{H \; H \\ | \; | \\ H-C-C-OH \\ | \; | \\ H \; H}}{} \xrightarrow[\text{agent}]{\text{oxidizing}} \underset{\substack{H \; O \\ | \; \parallel \\ H-C-C-H \\ | \\ H}}{} \longrightarrow \underset{\substack{H \\ | \\ H-C-C \\ | \quad\;\; \diagdown \\ H \quad\quad OH}}{\overset{O}{}}$$

(secondary alcohol) ⟶ (ketone)

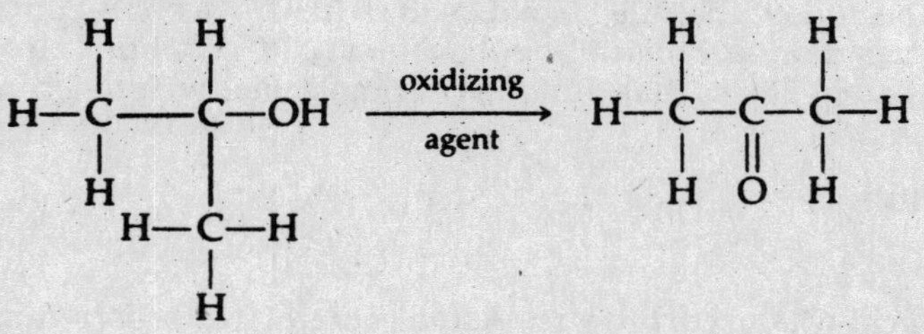

$$\underset{\substack{H \quad H \\ | \quad | \\ H-C-\!\!-C-OH \\ | \quad | \\ H \quad | \\ H-C-H \\ | \\ H}}{} \xrightarrow[\text{agent}]{\text{oxidizing}} \underset{\substack{H \quad\quad H \\ | \quad\quad | \\ H-C-C-C-H \\ | \quad \parallel \quad | \\ H \quad O \quad H}}{}$$

(tertiary alcohol) ⟶ (ketone)

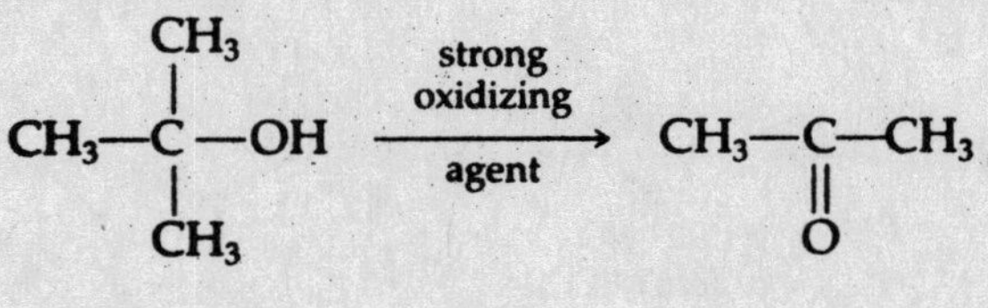

$$\underset{\substack{CH_3 \\ | \\ CH_3-C-OH \\ | \\ CH_3}}{} \xrightarrow[\text{agent}]{\substack{\text{strong} \\ \text{oxidizing}}} \underset{\substack{CH_3-C-CH_3 \\ \parallel \\ O}}{}$$

Double bond will go to make the most stable bond.

Substitution

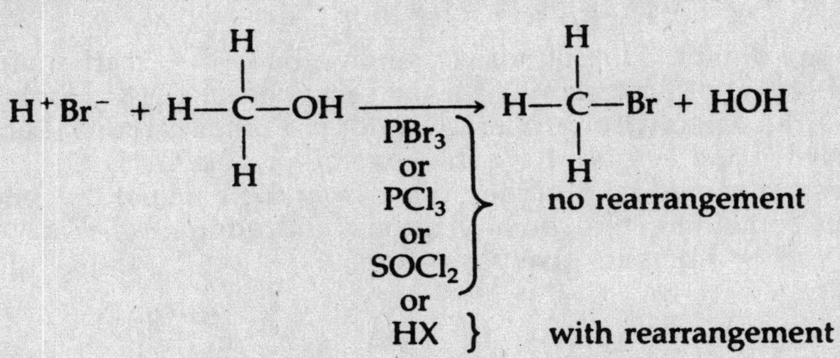

$$H^+Br^- + H-\overset{\overset{\displaystyle H}{|}}{\underset{\underset{\displaystyle H}{|}}{C}}-OH \xrightarrow{\hspace{1cm}} H-\overset{\overset{\displaystyle H}{|}}{\underset{\underset{\displaystyle H}{|}}{C}}-Br + HOH$$

$$\left.\begin{array}{c} PBr_3 \\ or \\ PCl_3 \\ or \\ SOCl_2 \end{array}\right\} \quad \text{no rearrangement}$$

$$\left.\begin{array}{c} or \\ HX \end{array}\right\} \quad \text{with rearrangement}$$

The most typical substitution reaction of alcohols is the substitution of the OH group by a halogen (by reaction of the alcohol with the halogen acid). The rate of the substitution reaction is the reverse order of the acid strengths: 3° > 2° > 1° (this follows the base strengths; the H$^+$ attacks first). This is in agreement with the concept that the carbon of the tertiary alcohol has the greatest electron density and will facilitate the release of the negative OH group or form a more stable carbocation.

Examples:

$$\boxed{\begin{array}{c} \textbf{Oxidizing Agents} \\[4pt] HI > HBr > \begin{pmatrix} HCl \\ ZnCl_2 \end{pmatrix} \end{array}}$$

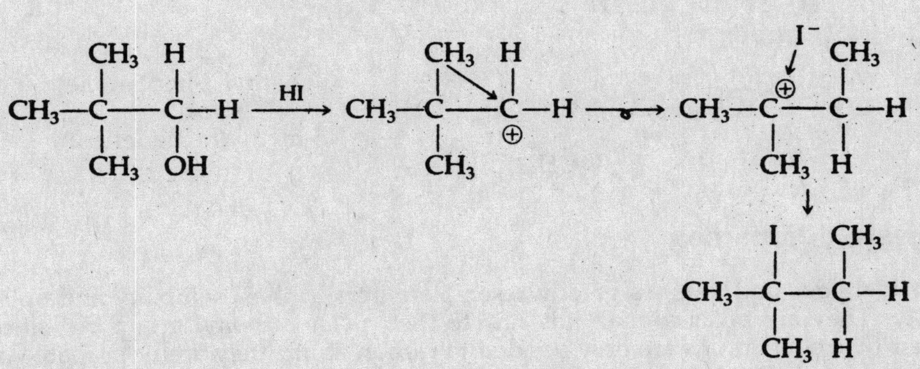

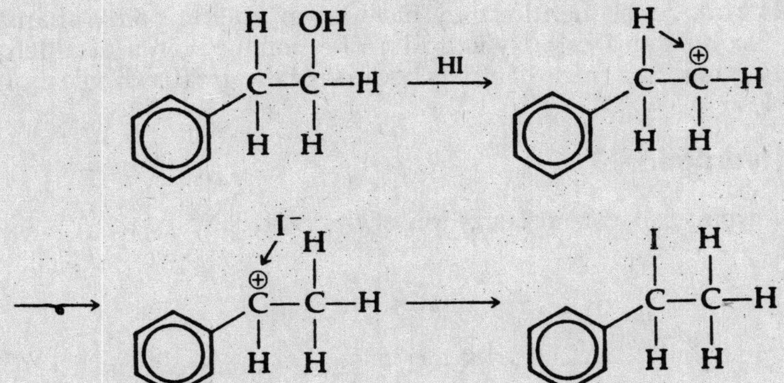

ALDEHYDES AND KETONES

Nomenclature

Aldehydes are organic compounds containing the $C = O$ (carbonyl) group attached to only one other carbon (with the exception of CH_2O, formaldehyde). *Ketones* have the carbonyl group attached to two other carbons. Saturated aliphatic aldehydes and ketones have the general formula $C_nH_{2n}O$.

Aldehydes are named by dropping the *-e* from the name of the longest chain hydrocarbon containing the carbonyl group and adding *-al*. Side chains are named and carbon numbers given as before.

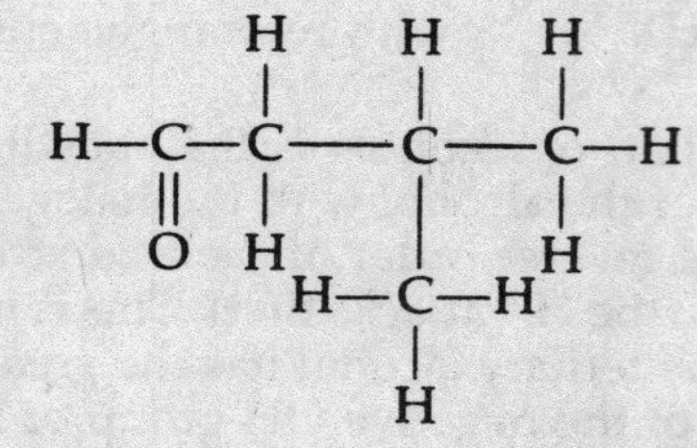

(3-methylbutanal)

Ketones end in *-one*, and position of the carbonyl group is indicated with the lowest possible number.

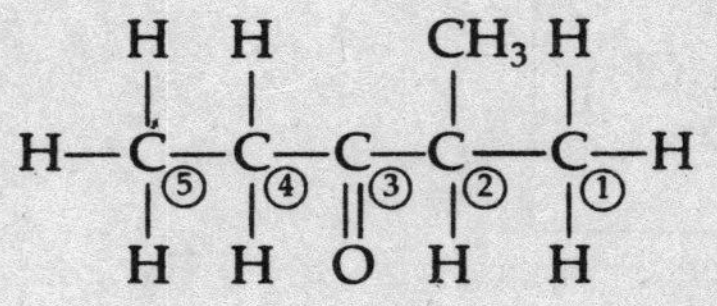

(2-methylpentanone-3)
or
(2-methyl-3-pentanone)

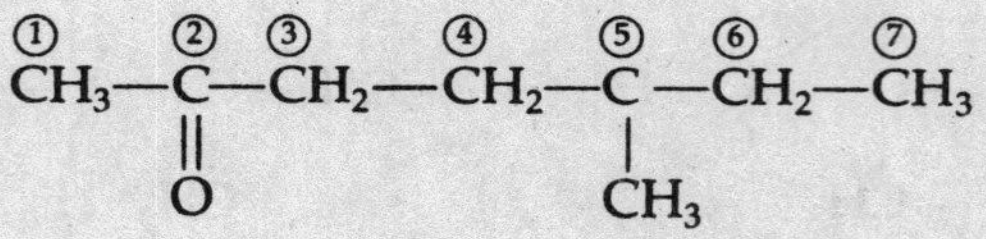

(5-methyl-2-heptanone)
or
(5-methylheptanone-2)

Physical Properties

Aldehydes and ketones greatly resemble ethers in their solubility and volatility. They are polar compounds due to their polar carbonyl group but since their hydrogen atoms are only bonded to carbon atoms they are not capable of intermolecular hydrogen bonding. This makes them less polar than their comparable alcohols and, consequently, they have lower boiling points than their corresponding alcohols and carboxylic acids. The boiling points of aldehydes and ketones are higher than those of ethers because of the greater dipole moment of their molecules.

Acidity of α Hydrogen

The carbonyl group causes a polarization of the molecule.

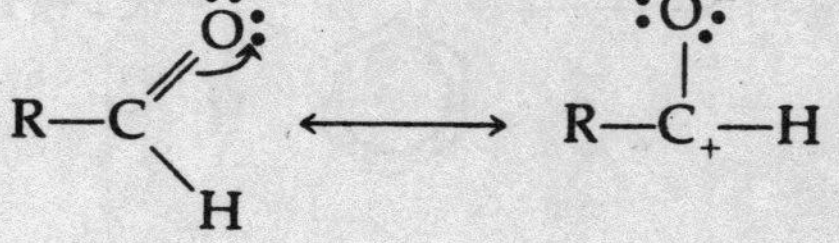

(resonance form)

This, in turn, tends to make the α carbon (the one next to the carbonyl group) slightly positive. This causes the relatively easy replacement of the α hydrogen by halogens.

Carbanions

When an organic compound loses a hydrogen ion or a proton, the resulting ion containing a carbon atom with an unshared electron pair is called a carbanion.

$$H : C \diagdown \quad \text{base} \quad H^+ + \ :C \diagdown$$

$$\text{carbanion}$$

In general, base-induced carbanion formation depends upon two factors: the basic strength of the attaching reagent and the structure of the molecule which is to undergo the reaction.

$$R-\underset{\underset{R}{|}}{\overset{\overset{H}{|}}{C}}-\overset{\overset{O}{\|}}{C}-Y \longleftrightarrow R-\underset{\underset{R}{|}}{\overset{\overset{H}{|}}{C}}-\overset{\overset{O^-}{|}}{\underset{+}{C}}-Y \xrightarrow{\text{base}} R-\underset{\underset{R}{|}}{\overset{\overset{..}{C}}{}}-\overset{\overset{O}{\|}}{C}-Y + \text{base}-H^+$$

$$\text{(resonance form)} \qquad \text{carbanion}$$

The ease of carbanion formation from the various carbonyl compounds decreases in order: aldehydes, ketones, esters, amides, and acids. The more electron-sharing Y becomes, the less likely the carbonyl group is to withdraw electrons from the α carbon atom.

Nucleophilic addition reactions are addition reactions of negative (positive-seeking) or electron donors to a positive center in a molecule. In the addition reactions to carbonyl compounds it is the + carbon that initiates the reaction.

$$R-\underset{+}{\overset{\overset{O^-}{|}}{C}}-H$$

Aldehydes are more reactive than ketones because the carbon of an aldehyde is more positive than that of a ketone.

$$R-\overset{\overset{O}{\|}}{C}-H + X^+Y^- \longrightarrow R-\underset{\underset{H}{|}}{\overset{\overset{OX}{|}}{C}}-Y$$

$$(H^+CN^-)$$
$$(Na^+HSO_3{}^-)$$
$$\text{(etc.)}$$

Oxidation

Aldehydes are more easily oxidized to acids than ketones are.

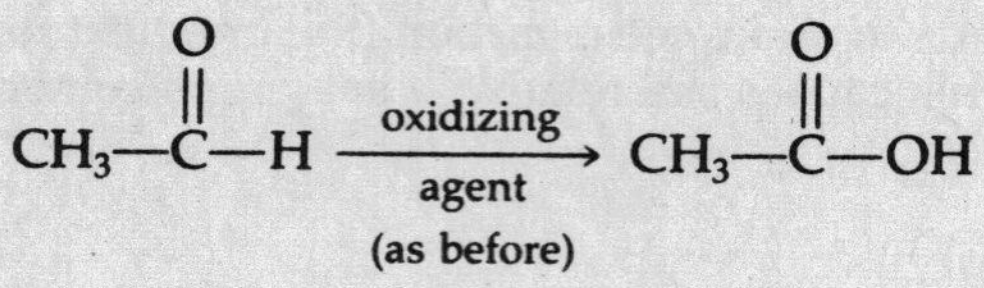

$$CH_3-\overset{\overset{\displaystyle O}{\|}}{C}-H \xrightarrow[\text{agent}]{\text{oxidizing}} CH_3-\overset{\overset{\displaystyle O}{\|}}{C}-OH$$

(as before)

Ketones require stronger oxidizing agents and result in two acid molecules with cleavage of the carbon chain on either side of the carbonyl group.

ETHERS

General Description

Simple ethers have the general formula $C_nH_{2n+2}O$ and are, therefore, isomers of the alcohols. Ethers contain two alkyl radicals connected by an oxygen atom.

$$R_1-O-R_2$$

If the two radicals are the same, then it is called a "simple" ether; if the two radicals are different, then it is called a "mixed" ether.

Nomenclature

Ethers can be named by stating the names of the two radicals and adding the word ether. In the IUPAC system, the group R—O— is known as *-al*.

Examples:

$$CH_3-O-CH_2CH_3 \qquad \text{(methyl ethyl ether)}$$
$$CH_2CH_3-O-CH_2CH_3 \qquad \text{(ethyl ether)}$$

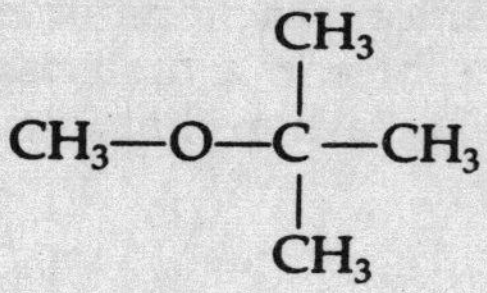

$$CH_3-O-\overset{\overset{\displaystyle CH_3}{|}}{\underset{\underset{\displaystyle CH_3}{|}}{C}}-CH_3 \qquad \text{(methyl tert-butyl ether)}$$

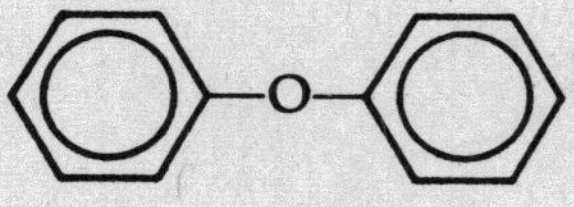

(phenyl ether)

Physical Properties

The C—O—C bond angle is 110° and thus, the dipole moments of the two C—O bonds do not cancel each other.

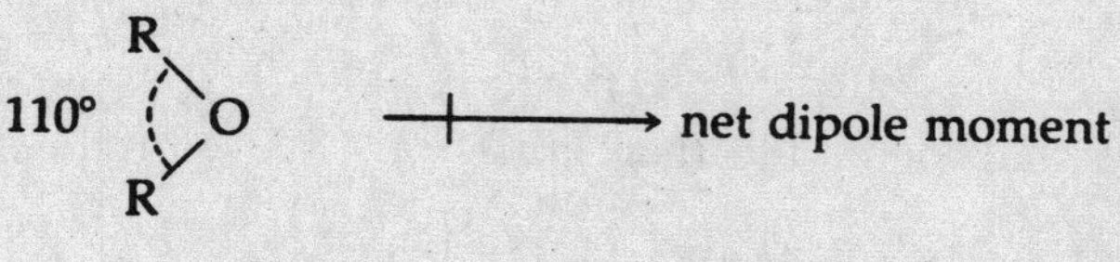

This weak polarity, however, does not appreciably affect the boiling points of ethers, which are about the same as those of alkanes of comparable molecular weights.

Ethers do not contain hydrogen bonded to oxygen atoms; hence, there is no tendency for proton bonding and their boiling points are close to those of hydrocarbons. The solubility of ethers is greater than the solubility of hydrocarbons and resembles the solubility of alcohols of similar molecular weights. This last property is probably due to the unshared electrons on the oxygen atom resulting in co-association of HOH on R—O—R.

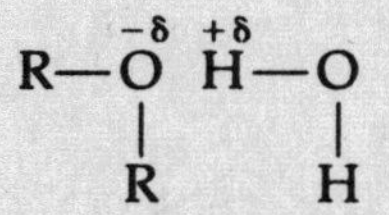

$$R-\overset{-\delta}{O} \ \overset{+\delta}{H}-O$$
$$\quad | \qquad \quad |$$
$$\quad R \qquad \quad H$$

PHENOLS

General Description

Phenols are compounds having an —OH (hydroxyl) group attached directly to an aromatic benzene nucleus.

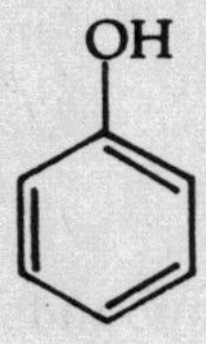

(phenol)

Phenol is one of the oldest disinfectants and the reference compound to which other germicidal substances are compared (phenol coefficient). The OH group in phenol is ortho-para-directing.

Nomenclature

Phenols are named as derivatives of phenol C_6H_5OH.

Examples:

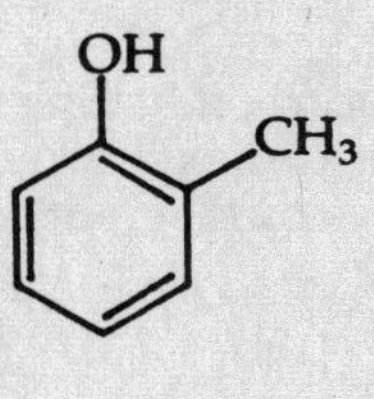

o-methylphenol
or
2-methylphenol

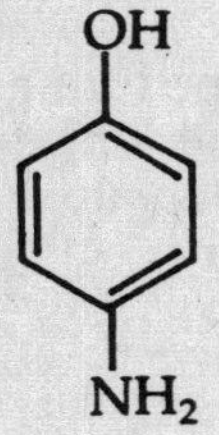

p-aminophenol
or
4-aminophenol

Physical Properties

Pure phenols are colorless solids or liquids, although they are usually found colored red by oxidation products. Their boiling points are higher than those of their aliphatic analogues. So-called "liquid phenol" is 90% phenol and 10% water due to the low solubility (8%) of phenol in water at room temperature.

Acidity

Phenols are considerably more acidic than alcohols or water due to resonance within the ring. Phenols containing strong electron-attracting groups in the nucleus (nitro group) will be far stronger acids. In the mononitrophenols the effect of the nitro group is greater in the ortho and para positions than in the meta position. Combinations of nitro groups in the ortho and para positions produce strong phenolic acids:

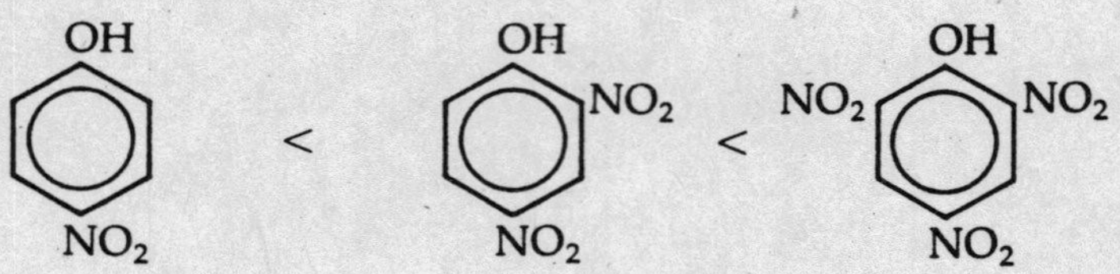

Hydrogen Bonding

Hydrogen bonding in phenols is limited since the oxygen atom of the OH group donates electrons into the ring and thus tends to be positive.

CARBOXYLIC ACIDS

General Description

Carboxylic acids are organic compounds that transfer protons more readily than the HOH molecule does. They are characterized by the presence of a carboxyl group.

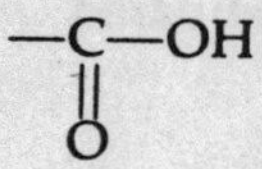

Acids may be saturated or unsaturated, aromatic or aliphatic, and with or without substituted groups on the chain. Amides, esters, and salts are examples of acid derivatives. "Fatty acids" are produced by the hydrolysis of fats.

Nomenclature

The -*e* is dropped from the name of the hydrocarbon having the same number of carbons as the longest chain containing the carboxyl group and -*oic acid* is added. The carbon atom of the carboxyl group is numbered 1 when numbering the longest chain.

Example:

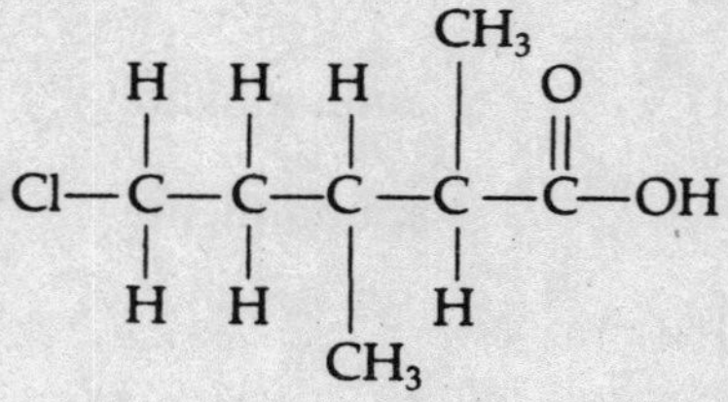

(2,3-dimethyl-5-chloropentanoic acid)

Acidity: Effect on Substitution

The carboxylic acids are relatively weak acids although some of their derivatives are strong acids.

$$R-\overset{\overset{\displaystyle O}{\|}}{C}-OH \longleftrightarrow R-\overset{\overset{\displaystyle OH}{|}}{C}=O$$

The acid radical can exist in two equivalent resonance structures

$$R-\overset{\overset{\displaystyle O}{\|}}{C}-O^- \longleftrightarrow R-\overset{\overset{\displaystyle O^-}{|}}{C}=O$$

and tends to be more stable than the acid (hence contributing to the formation of H_3O^+, the hydronium ion).

$$R-\overset{\overset{\displaystyle O}{\|}}{C}-OH + H_2O \rightarrow H_3O^+ + R-\overset{\overset{\displaystyle O}{\|}}{C}-O^-$$

Substitution of chlorine on the α carbon results in a far greater degree of ionization and a much stronger acid.

$$CL\leftarrow\overset{\overset{\displaystyle Cl}{\uparrow}}{\underset{\underset{\displaystyle Cl}{\downarrow}}{C}}_+-\overset{\overset{\displaystyle O}{\|}}{C}_+\leftarrow OH\underset{+}{}$$

Hydrogen Bonding and Dimerization

Measurement of the molecular weight of acetic acid in the vapor or in the liquid state gives a molecular weight of 120 (acetic acid = CH_3COOH). The acid thus exists as a *dimer*. This dimerization or molecular association is due to hydrogen bonding—that is, the protons of the hydroxyl groups accept electrons from the carbonyl radicals, forming hydrogen bonds between two acid molecules.

$$CH_3-C\overset{O\rightarrow H-O}{\underset{O-H\leftarrow O}{}}C-CH_3$$

(dimerization of CH_3COOH)

NUCLEOPHILIC REACTIONS

Inspection of the formula of an acid reveals that there are five basic reactions that can take place.

$$\underset{5}{R}-\underset{3}{\overset{\overset{\displaystyle O}{\|}}{C}}-\underset{1}{\overset{\overset{\displaystyle 2}{OH}}{}}\overset{4}{}$$

1. **Replacement of ionizable hydrogen.**
   Examples:

$$R-\overset{\overset{\displaystyle O}{\|}}{C}-OH + Na \longrightarrow R-\overset{\overset{\displaystyle O}{\|}}{C}-ONa + H_2$$

$$R-\overset{\overset{\displaystyle O}{\|}}{C}-OH + NaOH \longrightarrow R-\overset{\overset{\displaystyle O}{\|}}{C}-ONa + HOH$$

   (salt)

2. **Replacement of the OH group.**
   Examples:

   (esterification)

$$R-\overset{\overset{\displaystyle O}{\|}}{C}-OH + HOR_1 \longrightarrow R-\overset{\overset{\displaystyle O}{\|}}{C}-OR_1 + HOH$$

   (ester)

$$R-\overset{\overset{\displaystyle O}{\|}}{C}-OH + PCl_3 \longrightarrow R-\overset{\overset{\displaystyle O}{\|}}{C}-Cl + P(OH)_3$$

   (PBr$_3$)   (acid chloride)
   (SOCl$_2$)

3. **Reaction of the carbonyl group.**
   Example:

$$R-\overset{\overset{\displaystyle O}{\|}}{C}-O^-NH_4^+ \overset{\Delta}{\longrightarrow} R-\overset{\overset{\displaystyle O}{\|}}{C}-NH_2 + H_2O$$

   (amide)

4. **Elimination of the carboxyl group.**
   Examples:

$$R-\overset{\overset{\displaystyle O}{\|}}{C}-O^-Na^+ + NaOH \overset{\Delta}{\longrightarrow} RH + Na_2CO_3$$

$$R-\overset{\overset{\displaystyle O}{\|}}{C}-OH \xrightarrow[\text{LiAlH}_4]{\text{reduction, HOH}} R-CH_2-OH \text{ (1° alc.)}$$

5. **Halogen substitution in the alkyl radical.**
   Example:

$$R-\overset{\overset{\displaystyle O}{\|}}{C}-OH \xrightarrow[\text{PCl}_5]{\text{Cl}_2} R-\overset{\overset{\displaystyle O}{\|}}{\underset{\underset{\displaystyle Cl}{|}}{C}}-OH$$

   also

$$\xrightarrow[\text{PBr}_5]{\text{Br}_2}$$

OVERALL Ka

$$\text{alkane} < \text{alkene} < \text{alkyne} < -\overset{R}{\underset{|}{C}}-\overset{|}{\underset{|}{C}}- < \text{alc.} < H_2O < \text{phenol} <$$

$$\overset{10^{-42}}{} \quad \overset{10^{-36}}{} \quad \overset{10^{-25}}{} \quad \overset{10^{-20}}{} \quad \overset{10^{-18}}{} \quad \overset{10^{-14}}{} \quad \overset{10^{-10}}{}$$

$$< -\overset{O}{\underset{OH}{\overset{\|}{C}}} \quad < R:^- < :NH_2^-$$

$$\xrightarrow{\quad 10^{-4} \quad} \text{Basicity decreasing}$$

Other Organic Compounds of Biological Importance

AMINES

General Description

Aliphatic amines may be considered *amino* derivatives of alkane hydrocarbons or alkyl derivatives of ammonia (NH_3). This means that one, two, or three of the hydrogens from ammonia may be replaced by alkyl radicals.

$$\begin{array}{ccc}
\overset{H}{\underset{|}{R-N-H}} & \overset{R}{\underset{|}{R-N-H}} & \overset{R}{\underset{|}{R-N-R}} \\
\text{primary amine} & \text{secondary amine} & \text{tertiary amine}
\end{array}$$

Amines of each class unite with water to form addition products (may be considered substitution products of NH_4OH).

$$\begin{array}{ccc}
\left[\begin{array}{c} H \\ | \\ R-N-H \\ | \\ H \end{array}\right]^+ OH^- &
\left[\begin{array}{c} R \\ | \\ R-N-H \\ | \\ H \end{array}\right]^+ OH^- &
\left[\begin{array}{c} R \\ | \\ R-N-H \\ | \\ R \end{array}\right]^+ OH^- \\
\text{primary ammonium base} & \text{secondary ammonium base} & \text{tertiary ammonium base}
\end{array}$$

One more type of ammonium base, in which all four of the hydrogens have been replaced by alkyl radicals, has been prepared:

$$\left[\begin{array}{c} R \\ | \\ R-N-R \\ | \\ R \end{array}\right]^+ OH^-$$

tetraalkylammonium

Amines are substances of great importance since they are widely distributed in nature; proteins of both plant and animal origin yield amines as their derivatives. Amines are also widely used in the laboratory as basic catalysts.

Nomenclature

STRUCTURE	NAME	TYPE
$CH_3-\underset{\underset{NH_2}{\mid}}{\overset{\overset{H}{\mid}}{C}}-CH_3$	2-aminopropane	primary
$H-\underset{\underset{H}{\mid}}{\overset{\overset{H}{\mid}}{C}}-\underset{\underset{CH_3}{\mid}}{\overset{\overset{CH_3}{\mid}}{C}}-\underset{\underset{H}{\mid}}{\overset{\overset{H}{\mid}}{C}}-NH_2$	2-aminodimethylpropane or 1-amino-2,2-dimethylpropane	primary
$C_2H_5-\underset{\underset{H}{\mid}}{\overset{\overset{CH_3}{\mid}}{C}}-\underset{}{\overset{\overset{H}{\mid}}{N}}-C_2H_5$	ethyl-sec-butylamine	secondary
$CH_3-\underset{\underset{CH_3}{\mid}}{\overset{\overset{H}{\mid}}{C}}-\underset{\underset{H}{\mid}}{\overset{\overset{H}{\mid}}{C}}-\underset{}{\overset{\overset{CH_3}{\mid}}{N}}-C_2H_5$	methyl ethyl isobutylamine or 1-(methyl ethyl amino)- 2-methylpropane	tertiary
$C_2H_5-\underset{\underset{C_2H_5}{\mid}}{N}-C_2H_5$	triethylamine	tertiary
aminobenzene (NH_2 on benzene ring)	aminobenzene (aniline)	primary aromatic

Physical Properties

The lower members of the family are gases and highly soluble in water. Those with 3 to 11 carbons are liquids at room temperature. Amines of low molecular weight have an odor similar to that of ammonia.

Amines have lower boiling points than alcohols of corresponding molecular weights because there is less hydrogen bonding.

Basicity

The unshared electron pair on the nitrogen atom causes the amines to be basic (Lewis base). Amines react with water to form ammonium bases and with acids to form salts.

Example:

$$C_2H_5NH_2 + HCl \rightarrow C_2H_5NH_3{}^+Cl^- \text{ (ethylamine hydrochloride)}$$

Aliphatic amines of all three classes have Kb's of the order of 10^{-3} to 10^{-4}; they are, therefore, stronger bases than ammonia. Aromatic amines are, on the other hand, weaker bases and show the *ortho effect*.

electron-donating groups in the o- and p-positions will increase basicity

Electron-withdrawing groups in the o- and p-positions will decrease basicity

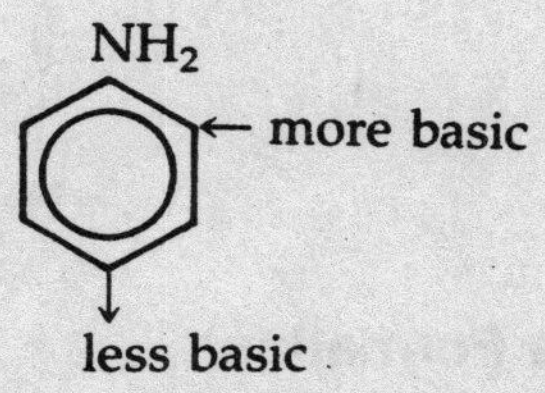

Examples:

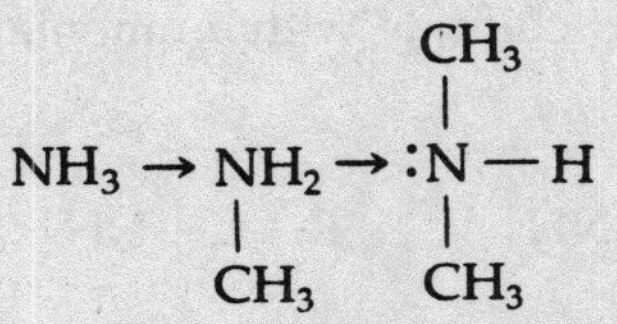

(more alkyl electron-pushing groups)

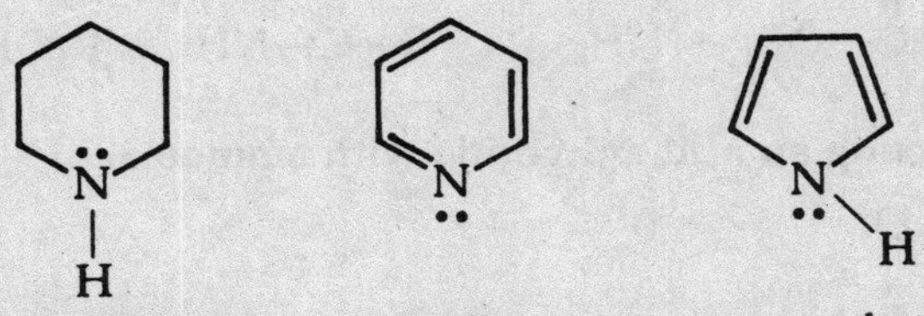

piperdine > pyridine > pyrrole

N electron pair sp^3 sp^2 sp^2 in π cloud

Carbonium Ion Stability

Many of the amine reactions involve the donation of the unshared nitrogen electron pair to a more polarized + carbon atom. A carbonium ion and a negative ion are formed in many cases.

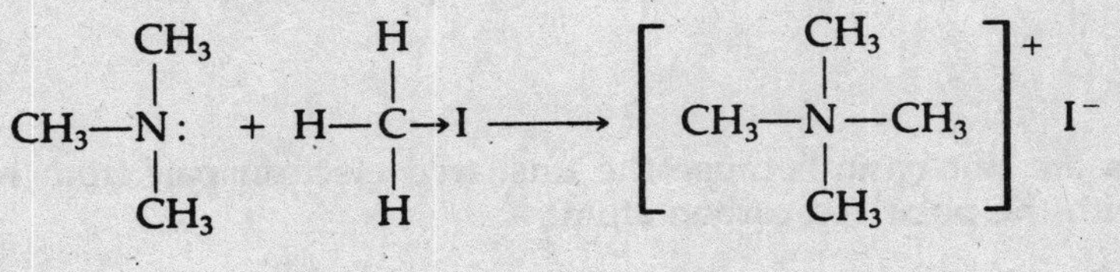

$$\underset{\underset{H}{|}}{\overset{\overset{R}{|}}{H-N:}} + \underset{\underset{H}{|}}{\overset{\overset{O^-}{|}}{_+C-R}} \longrightarrow \underset{\underset{H}{|}}{\overset{\overset{R}{|}}{H-N^+}} \underset{\underset{H}{|}}{\overset{\overset{O^-}{|}}{-C-R}}$$

resonance $\downarrow$ $\downarrow -H_2O$

$$\underset{\underset{H}{|}}{\overset{\overset{O}{\parallel}}{C-R}} \qquad R-N=\underset{\underset{C_2H_5}{|}}{\overset{\overset{H}{|}}{C}}$$

Amide Formation

Acid amides may be made in four ways:

1. Reacting an acid chloride with ammonia.

$$R-\overset{\overset{O}{\parallel}}{C}-Cl + 2NH_3 \qquad R-\overset{\overset{O}{\parallel}}{C}-NH_2 + NH_4Cl$$

2. Reacting an ester with ammonia.

$$R-\overset{\overset{O}{\parallel}}{C}-OR_1 + NH_3 \qquad R-\overset{\overset{O}{\parallel}}{C}-NH_2 + R_1OH$$

3. Reacting an acid anhydride with ammonia.

$$\begin{matrix} R-\overset{\overset{O}{\parallel}}{C} \\ \qquad\quad O + 2NH_3 \\ R-\underset{\underset{O}{\parallel}}{C} \end{matrix} \qquad R-\overset{\overset{O}{\parallel}}{C}-NH_2 + R-\underset{\underset{O}{\parallel}}{C}-O^-NH_4^+$$

4. From the ammonium salt of an acid.

$$R-\underset{\underset{O}{\parallel}}{C}-O^-NH_4^+ \xrightarrow{\text{heat}} R-\overset{\overset{O}{\parallel}}{C}-NH_2 + HOH$$

Amides are not basic because the unshared electron pair from nitrogen is shared with the polarized carbon atom.

Alkylation

Amines are alkylated by substituting alkyl groups for hydrogen atoms on the nitrogen atom.

$$R—NH_2 + R_1—Cl \longrightarrow \left[\begin{matrix} & H & \\ & | & \\ R—&N&—R_1 \\ & | & \\ & H & \end{matrix} \right]^+ Cl^- \xrightarrow[NaOH]{} \begin{matrix} H \\ | \\ R—N—R_1 \end{matrix}$$

Excess RNH_2 prevents, to a certain extent, multiple alkylation. The process above, however, may be continued in order to produce tertiary amines.

ACID DERIVATIVES

Amides

An amide is an acid derivative in which the OH of the carboxyl group has been replaced by an amino (NH_2) group.

$$\begin{matrix} O & H \\ \| & | \\ R—C—N—H \end{matrix} \qquad \begin{matrix} O & H & O \\ \| & | & \| \\ R—C—N—C—R \end{matrix} \qquad \begin{matrix} O & & O \\ \| & & \| \\ R—C—N—C—R \\ & | \\ & C=O \\ & | \\ & R \end{matrix}$$

(primary amide)   (secondary amide)   (tertiary amide)

Primary amides are of great importance. In a primary amide one or both of the hydrogen atoms may be replaced by alkyl radicals. Such replacements yield mono- and disubstituted amides.

$$\begin{matrix} O & H \\ \| & | \\ R—C—N—R_1 \end{matrix} \qquad\qquad \begin{matrix} O & R_2 \\ \| & | \\ R—C—N—R_1 \end{matrix}$$

(monosubstituted amide)   (disubstituted amide)

Nomenclature of Amides

$$\begin{matrix} O \\ \| \\ H—C—NH_2 \end{matrix}$$
(methanamide)
or
(formamide)

$$\begin{matrix} O \\ \| \\ CH_3—C—NH_2 \end{matrix}$$
(acetamide)

$$\begin{matrix} O \\ \| \\ C_2H_5—C—NH_2 \end{matrix}$$
(propionamide)

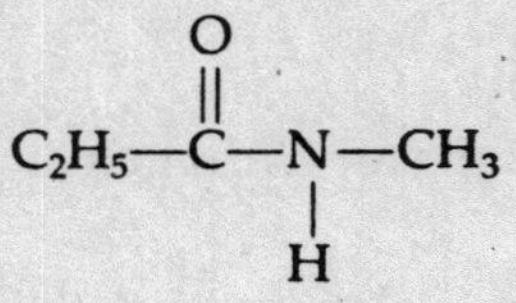

$$C_2H_5-\overset{\overset{O}{\|}}{C}-\underset{\underset{H}{|}}{N}-CH_3 \qquad \text{(N-methyl propionamide)}$$

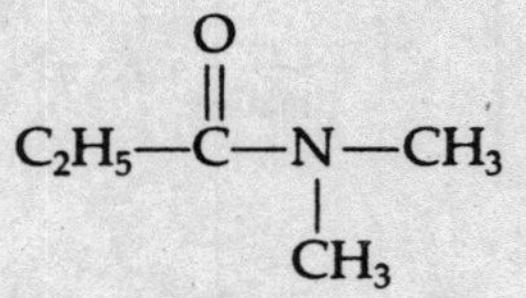

$$C_2H_5-\overset{\overset{O}{\|}}{C}-\underset{\underset{CH_3}{|}}{N}-CH_3 \qquad \text{(N,N-diethyl propionamide)}$$

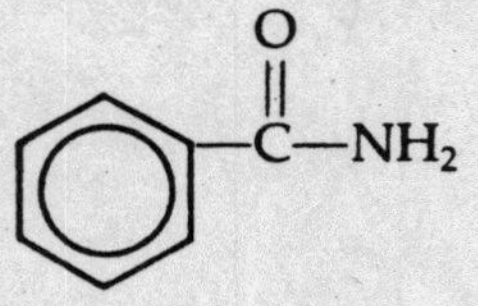

$$\text{(benzamide)}$$

Physical Properties of Amides

Amides are solid (with one exception). Hydrogen bonding leads to high melting and boiling points. Lower members of the family are soluble in water. Because of their high boiling points, amides of 8 or more carbons are distilled at reduced pressures to prevent decomposition.

Preparation of Amides

(See amines)

Electronic Structure (Resonance Forms) of Amides

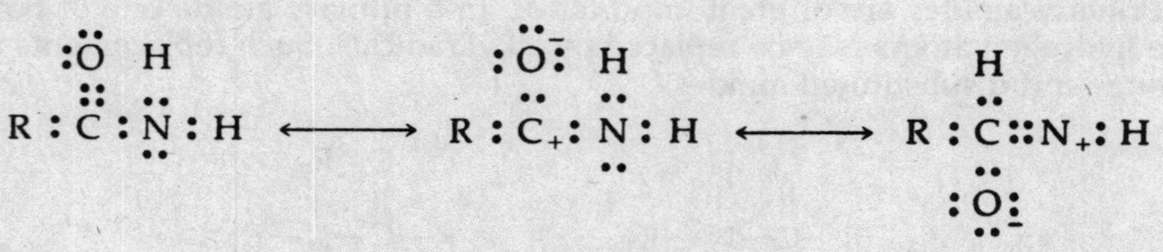

$$R:\overset{\overset{\cdot\cdot}{O}}{\underset{\cdot\cdot}{C}}:\underset{\cdot\cdot}{N}:H \quad H \longleftrightarrow \quad R:\underset{\cdot\cdot}{C_+}:\underset{\cdot\cdot}{N}:H \quad H \longleftrightarrow \quad R:C::N_+:H$$

Many chemical properties of amides can be explained by the three following resonance forms:

Esters

Esters are organic compounds formed by the reaction of an acid and an alcohol.

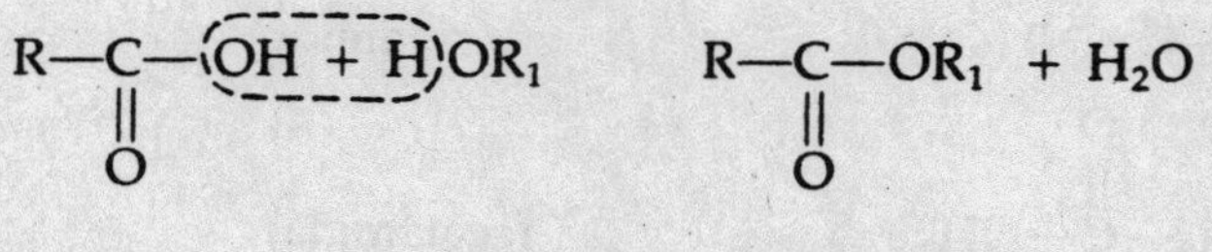

$$R-\overset{}{\underset{\overset{\|}{O}}{C}}-(OH + H)OR_1 \qquad R-\overset{}{\underset{\overset{\|}{O}}{C}}-OR_1 + H_2O$$

Depending on the structure of the acid and the alcohol, a great variety of esters are possible.

Nomenclature of Simple Esters

$$CH_3-\underset{\underset{O}{\|}}{C}-OCH_2CH_3 \qquad \text{(ethyl ethanoate or ethyl acetate)}$$

$$CH_3CH_2-\underset{\underset{O}{\|}}{C}-OCH_3 \qquad \text{(methyl propanoate)}$$

Physical Properties of Esters

Esters have normal boiling points but their solubility in water is less than would be expected from the amount of oxygen present. Volatile esters have low molecular weight, a pleasant odor, and are used to make perfumes, etc.

Chemical Reactions of Esters

The reactions of esters depend mostly on the scission of the linkage between the carbonyl group (C=O) and the alkoxy group (O—R). or between the alkyl group and the oxygen atom.

1. Hydrolysis: $R-\underset{\underset{O}{\|}}{C}-OR_1 + HOH \xrightarrow{H^+} R-\underset{\underset{O}{\|}}{C}-OH + R_1OH$ (OH$^-$ to form salt)

2. Alcoholysis: $R-\underset{\underset{O}{\|}}{C}-OR_1 + HOR_2 \xrightarrow{H^+} R-\underset{\underset{O}{\|}}{C}-OR_2$ (transesterification)

3. Amide Formation: See amides or amines

Fats and Oils

Fats and oils are esters of a higher fatty acid and glycerol.

$$\begin{array}{c} H \\ | \\ H-C-OH \\ | \\ H-C-OH \\ | \\ H-C-OH \\ | \\ H \end{array}$$

Fats are solid or semisolid at room temperature, but oils are liquid. Fats and oils differ in the degree of unsaturation of the acid part of the molecule—the acids of fats are predominantly of the saturated type, whereas those of oils have a higher degree of unsaturation. *Hydrolysis* of fats and oils yields acids and glycerol.

$$H-\overset{\overset{\displaystyle H}{|}}{\underset{\underset{\displaystyle H}{|}}{C}}-O-\overset{\overset{\displaystyle O}{\|}}{C}-R_1$$

$$H-\overset{}{\underset{}{C}}-O-\overset{\overset{\displaystyle O}{\|}}{C}-R_1$$

$$H-\overset{}{\underset{\underset{\displaystyle H}{|}}{C}}-O-\overset{\overset{\displaystyle }{\|}}{\underset{\displaystyle O}{C}}-R_3$$

(ester)   **+ 3H₂O** $\longrightarrow$

$$H-\overset{\overset{\displaystyle H}{|}}{\underset{\underset{\displaystyle H}{|}}{C}}-OH$$

$$H-\overset{}{\underset{}{C}}-OH$$

$$H-\overset{}{\underset{}{C}}-OH$$

(glycerol)   **+**

$$R_1-\overset{\overset{\displaystyle O}{\|}}{C}-OH$$

$$R_2-\overset{}{\underset{\underset{\displaystyle O}{\|}}{C}}-OH$$

$$R_3-\overset{}{\underset{\underset{\displaystyle O}{\|}}{C}}-OH$$

(acids)

Saponification

The saponification number of a fat is the number of mg of KOH required to complete saponification (hydrolysis with salt formation—the salt is a soap). The saponification number of a fat reflects its molecular weight and decreases as the molecular weight increases.

AMINO ACIDS AND PROTEINS

Amino Acids

An amino acid is a compound which contains both an amino group (NH_2) and an acid group (COOH). The position of the amino group can be α, β, γ, etc.

There are at best 21 (all needed) α amino acids that are the main constituents of both plant and animal proteins. In this group of 21 there are about 10 that are essential in human nutrition since the body does not make them. If any of them are lacking, some important biochemical reaction will fail to take place.

An amino acid that has an excess of carboxylic groups will be acidic; an amino acid with excess NH_2 will be basic.

$$\begin{array}{c} COOH \\ | \\ H-C-NH_2 \\ | \\ H-C-OH \\ | \\ H-C-H \\ | \\ COOH \end{array}$$

Acidic
(hydroxyglutamic acid)

$$\begin{array}{c} COOH \\ | \\ CH_2 \\ | \\ NH_2 \end{array}$$

Neutral
(glycine)

$$\begin{array}{c} COOH \\ | \\ H-C-NH_2 \\ | \\ (CH_2)_4 \\ | \\ NH_2 \end{array}$$

Basic
(lysine)

Proteins

Proteins are complex substances produced by, or associated with, living matter. Proteins contain the elements C, H, O, N, usually S, and sometimes P. An average composition of protein is, by weight:

C = 51%	N = 16%	S = 1%
O = 24%	H = 7%	P = 0.4%

The end products of protein hydrolysis are the amino acids. Proteins are formed when two molecules of amino acids link together with an "amide bond" to form a peptide.

$$H-N-CH_2-COOH$$

$$\longrightarrow NH_2-CH_2CO-NH-CH_2-CO-NH-CH_2COOH + 2H_2O$$

The structure of proteins may be studied on several levels.

1°. The way in which the atoms of protein molecules are joined to one another by covalent bonds to form chains.

2°. The spatial arrangement of chains to form coils, sheets, or compact spheroids, with hydrogen bonds holding together different chains or different parts of the same chain.

3°. The weaving together of coiled chains to form ropes, or the clumping together of individual molecules to form aggregates.

The irreversible precipitation of proteins caused by heat is called *denaturation*. Denaturation uncoils the protein, destroys its characteristic shape, and with it its characteristic biological activity. The extreme ease with which proteins are denatured increases the difficulty of their study.

Hydrolysis of Proteins

Hydrolysis is the breakdown of proteins (which are highly complex compounds) into compounds of lower molecular weight. Alpha (α) amino acids are one of the major products of protein hydrolysis.

Dipolar Ions

The amino acids contain two reactive groups, amino and carboxyl, each of which so modifies the character of the other that these substances cannot be considered merely as amines and acids. The acidic character is neutralized by the basicity of the amino group and the molecule exists mostly as an internal salt. The carboxyl group has the ability to lose a proton which the amino group may accept.

The dipole ion is called a *zwitterion*. The zwitterion is amphoteric, so it may gain or lose a proton.

In Acid: $NH_3{}^+CH_2COO^- + H_3O^+ \rightleftharpoons [NH_3CH_2COOH]^+ + H_2O$

In Base: $NH_3{}^+CH_2COO^- + OH^- \rightleftharpoons [NH_2CH_2COO]^- + H_2O$

An amino acid will thus form either a cation or an anion depending on the pH of the solution. The pH at which an amino acid has an equal tendency to form a positive or negative ion is called its *isoelectric point*.

The pH at isoelectric point of some amino acids is listed below:

glycine	6.0
tyrosine	5.7
aspartic acid	2.8
arginine	10.9

Electrophoresis

This is a method of separating protein fractions by taking advantage of the different rates of diffusion under an electromotive force. Different proteins have different proportions of acidic and basic side chains and different isoelectric points. In a particular pH solution, some molecules move toward a cathode and others toward an anode. Depending upon their size, shape, and charge, different proteins move at different rates.

Those with fewer acid chains than base chains → positive
more acid chains than base chains → negative
equal acid chains and base chains → (will not move)

Common Amino Acids Found in Proteins

NAME | STRUCTURE

glycine

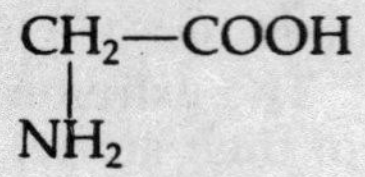

$$CH_2-COOH$$
$$|$$
$$NH_2$$

alanine

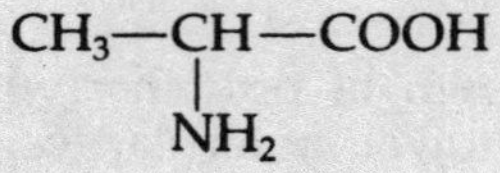

$$CH_3-CH-COOH$$
$$|$$
$$NH_2$$

phenylalanine

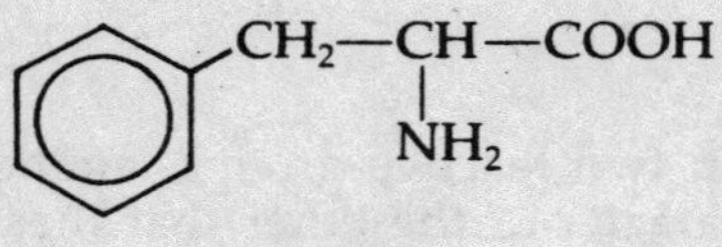

$$CH_2-CH-COOH$$
$$|$$
$$NH_2$$

valine

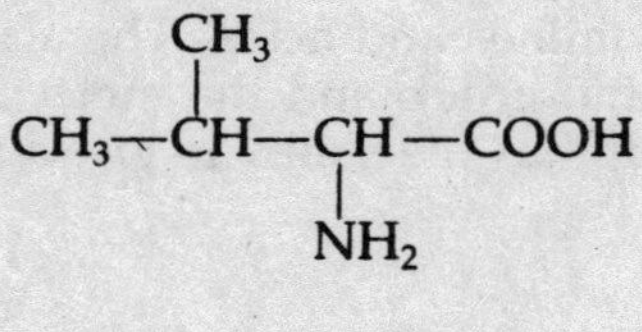

$$CH_3$$
$$|$$
$$CH_3-CH-CH-COOH$$
$$|$$
$$NH_2$$

leucine

$$CH_3$$
$$|$$
$$CH_3-CH-CH_2-CH-COOH$$
$$|$$
$$NH_2$$

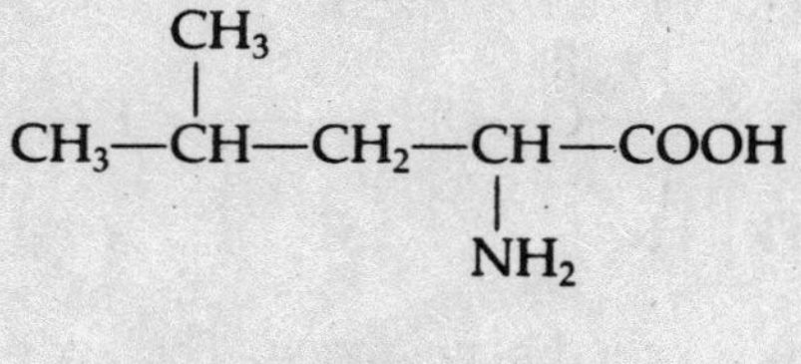

isoleucine

$$CH_3$$
$$|$$
$$CH_3-CH_2-CH-CH-COOH$$
$$|$$
$$NH_2$$

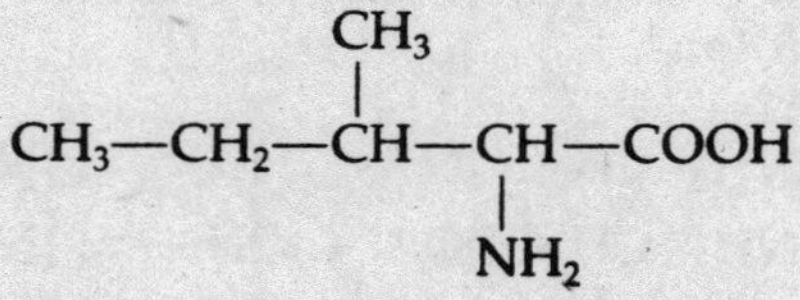

tyrosine

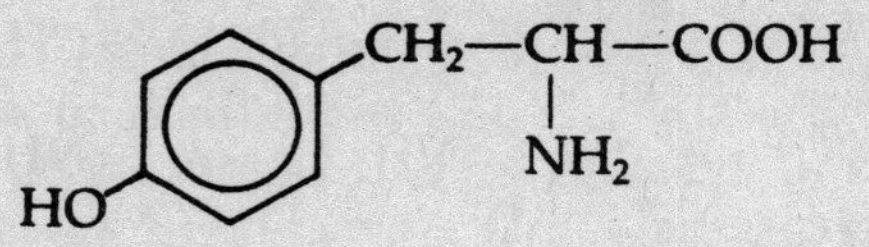

tryptophan

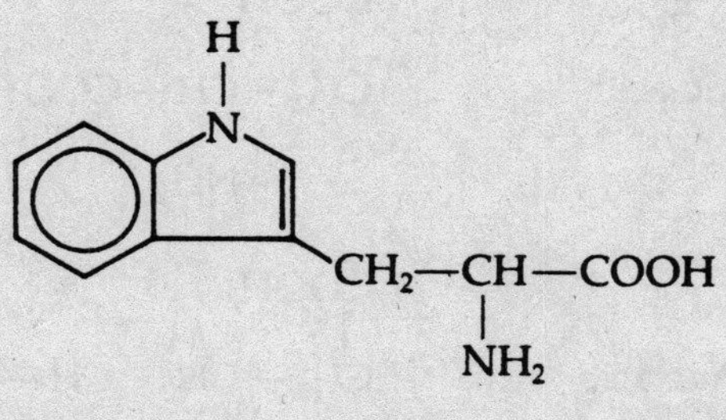

serine

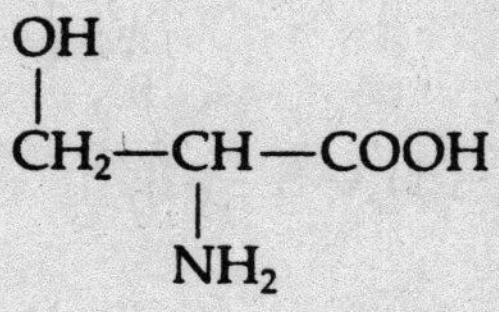

threonine

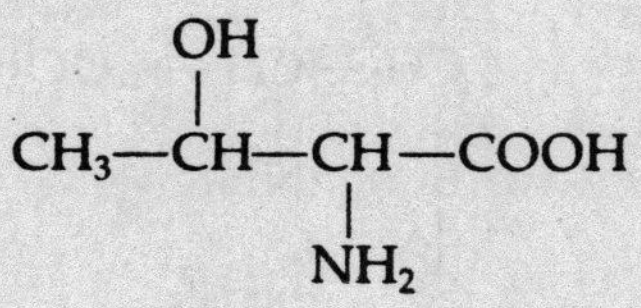

arginine

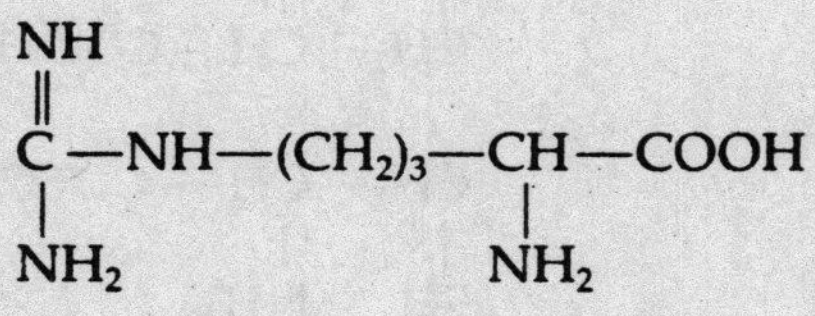

proline

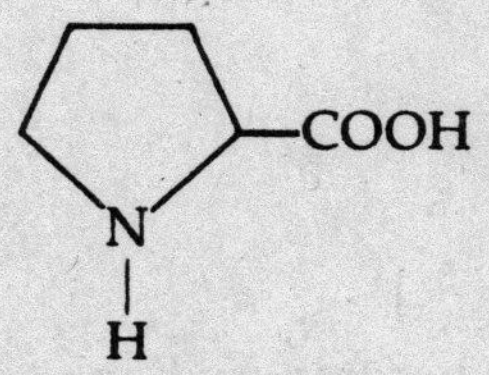

hydroxyproline

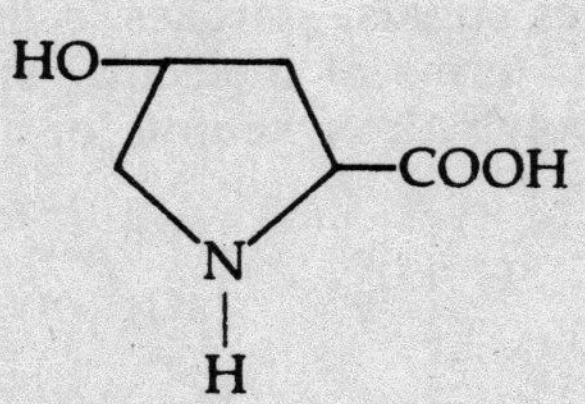

histidine

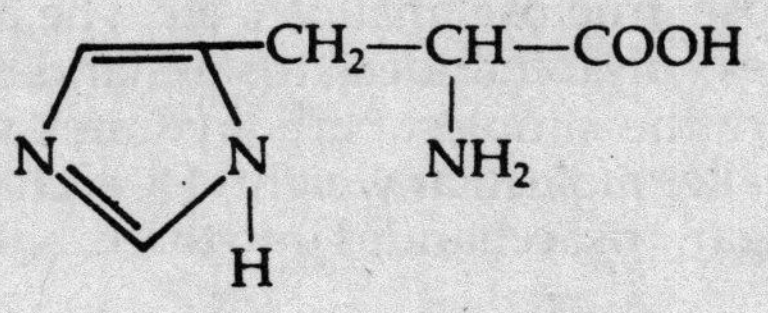

lysine

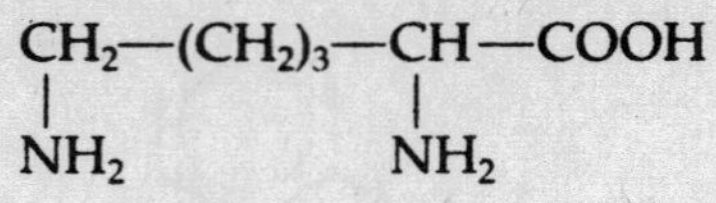

$$CH_2-(CH_2)_3-CH-COOH$$
$$\quad\quad\quad\quad\quad NH_2 \quad\quad\quad NH_2$$

aspartic acid

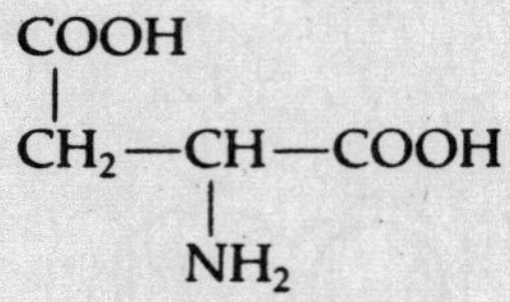

$$COOH$$
$$CH_2-CH-COOH$$
$$\quad\quad\quad NH_2$$

glutamic acid

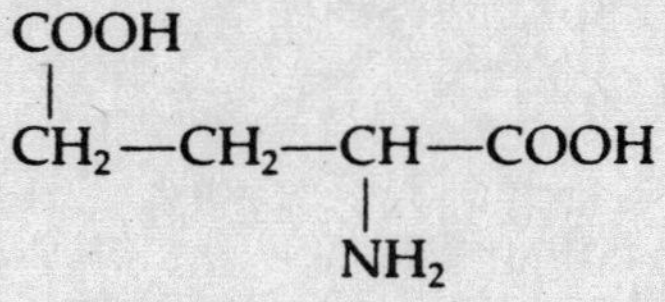

$$COOH$$
$$CH_2-CH_2-CH-COOH$$
$$\quad\quad\quad\quad\quad\quad NH_2$$

methionine

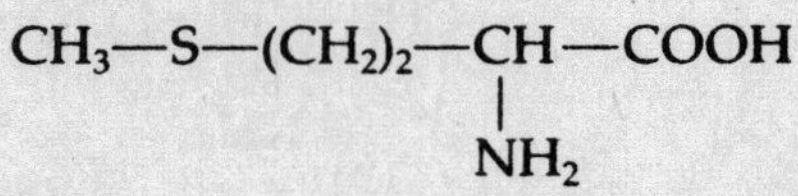

$$CH_3-S-(CH_2)_2-CH-COOH$$
$$\quad\quad\quad\quad\quad\quad\quad\quad NH_2$$

cystine

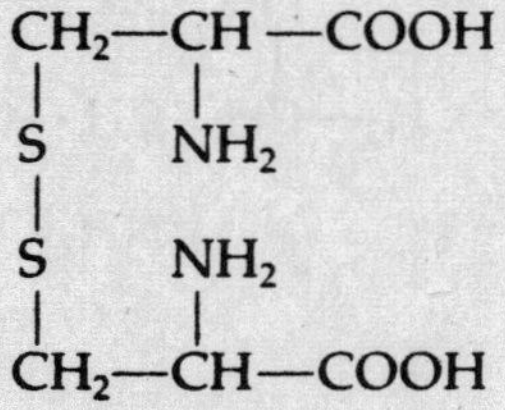

$$CH_2-CH-COOH$$
$$\quad S \quad\quad NH_2$$
$$\quad S \quad\quad NH_2$$
$$CH_2-CH-COOH$$

cysteine

$$CH_2-CH-COOH$$
$$\quad SH \quad\quad NH_2$$

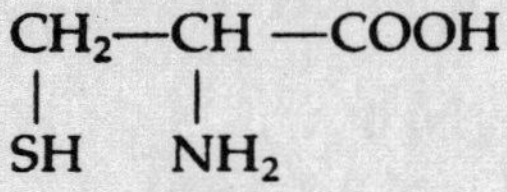

CARBOHYDRATES

General Description

Carbohydrates are compounds composed only of C, H, and O and have the general formula $C_nH_{2n}O_n$ (although not all carbohydrates adhere strictly to this formula). The class includes sugars, starches, celluloses, and other substances closely related to them. In terms of molecular structure, a carbohydrate is a polyhydroxyaldehyde, a polyhydroxyketone, or a compound which will yield them on hydrolysis.

Nomenclature

The names of carbohydrates are characterized by the ending -*ose;* we have sugars such as glucose, fructose, maltose, etc. The main groups of carbohydrates are monosaccharides, disaccharides, trisaccharides, and polysaccharides. The monosaccharides are the simplest carbohydrates which cannot be hydrolyzed into anything of smaller molecular weight. Disaccharides can be hydrolyzed into two molecules of sugar, trisaccharides into three, and polysaccharides into many.

MONOSACCHARIDES
  Pentoses ($C_5H_{10}O_5$)
    aldo:
      arabinose
      xylose
      lyxose
      ribose
    keto:
      none of any importance
  Hexoses ($c_6H_{12}O_6$)
    aldo:
      glucose
      gulose
      mannose
      galactose
      talose
      allose
      altrose
      idose
    keto:
      fructose
      sorbose

DISACCHARIDES ($C_{12}H_{22}O_{11}$)
  sucrose
  lactose
  maltose
  cellobiose

TRISACCHARIDE ($C_{18}H_{32}O_{16}$)
  raffinose

POLYSACCHARIDES
  Pentosans ($C_5H_8O_4)_n$
    araban
    xylan
  Hexosans ($C_6H_{10}O_5)_n$
    starch
    glycogen
    inulin
    cellulose
  Derived carbohydrates
    hemicelluloses
    gums
    mucilages
    pectic substances

Cyclic Structure and Conformation of Hexoses

The straight-chain structural formula for the hexoses does not adequately show the space relationships within the molecule, particularly on the last two carbons.

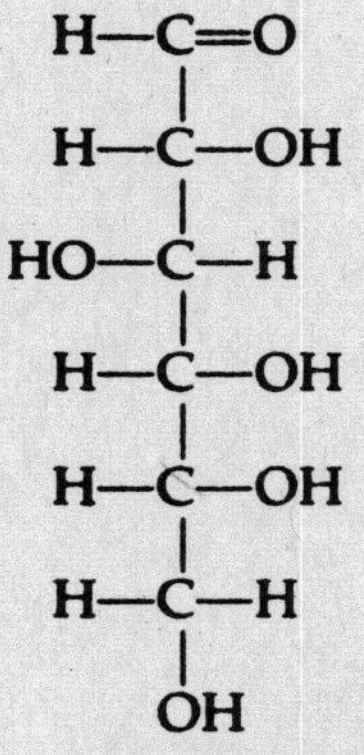

(straight chain)

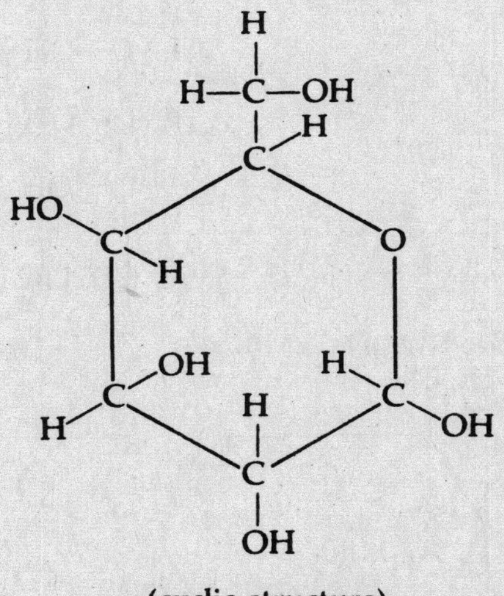

(cyclic structure)

The aldohexoses have 4 asymmetric carbon rings and there are 16 stereoisomers. The tautomeric forms of a hexose (as shown above) "explain" why glucose, for instance, does not form an addition product with sodium bisulfite or redden Schiff's reagent.

Epimers and Anomers

Two aldoses which are identical except for the configuration at the asymmetric carbon alpha to the aldehyde group are *epimers*.

$$
\begin{array}{ccc}
\begin{array}{c}
\text{CHO} \\
| \\
\text{H}-\text{C}-\text{OH} \\
| \\
\text{HO}-\text{C}-\text{H} \\
| \\
\text{H}-\text{C}-\text{OH} \\
| \\
\text{H}-\text{C}-\text{OH} \\
| \\
\text{H}-\text{C}-\text{OH} \\
| \\
\text{H}
\end{array}
& \longrightarrow
\begin{array}{c}
\text{H}-\text{C}=\text{NNHC}_6\text{H}_5 \\
| \\
\text{C}=\text{NNHC}_6\text{H}_5 \\
| \\
\text{HO}-\text{C}-\text{H} \\
| \\
\text{H}-\text{C}-\text{OH} \\
| \\
\text{H}-\text{C}-\text{OH} \\
| \\
\text{H}-\text{C}-\text{OH} \\
| \\
\text{H}
\end{array}
\longleftarrow &
\begin{array}{c}
\text{CHO} \\
| \\
\text{HO}-\text{C}-\text{H} \\
| \\
\text{HO}-\text{C}-\text{H} \\
| \\
\text{H}-\text{C}-\text{OH} \\
| \\
\text{H}-\text{C}-\text{OH} \\
| \\
\text{H}-\text{C}-\text{OH} \\
| \\
\text{H}
\end{array}
\end{array}
$$

(epimers give the
same osazone)

Epimers differ only in configuration about C-2. One way in which a pair of aldoses can be identified as epimers is if they form the same osazone.

A pair of diastereomers differing in configuration about C-1 are called *anomers*. The anomers are called α and β. α isomers have the hydroxyl group on the right for the d-family and on the left for the l-family.

$$
\begin{array}{c}
\text{CHO} \\
| \\
\text{H}-\text{C}-\text{OH} \\
| \\
\text{HO}-\text{C}-\text{H} \\
| \\
\text{H}-\text{C}-\text{OH} \\
| \\
\text{H}-\text{C}-\text{OH} \\
| \\
\text{CH}_2\text{OH}
\end{array}
$$

open structure
of D-(+)-glucose

TWO CYCLIC HEMIACETAL FORMS

α-Anomer
β-anomer

(α-D-(+)-glucopyranose)   (β-form)

Glycoside Linkage: Hydrolysis

Aldehydes react with alcohols in the presence of acids to form acetals; hemiacetals are intermediate in the reaction. In sugars, the aldehyde group of the sugar first reacts with the alcohol group of the fifth carbon atom to form a 6-

member ring. The hemiacetal then reacts with methyl alcohol or the alcohol of another ring to form the acetal. These acetals are called glycosides and can be acid hydrolyzed or base hydrolyzed back to their original form.

(methyl α-D-glycoside)

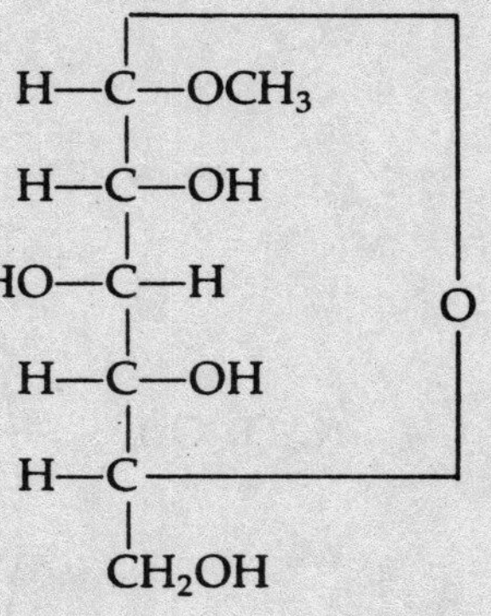

$$
\begin{array}{l}
H-C-OCH_3 \\
H-C-OH \\
HO-C-H \\
H-C-OH \\
H-C \\
\quad CH_2OH
\end{array}
$$

Common Carbohydrates

NAME	FORMULA	STRUCTURE
glucose	$C_6H_{12}O_6$	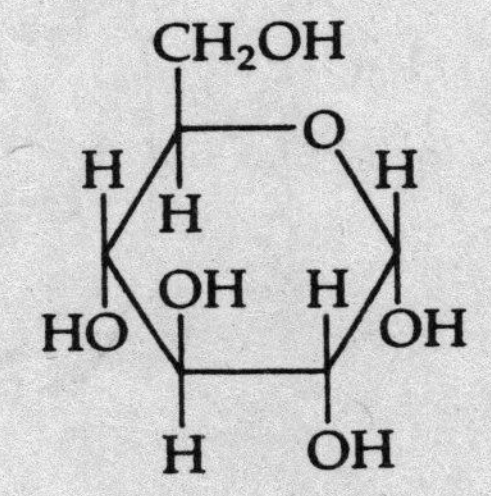
fructose	$C_6H_{12}O_6$	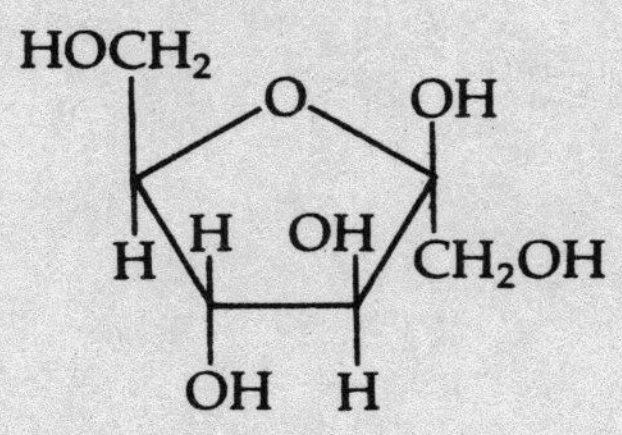
sucrose	$C_{12}H_{22}O_{11}$	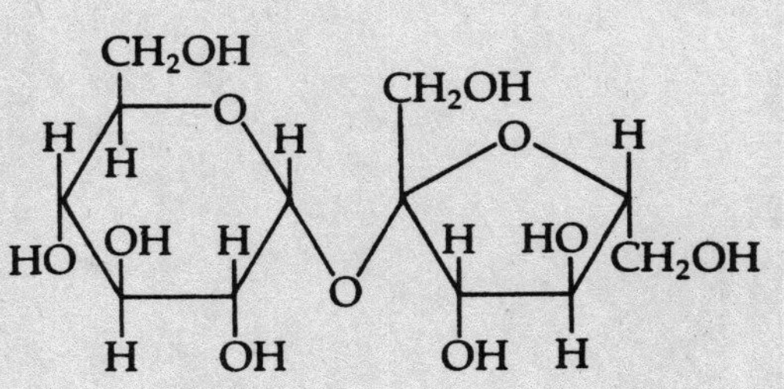
lactose	$C_{12}H_{22}O_{11}$	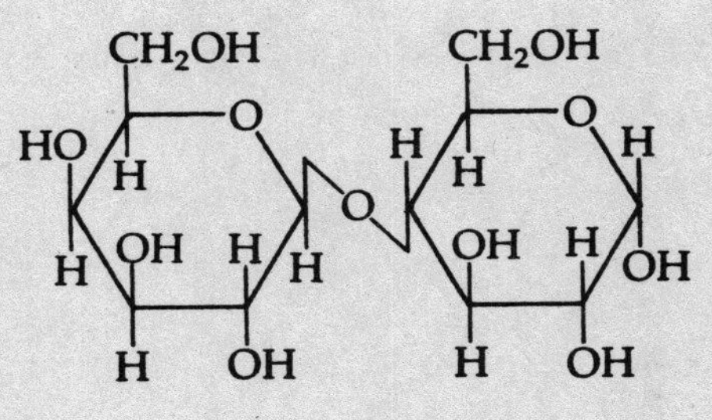

maltose $C_{12}H_{22}O_{11}$

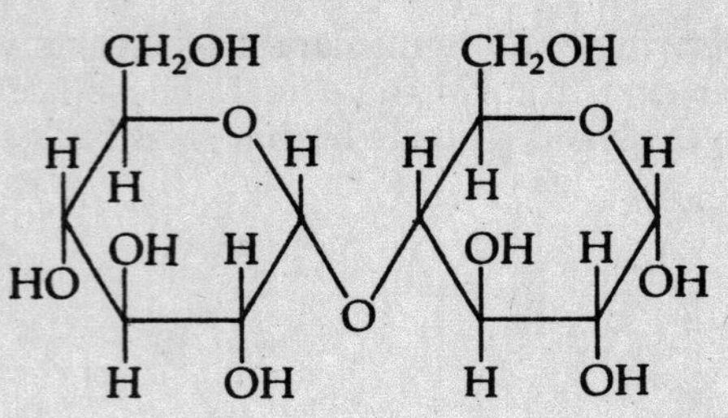

starch $(C_6H_{10}O_5)_n$

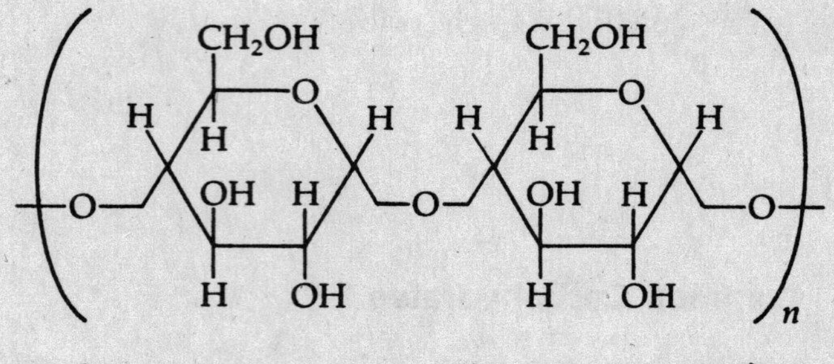

cellulose $(C_6H_{10}O_5)_n$

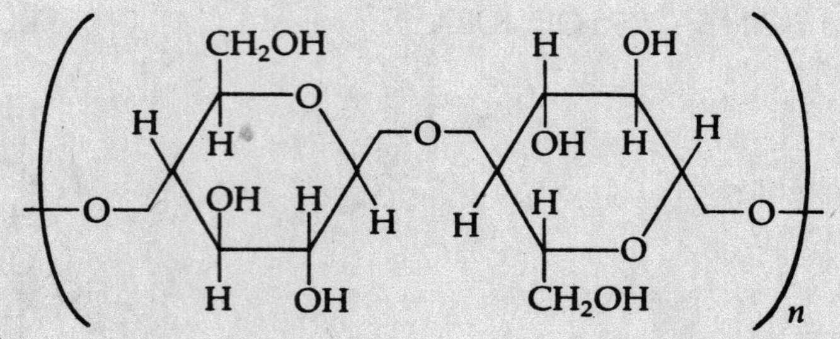

Organic Chemistry Review Practice Test

ANSWER SHEET

1 Ⓐ Ⓑ Ⓒ Ⓓ Ⓔ	17 Ⓐ Ⓑ Ⓒ Ⓓ Ⓔ	33 Ⓐ Ⓑ Ⓒ Ⓓ Ⓔ	49 Ⓐ Ⓑ Ⓒ Ⓓ Ⓔ	65 Ⓐ Ⓑ Ⓒ Ⓓ Ⓔ
2 Ⓐ Ⓑ Ⓒ Ⓓ Ⓔ	18 Ⓐ Ⓑ Ⓒ Ⓓ Ⓔ	34 Ⓐ Ⓑ Ⓒ Ⓓ Ⓔ	50 Ⓐ Ⓑ Ⓒ Ⓓ Ⓔ	66 Ⓐ Ⓑ Ⓒ Ⓓ Ⓔ
3 Ⓐ Ⓑ Ⓒ Ⓓ Ⓔ	19 Ⓐ Ⓑ Ⓒ Ⓓ Ⓔ	35 Ⓐ Ⓑ Ⓒ Ⓓ Ⓔ	51 Ⓐ Ⓑ Ⓒ Ⓓ Ⓔ	67 Ⓐ Ⓑ Ⓒ Ⓓ Ⓔ
4 Ⓐ Ⓑ Ⓒ Ⓓ Ⓔ	20 Ⓐ Ⓑ Ⓒ Ⓓ Ⓔ	36 Ⓐ Ⓑ Ⓒ Ⓓ Ⓔ	52 Ⓐ Ⓑ Ⓒ Ⓓ Ⓔ	68 Ⓐ Ⓑ Ⓒ Ⓓ Ⓔ
5 Ⓐ Ⓑ Ⓒ Ⓓ Ⓔ	21 Ⓐ Ⓑ Ⓒ Ⓓ Ⓔ	37 Ⓐ Ⓑ Ⓒ Ⓓ Ⓔ	53 Ⓐ Ⓑ Ⓒ Ⓓ Ⓔ	69 Ⓐ Ⓑ Ⓒ Ⓓ Ⓔ
6 Ⓐ Ⓑ Ⓒ Ⓓ Ⓔ	22 Ⓐ Ⓑ Ⓒ Ⓓ Ⓔ	38 Ⓐ Ⓑ Ⓒ Ⓓ Ⓔ	54 Ⓐ Ⓑ Ⓒ Ⓓ Ⓔ	70 Ⓐ Ⓑ Ⓒ Ⓓ Ⓔ
7 Ⓐ Ⓑ Ⓒ Ⓓ Ⓔ	23 Ⓐ Ⓑ Ⓒ Ⓓ Ⓔ	39 Ⓐ Ⓑ Ⓒ Ⓓ Ⓔ	55 Ⓐ Ⓑ Ⓒ Ⓓ Ⓔ	71 Ⓐ Ⓑ Ⓒ Ⓓ Ⓔ
8 Ⓐ Ⓑ Ⓒ Ⓓ Ⓔ	24 Ⓐ Ⓑ Ⓒ Ⓓ Ⓔ	40 Ⓐ Ⓑ Ⓒ Ⓓ Ⓔ	56 Ⓐ Ⓑ Ⓒ Ⓓ Ⓔ	72 Ⓐ Ⓑ Ⓒ Ⓓ Ⓔ
9 Ⓐ Ⓑ Ⓒ Ⓓ Ⓔ	25 Ⓐ Ⓑ Ⓒ Ⓓ Ⓔ	41 Ⓐ Ⓑ Ⓒ Ⓓ Ⓔ	57 Ⓐ Ⓑ Ⓒ Ⓓ Ⓔ	73 Ⓐ Ⓑ Ⓒ Ⓓ Ⓔ
10 Ⓐ Ⓑ Ⓒ Ⓓ Ⓔ	26 Ⓐ Ⓑ Ⓒ Ⓓ Ⓔ	42 Ⓐ Ⓑ Ⓒ Ⓓ Ⓔ	58 Ⓐ Ⓑ Ⓒ Ⓓ Ⓔ	74 Ⓐ Ⓑ Ⓒ Ⓓ Ⓔ
11 Ⓐ Ⓑ Ⓒ Ⓓ Ⓔ	27 Ⓐ Ⓑ Ⓒ Ⓓ Ⓔ	43 Ⓐ Ⓑ Ⓒ Ⓓ Ⓔ	59 Ⓐ Ⓑ Ⓒ Ⓓ Ⓔ	75 Ⓐ Ⓑ Ⓒ Ⓓ Ⓔ
12 Ⓐ Ⓑ Ⓒ Ⓓ Ⓔ	28 Ⓐ Ⓑ Ⓒ Ⓓ Ⓔ	44 Ⓐ Ⓑ Ⓒ Ⓓ Ⓔ	60 Ⓐ Ⓑ Ⓒ Ⓓ Ⓔ	76 Ⓐ Ⓑ Ⓒ Ⓓ Ⓔ
13 Ⓐ Ⓑ Ⓒ Ⓓ Ⓔ	29 Ⓐ Ⓑ Ⓒ Ⓓ Ⓔ	45 Ⓐ Ⓑ Ⓒ Ⓓ Ⓔ	61 Ⓐ Ⓑ Ⓒ Ⓓ Ⓔ	77 Ⓐ Ⓑ Ⓒ Ⓓ Ⓔ
14 Ⓐ Ⓑ Ⓒ Ⓓ Ⓔ	30 Ⓐ Ⓑ Ⓒ Ⓓ Ⓔ	46 Ⓐ Ⓑ Ⓒ Ⓓ Ⓔ	62 Ⓐ Ⓑ Ⓒ Ⓓ Ⓔ	78 Ⓐ Ⓑ Ⓒ Ⓓ Ⓔ
15 Ⓐ Ⓑ Ⓒ Ⓓ Ⓔ	31 Ⓐ Ⓑ Ⓒ Ⓓ Ⓔ	47 Ⓐ Ⓑ Ⓒ Ⓓ Ⓔ	63 Ⓐ Ⓑ Ⓒ Ⓓ Ⓔ	79 Ⓐ Ⓑ Ⓒ Ⓓ Ⓔ
16 Ⓐ Ⓑ Ⓒ Ⓓ Ⓔ	32 Ⓐ Ⓑ Ⓒ Ⓓ Ⓔ	48 Ⓐ Ⓑ Ⓒ Ⓓ Ⓔ	64 Ⓐ Ⓑ Ⓒ Ⓓ Ⓔ	80 Ⓐ Ⓑ Ⓒ Ⓓ Ⓔ

ORGANIC CHEMISTRY PRACTICE TEST

1.
$$H-\overset{\overset{\displaystyle H}{|}}{\underset{\underset{\displaystyle H}{|}}{C}}-\overset{\overset{\displaystyle H}{|}}{\underset{\underset{\displaystyle H}{|}}{C}}-\overset{\overset{\displaystyle H}{|}}{\underset{\underset{\displaystyle H}{|}}{C}}-\overset{\overset{\displaystyle H}{|}}{\underset{\underset{\displaystyle H}{|}}{C}}-H$$

How many different alkanes are there with the formula C_4H_{10}; that is, how many structural isomers exist for the formula C_4H_{10} (including the one above)?

A) 1 B) 2 C) 3 D) 4

2. Which of the following is the formula for 1,2-dichlorotetrafluorethane (Freon-114)?

A) $Cl-\overset{\overset{\displaystyle H}{|}}{\underset{\underset{\displaystyle F}{|}}{C}}-\overset{\overset{\displaystyle F}{|}}{\underset{\underset{\displaystyle Cl}{|}}{C}}-\overset{\overset{\displaystyle H}{|}}{\underset{\underset{\displaystyle H}{|}}{C}}-F$ C) $Cl-\overset{\overset{\displaystyle F}{|}}{\underset{\underset{\displaystyle F}{|}}{C}}-\overset{\overset{\displaystyle H}{|}}{\underset{\underset{\displaystyle H}{|}}{C}}-H$

B) $F-\overset{\overset{\displaystyle F}{|}}{\underset{\underset{\displaystyle H}{|}}{C}}-\overset{\overset{\displaystyle H}{|}}{\underset{\underset{\displaystyle H}{|}}{C}}-H$ D) $Cl-\overset{\overset{\displaystyle F}{|}}{\underset{\underset{\displaystyle F}{|}}{C}}-\overset{\overset{\displaystyle F}{|}}{\underset{\underset{\displaystyle F}{|}}{C}}-Cl$

3. The structural formula for 2,2,3-trimethylhexane is

A) $CH_3-\overset{\overset{\displaystyle CH_3}{|}}{\underset{\underset{\displaystyle CH_3}{|}}{C}}-\overset{\overset{\displaystyle CH_3}{|}}{CH}-CH_2-CH_3$ C) $CH_3-\overset{\overset{\displaystyle CH_3}{|}}{\underset{\underset{\displaystyle CH_3}{|}}{C}}-\overset{\overset{\displaystyle CH_3}{|}}{CH}-CH_2-CH_2-CH_3$

B) $CH_3-\overset{\overset{\displaystyle CH_3}{|}}{\underset{\underset{\displaystyle CH_3}{|}}{C}}-CH_2-\overset{\overset{\displaystyle CH_3}{|}}{CH}-CH_3$ D) $CH_3-\overset{\overset{\displaystyle CH_3}{|}}{CH}-CH_2-\overset{\overset{\displaystyle CH_3}{|}}{\underset{\underset{\displaystyle CH_3}{|}}{C}}-CH_3$

4. How many structural isomers are possible for the formula $C_2H_4Cl_2$?

A) 1 B) 2 C) 3 D) 4 E) 6

5. The compound below is used to combat rats by making male rats sterile after one dose. Name it.

$$Cl-CH_2-CH_2-\overset{\overset{\displaystyle OH}{|}}{CH_2}-OH$$

A) 1,2-dihydroxy-3-chloropropane
B) 1-chloro-2,3-dihydroxypropane
C) 2-hydroxypropane
D) 1-chloropropanediol
E) 3-chloro-1,2-propanediol

6. How many structural isomers exist for the formula C_6H_{14}?

A) 3 B) 4 C) 5 D) 6 E) 8

7. The name of the compound below is

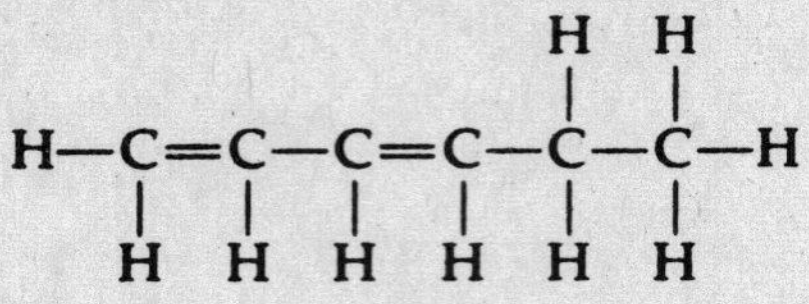

$$H-C=C-C=C-C-C-H$$

(with H atoms shown above and below the carbon chain)

A) hexadiene
B) 1,2,3,4-hexadiene
C) 3,5-hexadiene
D) 1,3-hexadiene
E) 3,4-hexadiene

8. How many geometrical isomers are possible for the compound shown below? (The rotation about the double bond is restricted.)

$$CH_3—CH=CH—CH_3$$

A) 1   B) 2   C) 3   D) 4   E) 6

9. Menthol (2-isopropyl-5-methylcyclohexanol) is used in a variety of commercial products. Which of the following is the structural formula for menthol?

A)

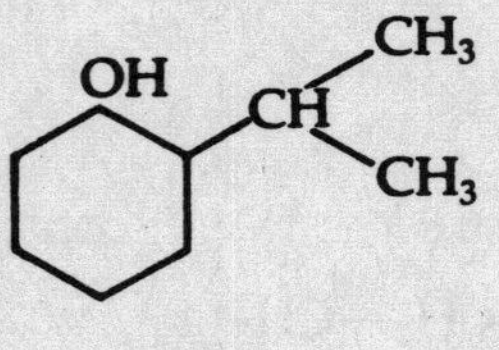

B)

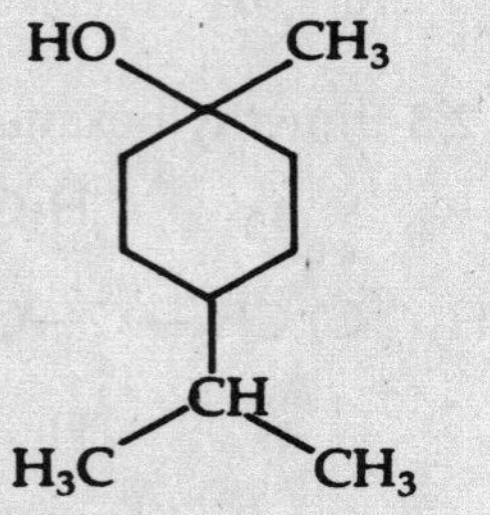

C)

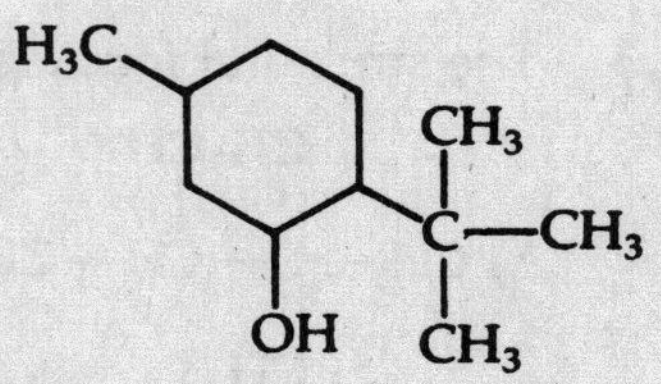

D)

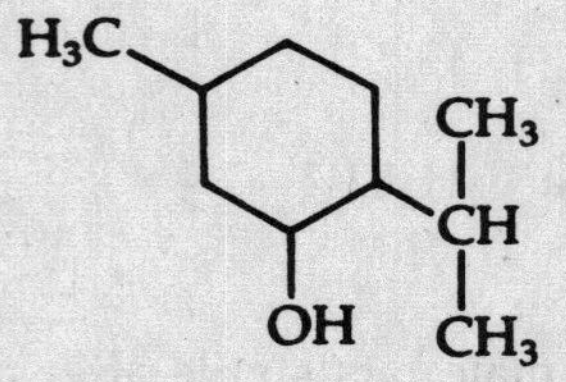

E)

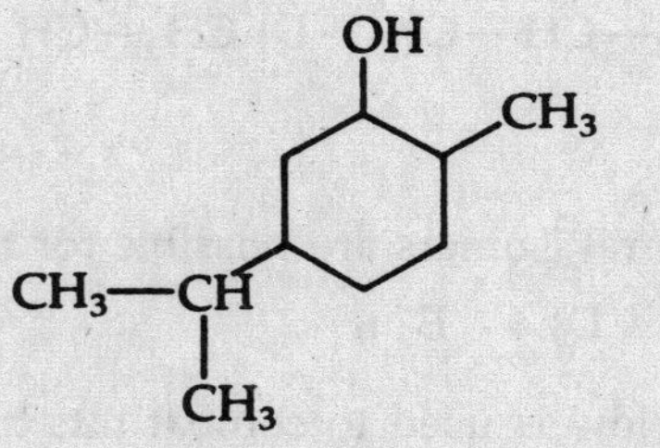

10. If an ester such as methyl acetate, CH_3COOCH_3, is heated in the presence of an acid catalyst, it is hydrolyzed readily to methyl alcohol, CH_3OH, and acetic acid, CH_3COOH. Which reaction is missing from the mechanism shown below for this hydrolysis?

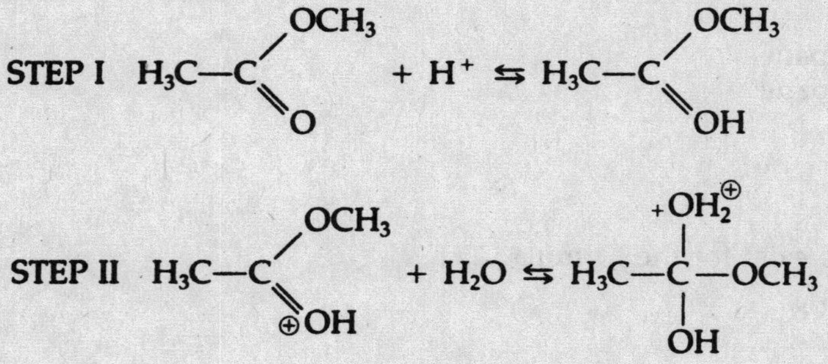

STEP I $H_3C—C(OCH_3)(O)$ $+ H^+ \leftrightarrows H_3C—C(OCH_3)(OH)$

STEP II $H_3C—C(OCH_3)(\oplus OH)$ $+ H_2O \leftrightarrows H_3C—C(OCH_3)(OH)(^+OH_2^{\oplus})$

STEP III $\quad$ H$_3$C—C(—OCH$_3$)(—$\overset{\oplus}{O}$H$_2$)(—OH) $\rightleftarrows$ H$_3$C—C(—OH)(—OH)—$\overset{\oplus}{O}$(—H)(—CH$_3$)

STEP IV $\quad$ H$_3$C—C(—$\overset{\oplus}{O}$H)(—OH) $\rightleftarrows$ H$_3$C—C(=O)(—OH) + H$^{\oplus}$

A) CH$_3$OH + H$_3$C—C(—$\overset{\oplus}{O}$H)(—OH) $\rightleftarrows$ H$_3$C—C(—OH)(—H)—$\overset{\oplus}{O}$(—H)(—CH$_3$)

B) H$_3$C—C(—OH)(—OH)—O(—H)(—CH$_3$) $\rightleftarrows$ H$_3$C—C(—OH)(=O) + CH$_3$OH

C) H$_3$C—C(—OH)(—OH)—$\overset{\oplus}{O}$(—H)(—CH$_3$) $\rightleftarrows$ H$_3$C—C(—OH)—OH + CH$_3\overset{\oplus}{O}$H

D) H$_3$C—C(—OH)—$\overset{\oplus}{O}$(—H)(—CH$_3$) $\rightleftarrows$ H$_3$C—C(=$\overset{\oplus}{O}$H)(—OH) + CH$_3$OH

E) none of the above

11. Examine the following statements about amino acids.

$$\text{H—C}(\text{—COO}^-)(\text{—NH}_3^+)(\text{—R})$$

1. Amino acids are generally water soluble.
2. Amino acids are generally soluble in organic solvents.
3. Amino acids are low-melting solids.

Which of the above is (are) correct?
A) 1 and 3 $\quad$ B) 1 only $\quad$ C) 2 and 3 $\quad$ D) 2 only

12. The compound dopa has recently been used successfully in treating cases of Parkinson's disease. If you knew that dopa was an amino acid, which of the compounds on the following page might possibly be dopa?

1. HO—⟨benzene ring⟩—CH₂—CH—COOH
    with NH₂ below the CH

$$\text{1.} \quad HO-\!\!\bigcirc\!\!-CH_2-\underset{\underset{NH_2}{|}}{CH}-COOH$$

$$\text{2.} \quad HO-\!\!\underset{\underset{HO}{}}{\bigcirc}\!\!-CH_2-\underset{\underset{NH_2}{|}}{CH}-COOH$$

$$\text{3.} \quad H-\!\!\underset{\underset{HO}{}}{\bigcirc}\!\!-CH_2-CH_2-NH_2$$

$$\text{4.} \quad HO-\!\!\underset{\underset{HO}{}}{\bigcirc}\!\!-\underset{\overset{OH}{|}}{CH}-CH_2-NH_2$$

A) 1 and 2   B) 3 and 4   C) 2, 3, and 4   D) 1   E) 4

13. Consider that 1 mole of an unknown polypeptide was hydrolyzed so it degraded to the corresponding amino acids. An amino acid analyzer showed that 2 moles of valine and 2 moles of cisteine were formed. Which of the following polypeptides fits the analysis?

A) ⁺H₃N CHC—NCHC—NCHC—NCHC—NCHCO₂⁻
   with side chains:
   CH₂ (HS), CH (H₃C CH₃), CH₂ (SH), CH₃, CH (H₃C CH₃)

$$\text{A)}\ ^{+}H_3N\,CH\underset{\underset{HS}{\underset{|}{CH_2}}}{\overset{\overset{O}{\|}}{C}}\!-\!N\underset{\underset{H_3C\ CH_3}{\overset{|}{CH}}}{\overset{\overset{H}{|}}{C}}H\overset{\overset{O}{\|}}{C}\!-\!NCH\underset{\underset{SH}{\overset{|}{CH_2}}}{\overset{\overset{O}{\|}}{C}}\!-\!N\underset{\underset{}{CH_3}}{C}H\overset{\overset{O}{\|}}{C}\!-\!NCH\underset{\underset{H_3C\ CH_3}{\overset{|}{CH}}}{CO_2^-}$$

$$\text{B)}\ ^{+}H_3NCH\underset{\underset{SH}{\overset{|}{CH_2}}}{\overset{\overset{O}{\|}}{C}}\!-\!NCH\underset{CH_3}{\overset{\overset{O}{\|}}{C}}\!-\!NCH\underset{\underset{H_3C\ CH_3}{\overset{|}{CH}}}{\overset{\overset{O}{\|}}{C}}\!-\!NCH\underset{CH_3}{\overset{\overset{O}{\|}}{C}}\!-\!NCH\underset{\underset{SH}{\overset{|}{CH_2}}}{CO_2^-}$$

$$\text{C)}\ ^{+}H_3NCH\underset{CH_3}{\overset{\overset{O}{\|}}{C}}\!-\!NCH\underset{\underset{H_3C\ CH_3}{\overset{|}{CH}}}{\overset{\overset{O}{\|}}{C}}\!-\!NCH\underset{H}{\overset{\overset{O}{\|}}{C}}\!-\!NCH\underset{\underset{SH}{\overset{|}{CH_2}}}{CO_2^-}$$

D) 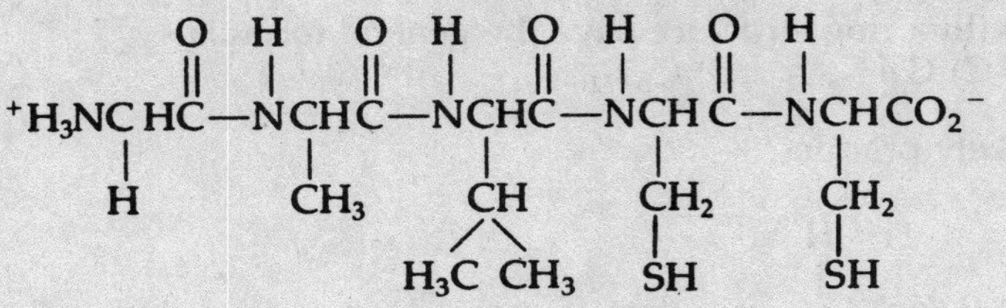 ^+H_3NC HC—NCHC—NCHC—NCHC—NCHCO$_2^-$

(with O H groups and side chains: H, CH$_3$, CH (H$_3$C CH$_3$), CH$_2$ SH, CH$_2$ SH)

14. The starting material in the preparation of one important type of silicone rubber is dimethyldichlorosilane $(CH_3)_2SiCl_2$. Which one of the following structures is the Lewis structure for dimethyldichlorosilane?

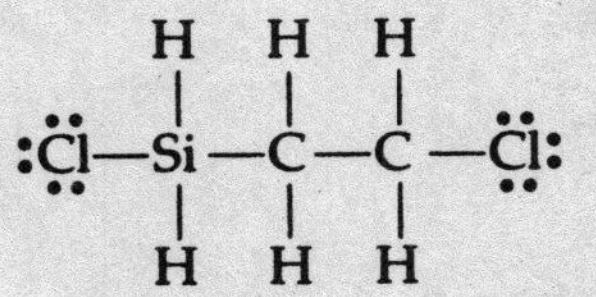

A) 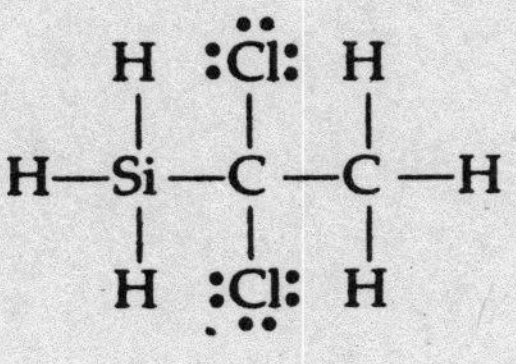 H—Si—C—C—H (with H, :Cl:, H substituents)

B) :Cl—Si—C—C—Cl: (with H substituents)

C) :Cl—C—Si—C—Cl: (with H substituents)

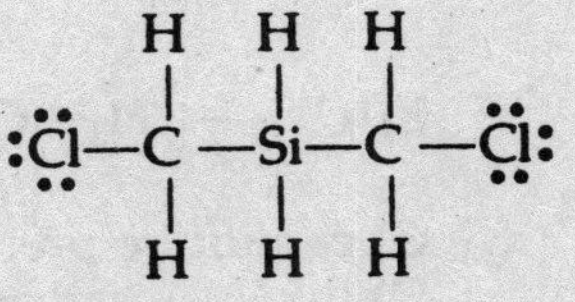

D) 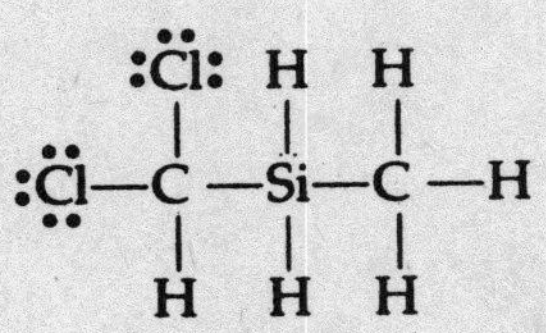 :Cl—C—Si—C—H (with :Cl:, H substituents)

E) 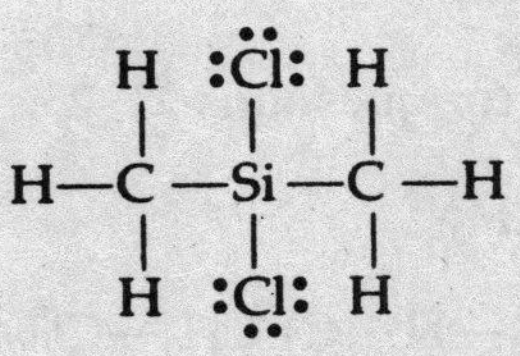 H—C—Si—C—H (with H, :Cl: substituents)

15. The ratio of *hydrogen weight to carbon weight* is greatest in which type of compound?
   A) unsaturated hydrocarbon (one double bond)
   B) aromatic hydrocarbon
   C) monosubstituted halogenated saturated hydrocarbon
   D) saturated aliphatic hydrocarbon
   E) phenol

16. Branching in alkanes reduces the boiling point of alkanes since it tends to
   A) increase hydrogen bonding
   B) decrease hydrogen bonding
   C) increase Van der Waals forces
   D) decrease Van der Waals forces
   E) none of the above

17. The oxidation products of the oxidation of alkanes at high temperature (with O_2 available) are
   A) $CO + H_2$ B) $C + H_2$ C) $CO_2 + H_2O$ D) $CO + H_2O$
   E) none of the above

18. The reaction

$$CH_4 + Cl_2 \xrightarrow{300°C} CH_4Cl_2$$

   A) occurs with great speed
   B) occurs very slowly
   C) does not occur
   D) is a first-order reaction

19. Saturated hydrocarbons with a ring structure have the general formula
A) C_nH_{2n+2} B) C_nH_{2n} C) C_nH_{2n-2} D) C_nH_{2n-1}

20. Which will be the most likely product?

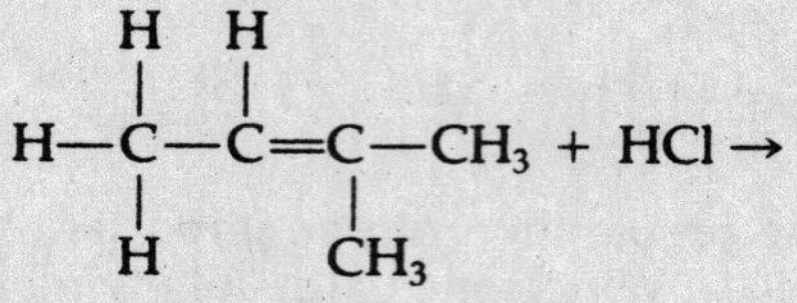

$$\begin{array}{ccc} & H & H \\ & | & | \\ H-C-C & = & C-CH_3 + HCl \rightarrow \\ & | & | \\ & H & CH_3 \end{array}$$

A) 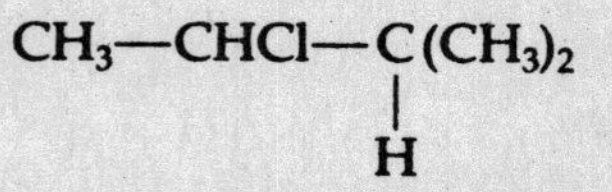 $CH_3-CHCl-C(CH_3)_2$
   |
   H

B) $CH_3-CH_2-C(Cl)(CH_3)_2$

C) cannot be predicted
D) involves carbanion formation
E) none of the above

The following choices are offered for questions 21–25.

$$\begin{array}{ccc} & CH_3 & CH_3 \\ & | & | \\ A)\ CH_3CH_2OH \quad B)\ CH_3-C-H \quad C)\ CH_3-CH_2-C-CH_3 \\ & | & | \\ & OH & OH \end{array}$$

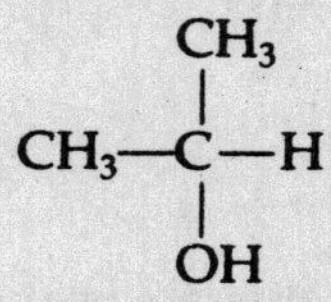

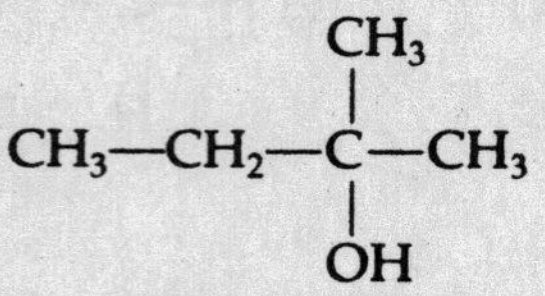

D) 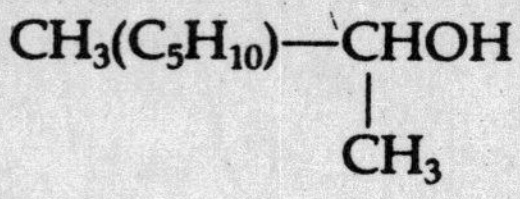 $CH_3(C_5H_{10})-CHOH$ E) not shown
                |
                CH_3

21. The strongest acid is _____ .

22. _____ forms fats.

23. OH is most easily replaced in _____ .

24. _____ has the lowest solubility in water.

25. _____ oxidizes to an aldehyde.

26. Ethers are isomeric to
A) aldehydes B) acids C) ketones D) esters
E) none of the above

27. If ethers had a symmetric structure they would
A) have a dipole moment
B) have no dipole moment
C) have no oxygen
D) none of the above

28. The oxidation of dimethyl ethanol will first yield
A) $CO_2 + H_2O$
B) CH_3COOH
C) CH_3COCH_3
D) CH_3-O-CH_3

29. The chief point of reaction in aldehydes is
    A) the alkyl radical
    B) the unpolarized carbonyl group
    C) the polarized carbonyl group
    D) none of the above

30. The carbonyl group is primarily
    A) free radical
    B) electrophilic
    C) neutrophilic
    D) both B and C above
    E) none of the above

31. Which of the following statements is true?
    A) aldehydes reduce Fehling's but not Tollens
    B) aldehydes reduce Tollens but not Fehling's
    C) aldehydes reduce neither Fehling's nor Tollens
    D) aldehydes reduce both Fehling's and Tollens

32. Two important properties of rubber are its flexibility and toughness, and these properties are greatly improved by vulcanization. Sulfur chloride (S_2Cl_2) is used industrially as a solvent for sulfur during vulcanization of many rubber products. Which one of the following Lewis electron dot structures represents the structure of sulfur chloride?

    A) $\ddot{\underset{..}{Cl}} : \ddot{\underset{..}{S}} : \ddot{\underset{..}{S}} : \ddot{\underset{..}{Cl}} :$ B) $S : \ddot{\underset{..}{Cl}} : \ddot{\underset{..}{S}} : Cl :$ C) $\ddot{\underset{..}{S}} :: \ddot{\underset{..}{Cl}} : \ddot{\underset{..}{Cl}} :: \ddot{\underset{..}{S}}$

    D) $: S \overset{\ddot{S}}{\underset{\ddot{Cl}}{\cdot \cdot}} \ddot{Cl} :$ E) $Cl : \ddot{\underset{..}{S}} : \ddot{\underset{..}{S}} : Cl$

33. Iodine (I_2) and iodine-containing compounds are widely used in medicine because of their antiseptic properties. One of the iodine-containing compounds used as an antiseptic is iodole (HC_4NI_4). Identify the Lewis structure for iodole.

    A) $: I - \overset{:\ddot{I}:}{\underset{:\ddot{I}:}{C}} - C \equiv C - \overset{:\ddot{I}:}{\underset{H}{C}} \equiv N :$ B) $\overset{:\ddot{I}:}{C} = C - \overset{:\ddot{I}:}{\underset{:\ddot{I}:}{C}} = C = \ddot{\underset{..}{N}} - H$

    C) $: N \equiv C - \overset{:\ddot{I}:}{C} = C - \overset{:\ddot{I}:}{\underset{:\ddot{I}: \; :\ddot{I}:}{C}}$ D) (ring structure)

    E) $H - N = C - \overset{}{\underset{:\ddot{I}: \; :\ddot{I}:}{C}} \equiv C - C - \ddot{\underset{..}{I}} :$

34. Which of the following Lewis diagrams is/are incorrect?

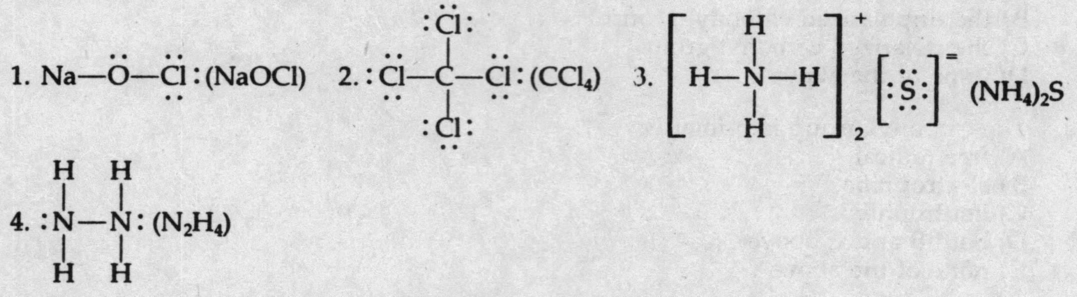

1. Na—Ö—Cl̈: (NaOCl)   2. :Cl̈—C—Cl̈: (CCl₄)   3. $\left[\begin{array}{c} H \\ | \\ H—N—H \\ | \\ H \end{array} \right]^+_2 \left[:\ddot{S}: \right]^= $ (NH₄)₂S

4. :N—N: (N₂H₄) (with H atoms above and below each N)

A) 1   B) 2, 3   C) 4   D) 1, 3   E) all are correct

35. Chlorine dioxide (ClO₂) is used in the manufacture of sodium chlorite. Which one of the following diagrams represents the Lewis structure of chlorine dioxide?

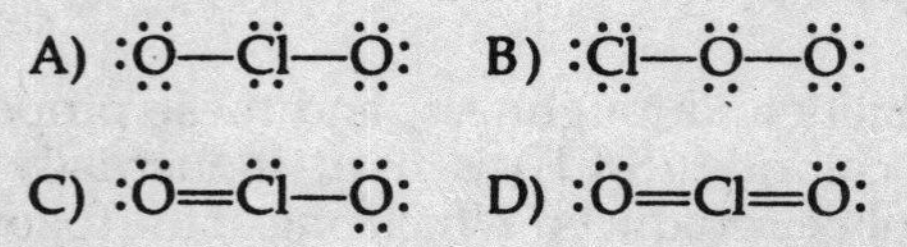

A) :Ö—Cl̈—Ö: B) :Cl̈—Ö—Ö:

C) :Ö=Cl̈—Ö: D) :Ö=Cl=Ö:

E) no Lewis structure can be drawn for chlorine dioxide

36. N₂O has a linear asymmetrical structure that may be thought of as a hybrid of two resonant forms. If a resonance form must have a satisfactory Lewis structure, which two of the five structures below are the two resonance forms of N₂O?

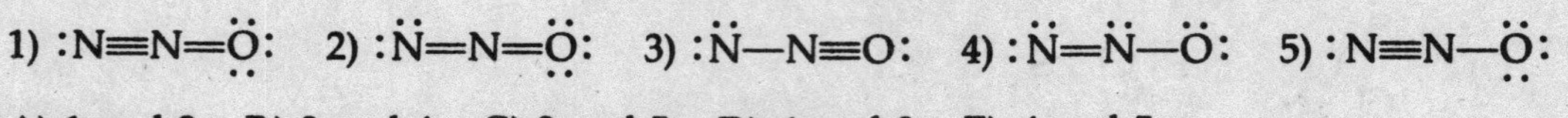

1) :N≡N=Ö: 2) :N̈=N=Ö: 3) :N̈—N≡O: 4) :N̈=N̈—Ö: 5) :N≡N—Ö:

A) 1 and 2   B) 3 and 4   C) 2 and 5   D) 1 and 3   E) 4 and 5

37. TNT explodes violently when properly detonated. The most common type of detonator is a percussion cap containing mercury fulminate, which explodes when struck. The fulminate ion is isoelectronic and isostructural with N₃⁻; both anions are best formulated as resonance hybrids. Which of the following resonant structures could contribute to the structure of the fulminate ion?

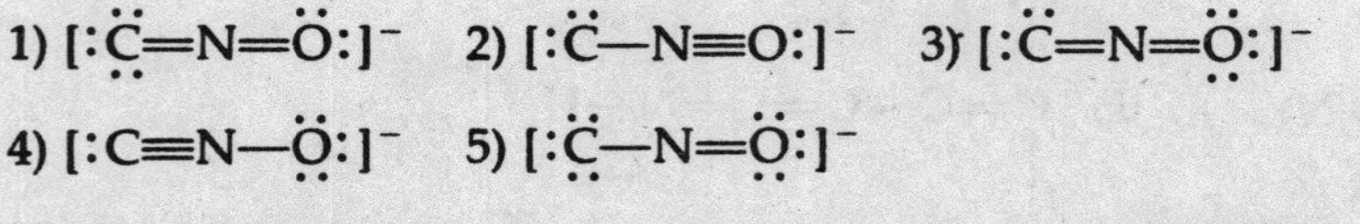

1) [:C̈=N=Ö:]⁻   2) [:C̈—N≡O:]⁻   3) [:C̈=N=Ö:]⁻

4) [:C≡N—Ö:]⁻   5) [:C̈—N=Ö:]⁻

A) 1 and 4   B) 3 and 5   C) 2 and 3   D) 1, 2, and 4   E) 3, 4, and 5

38. Carbon monoxide bonds to a variety of metals to form metal carbonyls. In how many different ways could carbon monoxide be bonded through its lone pairs to iron atoms in carboxyhemoglobin?

A) 1   B) 2   C) 3   D) 4   E) 5

39. An electron pair donor is called a Lewis base. Which one of the following species would be the least likely to act as a Lewis base?

A) PCl₃   B) CN⁻   C) I⁻   D) I⁺   E) SCl₂

40. An electron pair acceptor is called a Lewis acid. Which one of the following would not be regarded as a Lewis acid?

A) AlF₃   B) Ag⁺   C) SO₃   D) BH₄   E) SiCl₄

41. Arsenic compounds bond strongly with SH groups such as those in the sulfhydryl enzymes of the body tissues. Which of the following molecules would you choose as a possible antidote for Lewisite, an arsenic-containing gas?

A) $H_3C—S—CH_3$

B) $H_3C—S—S—CH_3$

C) $H_2C—CH—CH_2$
 $\quad\quad\;$|$\quad$|$\quad\quad$|
 $\quad\;$ SH $\;$ SH $\;$ OH

D) $H_2C—CH_2—CH_2—CH_2—CH_2—CH_2$
 $\quad\;$|$\quad\quad\quad\quad\quad\quad\quad\quad\quad\quad$|
 $\quad\;$ OH $\quad\quad\quad\quad\quad\quad\quad\quad\quad$ OH

E) $H_2C—CH_2—CH_2—CH_2—CH—CH_2—CH_2—CH_2—CH_2$
 $\quad\;$|$\quad\quad\quad\quad\quad\quad\quad\quad$|$\quad\quad\quad\quad\quad\quad\quad$|
 $\quad\;$ N $\quad\quad\quad\quad\quad\quad\quad\;$ N $\quad\quad\quad\quad\quad\quad\;$ N
 $\quad$/ \ $\quad\quad\quad\quad\quad\quad\;$ / \ $\quad\quad\quad\quad\quad\;$ / \
 $\;$ H $\;$ H $\quad\quad\quad\quad\quad\;$ H $\;$ H $\quad\quad\quad\quad\;$ H $\;$ H

42. Consider the following Pauling electronegativity data:

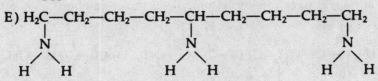

Atom	Electronegativity Value
H	2.1
B	2.0
C	2.5
N	3.0
F	4.0
S	2.5

Which of the following orders listed below would you expect to be the correct one for decreasing ionic character of the bonds indicated?

A) H—F > H—N > H—B > H—C = H—S
B) H—N > H—F > H—B > H—C > H—S
C) H—S > H—N > H—F > H—C > H—B
D) H—N > H—S > H—B > H—F > H—C
E) H—F > H—N > H—S = H—C > H—B

43. What is the structure of beryllium chloride if its dipole moment is known to be zero?

A) linear: Cl—Cl—Be

B) linear: Cl—Be—Cl

C) bent:
 $\quad\quad$ Cl
 $\quad\quad$ / \
 $\quad$ Cl $\quad$ Be

D) bent:
 $\quad\quad$ Be
 $\quad\quad$ / \
 $\quad$ Cl $\quad$ Cl

E) linear: Be—Cl—Cl

44. The reaction that reduces the carbon chain by one carbon is

A) ionization B) esterification C) hydrolysis D) decarboxylation E) dimerization

45.

$$
\begin{array}{cccc}
\text{H} & \text{H} & \text{Cl} & \text{O} \\
| & | & | & \| \\
\text{H}-\text{C}-\text{C}-\text{C}-\text{C}-\text{OH} \\
| & | & | \\
\text{OH} & \text{CH}_3 & \text{CH}_3
\end{array}
$$

The correct name for this acid is
A) 1-hydroxy-2-methyl-3-chloro-3-methyl butanoic acid
B) 1-methyl-1-chloro-2-methyl-3-hydroxy pentanoic acid
C) 1-methyl-1-chloro-2-methyl-3-hydroxy butanoic acid
D) 1-chloro-1-methyl-2-methyl-2-methanol butanoic acid
E) none of the above

46. Which of the following acids will have the lowest pH in a .1 molar solution?

$$
\text{A) } CH_3-\overset{\overset{\textstyle O}{\|}}{C}-OH \quad
\text{B) } H-\overset{\overset{\textstyle H}{|}}{\underset{\underset{\textstyle Cl}{|}}{C}}-\overset{\overset{\textstyle O}{\|}}{C}-OH \quad
\text{C) } Cl-\overset{\overset{\textstyle H}{|}}{\underset{\underset{\textstyle Cl}{|}}{C}}-\overset{\overset{\textstyle O}{\|}}{C}-OH \quad
\text{D) } Cl-\overset{\overset{\textstyle Cl}{|}}{\underset{\underset{\textstyle Cl}{|}}{C}}-\overset{\overset{\textstyle O}{\|}}{C}-OH
$$

$$
\text{E) } H-\overset{\overset{\textstyle H}{|}}{\underset{\underset{\textstyle Br}{|}}{C}}-\overset{\overset{\textstyle O}{\|}}{C}-OH
$$

47.

$$
\text{CH}_3-C\overset{O \rightarrow H-O}{\underset{OH \leftarrow O}{\Big\langle}}C-\text{CH}_3
$$

The molecule above is called
A) peptide   B) cyclic ester   C) dimer   D) acid anhydride   E) none of these

48. Which of the equations below represents the mechanism for ester formation?

A) $R_1-\overset{}{\underset{\underset{\textstyle O}{\|}}{C}}-OH + HOR$ B) $R_1-\overset{}{\underset{\underset{\textstyle O}{\|}}{C}}-OH + HOR$ C) $R_1=\overset{}{\underset{\underset{\textstyle O}{|}}{C}}-OH + HOR$

D) $R_1=\overset{}{\underset{\underset{\textstyle O}{\|}}{C}}-OH + HOR$ E) none of these

49. Sucrose is a
A) reducing sugar
B) monosaccharide
C) disaccharide
D) sugar substitute
E) sugar with an aldehyde group

50. Which of the following compounds shows cis-trans isomerism and zero dipole moment?

$$
\text{A) } \overset{Cl}{\underset{H}{\Big\rangle}}C=C\overset{Cl}{\underset{H}{\Big\langle}} \quad
\text{B) } \overset{H}{\underset{H}{\Big\rangle}}C=C\overset{Cl}{\underset{Cl}{\Big\langle}} \quad
\text{C) } \overset{Cl}{\underset{H}{\Big\rangle}}C=C\overset{H}{\underset{Cl}{\Big\langle}} \quad
\text{D) } \overset{H}{\underset{Cl}{\Big\rangle}}C=C\overset{H}{\underset{Cl}{\Big\langle}}
$$

E) none of the above

51. The product of the reaction of an acid with an amine is
    A) an amino acid   B) an amide   C) a salt   D) a cyanogen compound
    E) none of the above

52. 1.
$$
\begin{array}{c}
O \\
\| \\
C-OH \\
| \\
CH_2 \\
| \\
CH_2NH_2
\end{array}
$$
2.
$$
\begin{array}{c}
O \\
\| \\
C-OH \\
| \\
CH(NH_2) \\
| \\
C-OH \\
\| \\
O
\end{array}
$$
3.
$$
\begin{array}{c}
O \\
\| \\
C-OH \\
| \\
H-C-NH_2 \\
| \\
H-C-NH_2 \\
| \\
H
\end{array}
$$
4.
$$
\begin{array}{c}
O \\
\| \\
C-OH \\
| \\
H-C-NH_2 \\
| \\
H-C-NH_2 \\
| \\
H-C-NH_2 \\
| \\
C=O \\
| \\
OH
\end{array}
$$

   The order of decreasing pH is
   A) 4, 3, 2, 1   B) 1, 2, 3, 4   C) 1, 2, 4, 3   D) 4, 3, 1, 2   E) 4, 1, 3, 2

53. The average percentage of nitrogen found in a protein is
    A) 0–5%   B) 5–10%   C) 10–20%   D) 20–30%   E) more than 30%

54. The dipole ion formed by amino acids is a
    A) Lucas ion   B) Friedel ion   C) Lewis ion   D) peptide ion   E) none of these

55. The isoelectric point of an amino acid is the pH at which
    A) it reacts with another amino acid molecule
    B) forms a zwitterion
    C) will form a cation over an anion
    D) will form an anion over a cation
    E) none of the above

56. The method of separating protein fractions by taking advantage of the different rates of
    diffusion under the action of an electromotive force is called
    A) electrodistillation   B) electroplating   C) electrophoresis   D) vacuum distillation
    E) none of the above

57. What type of bond structure is present in the carbon-hydrogen bond?
    A) sigma   B) pi   C) neither of these

58. The net charge of which of the following is negative?
    A) carbonium ion   B) carbanion   C) both   D) neither

59. What is the product of the oxidation of a primary alcohol?
    A) an aldehyde   B) an alcohol   C) a ketone   D) none of these

60. Which of the following statements is correct?
    A) alcohols have a higher boiling point than their corresponding alkanes because of hydrogen bonding
    B) alcohols have a higher boiling point than their corresponding alkanes because of the increased molecular size
    C) alcohols have a lower boiling point than their corresponding alkanes because of hydrogen bonding
    D) alcohols have a lower boiling point than their corresponding alkanes because of the increased molecular size

61. Both aldehydes and ketones
    A) contain no double bonds
    B) contain no oxygen atoms
    C) are susceptible to nucleophilic attack
    D) are saturated
    E) none of the above

62. Enantiomers
    A) cannot be separated
    B) do not rotate the plane of polarized light
    C) contain asymmetric carbons
    D) none of these

63. Which of the following will not be affected by polarity in a molecule?
    A) solubility
    B) reactivity with nucleophilic agents
    C) reactivity with electrophilic agents
    D) melting and boiling points
    E) none of these

64. Which of the following hybrid types is present in alkanes?
    A) SP^1 B) SP^2 C) SP^3 D) SP^4 E) none of these

65. What charge does the carbonyl carbon on a ketone have?
    A) slightly positive   B) slightly negative   C) no charge

66. Where in the structure below would the most acidic hydrogen be found?

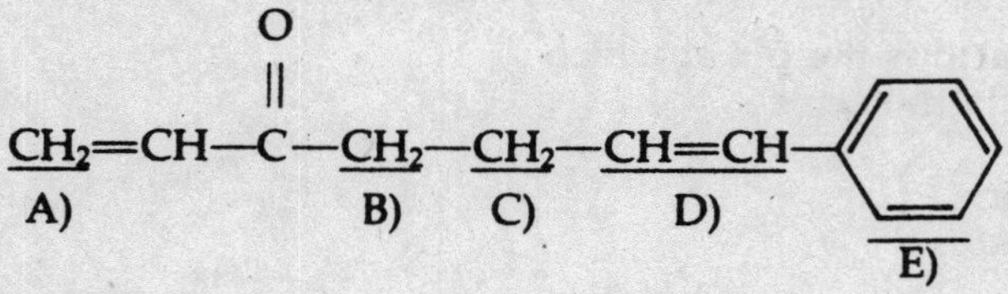

$$O$$
$$\|$$
$$CH_2{=}CH{-}C{-}CH_2{-}CH_2{-}CH{=}CH{-}$$
    A)   B)   C)   D)
                                        E)

67. Which of the following compounds shows optical isomerism?
    A) $CH_2OH{-}CHOH{-}CH_2OH$ B) $CCl_2{-}BrF_2$
    C) $CH_3{-}CH_2OH$ D) $CH_3{-}CHOH{-}CH_2{-}CH_3$
    E) none of these

68. If it is known that the CO_2 molecule has no dipole moment, we may correctly conclude that it is
    A) covalently bonded   B) planar   C) ionically bonded
    D) linear and symmetrical   E) planar and angular

69. Which of the following groups is not meta directing on a benzene ring?
    A) NH_2 B) COOH   C) CHO   D) COOCH

70. Dextrorotatory and levorotatory isomers are contained in what ratio in a racemic mixture?
    A) 1:2   B) 2:1   C) 2:3   D) none of these

71. Name the structure below.

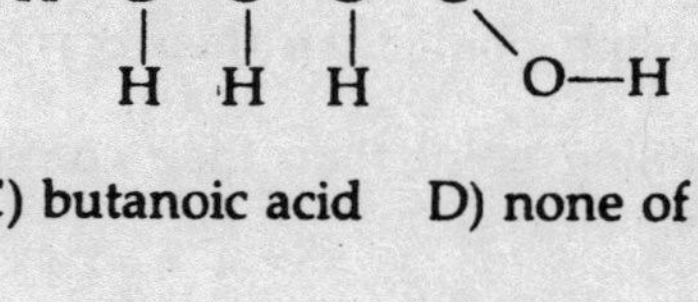

$$H\ H\ H\quad\ O$$
$$H{-}C{-}C{-}C{-}C$$
$$H\ H\ H\quad O{-}H$$

    A) butanol   B) butanal   C) butanoic acid   D) none of these

The following choices are offered for Questions 72–76

A) not shown   B) $R-\overset{\overset{\displaystyle O}{\|}}{C}-R_1$ C) $R-\overset{\overset{\displaystyle O}{\|}}{C}-O-R_1$ D) R—OH   E) R—O—R$_1$

72. What is the functional group of an organic acid?

73. What is the functional group of an ester?

74. What is the functional group of a ketone?

75. What is the functional group of an alcohol?

76. What is the functional group of an aldehyde?

77. Which of the following are the products of the fermentation of glucose?
     A) CO_2 and H_2O B) CO_2 and C_2H_5OH C) CO_2 and CH_3OH D) none of these

78. A reducing sugar contains
     A) an acid structure   B) a ketone structure
     C) an ester structure   D) an aldehyde structure
     E) an alcohol structure

79. Shortening and margarine are made from animal fats and vegetable oils. The treatment used to decrease rancidity is called
     A) hydrogenation   B) esterification   C) oxidation   D) desaturation

80. Which of the following acids has the highest pK_a?
     A) CH_3COOH B) CF_3COOH C) $NCCH_2COOH$ D) CCl_3COOH

ORGANIC CHEMISTRY ANSWER KEY

1. B	21. A	41. C	61. C
2. D	22. E	42. E	62. C
3. C	23. C	43. B	63. E
4. B	24. D	44. D	64. C
5. E	25. A	45. E	65. A
6. C	26. E	46. D	66. B
7. D	27. B	47. C	67. D
8. B	28. C	48. B	68. D
9. D	29. C	49. E	69. A
10. D	30. B	50. C	70. D
11. B	31. D	51. C	71. C
12. A	32. A	52. D	72. A
13. A	33. D	53. C	73. C
14. E	34. A	54. E	74. B
15. D	35. E	55. B	75. D
16. D	36. C	56. C	76. A
17. C	37. D	57. A	77. B
18. C	38. B	58. B	78. D
19. B	39. D	59. A	79. A
20. B	40. D	60. A	80. A

CHAPTER SEVEN
Physics Review

Mechanics

PREFIXES AND UNITS USED IN MECHANICS

The most commonly used prefixes in mechanics are:

micro --------- 10^{-6} -------- μ
milli --------- 10^{-3} ------- m
kilo --------- 10^3 -------- k
mega --------- 10^6 ------- M

The most common units used in mechanics are

length ---------------- meters, inches, cm, etc.
area ---------------- m^2, in^2, etc.
volume ---------------- m^3, cm^3, in^3, etc.
mass ---------------- grams, kilograms, slugs, etc.
weight, force ---------- dynes, newtons, pounds, etc.
energy, work ---------- ergs, joules, ft-lbs, etc.
speed, velocity ---------- ft/sec, m/sec, etc.
acceleration ---------- ft/sec^2, m/sec^2, etc.
density ---------------- g/cm^3, lbs/in^3, etc.
pressure ---------------- g/cm^2, lbs/in^2, etc.
momentum (linear) ------- (g-cm)/sec, (kg-m)/sec, etc.

VECTORS

Vector Addition (Graphic)

Vectors are added by completing the appropriate parallelogram, as shown below.

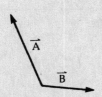 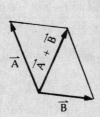 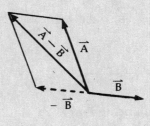

Addition of Vectors by Components

A vector $\vec{V}$ may be broken down into its horizontal and vertical components by

$$\vec{V}_x = |\vec{V}| \cos \theta$$
$$\vec{V}_y = |\vec{V}| \sin \theta$$

where $|\vec{V}|$ represents the length of vector $\vec{V}$ (its magnitude) and θ is the measure of the angle it makes with the horizontal.

To add two or more vectors, simply add their horizontal components together and their vertical components together. The magnitude of the resulting vector is given by

$$\vec{U} = \sqrt{(\vec{U}_x)^2 + (\vec{U}_y)^2}$$

and its angle from the horizontal by

$$\theta = \arctan \frac{\vec{U}_y}{\vec{U}_x}$$

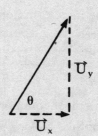

Force

$\vec{F} = m \cdot \vec{a}$; in pounds, newtons, or dynes.

$\vec{a}$ stands for the acceleration acting on the object. In the case of gravity, the value of the gravitational acceleration is 32.2 ft/sec² or 9.8 m/sec² and $\vec{F}$ is called the weight of the object.

Resultant Force

When several forces are acting on an object, the resultant is the one force that can replace all the forces and still have the same effect.

Example:

$F_2 = 50\# @ 150°$

$F_1 = 30\# @ 45°$

$F_3 = 40\# @ 270°$

F_1:
$F_{1_x} = 30 \cos 45° = 21.21$ $F_{1_y} = 30 \sin 45° = 21.21$
F_2:
$F_{2_x} = 50 \cos 150° = -43.30$ $F_{2_y} = 50 \sin 150° = 25.00$
F_3:
$F_{3_x} = 40 \cos 270° = 0.00$ $F_{3_y} = 40 \sin 270° = -40.00$

$R_x \qquad = -22.09$ $R_y \qquad = 6.21$

$R = \sqrt{(22.09)^2 + (6.21)^2} = 27.8\#$ $\phi = \tan^{-1} \dfrac{6.21}{-22.09} = 164.3°$

Balancing Force

The balancing force is one force that can nullify the effect of all the other forces in the system. The balancing force is exactly equal in magnitude to, but opposite in direction from, the resultant force.

Newton's Laws

The science of mechanics is based on the following three natural laws, clearly stated for the first time by Sir Isaac Newton and published in 1686 in his *Philosophiae Naturalis Principia Mathematica.*

1. Inertia: Every body continues in its state of rest, or of uniform motion in a straight line, unless acted upon by external forces.

2. $\vec{F} = m \cdot \vec{a}$: The rate of change of the velocity of a particle (acceleration) is equal to the resultant of all external forces divided by the mass of the particle, and is in the same direction as the resultant force.

3. Action-Reaction: Whenever one body exerts a force on another, the second body always exerts on the first a force which is equal in absolute magnitude, opposite in direction, and has the same line of action.

Static Equilibrium

When several forces act on an object simultaneously and their effects compensate one another, the result is that there is no translational or rotational motion. The object is said to be *in equilibrium;* this means that (1) the body either remains at rest or moves in a straight line with constant velocity, and (2) the body is either not rotating at all or is rotating at a constant rate. The conditions for equilibrium are given below.

1. Translational Equilibrium

$$\left.\begin{array}{l} \Sigma F_x = 0 \\ \Sigma F_y = 0 \\ \Sigma F_z = 0 \end{array}\right\}$$ The sum of the forces in each of the x, y, and z directions must equal 0.

2. Rotational Equilibrium (not rotating)

$$\Sigma M_p = 0 \Big\}$$ The sum of the moments (force times distance to a center for rotation) or torques about any point must equal 0.

Example 1:

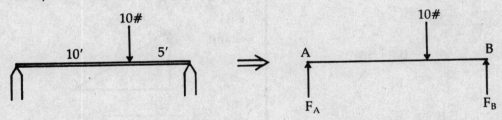

Find the force exerted by each support	$\Sigma M_A = 0$
	$(10\#)(10 \text{ ft}) - (F_B)(15 \text{ ft}) = 0$
	$F_B = 6\frac{2}{3}\#$

Note: Clockwise moments are assumed to be positive and counterclockwise moments negative.

$\Sigma F_y = 0$

$F_A + F_B - 10\# = 0$

$F_A + 6\frac{2}{3}\# - 10\# = 0$

$$F_A = 3\frac{1}{3}\#$$

(shortcut)

Since the distances are on a 10:5 or 2:1 ratio, the forces will be in a 1:2 ratio (reversed, the greater force at the least distance, and vice versa). So that F_A is 1/3 of 10 and F_B is 2/3 of 10.

Example 2:

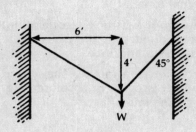

Find, in terms of W, the tension in each of the wires holding the weight.

$\underline{\Sigma F_x = 0}$

$$B_x - A_x = 0$$
$$B_x = A_x$$

From the proportional triangles we get:

$$\frac{A_x}{A_y} = \frac{6}{4} \text{ or } 2A_x = 3A_y$$

$$\text{or } \frac{2}{3}A_x = A_y$$

$$\frac{B_x}{B_y} = \frac{4}{4} \text{ or } B_x = B_y$$

$\underline{\Sigma F_y = 0}$

$$A_y + B_y - W = O$$
$$A_y + B_y = W$$
$$\frac{2}{3}A_x + B_y = W$$
$$\frac{2}{3}B_x + B_y = W$$
$$\frac{2}{3}B_y + B_y = W$$
$$\frac{5}{3}B_y = W$$
$$B_y = \frac{3}{5}W$$

from which we can obtain

$$B_x = \frac{3}{5}W$$
$$A_y = \frac{2}{5}W \text{ and } A_x = \frac{3}{5}W$$

Thus,

$$B = \sqrt{(B_x)^2 + (B_y)^2}$$
$$B = \frac{3\sqrt{2}}{5}W$$

and

$$A = \sqrt{(A_x)^2 + (A_y)^2}$$
$$A = \frac{\sqrt{13}}{5}W$$

(shortcut)

Some time may be saved if we see that the distances of the vertical forces on each side of W are on a 6:4 or a 3:2 ratio. In that case, their magnitudes are on a 2:3 ratio.

$$A_y = \frac{2}{5}W \text{ and } B_y = \frac{3}{5}W$$

We can then continue to find the other values in the usual manner.

MASS AND WEIGHT

Mass

Inertia is the property of a body by virtue of which a force is required to change its state of motion. Mass is a numerical measure of inertia.

Whenever a net unbalanced force acts on an object, it produces an acceleration in the direction of the force ($\vec{F} = m \cdot \vec{a}$). This acceleration is directly proportional to the magnitude of the force and inversely proportional to the mass of the object.

The center of mass of an object is the point about which the product of the mass and the moment arm for each and every part of the body add up to zero.

Gravitation and Gravity

In addition to the three laws of motion, Newton formulated the Law of Universal Gravitation:

> Every particle attracts every other particle in the universe with a force that is directly proportional to the product of the masses of the two particles and inversely proportional to the square of the distance between their centers of mass.

$$F = K_G \frac{m_1 \cdot m_2}{r^2}$$

$$(K_G = 6.670 \times 10^{-11}\, n \cdot m^2/kg^2)$$

On Earth all particles are attracted toward Earth by gravity. For earthbound particles, the value of r is nearly constant and it can be combined with K_G and M_{Earth} into a new constant, G. The force produced by the action of gravity on an object is called its *weight*.

$$W = G \cdot m$$

(G represents the acceleration due to gravity, and its value is 9.8 m/sec^2 or 32.2 ft/sec^2)

Example:
What is the weight of an object with mass 15 grams?

$$W = G \cdot m = (980\ cm/sec^2)(15\ grams) = 14{,}700\ dynes$$

UNIFORMLY ACCELERATED MOTION

Freely Falling Bodies and Projectiles

The most common example of uniformly accelerated motion is that of a body falling freely, that is, under the action of its weight alone.

$$v = at + v_o$$

$$d = \tfrac{1}{2}at^2 + v_o t + d_o$$

$$a = \frac{v_f - v_o}{t}$$

$$2ad = (v_f)^2 - (v_o)^2$$

For bodies being accelerated by gravity alone, we use a = 32.2 ft/sec^2 = 9.8 m/sec^2 = 980 cm/sec^2 (using whichever units fit the problem).

Upwardly thrown objects and projectiles are dealt with by using the same formulas (as long as their motion is strictly vertical). If the object or projectile has been imparted motion other than vertical, it must be broken down into its horizontal and vertical components. The vertical component of velocity is treated with the formulas above; the horizontal component remains constant until the object hits the ground.

Example 1:
An apple falls off a tree. What is its velocity at the end of .5 second and how far has it fallen during that time?

$$v = at + v_o$$
$$\;\; = (32.2 \text{ ft/sec}^2)(.5 \text{ sec}) + 0 = 16.1 \text{ ft/sec}$$
$$d = \tfrac{1}{2}at^2 + v_o t + d_o$$
$$\;\; = \tfrac{1}{2}(32.2 \text{ ft/sec}^2)(.25 \text{ sec}^2) + 0 + 0 = 4.025 \text{ ft}$$

(shortcut)

$$\text{average velocity} = \tfrac{1}{2}(v_f + v_o) = \tfrac{1}{2}(16.1 + 0) = 8.05 \text{ ft/sec}$$
$$d = (\text{average velocity})t = 8.05 \times .5 = 4.025 \text{ ft/sec}$$

Example 2:
A ball is thrown upward with an initial speed of 40 ft/sec. How high does it go and how long will it take for the ball to get back to the height from which it was thrown?
At the highest point, $v = 0$

$$v = 0 = at + v_o \qquad\qquad d = \tfrac{1}{2}at^2 + v_o t + d_o$$
$$0 \doteq -32t + 40$$
$$32t \doteq 40 \qquad\qquad\quad d \doteq \tfrac{1}{2}(32)(1.25)^2 + (40)(1.25) + 0$$
$$t \doteq 40/32 = 1.25 \text{ sec} \quad d \doteq 25 + 50 + 0 = 75$$
$$\therefore \underline{\text{it will rise approx. 75 feet.}}$$

Since it will take another 1.25 sec. to get back down from the highest point, the total time the ball was in the air from the time it was released to the time it returned to its original height was $1.25 + 1.25 = \underline{2.50 \text{ sec (approx.)}}$

Example 3:
A projectile is thrown with an initial speed of 1000 ft/sec in a direction 30° above the horizontal. Find the height to which it rises, the time of flight, and the horizontal range.
Initially:

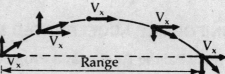

$$v_y = v \sin \theta = 1000\sin 30° = 500 \text{ ft/sec}$$
$$v_x = v \cos \theta = 1000\cos 30° = 866 \text{ ft/sec}$$

For highest point:

$$2ad = v_f{}^2 - v_o{}^2; \; 2(-32)d = 0^2 - 500^2$$
$$-64d = -250000$$
$$\underline{d \doteq 3{,}906 \text{ ft}}$$

For time of flight:
First find the time required to reach the highest point, and double it.

$$at = v_f - v_o; \quad -32t = 0 - 500$$
$$-32t = -500$$
$$t \doteq 16 \text{ sec} \quad \therefore \underline{\text{time of flight} \doteq 32 \text{ seconds}}$$

For horizontal range:
Since the total time of flight was 32 seconds, and the horizontal component of velocity was 866 ft/sec,

$$\text{range} = vt = 866 \times 32 \doteq 28,000 \text{ feet}$$

Motion on an Incline: Friction

Whenever an object moves while in contact with another, each body exerts a frictional force on the other, parallel to the surfaces and opposing the relative motion. The frictional force has the following properties:

- Friction is parallel to the surfaces sliding over one another.
- Friction is proportional to the magnitude of the *normal* force between the surfaces.
- Friction is relatively independent of the speed of sliding.
- Friction is dependent upon the nature of the surfaces and their condition.

Static Friction

When a force is applied to make an object slide over another, this force is opposed by friction. Up to a certain limiting value, no motion occurs and the magnitude of friction is equal to the applied force.

$$F = f_s \leq \mu_s N$$

The equality sign holds only when the applied force F, parallel to the surface, has such value that motion is about to start.

$$F = f_s + W\sin\theta$$
$$\text{where } f_s = \mu_s N$$

Example:
Determine the force parallel to the surface required to start moving a 10-newton block up a 30° incline if the coefficient of static friction between the block and the incline is .5.

$$W = 10 \text{ n} \Rightarrow N = 10 \cos30° = 8.66 \text{ n}$$
$$\Rightarrow W\sin\theta = 10 \sin30° = 5 \text{ n}$$
$$F = (.5)(8.66 \text{ n}) + 5 \text{ n} = 9.33 \text{ n}$$

Kinetic Friction

As soon as sliding begins, the friction force decreases. The force of sliding friction is given by:

$$f_k = \mu_k N$$

Angle of Repose

If a block rests on a plane and the plane is gradually tilted until the block just begins to slip, the angle of inclination of the plane is called the angle of repose or limiting angle. For this angle θ

$$\tan \theta = \mu_s$$

If the block slides down the plane with uniform speed

$$\tan \theta = \mu_k$$

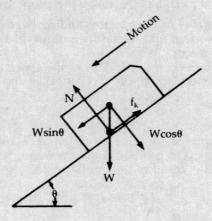

FORCES ON A BLOCK SLIDING DOWN AN INCINED
PLANE WITH CONSTANT SPEED ($f_k = \mu_k N$)

WORK, ENERGY, AND POWER

Work

The term "work" is used in physics in a very restricted sense. Work is done only when a force is exerted on a body while the body moves in such a way that the force has a component along the line of displacement of its point of application. Work is defined to be the product of the magnitude of the force component times the distance it moves the body.

$$W = F \cdot d$$

Work has the following properties:

- If the force is in the same direction as the motion, the work is positive.

- If the force is in a direction opposite to the motion, the work is negative.
- If the force is perpendicular to the motion, the work is 0.
- If there is no motion, the work is 0.
- If the object is moved and then returned to its starting place, the *net work* done is 0.

Energy

Kinetic Energy

Kinetic energy is a scalar quantity. The change in kinetic energy of a body depends only on the work done.

$$E_k = \tfrac{1}{2}mv^2$$

Gravitational Potential Energy

The gravitational potential energy of a body is the product of its weight (Gm) and the height of its center of gravity.

$$E_p = Wy = (Gm)(y)$$

Total Mechanical Energy

The sum of the kinetic and potential energies of a body is called its total mechanical energy. The *work* exerted on a body is the difference between its final and its initial total mechanical energies.

$$\text{work} = (\tfrac{1}{2}mv_f^2 + Gmy_f) - (\tfrac{1}{2}mv_o^2 + Gmy_o)$$

Power

The definition of work does not include the element of time. The *rate* of doing work is called *power*.

$$P = \frac{dW}{dt} \qquad P(\text{avg.}) = \frac{\Delta W}{\Delta t}$$

1 watt = 1 joule/sec
1 horsepower = 550 ft-lbs/sec $\Big\}$ units of power

$W = Pt$ shows that the kilowatt-hour, watt-hour, hp-min, etc., are units of work.

1 hp-hr = 1.98 × 10⁶ ft-lbs = 1.98 Mega-ft-lbs $\Big\}$
1 kw-hr = 3.6 × 10⁶ joules = 3.6 Megajoules $\Big/$ work

Power and Velocity

$$\overline{P} = \frac{\Delta W}{\Delta t} = F\frac{\Delta d}{\Delta t} = F\overline{v}$$

$$\text{or, } P = Fv$$

Thermodynamics: Bulk Properties of Matter

THERMODYNAMICS

Laws of Thermodynamics

1. If heat energy, Q, is furnished to a body, it will appear as an increase in the energy stored in the system (U_2—U_1) and as work done by the system.

$$Q = U_2 - U_1 + W$$

This law is also known as the *Law of Conservation of Energy*: energy can neither be created nor destroyed but can only be converted from one form into an equivalent quantity in another form.

2. No process is possible whose sole result is the absorption of heat from a reservoir at a single temperature and the conversion of this heat entirely into mechanical energy. As a special case: *no self-acting engine can transfer heat from a colder to a hotter body.*

3. Absolute zero may be approached but not reached.

4. Two bodies that are in thermal equilibrium with a third body are in thermal equilibrium with each other.

Units Used in Thermodynamics

Calorie: This represents the quantity of heat required to raise the temperature of 1 gram of water by 1°Centigrade.

$$1 \text{ cal} = 1/860 \text{ watt-hr} = 4.18605 \text{ joules}$$

Btu: This represents the quantity of heat required to raise the temperature of 1 pound-mass of water by 1°Fahrenheit.

$$1 \text{ Btu} = 778.26 \text{ ft-lb} = 251.996 \text{ cal}$$

Mechanical Equivalent of Heat

$1 \text{ cal} = \dfrac{1}{860} \text{ watt-hour} = 4.18605 \text{ joules}$
$1 \text{ Btu} = 778.26 \text{ ft-lb} = 251.996 \text{ cal}$

Heat Transfer

There are three ways in which heat may be transferred from one place to another: conduction, convection, and radiation.

Conduction

Conduction is heat transfer from molecule to molecule through a body or through bodies in contact. The rate of heat transfer depends on the temperature gradient (rate of change of temperature with respect to the distance x along the rod).

$$\text{temperature gradient} = \frac{dT}{dx} \approx \frac{\Delta T}{\Delta x}$$

The thermal conductivity of a rod is defined as the negative of the heat current per unit area perpendicular to the flow and per unit temperature gradient.

$$K = - \frac{H}{A(dT/dx)}$$

While the thermal conductivity of most materials is also a function of temperature (increasing slightly with increasing temperature), the variation due to temperature changes is small and can often be neglected. A material for which k is large is a good heat conductor, while one for which k is small is a poor conductor or a good insulator.

Convection

Convection is heat transfer due to movement of matter. This motion of matter is caused by changes in density or pressure. The heat lost or gained by a surface by convection per unit time is called the heat convection current, H, and is defined as the product of the area of the surface, A, the temperature difference between the surface and the main body of fluid, T, and the coefficient of natural convection for the particular surface, h.

$$H = hA \, \Delta T$$

Radiation

Radiation is heat transfer without the aid of material from one body to another. The term radiation refers to the continual emission of radiant energy by all bodies (the energy is carried by electromagnetic waves). Absorption is the process of converting radiant energy into energy of thermal motion once again.

Good absorbers are also good emitters and the best emitting surface is that which is the best absorber. Such a surface is called an *ideally black surface* and a body having it is called a *blackbody*.

The radiancy, or the rate at which energy is radiated from the surface of a body per unit time per unit area, is

$$W = e \, \sigma \, T^4 \qquad \text{(Stefan's Law)}$$

where

$\sigma = 5.672 \cdot 10^{-8} \text{ watt/m}^2 \cdot (^\circ K)^4$

e $= 1$ for a blackbody and a fraction (less than 1) for all other bodies

T $=$ Kelvin temperature

For any body the *emittance*, e, is the ratio of its radiation output to the radiation output of an equal area of blackbody at the same temperature.

Specific Heat

The specific heat of a substance is the heat per unit mass per degree required to raise the temperature of the substance. The specific heat of water varies very slightly with the temperature but for most purposes this variation can be neglected and C considered constant.

$$C = \frac{1}{m}\frac{dQ}{dT} \doteq \frac{\Delta Q}{m\Delta t} \quad \text{for water} = \begin{cases} 1 \text{ cal/g } ^\circ C \\ 1 \text{ Btu/lb } ^\circ F \end{cases}$$

Molar Heat Capacity

The molar heat capacity of a substance is the amount of heat per mole per degree required to raise its temperature.

Heat Lost or Gained

The heat lost or gained by a body when the temperature changes is the product of the specific heat, the mass, and the change in temperature.

$$Q = C \cdot m \cdot \Delta t$$

Heat of Fusion

The heat of fusion of a substance is the heat per unit mass required for changing its state from solid to liquid at its melting point.

Heat of Vaporization

The heat of vaporization of a substance is the heat per unit mass required for changing its state from liquid to vapor at its boiling point.

SOLIDS

The *density* of a homogeneous solid is defined as the ratio of its mass to its volume.

$$D = \frac{m}{V}$$

Elastic Properties

Elasticity is that property of a body that tends to resist deformations and to return the body to its original form after removal of the deforming force.

Within the limits of elasticity, stress is proportional to strain (elongation is proportional to the force).

$$F = -Ks \quad \text{(Hooke's Law)}$$

Tensile stress is the ratio of force to the cross-sectional area.
Tensile strain is the ratio of the elongation to the original length.
The stress required to produce a given strain is dependent on the nature of the material. An elastic modulus of the material is Young's modulus.

$$\textit{Young's modulus} = \frac{\text{tensile stress}}{\text{tensile strain}} \quad (Y = \frac{F/A}{\Delta L/L})$$

The modulus which relates hydrostatic pressure to the volume strain it produces is called the *bulk modulus*.

$$B = -\frac{dP}{dV/V} = -V\frac{dP}{dV}$$

Elastic limit is the smallest stress that produces an irreversible deformation in a material.

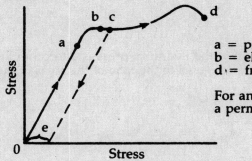

a = proportional limit
b = elastic limit
d = fracture point

For any point, c, beyond the elastic limit, a permanent deformation, e, will occur.

FLUIDS

Properties of Fluids

The density of a homogeneous fluid is the ratio of its mass to its volume.

$$D = \frac{m}{V}$$

The specific gravity, or relative density, of a substance is the ratio of the density of the substance to the density of water.

$$\text{specific gravity} = D_{(relative)} = \frac{D}{D_w}$$

Pressure is defined as the normal force on a surface per unit area.

$$P = \frac{F}{A}$$

At a depth h from the surface of a liquid the pressure produced by the weight of the liquid is given by

$$P = h \cdot D \cdot G$$

Pascal's Law

If an external force is applied to a confined liquid then the pressure produced by that force is transmitted, undiminished, to every point of the fluid and the walls of the container.

Pascal's Law is illustrated by the operation of a hydraulic press.

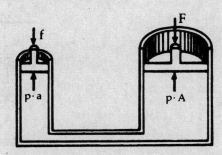

The pressure p = f/a is transmitted to the larger cylinder where p = F/A.

$$\frac{f}{a} = \frac{F}{A}$$

From the above equation it follows that the hydraulic press is a force-multiplying device with the multiplication factor equal to the ratio of the areas of the two pistons.

$$F = \frac{A}{a} \times f$$

Archimedes' Principle

A body wholly or partially submerged in a fluid, is buoyed up by a force equal to the weight of the displaced fluid. If the body is denser than the fluid, the volume it displaces is equal to its own volume and the body is totally submerged; if the body is less dense than the fluid, it floats partially submerged at the free upper surface of the fluid and displaces that volume of fluid that has the same weight as the body.

Example 1:

A body of mass 10 kg is hung by a string from a spring scale and lowered into a tank containing water, where it is totally submerged. If the body does not touch the sides or the bottom of the tank and the weight reading on the scale is 30 newtons, what is the volume of the body?

weight of body: 10 kg × 9.8 m/sec² = 98 newtons
buoyant force: 98 newtons − 30 newtons = 68 newtons
weight of water displaced = buoyant force = 68 n
mass of water displaced = 68 n/(9.8 m/sec²) = 6.94 kg
volume of body = volume of water displaced

$$V = \frac{m}{D} = \frac{6.94 \text{ kg}}{1 \text{ kg/l}} = 6.94 \text{ liters}$$
$$V = 6.94 \times 10^3 \text{ cm}^3$$

Example 2:

A tank containing water is placed on a scale which registers a total weight of 1000 newtons. A rock of weight 100 newtons and volume 5000 cubic centimeters is hung from the string and lowered into the water without touching the sides or bottom of the tank, as shown in the figure below. What will be the reading on the scale?

mass of body: 100/9.8 = 10.2 kg
volume of body = 5000/1000 = 5l
density of body = 10.2/5 = 2.04 kg/l
   (body will sink)
mass of water displaced = 5 kg
weight of water displaced = 49 n
buoyant force = 49 kg
scale reading = 1000 + 49 = 1049 kg

Viscosity

The viscosity of a fluid is a measure of its resistance to flow (a sort of internal "friction"). Its definition is usually given in terms of two parallel plates through a fluid: if F/A is the force per unit area needed to move one plate parallel to the other with relative speed v and if L is the distance between the two plates, then

$$\eta = \frac{F/A}{L/v}$$

Bernoulli's Equation

If a liquid has a small enough viscosity that the energy loss caused by it can be neglected, Bernoulli's Equation can be used to describe the pressure relationships within the fluid. Simply stated, Bernoulli's Equation establishes that the sum of the pressure head, the elevation head, and the velocity head is constant.

$$P_1 + Gy_1D + \tfrac{1}{2}v_1^2D = P_2 + Gy_2D + \tfrac{1}{2}v_2^2D$$

(P is the *absolute* pressure, not the gauge pressure.)

The venturi tube and the airfoil are two applications of this equation.

Venturi Tube

Velocity of a liquid (or gas) passing through a constriction increases, and the pressure consequently drops. If there is an opening in the venturi, as in the automobile carburetor, liquids can be sucked in.

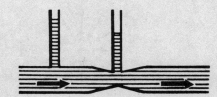

Airfoil

By forcing the air in the upper surface of the airfoil to travel a longer distance, it will need to move faster. This lowers the pressure in the upper surface and produces "lift."

Electricity

ELECTROSTATICS

Charge

The "natural" unit of charge is that carried by an electron or by a proton. For an electron

$$1e = 1.60207 \times 10^{-19} \text{ coulombs}$$

1 coulomb represents the aggregate charge of about 6×10^{18} electrons.

The "charge" of a body refers to its *excess* charge only. This is a very small part of the total positive or negative charge in a body.

Conductors and Insulators

A material that permits a charge transfer along or through itself is called a conductor. A material that impedes such a passage is called an insulator or dielectric.

Metals are generally good conductors and nonmetals are usually insulators. The positive valency of metals and the fact that they form positive ions in solution indicate that they will release one or more of their outer electrons. These "free electrons" then move along the conductor carrying the charge.

Coulomb's Law

$$F = k \frac{q \cdot q'}{r^2} \qquad \text{where } k \doteq 9 \times 10^{-9} \frac{n \cdot m^2}{coul^2}$$

Notice the similarity to Newton's Law of Universal Gravitation.

Field

An electric field exists at a point if an electrical force is exerted on a charged particle at the point. The electric field is defined in a manner similar to the gravitational field.

It is generally agreed to define the direction of the field as the direction of the electrical force vector on a *positive* point charge. The lines drawn in the diagram below represent the lines of force on this point charge and are called *electric lines of force.*

Field Intensity

The electric field intensity at a point in the neighborhood of an electric charge is the force acting on a unit charge at that point.

$$E = \frac{F}{q_t}$$

Substituting $F = k \frac{q \cdot q_t}{r^2}$, we get $E = k \frac{q}{r^2}$

Example:

Find the electric field intensity at a point 3 cm away from a charge of .01 coul in a vacuum.

$$E = 9 \times 10^9 \times \frac{.01}{(.03 \text{ m})^2} = 1 \times 10^{11} \text{ n/coul}$$

The diagram at right illustrates the lines of electric force between like and unlike charges.

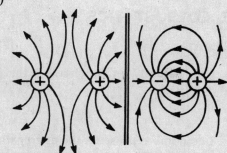

Potential

The potential difference (V) between two points A and B is the work per unit charge required to move a particle from one to the other.

$$V = \frac{W}{+q}$$

The work done in moving a charge from point A to point B, at different potentials, is

$$W_{AB} = q(V_B - V_A)$$

The electric field intensity at a point equals the negative of the potential gradient of the field at the point.

$$E = -\frac{\Delta V}{\Delta d}$$

Example:
5 joules of work are needed to move a .01-coulomb positive charge from point A to point B. What is the potential difference between point A and point B?

$$V = \frac{W}{q} = \frac{5 \text{ joules}}{.01 \text{ coul}} = 500 \text{ volts}$$

Electric Dipole

An electric dipole consists of two point charges of equal magnitude and opposite sign.

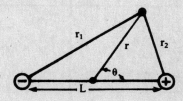

The potential at point P is given by

$$V_P = k\left(\frac{q}{r_1} - \frac{q}{r_2}\right)$$

If r >> L, the product of the charge, q, and the charge separation, L, is called the electric or *dipole moment*, p. The potential at P is then given by the formula

$$V_P = k \cdot p \cdot \frac{\cos \theta}{r^2}$$

The field is said to be outward when $\theta = 0°$; it is inward when $\theta = 180°$.

DC CIRCUITS

Basic Formulas

Ohm's Law $\quad I = \dfrac{V}{R}$ $\qquad$ amps = volts/ohms

Resistivity $\quad \rho = \dfrac{A \cdot R}{L}$ $\qquad$ res. $= \dfrac{\text{cross-sect. area} \times \text{Res.}}{\text{length}}$

Current $\quad I = \dfrac{q}{t}$ $\qquad$ amps = coulombs/seconds

Potential $\quad V = \dfrac{W}{q}$ $\qquad$ volts = joules/coulombs

Capacitance $\quad C = \dfrac{q}{V}$ $\qquad$ farads = coulombs/volts

Power $\quad P = V\dfrac{q}{t} = VI = I^2R = \dfrac{V^2}{R}$ $\quad$ (in watts)

Formulas for Circuit Components in Series and in Parallel

		IN SERIES	IN PARALLEL
Resistors		$I = I_1 = I_2 = I_3 = \ldots$ $V = V_1 + V_2 + V_3 + \ldots$ $R = R_1 + R_2 + R_3 + \ldots$	$I = I_1 + I_2 + I_3 + \ldots$ $V = V_1 = V_2 = V_3 = \ldots$ $\dfrac{1}{R} = \dfrac{1}{R_1} + \dfrac{1}{R_2} + \dfrac{1}{R_3} + \ldots$
Capacitors		$\dfrac{1}{C} = \dfrac{1}{C_1} + \dfrac{1}{C_2} + \dfrac{1}{C_3} + \ldots$ $V = V_1 + V_2 + V_3 + \ldots$ $q = q_1 = q_2 = q_3 = \ldots$	$C = C_1 + C_2 + C_3 + \ldots$ $V = V_1 = V_2 = V_3 = \ldots$ $q = q_1 + q_2 + q_3 + \ldots$
Batteries		$V = V_1 + V_2 + V_3 + \ldots$ $R = R_1 + R_2 + R_3 + \ldots$ (internal resistance)	(equal cells) $V = V_1 = V_2 = V_3 = \ldots$ $R = \dfrac{R_i}{N}$ (number of cells)

Example:
Find the total resistance due to the three resistors in the circuit below, the voltage drop across each resistor, and the current flow through each resistor and through the entire circuit.

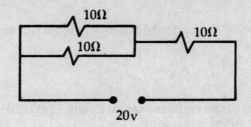

Combined resistance of two parallel resistors:

$$\frac{1}{R} = \frac{1}{10} + \frac{1}{10} \qquad \frac{1}{R} = \frac{1}{5} \qquad R = 5\Omega$$

Combined resistance in the whole circuit:

$$R = 5 + 10 = 15\Omega$$

Voltage drop across parallel resistors:

$$\frac{5}{15} \cdot 20 = 6\frac{2}{3} \text{ v}$$

Voltage drop across the 10-Ω resistor:

$$\frac{10}{15} \cdot 20 = 13\frac{1}{3} \text{ v}$$

Current flow through circuit (and through 10-Ω resistor):

$$I = \frac{V}{R} = \frac{20}{15} = 1\frac{1}{3} \text{ amp}$$

Current flow across each of the parallel resistors:

$$\frac{5}{10} \cdot 1\frac{1}{3} = \frac{2}{3} \text{ amp}$$

Kirchhoff's Rules

Not all networks can be reduced to simple series-parallel combinations as shown by the two circuits below. While no new principles are necessary to compute the currents in these networks, some new techniques are needed.

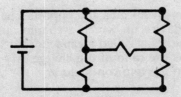

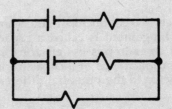

Point Rule

The algebraic sum of the currents *toward* any branch point is zero.

$$I = 0$$

Loop Rule

The algebraic sum of the emf's (voltages) in any loop equals the algebraic sum of the I·R products in the same loop.

Example:
Find the current through each of the resistors below.

(Disregard the internal resistances of the batteries.)

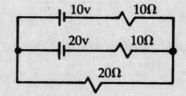

The circuit is separated into branches as follows:

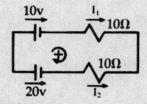 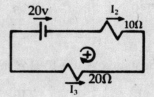

From Point Rule:

$$I_1 + I_2 + I_3 = 0$$

From Loop Rule:

$$10 - 20 = 10I_1 - 10I_2$$

and

$$20 = 10I_2 - 20I_3$$

This gives us 3 unknowns in 3 equations which can be solved.

$$I_1 = -.2a$$

$$I_2 = .8a$$

$$I_3 = -.6a$$

Capacitance

When two conductors in the same vicinity are given equal and opposite charges, the arrangement is called a capacitor. Any device on which a charge may be stored so as to possess electrical potential energy is called a capacitor.

The capacitance of a capacitor is defined as the ratio of the charge on either conductor to the potential difference between the two conductors.

$$C = \frac{q}{V}$$

The net charge on the capacitor is zero. When we refer to the charge of a capacitor we mean only the charge on one of the conductors.

Parallel-Plate Capacitor

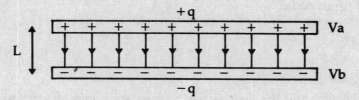

The most common and simplest type of capacitor consists of two conducting plates parallel to each other and separated by a distance that is small compared to the length and width of the plate. Practically the entire field is contained between the plates and, if the space is a vacuum, the field is uniform and depends on the charge per unit area on the plates. The electric field intensity is given by

$$E = \frac{q}{\epsilon_o A}$$

ϵ_o is called the *permittivity of free space* and is equal to $8.85 \cdot 10^{-12}$ farad/meter

Its capacitance in a vacuum is given by

$$C = \epsilon_o \frac{A}{L}$$

Energy of a Charged Capacitor

The energy of a charged capacitor is equal to the work it took to transfer charge, q, through the charging time. During the charging time, the potential changes from O to V, so the average value is $\frac{1}{2}V$. Thus

$$W = \tfrac{1}{2}qV = \tfrac{1}{2}CV^2 = \frac{q^2}{2C}$$

Dielectrics

Most parallel-plate capacitors have an insulating sheet of material called the dielectric. It serves three purposes.

1. The plates can be placed closer together with no fear of their touching one another.

2. They prevent sparking across the plates.

3. They increase the capacitance.

When a dielectric is placed between the plates, the capacitance has been found to be larger by a factor of ϵ_r (the dielectric constant or relative permittivity of the dielectric).

The following figure illustrates why a dielectric causes an increase in capacitance.

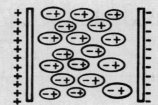

When a polar dielectric is placed between the charged plates, the molecules tend to align in the field. They thereby induce more charge to flow toward the plates.

AC CIRCUITS

Because of its economy of transmission, ac is used much more extensively than dc. This economy is made possible by the ease with which ac voltages may be stepped up or down.

The *effective value* or *RMS value* of a sinusoidal current is given by

$$I_{RMS} = \frac{1}{2} \cdot I_{max}$$

ın ac circuits

1. The current and the voltage are in phase for noninductive resistors.

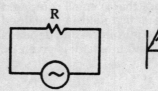
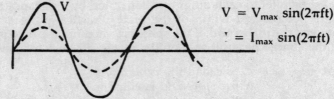

$$V = V_{max} \sin(2\pi ft)$$
$$I = I_{max} \sin(2\pi ft)$$

2. The current lags the voltage in inductive circuits by angles ranging from 0° to 90°, with the latter value achieved only by pure inductances.

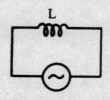
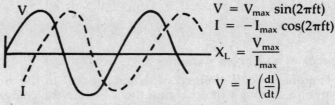

$$V = V_{max} \sin(2\pi ft)$$
$$I = -I_{max} \cos(2\pi ft)$$
$$X_L = \frac{V_{max}}{I_{max}}$$
$$V = L\left(\frac{dI}{dt}\right)$$

3. The current leads the voltage in capacitive circuits by angles ranging from 0° to 90°, with the latter value achieved only by pure capacitances.

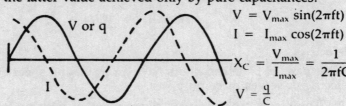

$$V = V_{max} \sin(2\pi ft)$$
$$I = I_{max} \cos(2\pi ft)$$
$$X_C = \frac{V_{max}}{I_{max}} = \frac{1}{2\pi fC}$$
$$V = \frac{q}{C}$$

The Combined R-L-C Series Circuit

Often ac circuits include resistance, inductive reactance and capacitive reactance. Let V's represent the maximum voltages and v's represent the instantaneous voltages.

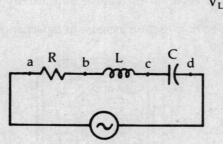
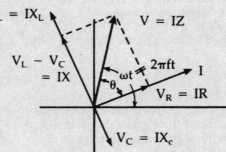

The potential difference across a resistor is in phase with the current in the resistor, thus

$$V_R = IR$$

The voltage in an inductor leads the current by 90° (the current lags the voltage), thus

$$V_L = IX_L$$

The voltage in a capacitor lags the current by 90° (the current leads the voltage), thus

$$V_C = IX_C$$

From the rotor diagram we see that $IX = V_L - V_C$ and by application of the Pythagorean Theorem,

$$\begin{aligned} V &= \sqrt{V_R^2 + (V_L - V_C)^2} \\ &= I\sqrt{R^2 + (X_L - X_C)^2} \\ &= I\sqrt{R^2 + X^2} \\ &= I \cdot Z \end{aligned}$$

The instantaneous voltages v_R, v_L, and v_C are given by the projections of V_R, V_L, and V_C on the vertical axis.

The line voltage and the line current are represented by

$$v = V\sin(\omega t) \quad \text{and} \quad i = I\sin(\omega t - \theta)$$

Example:

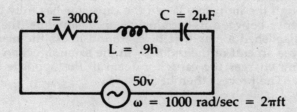

In the R-L-C circuit above, find V_R, V_L, V_C, and θ.

$$X_L = \omega L = 900 \ \Omega$$

$$X_C = \frac{1}{\omega C} = 500 \ \Omega$$

$$X = X_L - X_C = 400 \ \Omega$$

The impedance $Z_C = \sqrt{R^2 + X^2} = \sqrt{300^2 + 400^2} = 500 \ \Omega$

$$I = \frac{V}{Z} = \frac{50}{500} = .1 \ \text{amp}$$

The lag angle $\theta = \arctan\dfrac{X}{R} = 53°$

$$V = IR = 30 \ v$$
$$V_L = IX_L = 90 \ v$$
$$V_C = IX_C = 50 \ v$$

Series Resonance

The impedance Z of an R-L-C circuit depends on the frequency. There is one particular frequency at which $X_L = X_C$ and therefore $X = 0$. At that frequency Z is at a *minimum* and $Z = R$. At that frequency, since $I = V/R$, I is at a *maximum* and the frequency is called the *resonant frequency*.

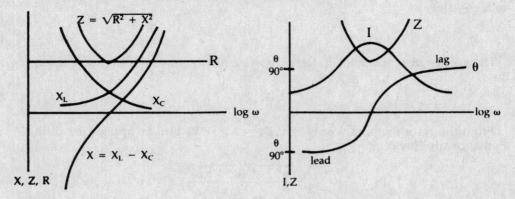

At the resonant frequency,

$$X_L = X_C \qquad L = \frac{1\omega}{C} \qquad \omega = \frac{1}{LC}$$

Note that in order to determine the resonant frequency the resistance R is not needed, an L-C circuit would be in resonance at the same frequency but with a greater value for I. Let us try to explain what happens in an L-C circuit at resonance.

If a charged capacitor is connected to a resistanceless inductor, the capacitor discharges through the inductor. When the capacitor has fully discharged, the potential difference between its terminals is 0; meanwhile, the current in the inductor has established a magnetic field around it. As the magnetic field decreases, it induces an emf in the inductor in the same direction as the current. This induced emf charges the capacitor again in the opposite direction as its original polarity. The process then begins anew.

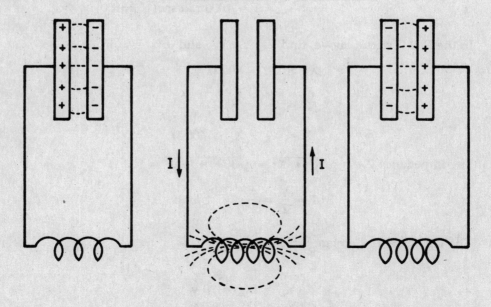

Wave Characteristics, Sound, and Optics

WAVE CHARACTERISTICS

Simple Harmonic Motion

Simple harmonic motion is motion of objects to and fro along a fixed path, repeating over and over a fixed series of motions and returning to each position and velocity after a definite time interval.

The *period*, T, in simple harmonic motion is the time interval spent in moving from one endpoint to the other and back again. The *displacement*, x, is the distance from the position of the oscillating body to the center of the path or rest point. The *frequency*, f, is the number of vibrations per unit time.

$$f = \frac{1}{T}$$

Hooke's Law

Simple harmonic motion follows Hooke's Law: The restoring force, F, is proportional to the displacement and opposite in direction.

$$F = -Kx \quad \text{and} \quad a = -\frac{K}{m}x$$

The acceleration is also proportional to the displacement and opposite in direction.

In undamped simple harmonic motion, the *sum of the kinetic and potential energies is constant*.

Simple Pendulum

A simple pendulum consists of a concentrated mass supported by a very light string. Its motion is roughly simple harmonic, and the period is given by

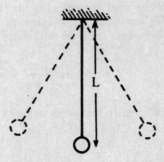

$$T = 2\pi\sqrt{\frac{L}{G}}$$

Reference Circle

Simple harmonic motion can be thought of as the projection of a point, P, moving along the circumference of a circle called the reference circle in a uniform manner.

The velocity of the simple harmonic motion is the projection of the tangential velocity, v_t, of point P.

The acceleration of the simple harmonic motion is the projection of the centripetal acceleration of P along the diameter joining with the center of the reference circle.

The location, x, of the simple harmonic motion is the projection of the location of point P on the reference circle.

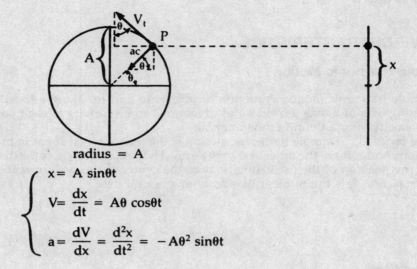

radius = A

$$\begin{cases} x = A \sin\theta t \\[2mm] V = \dfrac{dx}{dt} = A\theta \cos\theta t \\[2mm] a = \dfrac{dV}{dx} = \dfrac{d^2x}{dt^2} = -A\theta^2 \sin\theta t \end{cases}$$

Waves

Disturbances traveling through a medium are called waves. The *wavelength*, λ, is the distance between two successive particles in the same phase. The *frequency*, f, is the number of waves passing through a point per unit of time. The *period*, T, is the time required for one wave to pass through a given point.

$$f = \frac{1}{T}$$

Two particles are said to be in the same *phase* if they both have the same displacement and are moving in the same direction. The letter A is used to denote the *amplitude* or maximum deviation from the rest position. The relationship between time (t) and displacement (Y) at location x is given by

$$Y = A \sin\left(\frac{2\pi x}{\lambda} - \frac{2\pi t}{T}\right) = A \sin\left[\frac{2\pi}{\lambda}(c - vt)\right]$$

The relationship between velocity, frequency, and wavelength is given by the equation

$$c = f\lambda$$

Types of Waves

Transverse Waves

In transverse waves the medium particles vibrate in paths that are perpendicular to the wave movement. For a transverse wave on a string of mass per unit length μ and tension S,

$$v = \sqrt{\frac{S}{\mu}}$$

Longitudinal or Compressional Waves

In longitudinal waves the medium particles vibrate in paths that are parallel to the direction the wave travels. For a longitudinal or compressional wave in a medium of density ρ (in units of mass/unit volume) and bulk modulus B

$$v = \sqrt{\frac{B}{\rho}}$$

For a rod of Young's modulus Y

$$v = \sqrt{\frac{Y}{\rho}}$$

Intensity of Waves

The intensity of a wave is the energy transferred per unit time per unit area through a surface perpendicular to the direction of motion of the wave.

$$I = 2\pi^2 c\ \rho f^2 A^2$$

When waves from a point source or some other very small source travel uniformly in all directions unabsorbed, *the intensity varies inversely as the square of the distance*.

Superposition of Waves

When two or more waves travel simultaneously within the same medium, each wave travels as if the other or others were not present. Neither wave affects each other's propagation. The displacement at any point in the medium is the sum of the displacements of the individual waves.

$$Y = Y_1 + Y_2 + \ldots$$

When two waves of slightly different frequencies are superposed, *beats* occur. The number of beats per second equals the difference of the frequencies of the two waves.

Interference

The combining of two or more waves by superposition is called interference. If they arrive in phase, the interference is said to be constructive; if they arrive 180° out of phase the interference is said to be destructive. Many other combinations are possible.

The following figure shows the superposition of two waves of different frequency and amplitude.

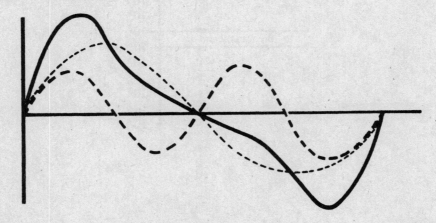

Resonance

When a periodic driving force is impressed upon a system whose natural vibration frequency is equal to that of the driving force, the amplitude of vibration builds up to very large values. At this point the system is said to be in resonance with the driving force.

Standing Waves

A stationary or standing wave is produced when two waves of equal frequency and amplitude travel in opposite directions in a medium. The points at which the amplitude is equal to zero are called *nodes*. The points at which the amplitude is a maximum (equal to the sum of both amplitudes) are called *antinodes*.

The following figure shows the particle velocities in a standing wave.

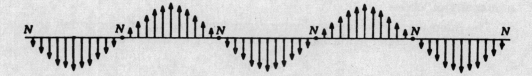

Classification of Electromagnetic Radiation

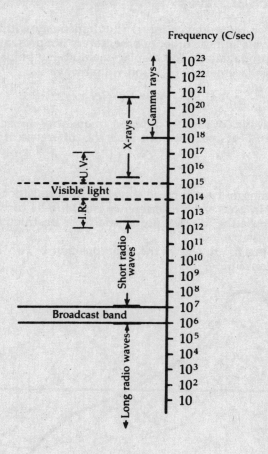

Planck's Law

The idea of a *quantum* or *photon* of energy (h·v) was introduced by Planck in 1901 to explain the energy spectrum of a blackbody.

$$E = h \cdot v \quad (\text{or } h \cdot f)$$

(where $h = 6.62 \times 10^{-34}$ joule-sec, known as Planck's Constant)

SOUND

Properties of Sound

A vibration of some object capable of being detected by the ear is called sound. Sound waves are longitudinal and range in frequency from 20 to 20,000 vibrations per second.

When a sound wave reaches the eardrum, it produces a vibration of air particles with definite frequency and force. This vibration can also be described as variations of the air pressure at the same point; as the air pressure rises above and sinks below the atmospheric pressure, the maximum deviation from atmospheric pressure is called the *pressure amplitude* and is proportional to the displacement amplitude.

Pitch is that attribute of sound which allows us to classify it as "high" or "low." Pitch is associated with the frequency of vibration.

The *quality* of a sound depends on its relative complexity. It is determined by the number of overtones present and their relative intensity vs. time curves.

The *intensity*, I, of a traveling wave is the average time rate of energy transport, r, per unit area

$$I = \frac{P^2}{2Dc}$$

(where P is the pressure amplitude, D is the average density of the medium and c is the velocity of the sound wave).

The *loudness* of the sound is the magnitude of the auditory sensation caused by it. The loudness of a sound depends upon both its intensity and its frequency. Loudness is a measure of the relative position of a sound between the threshold of hearing and the threshold of pain.

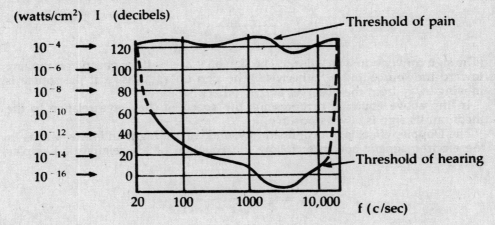

The *intensity level* of a sound is the logarithm of the ratio of its intensity to an arbitrarily chosen intensity. The units of intensity level are the *bel* and the *decibel*. (In one of those weird aberrations of nomenclature, it turns out that the decibel equals 10 bels.)

$$d\beta = 10 \log \frac{I}{I_o} \quad \text{(in decibels)}$$

(where I_o was arbitrarily chosen to equal 10^{-16} watts/cm²)

Speed of Sound

The velocity of sound waves (longitudinal waves) in air at 20°C is 344 m/sec or 1180 ft/sec. The motion of any single particle in the medium is simple harmonic and parallel to the direction of propagation. The effect of a temperature change in the velocity of propagation of sound waves in air is given by

$$\frac{c_1}{c_2} = \sqrt{\frac{T_1}{T_2}}$$

The speed of propagation of a longitudinal pulse in a fluid depends only on the bulk modulus, B, and the density, ρ, of the medium.

$$c = \sqrt{\frac{B}{\rho}}$$

The speed of propagation of a longitudinal pulse along a solid bar depends only on the Young's modulus, Y, and the density, ρ, of the bar.

$$c = \sqrt{\frac{Y}{\rho}}$$

Example:
Find the speed of propagation of sound at 30°C.

$$\frac{c_1}{c_2} = \sqrt{\frac{T_1}{T_2}} \qquad \frac{X}{1130} = \sqrt{\frac{303}{293}} \qquad X = 1149 \text{ ft/sec}$$

Doppler Effect

If there is relative motion between a sound source and an observer, the apparent frequency of the sound changes. The relationship between the frequency of the source and the apparent frequency is given by

$$f_{obs} = \frac{c \pm v_{obs}}{c \mp v_{sound}} \cdot f_{sound}$$

(The sign convention is as follows: The sign on v_{obs} is + if the observer is moving toward the source and − otherwise. The sign on v_{sound} is + if the source is moving away from the observer and − otherwise.)

In the above equation c represents the speed of the wave relative to the medium. Its sign is always positive.

The Doppler effect is not confined to sound waves. Light and other waves in the electromagnetic spectrum follow the equation of the relativistic Doppler effect.

$$f_B = f_A \cdot \sqrt{\frac{1 - (v/c)}{1 + (v/c)}}$$

In the above equation, c represents the speed of light relative to either A or B, and v represents the relative velocity of A and B.

The Doppler effect can be observed when a car is approaching or receding from an observer. The horn of the car appears to have a higher frequency when approaching and a lower frequency when receding. The Doppler effect is also used in calculating the velocity with which stars are moving toward or away from Earth and in determining the velocity of moving vehicles by police radar.

REFLECTION

Laws of Reflection

1. The incident ray, the reflected ray, and the normal to the reflecting surface all lie in the same plane.

2. The angle of reflection is equal to the angle of incidence.

Mirrors

Plane Mirrors

The images formed by plane mirrors are virtual, erect, of the same size as the object, and appear to be located as far behind the mirror as the object is in front of it.

In a plane mirror the image is perverted (that is, there is a left-to-right inversion relative to the object). When a plane mirror is rotated through a given angle, the reflected ray is deviated through twice as large an angle.

Spherical Mirrors

The principal focus of a spherical mirror is the point where rays parallel to the principal axis and very close to it are focused (converge). Concave mirrors have a real focus, while the focus of a convex mirror is virtual. The principal focus is located on the principal axis at a point halfway between the mirror and its center of curvature.

Concave mirrors form real and inverted images of objects located outside the principal focus. If the object is located between the principal focus and the mirror, the image is virtual, erect, and enlarged.

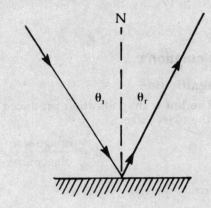

Convex mirrors produce only virtual, erect and smaller images.

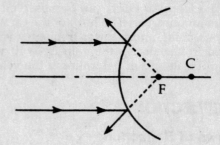

Calculations

Magnification

The linear magnification produced by a mirror is the ratio of the image size to the object size.

$$M = \frac{\text{image size}}{\text{object size}} = \frac{\text{image distance}}{\text{object distance}} = \frac{q}{p}$$

Mirror Equation

For concave and convex spherical mirrors

$$\frac{1}{p} + \frac{1}{q} = \frac{1}{f}$$

where p = object distance, q = image distance, f = focal length of mirror (r/2).

q is positive for real images (in front of mirror) and negative for virtual images (in back of mirror).

REFRACTION

Laws of Refraction

When a ray of light passes from one medium into another its speed changes. If it passes to a medium in which its speed is less than the medium from which it came, then the ray is bent towards the normal. If the light passes to a faster medium, then it is bent away from the normal.

The index of refraction of a substance relative to another is the ratio of the speed, v_1, of light in the first medium to the speed, v_2, of light in the second medium.

$$n = \frac{v_1}{v_2} = \frac{\sin \theta 1}{\sin \theta 2}$$

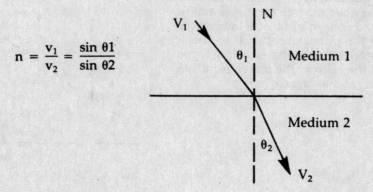

Critical Angle

The smallest angle for which all the light is *reflected* at the surface of separation is called the critical angle. This occurs when light passes from one medium into another in which its speed is greater. The formula for the critical incidence angle is

$$\sin \theta_{crit.} = \frac{1}{n}$$

Whenever the angle of incidence is greater than the critical angle, total internal reflection will occur.

Snell's Law

For monochromatic light

$$\frac{n_1}{n_2} = \frac{\sin \theta 1}{\sin \theta 2}$$

Lenses

Converging lenses (positive lenses) are thicker at the center and will converge parallel rays to a real focus.

Diverging lenses (negative lenses) are thinner at the center and will diverge parallel rays from a virtual focus.

Lens Equation

$$\frac{1}{p} + \frac{1}{q} = \frac{1}{f}$$

(p is the object distance, q is the image distance, and f is the focal length of the lens).

p is positive for real objects and negative for virtual objects. q is positive for real images and negative for virtual images. f is positive for converging lenses and negative for diverging lenses.

Lens Power

$$\text{Lens power (in } diopters) = \frac{1}{\text{focal length of lens in meters}}$$

Lenses in Contact with Each Other

When two lenses of focal lengths f_1 and f_2, are in contact with each other, the focal length of the combination is given by

$$\frac{1}{f} = \frac{1}{f_1} + \frac{1}{f_2}$$

Myopia and Hyperopia

Normal Eye: focuses at the retina.

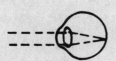

POSITION OF OBJECT	POSITION OF IMAGE	RELATIVE SIZE OF IMAGE	NATURE OF IMAGE
At infinity	At F	Very small	Real
Beyond 2F	Between F and 2F	Smaller	Real, inv.
At 2F	At 2F	Same	Real, inv.
Between F and 2F	Beyond 2F	Larger	Real, inv.
At F	At infinity		No image
Between F and the lens	Same side as object, farther back	Larger	Virtual, erect

Nearsighted (myopic) eye: focuses in front of the retina because the eyeball is too long for its lens. It can be corrected with a diverging lens.

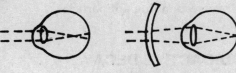

Corrected

Farsighted (hyperopic) eye: focuses beyond the retina because the eyeball is too short for its lens. It can be corrected with a converging lens.

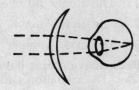

Corrected

Nuclear Physics

FUNDAMENTAL CONCEPTS

An atom is a very small, electrically neutral particle with a tiny but massive positive nucleus and one or more electrons orbiting at a relatively large distance. The following facts are helpful in predicting the composition of individual atoms:

1. The atomic number is the number of protons or electrons.
2. The number of protons and the number of electrons are equal.
3. The mass number is the total number of protons and neutrons.
4. The mass number minus the atomic number equals the number of neutrons.
5. The isotopes of an element differ from each other only in the number of neutrons in their nuclei.

The diameters of atoms are of the order of 10^{-8} cm (Å).
1 amu (atomic mass unit) is 1/12 the mass of $_6C^{12}$ or 1 amu = 1.660×10^{-24}g
The atomic mass, as stated in the periodic table of the elements, is the weighted average mass of the isotopes of the element expressed in amu's.

ELEMENTARY PARTICLES

The most well-known particles are the *nucleons*, which include the protons and neutrons, and the *leptons*, which include the electrons and photons. Their characteristics and mass are summarized in the following table.

PARTICLE	SYMBOL	MASS (AMU)	RELATIVE CHARGE
proton	p	1.007596	+1
neutron	n	1.008986	0
electron	e	0.0005488	−1
photon	γ	0	0

In addition to these, other particles (Ξ hyperons, Σ hyperons, λ hyperons, K mesons, π mesons, μ mesons, neutrinos, etc.) have been identified as well as their corresponding antiparticles.

RADIOACTIVE DECAY

Every atom is completely described by three numbers:

1. The atomic number, Z.
2. The atomic mass.
3. The mass number, A.

Radioactive atoms have an unfavorable ratio of neutrons to protons in their nuclei. The radiation emitted is that which tends to increase nuclear stability.

Alpha

$$_{92}U^{238} \longrightarrow 2\alpha^4 + {}_{90}Th^{234}$$

Ejection of an alpha particle (He nucleus) decreases the atomic number by 2 and the mass number by 4.

Beta

$$_{90}Th^{234} \longrightarrow {}_{-1}e^0 + {}_{91}Pa^{234}$$

Ejection of a beta particle (electron) increases the atomic number by 1 and leaves the mass number unaltered.

Half-Life

The rate at which radioactive decay occurs gives a measure of the nuclear stability of an isotope. This is usually expressed in terms of the half-life of the nucleus: the time it takes for half of a given quantity of an isotope to be transformed into something else. $t_{1/2}$ is a constant for each isotope, and does not depend on any conditions other than the isotope itself.

FISSION AND FUSION

Fission

Fission is the name of the process whereby the nucleus of a heavy atom splits into two or more nuclei of intermediate mass. The two nuclei weigh less than the original nucleus and this loss of mass causes the liberation of a tremendous amount of energy. For example, when uranium undergoes fission, barium, krypton, and other elements are produced. In addition, about 200 Mev are released as well as some neutrons. These neutrons then become free to strike other uranium nuclei and cause other fissions, giving rise to the possibility of a *chain reaction.*

Fusion

Much more matter can be converted into energy by fusion of light nuclei into heavier nuclei than by fission of heavy nuclei. Calculations show that the ratio of matter converted into energy by fusion to that by fission is about 7:1, and that the process is free from radioactive waste. The energy-liberating equations involved in fusion of hydrogen atoms are

$$_1H^1 + {}_1H^1 \longrightarrow {}_1H^2 + {}_1e^0$$

$$_1H^2 + {}_1H^1 \longrightarrow {}_2He^3 + \gamma \text{ radiation}$$

$$_2He^3 + {}_2He^3 \longrightarrow {}_2He^4 + {}_1H^1 + {}_1H^1$$

In order for the third reaction to occur, the first two reactions must occur twice. These reactions, known as the proton-proton chain, require temperatures of the order of 100 million degrees C to initiate.

ENERGY

Mass Defect

Nuclei always have slightly smaller masses than the sum of the masses of the particles which make them up. This missing mass, called the mass defect or deficit, is associated with the energy required for the binding of protons and neutrons into the nucleus. The following graph shows the relationship between mass defect per nucleon and mass number.

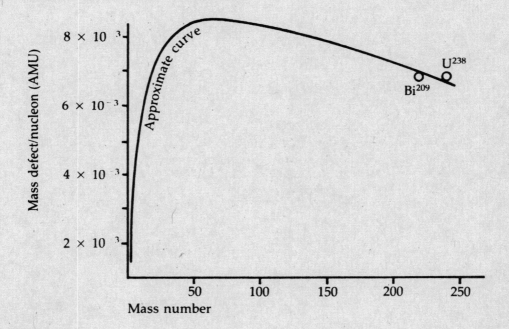

Binding Energy and Liberated Energy

Binding Energy

The binding energy in a nucleus can be calculated from the mass defect by applying Einstein's equation ($E = mc^2$).

Liberated Energy

When the sum of the final rest masses is less than the sum of the initial masses, the difference constitutes the liberated energy and may be calculated by Einstein's equation.

Physics Review Practice Test

ANSWER SHEET

1 Ⓐ Ⓑ Ⓒ Ⓓ	17 Ⓐ Ⓑ Ⓒ Ⓓ	33 Ⓐ Ⓑ Ⓒ Ⓓ	49 Ⓐ Ⓑ Ⓒ Ⓓ	65 Ⓐ Ⓑ Ⓒ Ⓓ
2 Ⓐ Ⓑ Ⓒ Ⓓ	18 Ⓐ Ⓑ Ⓒ Ⓓ	34 Ⓐ Ⓑ Ⓒ Ⓓ	50 Ⓐ Ⓑ Ⓒ Ⓓ	66 Ⓐ Ⓑ Ⓒ Ⓓ
3 Ⓐ Ⓑ Ⓒ Ⓓ	19 Ⓐ Ⓑ Ⓒ Ⓓ	35 Ⓐ Ⓑ Ⓒ Ⓓ	51 Ⓐ Ⓑ Ⓒ Ⓓ	67 Ⓐ Ⓑ Ⓒ Ⓓ
4 Ⓐ Ⓑ Ⓒ Ⓓ	20 Ⓐ Ⓑ Ⓒ Ⓓ	36 Ⓐ Ⓑ Ⓒ Ⓓ	52 Ⓐ Ⓑ Ⓒ Ⓓ	68 Ⓐ Ⓑ Ⓒ Ⓓ
5 Ⓐ Ⓑ Ⓒ Ⓓ	21 Ⓐ Ⓑ Ⓒ Ⓓ	37 Ⓐ Ⓑ Ⓒ Ⓓ	53 Ⓐ Ⓑ Ⓒ Ⓓ	69 Ⓐ Ⓑ Ⓒ Ⓓ
6 Ⓐ Ⓑ Ⓒ Ⓓ	22 Ⓐ Ⓑ Ⓒ Ⓓ	38 Ⓐ Ⓑ Ⓒ Ⓓ	54 Ⓐ Ⓑ Ⓒ Ⓓ	70 Ⓐ Ⓑ Ⓒ Ⓓ
7 Ⓐ Ⓑ Ⓒ Ⓓ	23 Ⓐ Ⓑ Ⓒ Ⓓ	39 Ⓐ Ⓑ Ⓒ Ⓓ	55 Ⓐ Ⓑ Ⓒ Ⓓ	71 Ⓐ Ⓑ Ⓒ Ⓓ
8 Ⓐ Ⓑ Ⓒ Ⓓ	24 Ⓐ Ⓑ Ⓒ Ⓓ	40 Ⓐ Ⓑ Ⓒ Ⓓ	56 Ⓐ Ⓑ Ⓒ Ⓓ	72 Ⓐ Ⓑ Ⓒ Ⓓ
9 Ⓐ Ⓑ Ⓒ Ⓓ	25 Ⓐ Ⓑ Ⓒ Ⓓ	41 Ⓐ Ⓑ Ⓒ Ⓓ	57 Ⓐ Ⓑ Ⓒ Ⓓ	73 Ⓐ Ⓑ Ⓒ Ⓓ
10 Ⓐ Ⓑ Ⓒ Ⓓ	26 Ⓐ Ⓑ Ⓒ Ⓓ	42 Ⓐ Ⓑ Ⓒ Ⓓ	58 Ⓐ Ⓑ Ⓒ Ⓓ	74 Ⓐ Ⓑ Ⓒ Ⓓ
11 Ⓐ Ⓑ Ⓒ Ⓓ	27 Ⓐ Ⓑ Ⓒ Ⓓ	43 Ⓐ Ⓑ Ⓒ Ⓓ Ⓔ	59 Ⓐ Ⓑ Ⓒ Ⓓ	75 Ⓐ Ⓑ Ⓒ Ⓓ
12 Ⓐ Ⓑ Ⓒ Ⓓ	28 Ⓐ Ⓑ Ⓒ Ⓓ	44 Ⓐ Ⓑ Ⓒ Ⓓ	60 Ⓐ Ⓑ Ⓒ Ⓓ	76 Ⓐ Ⓑ Ⓒ Ⓓ
13 Ⓐ Ⓑ Ⓒ Ⓓ	29 Ⓐ Ⓑ Ⓒ Ⓓ	45 Ⓐ Ⓑ Ⓒ Ⓓ	61 Ⓐ Ⓑ Ⓒ Ⓓ	77 Ⓐ Ⓑ Ⓒ Ⓓ
14 Ⓐ Ⓑ Ⓒ Ⓓ	30 Ⓐ Ⓑ Ⓒ Ⓓ	46 Ⓐ Ⓑ Ⓒ Ⓓ	62 Ⓐ Ⓑ Ⓒ Ⓓ	78 Ⓐ Ⓑ Ⓒ Ⓓ
15 Ⓐ Ⓑ Ⓒ Ⓓ	31 Ⓐ Ⓑ Ⓒ Ⓓ	47 Ⓐ Ⓑ Ⓒ Ⓓ	63 Ⓐ Ⓑ Ⓒ Ⓓ	79 Ⓐ Ⓑ Ⓒ Ⓓ
16 Ⓐ Ⓑ Ⓒ Ⓓ	32 Ⓐ Ⓑ Ⓒ Ⓓ	48 Ⓐ Ⓑ Ⓒ Ⓓ	64 Ⓐ Ⓑ Ⓒ Ⓓ	80 Ⓐ Ⓑ Ⓒ Ⓓ

PHYSICS PRACTICE TEST

1. Compute the energy of a photon of blue light (wavelength 4,500 Å) in joules. Planck's Constant = 6.62×10^{-34} joule-sec.
   A) 4.41×10^{-19} B) 4.41×10^{-18} C) 2.10×10^{-9} D) 6.62×10^{-34}

2. What particle, X, is released in the reaction

   $$_{88}Ra^{226} \longrightarrow X + {}_{86}Rn^{222}$$

   A) β   B) α   C) λ   D) a proton

3. The force between two charges is F. If the distance between the charges is doubled, the force will be
   A) F/2   B) F/4   C) 2F   D) F

4. Pressure in a liquid
   A) decreases with depth
   B) is variable at different points at different levels
   C) is variable at all points at the same level
   D) is the same at all points at the same level

5. When a bullet is fired upwards, it gains
   A) velocity   B) momentum   C) kinetic energy   D) potential energy

6. Let M represent the mass of the earth and r its radius (assumed to be uniformly standard). The ratio of g (the gravitational acceleration) to G (the gravitation constant) is
   A) M/r^2 B) Mr^2 C) r^2/M D) Mm^2/r^2

7. If a lens has focal length f in air, in water its focal length will be
   A) < R   B) > R   C) R   D) decreasing with depth

8. Find the resistance in a 120-v, 60-watt lightbulb.
   A) 120 Ω   B) 60 Ω   C) 240 Ω   D) 30 Ω

9. On a foggy night street lights appear to have rings around them. These are due to
   A) refraction of light by water droplets
   B) reflection of light by water droplets
   C) diffraction of light by water droplets
   D) magnification of light by water droplets

10. If $_{83}Bi^{210}$ emits a beta particle, the atomic number for the new element is
    A) 81   B) 82   C) 83   D) 84

11. If the length of a pendulum is quadrupled, its period is
    A) divided by 4   B) cut in half   C) doubled   D) quadrupled

12. As air temperature increases
    A) sound frequency decreases   C) sound speed increases
    B) sound frequency increases   D) sound speed decreases

13. The vision of myopic (nearsighted) individuals can be corrected with which of the following types of lenses?
    A) convex   B) converging   C) biconvex   D) biconcave

14. A fireman climbed a ladder 60 feet tall. If the weight of the fireman is 200 pounds, how much work did he do against gravity?
    A) 260 ft-lbs   B) 3.3×10^3 ft-lbs   C) 1200 ft-lbs   D) 12,000 ft-lbs

15. If an object is thrown straight up into the air with an initial velocity of 160 ft/sec, in how many seconds will it return?
    A) 2   B) 5   C) 10   D) 20

16. An atom undergoing beta decay will produce
    A) an atom of greater atomic number
    B) an isotope of the original element
    C) an ion of more positive charge of the same element
    D) none of these

17. If a radioactive isotope of silver has a half-life of 20 days, what part of the original amount will remain after 40 days?
    A) ½   B) ¼   C) none   D) depends on the original quantity

18. The velocity of sound in a vacuum is _____ in air.
    A) the same as   B) greater than   C) less than   D) none of these

19. When crossing a bridge, marching soldiers are told not to march in cadence. The reason for this is that
    A) vibrations induced through resonance may damage the bridge
    B) the soldiers can pay more attention to being careful when they do not have to worry about other things.
    C) the bridge surface produces more friction and therefore can cause greater wear on the soles
    D) none of these

20. In the diagram at right, the equivalent resistance is
    A) 11 Ω
    B) 2 Ω
    C) 1 Ω
    D) 6 Ω

21. The voltage drop across CD is
    A) 10 v
    B) 2 v
    C) 5 v
    D) none of these

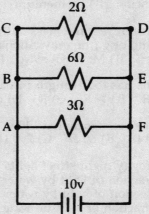

22. If 3 joules of work are necessary to move a 15-coulomb charge from point A to point B .5 meters apart, the potential difference between A and B is
    A) 30 v   B) 15 v   C) 2.5 v   D) .2 v

23. If a sphere weighing 2 pounds is rolled up the incline as shown, by how much does its potential energy increase?
    A) 10 ft-lbs   C) 6 ft-lbs
    B) 8 ft-lbs   D) 7 ft-lbs

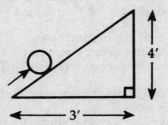

24. A small object lies 6 inches outside the vertex of a concave mirror whose radius of curvature is 18 inches. Find the image magnification.
    A) .67   B) 1   C) 1.5   D) 3

25. A ball falls 144 feet from rest. What will be its average velocity?
    A) ½final velocity   C) ½at²
    B) √final velocity   D) (final velocity)²

26. How long would a 2-amp current need to pass 40 coulombs through a point in a wire?
    A) 40 sec   B) 80 sec   C) 2 √5 sec   D) 20 sec

27. Which of the following is always true about electrical resistance?
    A) it decreases with an increase in temperature
    B) it is proportional to the square of the conductor's length
    C) it is inversely proportional to the cross-sectional area
    D) it can only be measured with an ohmmeter.

28. When a bullet hits a target, the kind of energy exerted is
    A) inertia   B) kinetic   C) potential   D) mass energy

29. If 50 grams of material occupy 34 cm³, how much volume would 25 grams occupy (assuming constant density)?
    A) 1 9/34 cm³   B) 12 cm³   C) 17 cm³   D) 19 cm³

30. If the cross-sectional area of a steel rod is 50 sq in and 1000 pounds are applied to it as a stretching force, by what percentage would the rod be stretched? (Young's modulus = 28 × 10⁶ lbs/sq in)
    A) 7.14   B) 7.14 × 10⁻²   C) 7.14 × 10⁻⁶   D) 7.14 × 10⁻⁴

31. If a block of volume 40 cm³ floats halfway submerged in a tank full of a liquid with density 1.5, what is the mass of the block?
    A) 60 g   B) 30 g   C) 26.67 g   D) 21.5 g

32. A longitudinal wave of frequency 40 h has a wavelength of 36 feet. Find the speed of propagation of the wave.
    A) 1440 ft/sec   B) 1680 ft/sec   C) 1720 ft/sec   D) none of these

33. Which of the following causes hyperopia (farsightedness)?
    A) shortened focal length of the eye lens
    B) decrease in the transparency of the eye lens
    C) lengthened focal length of the eye lens
    D) an increase in the pressure of the viscous fluid

34. What is the index of refraction of a substance whose critical angle is 30°?
    A) 30   B) .033   C) 2   D) .5

35. What force is needed to raise 300 lbs by means of the pulley system shown at right?
    A) 60 lbs   C) 100 lbs
    B) 75 lbs   D) 125 lbs

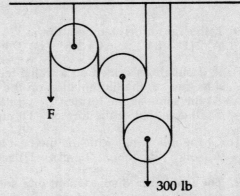

36. Which of the following is a description of a sound wave in air?
    A) longitudinal   B) transverse   C) torsional   D) shearing

37. If an object moves with constant velocity of 32 ft/sec, its acceleration is (in ft/sec²)
    A) 0   B) 16   C) 32   D) none of these

38. What happens as a person approaches a plane mirror?
    A) image size will decrease   C) image will be refracted
    B) focal length will increase   D) image size will increase

39. Uranium-235 has atomic number 92. How many neutrons does U-235 have in its nucleus?
    A) 46   B) 92   C) 143   D) 235

40. When standing waves are set up on a string, the parts of the string that never move from their equilibrium position are called
    A) equilibrants   B) nodes   C) crests   D) nadirs

41. What is the effect on the kinetic energy of an object whose velocity is doubled?
    A) doubled   B) increased by 200%   C) quadrupled   D) increased by a factor of $\sqrt{2}$

42. What is the force necessary to balance the earth's gravitational pull on an object of mass 10 kg?
    A) 9.8 n   B) 10 n   C) 98 n   D) 10,000 n

43. A particle is in equilibrium if the total force acting on it is
    A) zero   B) positive   C) less than its weight   D) negative   E) equal to its magnetic field strength

44. The electric field intensity between two parallel plates which are oppositely charged
    A) varies directly as the square of the distance
    B) varies directly with the distance
    C) is fixed and depends only upon the charges
    D) none of these is correct

45. The distance betwen two consecutive points in the same phase on a wave is called
    A) amplitude   B) period   C) wavelength   D) node

46. What would be the effect on the acceleration of an object due to gravity if the mass of the object were quadrupled?
    A) double   B) quadruple   C) eightfold   D) none

47. Which of the following is not a measure of force?
    A) ounce   B) gram   C) newton   D) dyne

48. How long will it take a ball dropped from a height of 144 feet to reach the ground?
    A) 1 second   B) 2 seconds   C) 3 seconds   D) 4 seconds

49. If the Fahrenheit temperature is 32°, what is the Kelvin temperature?
    A) 241°   B) 273°   C) 295°   D) 373°

50. A flashlight is shined on a wall 4 feet away. If the same flashlight were to shine on a wall 8 feet away, the illumination on the latter wall would be
    A) the same as the former   C) half that of the former
    B) double that of the former   D) one-fourth that of the former

51. Of the following, which is the best transmitter of sound?
    A) solid   B) liquid   C) gas   D) vacuum

52. The maximum displacement of a sound wave in any one direction from the center line is called
    A) displacement   B) wavelength   C) phase   D) amplitude

53. An automobile slows down from 60 ft/sec to 40 ft/sec in 10 seconds. Its deceleration is
    A) 20 ft/sec² B) 10 ft/sec² C) 2 ft/sec² D) none of these

54. The product of the combination of an electron and a positron is
    A) a gamma ray B) an alpha particle C) a neutron D) a beta particle

55. The time it takes for 3/4 of a radioactive substance to decay is
    A) 1½ half-lives B) 2 half-lives C) 3 half-lives D) none of these

56. In the diagram at right, the image
    of the object will be located at
    A) A B) B C) C D) D

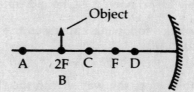

57. As a floating ice cube melts in a glass of water
    A) the level of the water will decrease
    B) the level of the water will increase
    C) the level of the water will remain the same
    D) the level of the water will first increase and later decrease

58. The effective value of a sinusoidal alternating voltage equals its maximum voltage multiplied by
    A) .5 B) .707 C) 1.414 D) 2

59. The eye being too short from front to back causes
    A) aberrations B) nearsightedness C) hyperopia D) glaucoma

Questions 60–62 are based on the following diagram.

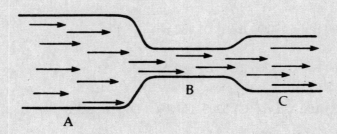

60. Which section of pipe has the least pressure exerted by the liquid on the walls?
    A) A B) B C) C D) equal in all

61. For which section of pipe is the volume per unit time of liquid flowing through the greatest?
    A) A B) B C) C D) equal in all

62. In which section of pipe is the velocity of the liquid the greatest?
    A) A B) B C) C D) equal in all

63. Two particles have equal masses and equal velocities. They also have equal
    A) acceleration B) potential energy C) momentum D) all of these

64. Which of the following sounds is most likely to be audible to most people?
    A) 5 cps B) 5,000 cps C) 50,000 cps D) 500,000 cps

65. Roy and Jose are balanced on a seesaw. They have equal
    A) masses   B) weights   C) moment arms   D) torques

66. A capacitor is connected to an ac voltage source. If the voltage is doubled the reactance will be
    A) doubled   B) halved   C) quadrupled   D) quartered

67. A capacitor is connected to an ac voltage source. If the frequency is doubled the capacitive reactance will be
    A) doubled   B) halved   C) quadrupled   D) quartered

68. Which of the following expresses the relationship between frequency (f), speed (v) and wavelength (λ)?
    A) $\lambda = fv$ B) $\lambda = f/v$ C) $\lambda = v/f$ D) $\lambda = 1/vf$

69. Of the following, the waves with the shortest wavelength are
    A) short-wave radio   B) gamma rays   C) ultraviolet   D) infrared

Questions 70–73 are based on the following diagram.

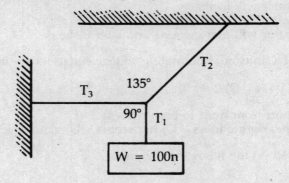

70. $T_1 = $ _____ ?
    A) 980 kg   B) 100 n   C) 3200 lbs   D) 980 n

71. $T_3 = $ _____ ?
    A) 980 kg   B) 100 n   C) 3200 lbs   D) 980 n

72. $T_2 = $ _____ ?
    A) $980 \sqrt{2}$ kg   B) $100 \sqrt{2}$ n   C) $3200 \sqrt{3}$ lbs   D) $980 \sqrt{3}$ n

73. Doubling the value of W will
    A) double T_1 and T_2 but not T_3 C) double T_1 and T_3, and quadruple T_2
    B) double T_1 only   D) double T_1, T_2, and T_3

Questions 74–76 are based on the diagram at right.

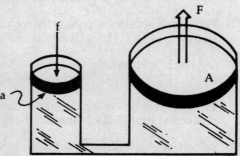

The accompanying diagram represents a confined body of liquid connecting two cylinders of cross-sectional areas, a and A, each fitted with a piston. Upon applying force f to the smaller piston, a greater force, F, will be exerted by the larger one such that the pressures at the two cylinders are equal.

74. If the area a is 1/5 as great as area A, the ratio of F to f will be
    A) .2:1   B) .5:1   C) 2:1   D) 5:1

75. If the ratio of the radius of the smaller cylinder to the radius of the larger cylinder is 1:2, the ratio of F to f will be
    A) 2:1   B) 4:1   C) 16:1   D) 1:2

76. The mechanical advantage of a machine is defined as the ratio of the force exerted by the machine to the force applied. Disregarding friction, the mechanical advantage of this hydraulic press is
    A) A:a   B) a:f   C) f:F   D) a:A

77. If $_{94}Pu^{242}$ undergoes successive alpha and beta emissions, the result will be
    A) $_{94}Pu^{238}$ B) $_{92}U^{238}$ C) $_{92}U^{239}$ D) $_{93}Np^{238}$

78. A girl is holding a 10-lb bag of potatoes at a height of 4 feet off the ground. How much work is she doing?
    A) 40 ft-lb.   B) 2.5 ft-lb.   C) 2.5 lb-ft.   D) none

79. A rifle fires a bullet horizontally with an initial velocity of 900 ft/sec. At the same instant a slug is dropped from the same height as the rifle. Under the conditions just described
    A) the bullet will hit the ground first
    B) the slug will hit the ground first
    C) both will hit the ground at the same time
    D) it is impossible to predict since it depends on the air density (causing friction) on the given day

80. The coefficient of friction between a 30-kg block and the floor is .1. The work required in moving the block 10 m is
    A) 294 j   B) 2940 j   C) 29.4 j   D) 29,400 j

PHYSICS ANSWER KEY

1. A	21. A	41. C	61. D
2. B	22. D	42. C	62. B
3. B	23. B	43. A	63. C
4. D	24. C	44. D	64. B
5. D	25. A	45. C	65. D
6. A	26. D	46. D	66. A
7. B	27. C	47. B	67. B
8. C	28. B	48. C	68. C
9. A	29. C	49. B	69. B
10. D	30. D	50. D	70. B
11. C	31. B	51. A	71. B
12. C	32. A	52. D	72. B
13. D	33. C	53. D	73. D
14. D	34. C	54. A	74. D
15. C	35. B	55. B	75. B
16. A	36. A	56. B	76. A
17. B	37. A	57. C	77. D
18. D	38. D	58. B	78. D
19. A	39. C	59. C	79. C
20. C	40. B	60. B	80. A

Sample Test
ANSWER SHEET

Science Knowledge

Biology

1 Ⓐ Ⓑ Ⓒ Ⓓ Ⓔ	11 Ⓐ Ⓑ Ⓒ Ⓓ Ⓔ	21 Ⓐ Ⓑ Ⓒ Ⓓ Ⓔ	31 Ⓐ Ⓑ Ⓒ Ⓓ Ⓔ
2 Ⓐ Ⓑ Ⓒ Ⓓ Ⓔ	12 Ⓐ Ⓑ Ⓒ Ⓓ Ⓔ	22 Ⓐ Ⓑ Ⓒ Ⓓ Ⓔ	32 Ⓐ Ⓑ Ⓒ Ⓓ Ⓔ
3 Ⓐ Ⓑ Ⓒ Ⓓ Ⓔ	13 Ⓐ Ⓑ Ⓒ Ⓓ Ⓔ	23 Ⓐ Ⓑ Ⓒ Ⓓ Ⓔ	33 Ⓐ Ⓑ Ⓒ Ⓓ Ⓔ
4 Ⓐ Ⓑ Ⓒ Ⓓ Ⓔ	14 Ⓐ Ⓑ Ⓒ Ⓓ Ⓔ	24 Ⓐ Ⓑ Ⓒ Ⓓ Ⓔ	34 Ⓐ Ⓑ Ⓒ Ⓓ Ⓔ
5 Ⓐ Ⓑ Ⓒ Ⓓ Ⓔ	15 Ⓐ Ⓑ Ⓒ Ⓓ Ⓔ	25 Ⓐ Ⓑ Ⓒ Ⓓ Ⓔ	35 Ⓐ Ⓑ Ⓒ Ⓓ Ⓔ
6 Ⓐ Ⓑ Ⓒ Ⓓ Ⓔ	16 Ⓐ Ⓑ Ⓒ Ⓓ Ⓔ	26 Ⓐ Ⓑ Ⓒ Ⓓ Ⓔ	36 Ⓐ Ⓑ Ⓒ Ⓓ Ⓔ
7 Ⓐ Ⓑ Ⓒ Ⓓ Ⓔ	17 Ⓐ Ⓑ Ⓒ Ⓓ Ⓔ	27 Ⓐ Ⓑ Ⓒ Ⓓ Ⓔ	37 Ⓐ Ⓑ Ⓒ Ⓓ Ⓔ
8 Ⓐ Ⓑ Ⓒ Ⓓ Ⓔ	18 Ⓐ Ⓑ Ⓒ Ⓓ Ⓔ	28 Ⓐ Ⓑ Ⓒ Ⓓ Ⓔ	38 Ⓐ Ⓑ Ⓒ Ⓓ Ⓔ
9 Ⓐ Ⓑ Ⓒ Ⓓ Ⓔ	19 Ⓐ Ⓑ Ⓒ Ⓓ Ⓔ	29 Ⓐ Ⓑ Ⓒ Ⓓ Ⓔ	
10 Ⓐ Ⓑ Ⓒ Ⓓ Ⓔ	20 Ⓐ Ⓑ Ⓒ Ⓓ Ⓔ	30 Ⓐ Ⓑ Ⓒ Ⓓ Ⓔ	

Inorganic Chemistry

1 Ⓐ Ⓑ Ⓒ Ⓓ Ⓔ	6 Ⓐ Ⓑ Ⓒ Ⓓ Ⓔ	11 Ⓐ Ⓑ Ⓒ Ⓓ Ⓔ	16 Ⓐ Ⓑ Ⓒ Ⓓ Ⓔ	21 Ⓐ Ⓑ Ⓒ Ⓓ Ⓔ
2 Ⓐ Ⓑ Ⓒ Ⓓ Ⓔ	7 Ⓐ Ⓑ Ⓒ Ⓓ Ⓔ	12 Ⓐ Ⓑ Ⓒ Ⓓ Ⓔ	17 Ⓐ Ⓑ Ⓒ Ⓓ Ⓔ	22 Ⓐ Ⓑ Ⓒ Ⓓ Ⓔ
3 Ⓐ Ⓑ Ⓒ Ⓓ Ⓔ	8 Ⓐ Ⓑ Ⓒ Ⓓ Ⓔ	13 Ⓐ Ⓑ Ⓒ Ⓓ Ⓔ	18 Ⓐ Ⓑ Ⓒ Ⓓ Ⓔ	23 Ⓐ Ⓑ Ⓒ Ⓓ Ⓔ
4 Ⓐ Ⓑ Ⓒ Ⓓ Ⓔ	9 Ⓐ Ⓑ Ⓒ Ⓓ Ⓔ	14 Ⓐ Ⓑ Ⓒ Ⓓ Ⓔ	19 Ⓐ Ⓑ Ⓒ Ⓓ Ⓔ	24 Ⓐ Ⓑ Ⓒ Ⓓ Ⓔ
5 Ⓐ Ⓑ Ⓒ Ⓓ Ⓔ	10 Ⓐ Ⓑ Ⓒ Ⓓ Ⓔ	15 Ⓐ Ⓑ Ⓒ Ⓓ Ⓔ	20 Ⓐ Ⓑ Ⓒ Ⓓ Ⓔ	

Organic Chemistry

1 Ⓐ Ⓑ Ⓒ Ⓓ Ⓔ	6 Ⓐ Ⓑ Ⓒ Ⓓ Ⓔ	11 Ⓐ Ⓑ Ⓒ Ⓓ Ⓔ	16 Ⓐ Ⓑ Ⓒ Ⓓ Ⓔ	21 Ⓐ Ⓑ Ⓒ Ⓓ Ⓔ
2 Ⓐ Ⓑ Ⓒ Ⓓ Ⓔ	7 Ⓐ Ⓑ Ⓒ Ⓓ Ⓔ	12 Ⓐ Ⓑ Ⓒ Ⓓ Ⓔ	17 Ⓐ Ⓑ Ⓒ Ⓓ Ⓔ	22 Ⓐ Ⓑ Ⓒ Ⓓ Ⓔ
3 Ⓐ Ⓑ Ⓒ Ⓓ Ⓔ	8 Ⓐ Ⓑ Ⓒ Ⓓ Ⓔ	13 Ⓐ Ⓑ Ⓒ Ⓓ Ⓔ	18 Ⓐ Ⓑ Ⓒ Ⓓ Ⓔ	23 Ⓐ Ⓑ Ⓒ Ⓓ Ⓔ
4 Ⓐ Ⓑ Ⓒ Ⓓ Ⓔ	9 Ⓐ Ⓑ Ⓒ Ⓓ Ⓔ	14 Ⓐ Ⓑ Ⓒ Ⓓ Ⓔ	19 Ⓐ Ⓑ Ⓒ Ⓓ Ⓔ	24 Ⓐ Ⓑ Ⓒ Ⓓ Ⓔ
5 Ⓐ Ⓑ Ⓒ Ⓓ Ⓔ	10 Ⓐ Ⓑ Ⓒ Ⓓ Ⓔ	15 Ⓐ Ⓑ Ⓒ Ⓓ Ⓔ	20 Ⓐ Ⓑ Ⓒ Ⓓ Ⓔ	25 Ⓐ Ⓑ Ⓒ Ⓓ Ⓔ

Physics

1 Ⓐ Ⓑ Ⓒ Ⓓ Ⓔ	11 Ⓐ Ⓑ Ⓒ Ⓓ Ⓔ	21 Ⓐ Ⓑ Ⓒ Ⓓ Ⓔ	31 Ⓐ Ⓑ Ⓒ Ⓓ Ⓔ
2 Ⓐ Ⓑ Ⓒ Ⓓ Ⓔ	12 Ⓐ Ⓑ Ⓒ Ⓓ Ⓔ	22 Ⓐ Ⓑ Ⓒ Ⓓ Ⓔ	32 Ⓐ Ⓑ Ⓒ Ⓓ Ⓔ
3 Ⓐ Ⓑ Ⓒ Ⓓ Ⓔ	13 Ⓐ Ⓑ Ⓒ Ⓓ Ⓔ	23 Ⓐ Ⓑ Ⓒ Ⓓ Ⓔ	33 Ⓐ Ⓑ Ⓒ Ⓓ Ⓔ
4 Ⓐ Ⓑ Ⓒ Ⓓ Ⓔ	14 Ⓐ Ⓑ Ⓒ Ⓓ Ⓔ	24 Ⓐ Ⓑ Ⓒ Ⓓ Ⓔ	34 Ⓐ Ⓑ Ⓒ Ⓓ Ⓔ
5 Ⓐ Ⓑ Ⓒ Ⓓ Ⓔ	15 Ⓐ Ⓑ Ⓒ Ⓓ Ⓔ	25 Ⓐ Ⓑ Ⓒ Ⓓ Ⓔ	35 Ⓐ Ⓑ Ⓒ Ⓓ Ⓔ
6 Ⓐ Ⓑ Ⓒ Ⓓ Ⓔ	16 Ⓐ Ⓑ Ⓒ Ⓓ Ⓔ	26 Ⓐ Ⓑ Ⓒ Ⓓ Ⓔ	36 Ⓐ Ⓑ Ⓒ Ⓓ Ⓔ
7 Ⓐ Ⓑ Ⓒ Ⓓ Ⓔ	17 Ⓐ Ⓑ Ⓒ Ⓓ Ⓔ	27 Ⓐ Ⓑ Ⓒ Ⓓ Ⓔ	37 Ⓐ Ⓑ Ⓒ Ⓓ Ⓔ
8 Ⓐ Ⓑ Ⓒ Ⓓ Ⓔ	18 Ⓐ Ⓑ Ⓒ Ⓓ Ⓔ	28 Ⓐ Ⓑ Ⓒ Ⓓ Ⓔ	38 Ⓐ Ⓑ Ⓒ Ⓓ Ⓔ
9 Ⓐ Ⓑ Ⓒ Ⓓ Ⓔ	19 Ⓐ Ⓑ Ⓒ Ⓓ Ⓔ	29 Ⓐ Ⓑ Ⓒ Ⓓ Ⓔ	
10 Ⓐ Ⓑ Ⓒ Ⓓ Ⓔ	20 Ⓐ Ⓑ Ⓒ Ⓓ Ⓔ	30 Ⓐ Ⓑ Ⓒ Ⓓ Ⓔ	

Science Problems

1 Ⓐ Ⓑ Ⓒ Ⓓ Ⓔ	15 Ⓐ Ⓑ Ⓒ Ⓓ Ⓔ	29 Ⓐ Ⓑ Ⓒ Ⓓ Ⓔ	43 Ⓐ Ⓑ Ⓒ Ⓓ Ⓔ	57 Ⓐ Ⓑ Ⓒ Ⓓ Ⓔ
2 Ⓐ Ⓑ Ⓒ Ⓓ Ⓔ	16 Ⓐ Ⓑ Ⓒ Ⓓ Ⓔ	30 Ⓐ Ⓑ Ⓒ Ⓓ Ⓔ	44 Ⓐ Ⓑ Ⓒ Ⓓ Ⓔ	58 Ⓐ Ⓑ Ⓒ Ⓓ Ⓔ
3 Ⓐ Ⓑ Ⓒ Ⓓ Ⓔ	17 Ⓐ Ⓑ Ⓒ Ⓓ Ⓔ	31 Ⓐ Ⓑ Ⓒ Ⓓ Ⓔ	45 Ⓐ Ⓑ Ⓒ Ⓓ Ⓔ	59 Ⓐ Ⓑ Ⓒ Ⓓ Ⓔ
4 Ⓐ Ⓑ Ⓒ Ⓓ Ⓔ	18 Ⓐ Ⓑ Ⓒ Ⓓ Ⓔ	32 Ⓐ Ⓑ Ⓒ Ⓓ Ⓔ	46 Ⓐ Ⓑ Ⓒ Ⓓ Ⓔ	60 Ⓐ Ⓑ Ⓒ Ⓓ Ⓔ
5 Ⓐ Ⓑ Ⓒ Ⓓ Ⓔ	19 Ⓐ Ⓑ Ⓒ Ⓓ Ⓔ	33 Ⓐ Ⓑ Ⓒ Ⓓ Ⓔ	47 Ⓐ Ⓑ Ⓒ Ⓓ Ⓔ	61 Ⓐ Ⓑ Ⓒ Ⓓ Ⓔ
6 Ⓐ Ⓑ Ⓒ Ⓓ Ⓔ	20 Ⓐ Ⓑ Ⓒ Ⓓ Ⓔ	34 Ⓐ Ⓑ Ⓒ Ⓓ Ⓔ	48 Ⓐ Ⓑ Ⓒ Ⓓ Ⓔ	62 Ⓐ Ⓑ Ⓒ Ⓓ Ⓔ
7 Ⓐ Ⓑ Ⓒ Ⓓ Ⓔ	21 Ⓐ Ⓑ Ⓒ Ⓓ Ⓔ	35 Ⓐ Ⓑ Ⓒ Ⓓ Ⓔ	49 Ⓐ Ⓑ Ⓒ Ⓓ Ⓔ	63 Ⓐ Ⓑ Ⓒ Ⓓ Ⓔ
8 Ⓐ Ⓑ Ⓒ Ⓓ Ⓔ	22 Ⓐ Ⓑ Ⓒ Ⓓ Ⓔ	36 Ⓐ Ⓑ Ⓒ Ⓓ Ⓔ	50 Ⓐ Ⓑ Ⓒ Ⓓ Ⓔ	64 Ⓐ Ⓑ Ⓒ Ⓓ Ⓔ
9 Ⓐ Ⓑ Ⓒ Ⓓ Ⓔ	23 Ⓐ Ⓑ Ⓒ Ⓓ Ⓔ	37 Ⓐ Ⓑ Ⓒ Ⓓ Ⓔ	51 Ⓐ Ⓑ Ⓒ Ⓓ Ⓔ	65 Ⓐ Ⓑ Ⓒ Ⓓ Ⓔ
10 Ⓐ Ⓑ Ⓒ Ⓓ Ⓔ	24 Ⓐ Ⓑ Ⓒ Ⓓ Ⓔ	38 Ⓐ Ⓑ Ⓒ Ⓓ Ⓔ	52 Ⓐ Ⓑ Ⓒ Ⓓ Ⓔ	66 Ⓐ Ⓑ Ⓒ Ⓓ Ⓔ
11 Ⓐ Ⓑ Ⓒ Ⓓ Ⓔ	25 Ⓐ Ⓑ Ⓒ Ⓓ Ⓔ	39 Ⓐ Ⓑ Ⓒ Ⓓ Ⓔ	53 Ⓐ Ⓑ Ⓒ Ⓓ Ⓔ	
12 Ⓐ Ⓑ Ⓒ Ⓓ Ⓔ	26 Ⓐ Ⓑ Ⓒ Ⓓ Ⓔ	40 Ⓐ Ⓑ Ⓒ Ⓓ Ⓔ	54 Ⓐ Ⓑ Ⓒ Ⓓ Ⓔ	
13 Ⓐ Ⓑ Ⓒ Ⓓ Ⓔ	27 Ⓐ Ⓑ Ⓒ Ⓓ Ⓔ	41 Ⓐ Ⓑ Ⓒ Ⓓ Ⓔ	55 Ⓐ Ⓑ Ⓒ Ⓓ Ⓔ	
14 Ⓐ Ⓑ Ⓒ Ⓓ Ⓔ	28 Ⓐ Ⓑ Ⓒ Ⓓ Ⓔ	42 Ⓐ Ⓑ Ⓒ Ⓓ Ⓔ	56 Ⓐ Ⓑ Ⓒ Ⓓ Ⓔ	

Skills Analysis: Reading

1 Ⓐ Ⓑ Ⓒ Ⓓ Ⓔ	15 Ⓐ Ⓑ Ⓒ Ⓓ Ⓔ	29 Ⓐ Ⓑ Ⓒ Ⓓ Ⓔ	43 Ⓐ Ⓑ Ⓒ Ⓓ Ⓔ	57 Ⓐ Ⓑ Ⓒ Ⓓ Ⓔ
2 Ⓐ Ⓑ Ⓒ Ⓓ Ⓔ	16 Ⓐ Ⓑ Ⓒ Ⓓ Ⓔ	30 Ⓐ Ⓑ Ⓒ Ⓓ Ⓔ	44 Ⓐ Ⓑ Ⓒ Ⓓ Ⓔ	58 Ⓐ Ⓑ Ⓒ Ⓓ Ⓔ
3 Ⓐ Ⓑ Ⓒ Ⓓ Ⓔ	17 Ⓐ Ⓑ Ⓒ Ⓓ Ⓔ	31 Ⓐ Ⓑ Ⓒ Ⓓ Ⓔ	45 Ⓐ Ⓑ Ⓒ Ⓓ Ⓔ	59 Ⓐ Ⓑ Ⓒ Ⓓ Ⓔ
4 Ⓐ Ⓑ Ⓒ Ⓓ Ⓔ	18 Ⓐ Ⓑ Ⓒ Ⓓ Ⓔ	32 Ⓐ Ⓑ Ⓒ Ⓓ Ⓔ	46 Ⓐ Ⓑ Ⓒ Ⓓ Ⓔ	60 Ⓐ Ⓑ Ⓒ Ⓓ Ⓔ
5 Ⓐ Ⓑ Ⓒ Ⓓ Ⓔ	19 Ⓐ Ⓑ Ⓒ Ⓓ Ⓔ	33 Ⓐ Ⓑ Ⓒ Ⓓ Ⓔ	47 Ⓐ Ⓑ Ⓒ Ⓓ Ⓔ	61 Ⓐ Ⓑ Ⓒ Ⓓ Ⓔ
6 Ⓐ Ⓑ Ⓒ Ⓓ Ⓔ	20 Ⓐ Ⓑ Ⓒ Ⓓ Ⓔ	34 Ⓐ Ⓑ Ⓒ Ⓓ Ⓔ	48 Ⓐ Ⓑ Ⓒ Ⓓ Ⓔ	62 Ⓐ Ⓑ Ⓒ Ⓓ Ⓔ
7 Ⓐ Ⓑ Ⓒ Ⓓ Ⓔ	21 Ⓐ Ⓑ Ⓒ Ⓓ Ⓔ	35 Ⓐ Ⓑ Ⓒ Ⓓ Ⓔ	49 Ⓐ Ⓑ Ⓒ Ⓓ Ⓔ	63 Ⓐ Ⓑ Ⓒ Ⓓ Ⓔ
8 Ⓐ Ⓑ Ⓒ Ⓓ Ⓔ	22 Ⓐ Ⓑ Ⓒ Ⓓ Ⓔ	36 Ⓐ Ⓑ Ⓒ Ⓓ Ⓔ	50 Ⓐ Ⓑ Ⓒ Ⓓ Ⓔ	64 Ⓐ Ⓑ Ⓒ Ⓓ Ⓔ
9 Ⓐ Ⓑ Ⓒ Ⓓ Ⓔ	23 Ⓐ Ⓑ Ⓒ Ⓓ Ⓔ	37 Ⓐ Ⓑ Ⓒ Ⓓ Ⓔ	51 Ⓐ Ⓑ Ⓒ Ⓓ Ⓔ	65 Ⓐ Ⓑ Ⓒ Ⓓ Ⓔ
10 Ⓐ Ⓑ Ⓒ Ⓓ Ⓔ	24 Ⓐ Ⓑ Ⓒ Ⓓ Ⓔ	38 Ⓐ Ⓑ Ⓒ Ⓓ Ⓔ	52 Ⓐ Ⓑ Ⓒ Ⓓ Ⓔ	66 Ⓐ Ⓑ Ⓒ Ⓓ Ⓔ
11 Ⓐ Ⓑ Ⓒ Ⓓ Ⓔ	25 Ⓐ Ⓑ Ⓒ Ⓓ Ⓔ	39 Ⓐ Ⓑ Ⓒ Ⓓ Ⓔ	53 Ⓐ Ⓑ Ⓒ Ⓓ Ⓔ	67 Ⓐ Ⓑ Ⓒ Ⓓ Ⓔ
12 Ⓐ Ⓑ Ⓒ Ⓓ Ⓔ	26 Ⓐ Ⓑ Ⓒ Ⓓ Ⓔ	40 Ⓐ Ⓑ Ⓒ Ⓓ Ⓔ	54 Ⓐ Ⓑ Ⓒ Ⓓ Ⓔ	68 Ⓐ Ⓑ Ⓒ Ⓓ Ⓔ
13 Ⓐ Ⓑ Ⓒ Ⓓ Ⓔ	27 Ⓐ Ⓑ Ⓒ Ⓓ Ⓔ	41 Ⓐ Ⓑ Ⓒ Ⓓ Ⓔ	55 Ⓐ Ⓑ Ⓒ Ⓓ Ⓔ	
14 Ⓐ Ⓑ Ⓒ Ⓓ Ⓔ	28 Ⓐ Ⓑ Ⓒ Ⓓ Ⓔ	42 Ⓐ Ⓑ Ⓒ Ⓓ Ⓔ	56 Ⓐ Ⓑ Ⓒ Ⓓ Ⓔ	

Skills Analysis: Quantitative

1 Ⓐ Ⓑ Ⓒ Ⓓ Ⓔ	15 Ⓐ Ⓑ Ⓒ Ⓓ Ⓔ	29 Ⓐ Ⓑ Ⓒ Ⓓ Ⓔ	43 Ⓐ Ⓑ Ⓒ Ⓓ Ⓔ	57 Ⓐ Ⓑ Ⓒ Ⓓ Ⓔ
2 Ⓐ Ⓑ Ⓒ Ⓓ Ⓔ	16 Ⓐ Ⓑ Ⓒ Ⓓ Ⓔ	30 Ⓐ Ⓑ Ⓒ Ⓓ Ⓔ	44 Ⓐ Ⓑ Ⓒ Ⓓ Ⓔ	58 Ⓐ Ⓑ Ⓒ Ⓓ Ⓔ
3 Ⓐ Ⓑ Ⓒ Ⓓ Ⓔ	17 Ⓐ Ⓑ Ⓒ Ⓓ Ⓔ	31 Ⓐ Ⓑ Ⓒ Ⓓ Ⓔ	45 Ⓐ Ⓑ Ⓒ Ⓓ Ⓔ	59 Ⓐ Ⓑ Ⓒ Ⓓ Ⓔ
4 Ⓐ Ⓑ Ⓒ Ⓓ Ⓔ	18 Ⓐ Ⓑ Ⓒ Ⓓ Ⓔ	32 Ⓐ Ⓑ Ⓒ Ⓓ Ⓔ	46 Ⓐ Ⓑ Ⓒ Ⓓ Ⓔ	60 Ⓐ Ⓑ Ⓒ Ⓓ Ⓔ
5 Ⓐ Ⓑ Ⓒ Ⓓ Ⓔ	19 Ⓐ Ⓑ Ⓒ Ⓓ Ⓔ	33 Ⓐ Ⓑ Ⓒ Ⓓ Ⓔ	47 Ⓐ Ⓑ Ⓒ Ⓓ Ⓔ	61 Ⓐ Ⓑ Ⓒ Ⓓ Ⓔ
6 Ⓐ Ⓑ Ⓒ Ⓓ Ⓔ	20 Ⓐ Ⓑ Ⓒ Ⓓ Ⓔ	34 Ⓐ Ⓑ Ⓒ Ⓓ Ⓔ	48 Ⓐ Ⓑ Ⓒ Ⓓ Ⓔ	62 Ⓐ Ⓑ Ⓒ Ⓓ Ⓔ
7 Ⓐ Ⓑ Ⓒ Ⓓ Ⓔ	21 Ⓐ Ⓑ Ⓒ Ⓓ Ⓔ	35 Ⓐ Ⓑ Ⓒ Ⓓ Ⓔ	49 Ⓐ Ⓑ Ⓒ Ⓓ Ⓔ	63 Ⓐ Ⓑ Ⓒ Ⓓ Ⓔ
8 Ⓐ Ⓑ Ⓒ Ⓓ Ⓔ	22 Ⓐ Ⓑ Ⓒ Ⓓ Ⓔ	36 Ⓐ Ⓑ Ⓒ Ⓓ Ⓔ	50 Ⓐ Ⓑ Ⓒ Ⓓ Ⓔ	64 Ⓐ Ⓑ Ⓒ Ⓓ Ⓔ
9 Ⓐ Ⓑ Ⓒ Ⓓ Ⓔ	23 Ⓐ Ⓑ Ⓒ Ⓓ Ⓔ	37 Ⓐ Ⓑ Ⓒ Ⓓ Ⓔ	51 Ⓐ Ⓑ Ⓒ Ⓓ Ⓔ	65 Ⓐ Ⓑ Ⓒ Ⓓ Ⓔ
10 Ⓐ Ⓑ Ⓒ Ⓓ Ⓔ	24 Ⓐ Ⓑ Ⓒ Ⓓ Ⓔ	38 Ⓐ Ⓑ Ⓒ Ⓓ Ⓔ	52 Ⓐ Ⓑ Ⓒ Ⓓ Ⓔ	66 Ⓐ Ⓑ Ⓒ Ⓓ Ⓔ
11 Ⓐ Ⓑ Ⓒ Ⓓ Ⓔ	25 Ⓐ Ⓑ Ⓒ Ⓓ Ⓔ	39 Ⓐ Ⓑ Ⓒ Ⓓ Ⓔ	53 Ⓐ Ⓑ Ⓒ Ⓓ Ⓔ	67 Ⓐ Ⓑ Ⓒ Ⓓ Ⓔ
12 Ⓐ Ⓑ Ⓒ Ⓓ Ⓔ	26 Ⓐ Ⓑ Ⓒ Ⓓ Ⓔ	40 Ⓐ Ⓑ Ⓒ Ⓓ Ⓔ	54 Ⓐ Ⓑ Ⓒ Ⓓ Ⓔ	68 Ⓐ Ⓑ Ⓒ Ⓓ Ⓔ
13 Ⓐ Ⓑ Ⓒ Ⓓ Ⓔ	27 Ⓐ Ⓑ Ⓒ Ⓓ Ⓔ	41 Ⓐ Ⓑ Ⓒ Ⓓ Ⓔ	55 Ⓐ Ⓑ Ⓒ Ⓓ Ⓔ	
14 Ⓐ Ⓑ Ⓒ Ⓓ Ⓔ	28 Ⓐ Ⓑ Ⓒ Ⓓ Ⓔ	42 Ⓐ Ⓑ Ⓒ Ⓓ Ⓔ	56 Ⓐ Ⓑ Ⓒ Ⓓ Ⓔ	

CHAPTER EIGHT

Sample Test

Science Knowledge

Select the one best answer from the alternatives given. There may be three, four, or five alternatives.

BIOLOGY

time—25 minutes

1. Osmosis is the process whereby molecules are moved across a semipermeable membrane from a region of high concentration to a region of lower concentration. Which of the following is the name of the process by which molecules are moved across a cell membrane against a concentration gradient through the expenditure of energy?
   A) diffusion   B) active transport   C) reverse osmosis   D) differential permeability

2. Which of the following glandular secretions passes into the circulatory system?
   A) pepsin   B) trypsin   C) ptyalin   D) insulin
   E) all of the above

3. Mesoderm is the primary germ layer which gives rise to muscles. Which of the following structures is *not* of mesodermal origin?
   A) stomach   B) spleen   C) blood cells   D) bones

4. When more than two stimuli are given to a muscle a partial merging of all the contractions may occur. This happens when the stimuli follow each other in rapid succession and the contractions take place before relaxation is completed. Contractions that are steadily sustained with no relaxation taking place between stimuli are known as
   A) tonus   B) tetany   C) "all or none" contractions   D) twitches

5. Structures exhibiting similarities attributable to common genetic and embryonic origins are
   A) similar structures   B) analogous structures   C) homologous structures   D) parallel structures

6. In a laboratory experiment a subject is made to hyperventilate. If the subject's blood pH is measured both before and immediately after hyperventilating
   A) no noticeable difference will be observed
   B) the pH will be lower after hyperventilating
   C) the pH will be higher after hyperventilating

213

7. The diagram at right illustrates a typical neuron. Impulses from other neurons are picked up by
   A) 1 B) 2 C) 3 D) 4

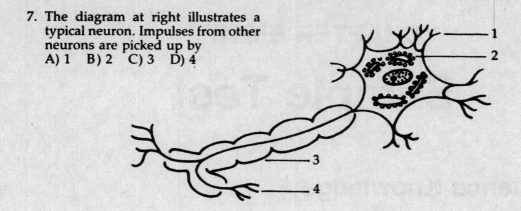

8. Which of the following movements are caused by flexors?
   A) opening the fists
   B) straightening the legs
   C) raising the head
   D) bending the arms at the elbow

9. Vigorous exercise usually causes muscle fatigue. Which of the following is a primary cause of muscle fatigue?
   A) ATP is used up
   B) lactic acid is accumulated in the muscle
   C) oxygen is used up, leaving an excess of carbon dioxide
   D) ADP accumulates in the muscle in excessive quantities

10. Which of the following is the result of the anaerobic breakdown of glucose?
    A) lactate B) pyruvate C) ethanol D) CO_2

11. Hemophilia is a bleeding disorder transmitted through a sex-linked recessive gene. Hemophilia
    A) can only be inherited by males
    B) can only be inherited by females
    C) can be inherited by males only if both parents are hemophiliacs
    D) can be inherited by females only if the mother is a carrier and the father is hemophiliac

12. Cilia and flagella have the same fibrillar arrangement in all organisms. The correct number of pairs of tubules is
    A) 7 outer, 2 inner
    B) 7 outer, 3 inner
    C) 9 outer, 2 inner
    D) 11 outer, 3 inner

13. "The rabbit died" was a popular way of letting women know of positive pregnancy test results. Present-day pregnancy tests are based on the chemical detection of
    A) estrogen B) progesterone C) LH D) chorionic gonadotropin

14. The main function of the large intestine is
    A) completion of the digestive process
    B) absorption of water
    C) absorption of nutrients
    D) breaking down of foods

15. A cell was examined and found to contain many Golgi bodies and a large quantity of rough endoplasmic reticulum. We would be justified in hypothesizing that the cell is involved in
    A) protein synthesis and exportation
    B) respiration
    C) fat storage
    D) ATP formation

16. During what stage of its development does the embryo consist of a hollow 1-cell-thick sphere of cells?
    A) morula B) blastula C) gastrula D) cleavage

17. Which of the following would be most likely to disturb a person's sense of balance?
    A) puncturing of both eardrums
    B) a blow on the head
    C) a malfunction of the sensory neurons of the inner ear
    D) temporary blindness caused by stepping out from a very dark room to a very brightly lit area

18. In order to lower blood pressure, a physician may give a patient a drug which
    A) thins out the blood   C) dilates the arterioles
    B) thickens the blood   D) decreases lymphatic drainage

19. The human male produces four gametes (sperm) from each sex cell during meiosis while the female only produces one gamete (egg) and three polar bodies. Which of the following best explains this disparity in gamete production?
    A) the egg contains more genetic material
    B) the sperm is haploid
    C) the egg is more mobile than the sperm
    D) the egg contains stored food

20. Eucaryotic animal and plant cells and animal viruses have a certain characteristic in common: they all
    A) reproduce mitotically
    B) are subject to mutations
    C) produce their own proteins
    D) contain DNA
    E) have nuclei

21. Human gametes are haploid in number of chromosomes as a result of reduction division. Which of the following processes restores the diploid number?
    A) fertilization   B) mitosis   C) duplication   C) meiosis   E) cleavage

22. The human brain is divided into two hemispheres, with the right hemisphere controlling the left half of the body and the left hemisphere controlling the right half of the body. The two cerebral hemispheres are connected by the
    A) anterior commissure   B) peduncle   C) corpus callosum   D) frontal ganglion

23. The pH of gastric juice ranges between 0.9 and 1.5 due to the hydrochloric acid secreted by the gastric mucosa. This acidity inhibits the effect of
    A) ptyalin   B) rennin   C) pepsin   D) lipase

24. Which of the following correctly describes the path of the nerve impulse in a reflex arc?
    A) reception via efferent neurons, conduction by the afferent system, propagation to the central nervous system
    B) reception via afferent neurons, conduction via sensory fibers to the central nervous system, propagation to the efferent neurons
    C) reception by the sensory fibers, conduction to the central nervous system via afferent neurons, propagation to the efferent neurons
    D) reception by the afferent neurons, direct transmission to the efferent neurons

25. Enzymes act as catalysts to trigger certain reactions. The effect of enzymes is specific, and each enzyme triggers only that reaction for which it was intended. This specificity of enzymes is dependent upon
    A) the lowering by the enzyme of the required activation energy
    B) the shape (molecular structure) of the active site and the substrate
    C) the ability of enzymes to increase the reaction rate
    D) all of the above

26. The gene for round peas is recessive to the gene for wrinkled peas. Two plants are crossed and 50% of their offspring are round. If W represents the gene for wrinkled and w represents the gene for round, what was the genotype of the two original plants?
A) WW × ww   B) Ww × Ww   C) WW × Ww   D) ww × Ww

27. A heterotroph is an organism that cannot synthesize all the complex organic molecules needed for metabolism from simpler molecules such as H_2O and CO_2. Man and other heterotrophic organisms obtain the needed complex molecules from other living organisms. Which of the following would not be classified as a heterotroph?
A) an ant   B) yeasts   C) green algae
D) none of the above

28. A cell separated from the embryo at the very early stages of development may develop into a complete organism. This will not happen after formation of the primary germ layers. The process which prevents the cell from developing into a complete organism after the very early stages of embryonic development is
A) determination   B) gastrulation   C) cleavage   D) induction

29.

Which structure in the above diagram of a generalized animal cell would be most influenced by a decreased oxygen supply?
A) 1   B) 2   C) 3   D) 4

30. During which of the following is ATP *not* utilized by cells?
A) active transport   B) muscle contraction   C) glycolysis   D) none of these

31. Langerhans first described the beta cells within the islets of Langerhans in the pancreas. These cells produce insulin which affects the metabolism of glucose directly, and of fats and proteins indirectly. Insulin stimulates the absorption of glucose by the cells and helps in the conversion of glucose to glycogen. Which of the following would correctly describe the levels of blood sugar and insulin one to two hours after a rich meal?
A) the blood sugar level would be high and the insulin level would be low
B) both levels would be high
C) both levels would be low
D) the blood sugar level would be low and the insulin level would be high

32. A person is having digestive problems. When he tried a diet consisting primarily of fats he lost a great deal of weight. When he changed his diet to one of protein only he recovered from his symptoms. Which of the organs below is probably malfunctioning?
A) the pancreas   B) the stomach   C) the gallbladder   D) the liver

33. Some blood cells defend the organism against diseases by destroying bacteria. Which of the following is a method used to destroy the invading bacteria?
A) complement activation   B) feedback inhibition   C) exocytosis   D) phagocytosis

34. Mutations, sexual reproduction, and independent assortment have which desirable effect over populations?
A) they stabilize the number of individuals
B) they increase genetic variation
C) they simplify classification

35. The term which refers to organisms living on dead organisms or products of living organisms is
    A) parasitism   B) commensalism   C) saprophytism   D) parallelism

36. Different ecological niches favor different body types. Mobile organisms are predisposed by their environment to bilateral symmetry since left and right are not usually inherently different whereas front and back and up and down are qualitatively different. What type of symmetry would be expected from a free-floating organism?
    A) spherical   B) bilateral   C) asymmetrical

37. An action potential is propagated along an axon or muscle cell membrane by selective voltage-dependent changes in the permeabilities to which two ions?
    A) oxygen and hydrogen   C) sodium and potassium
    B) potassium and nitrogen   D) sodium and chlorine

38. Human erythrocytes have a life span of approximately 4 months. Which of the following is responsible for their removal and destruction?
    A) pancreas   B) lymph nodes   C) liver   D) lungs   E) tonsils

INORGANIC CHEMISTRY

time—30 minutes

1. Gases respond to changes in pressure, volume, and temperature according to the Ideal Gas Law, $PV = nrT$. Under which of the following single-condition changes would the behavior of the gas be most likely to deviate from that predicted by the Ideal Gas Law?
   A) a great increase in temperature
   B) a great increase in pressure
   C) a great increase in volume
   D) none of the above changes would result in deviation from the behavior predicted by $PV = nrT$

2. How many grams of $H_2PO_2^-$ are produced by the balanced equation below when 27 grams of water are used?

   $$P_4 + 3OH^- + 3H_2O \longrightarrow 3H_2PO_2^- + PH_3$$
   (molecular weight data: P = 31, H = 1, O = 16)

   A) 65   B) $1\frac{1}{4}$ C) $97\frac{1}{2}$ D) 195

3. Barium sulfite, $BaSO_3$, is not very soluble in water. Its solubility increases greatly as HCl is added. The reason for the increase in solubility as acid is added is that
   A) H_2SO_3 is a weak acid
   B) $BaCl_2$ is insoluble
   C) HCl is not completely dissociated
   D) $Ba(OH)_2$ is a weak base

4. Consider the following reaction:

   $$Al^{+++} + 3OH^- = Al(OH)_3$$

   What is the change in the oxidation number of aluminum?
   A) 0   B) +1   C) +3   D) −3

5. Into which of the following pH ranges does molar HCl fall?
   A) $2 \leqslant pH \leqslant 4$ B) $1 < pH \leqslant 2$ C) $0 < pH \leqslant 1$ D) 0

6. .2 liters of .1 molar NaCl are electrolyzed. How many moles of chlorine gas are produced by the time the OH^- concentration reaches .05 moles/liter?
   A) .005   B) .05   C) .01   D) .1

7. A sample of a gas occupies 500 ml at 1 atm and 27°C. What volume will it occupy at 1.5 atm and 77°C.
   A) 350 ml   B) 372 ml   C) 389 ml   D) 401 ml

8. Suppose the value for the equilibrium constant for

$$A + 2B \rightleftharpoons 2C$$

(where A and C are liquid and B is a gas) is .252. The equilibrium constant for

$$2C \rightleftharpoons A + 2B$$

is
A) −.252   B) .252   C) 3.968   D) 2.748

9. The neutron has an important role in binding the nucleus. Neutron-proton attractions are stronger than neutron-neutron or proton-proton attractions. It has been postulated that protons and neutrons are bound by the exchange of a nuclear particle called a π meson. Lighter elements have a neutron-proton ratio of approximately 1. With increasing atomic number more and more protons are packed into a tiny nucleus, the electrostatic repulsion forces increase greatly, and an increasing excess of neutrons is needed to diminish their effect. Nuclei that have too high a neutron-proton ratio are unstable. An isotope with too high a neutron-proton ratio can gain stability by
   A) emitting a α particle   C) emitting a γ radiation
   B) emitting a β particle   D) absorbing neutrons

10. According to the Brönsted theory, which of the following can act as either an acid or a base?
    A) HI   B) PO_4^{---} C) $HSeO_4^-$ D) all of these   E) none of these

11. What volume of .063 N NaOH is required to neutralize 36 ml of .1 M H_2SO_4?
    A) 36 ml   B) 57 ml   C) 63 ml   D) 114 ml   E) 228 ml

12. When an automobile battery is being charged it is
    A) a voltaic cell   B) a Damell cell   C) a dry cell   D) a galvanic cell   E) an electrolytic cell

13. Suppose that the solubility of XY is .1 mole/liter. What is the solubility product for

$$XY \; (s) \rightleftharpoons X^+ + Y^-$$

A) 1×10^1 B) 1×10^{-1} C) 1×10^2 D) 1×10^{-2}

14. Which of the following causes the greatest lowering of the freezing point?
    A) .5 M NaCl   B) .5 M CH_3COONa C) .5 M KCl   D) .5 M $CaCl_2$

15. A flask contains 2 grams H_2 and 16 grams O_2. What part of the total pressure is the partial pressure of oxygen?
    A) ⅓ of the total   B) ½ of the total   C) ⅛ of the total   D) ⁸/₉ of the total

16. Find the potential for the equation

$$Fe^{++} + Ce^{++++} \longrightarrow Fe^{+++} + Ce^{+++}$$

if the electrode potentials for the half-reactions are:

$$Fe^{++} \; Fe^{+++} + e^-, \; E° = -.77 \; v$$
$$Ce^{+++} \; Ce^{++++} + e^-, \; E° = -1.61 \; v$$

A) $-.84$ v   B) $+.84$ v   C) -2.38 v   D) $+2.38$ v

17. Many of the physical properties of certain covalent compounds reflect the polar nature of their molecules—among these are surface tension, melting point, bond energy, and dipole moment. A molecule with positive and negative centers located at places other than the center of the molecule is called a dipole. The dipole moment of which of the following is *not* zero?
A) CCl_4 B) O_2 C) HCl   D) all have zero dipole moment

18.

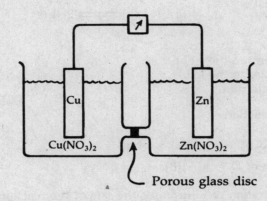

The voltaic cell above employs the copper-zinc reaction:

$$Cu^{++} + Zn \longrightarrow Cu + Zn^{++}$$

The flow of ions through the porous glass disc during cell reaction is:

If the porous glass disc were removed and the solutions allowed to mix freely
A) there would be a reversal in the direction of current flow
B) there would be an increase in the magnitude of the current
C) there would be no change in the direction and magnitude of current flow
D) the magnitude of the current will decrease to zero

19. The ionization constant for ammonia is 1.8×10^{-5}. Determine the concentration of hydroxide ions in a solution made by dissolving .02 mole of ammonium chloride in 100 ml of .15 M ammonia. (Assume that the addition of the solid does not change the volume of the solution.)
A) 1.23×10^{-5} B) 1.35×10^{-5} C) 1.8×10^{-5} D) 2.4×10^{-5}

20. An ideal gas is one whose behavior is described by the gas laws: Boyle's Law, Charles' Law, Dalton's Law, etc. Which of the following is an assumption of ideal gases in terms of the kinetic theory?
A) molecules collide without loss of energy
B) molecules have high attraction for each other

C) molecules occupy no volume.
D) all of the above

21. A solution is .1 M in Cl^- and .1 M in $C_2O_4^{--}$. If solid silver nitrate is gradually added to the solution, which will precipitate first?

K_{sp} of AgCl = 1.7×10^{-10} K_{sp} of Ag_2CrO_4 = 1.9×10^{-12}

A) AgCl   C) they will precipitate at the same time
B) Ag_2CrO_4 D) neither will precipitate

22. In any cubic lattice (simple, face-centered, or body-centered), a corner point in a unit cell is also a corner point of, and shared by, how many *other* unit cells?
A) 1   B) 3   C) 4   D) 7   E) 8

23. Increasing the pressure on the system

$$H_2(g) + I_2(g) \rightleftharpoons 2HI\,(g)$$

will
A) shift the equilibrium to the right
B) shift the equilibrium to the left
C) not affect the equilibrium

24. In the hypothetical reaction

$$A(g) + B(g) + 2C(g) \longrightarrow D(g) + 3E(g)$$

rate of formation of D = $k[A][B]^2$

doubling the concentration of B increases the rate of the reaction by a factor of
A) 1 (not affected)   B) 2   C) 4   D) 8

ORGANIC CHEMISTRY

time—30 minutes

1. Which of the following represents a resonance hybrid of $CH_3-C\equiv N-\overset{\|}{\underset{\|}{O}}=$?

A) $CH_3-C=N-\overset{\|}{\underset{\|}{O}}$ B) $CH_3-\overset{\|}{C}=N=\overset{\|}{O}=$

C) $CH_3-C=N=\overset{\|}{\underset{\|}{O}}=$ D) $CH_3-\overset{\|}{\underset{\|}{C}}-\overset{\|}{\underset{\|}{N}}-\overset{\|}{\underset{\|}{O}}=$

E) $CH_3-N=C=\overset{\|}{\underset{\|}{O}}=$

2. Which of the following compounds has the largest dipole moment?
A) CH_3Cl B) CH_3I C) CH_3Br D) CH_3F

3. How many pi bonds are present in the compound $CH_3CH_2CH_2CH_2CHO$?
A) zero   B) one   C) two   D) three   E) four

4. Which of the following compounds can have stereoisomers?
A) $CH_3CH_2CHClCH_2CH_3$ B) $CH_3CH_2CH(CH_3)CH_2CH_3$
C) $CH_2ClCH_2CH_2CH_2CH_3$ D) $CH_3CHClCH_2CH_2CH_3$
E) $CH_3CH_2CH_2CCl_2CH_3$

5. Racemic mixtures can be separated by
A) using a nuclear magnetic resonance spectrophotometer
B) forming diastereomers and using their difference in solubility
C) using the degree to which each compound can rotate plane-polarized light
D) evaporation for each isomer would usually have a sufficient difference in vapor pressure
E) using the difference in the rate of reaction of each isomer

6. The correct name for $CH_3CH(CH_3)CH(CH_3)CH_2CH_2CH_3$ is
A) nonane   B) 5,6-dimethylnonane   C) 2,3-dimethylnonane   D) 2,3-dimethylheptane
E) isoheptane

7. The main product from the reaction

$$CH_3CH(CH_3)CH_2CH_3 + Br_2 \xrightarrow[\text{gas phase}]{\text{uv}}$$

is
A) $CH_2BrCH(CH_3)CH_2CH_3$ B) $CH_3CBr(CH_3)CH_2CH_3$
C) $CH_3CH(CH_3)CHBrCH_3$ D) $CH_3CH(CH_3)CH_2CH_2Br$
E) $CH_3CH(CH_2Br)CHBrCH_3$

8. Which of the following free radicals is the most stable?
A) $\cdot CH_2CH(CH_3)CH_3$ B) $CH_3CH(CH_3)CH_2$
C) $CH_3\dot{C}(CH_3)CH_3$ D) $CH_3CH(CH_2)CH_3$

9. The correct name for $CH_2{=}CHCH(CH_3)CH_3$ is
A) 3-methyl-1-butene   B) 2-methyl-3-butene
C) 2-methyl-4-butene   D) 3-methyl-1-pentene
E) 1-pentene

10. Which of the following carbonium ions is the most stable?
A) $\overset{\oplus}{C}H_2C(CH_3)_2CH(CH_3)CH_3$ B) $CH_3\overset{\oplus}{C}(CH_3)_2CH(CH_3)CH_3$
C) $CH_3C(CH_3)_2\overset{\oplus}{C}(CH_3)CH_3$ D) $CH_3C(CH_3)_2CH(\overset{\oplus}{C}H_2)CH_3$
E) $CH_3C(CH_3)_2CH(CH_3)\overset{\oplus}{C}H_2$

11. Which of the following compounds may have cis-trans isomerism?

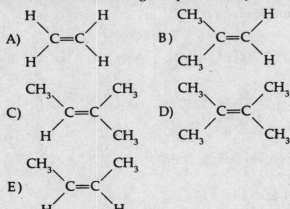

12. The structure of ortho-toluidine is

A) [structure: benzene ring with NH₂ and NH₂ groups ortho]

B) [structure: benzene ring with CH₃ and CH₃ groups ortho]

C) [structure: benzene ring with CH₃ and NH₂ groups meta]

D) [structure: benzene ring with NH₂ and NH₂ groups meta]

E) [structure: benzene ring with CH₃ and NH₂ groups ortho]

13. When HI reacts with $CH_2\!=\!CHCH_3$, the intermediate carbonium ion that is obtained is

A) $CH_3\overset{\oplus}{C}HCH_3$ B) $\overset{\oplus}{C}H_2CH_2CH_3$ C) $CH_2(I)\overset{\oplus}{C}HCH_3$ D) $\overset{\oplus}{C}H_2CH(I)CH_3$

E) $CH_2\overset{\oplus}{C}CH_3$

14. The shape about a carbon atom in benzene is best described as
    A) linear   B) trigonal planar   C) tetrahedral   D) trigonal bipyramidal   E) octahedral

15. When one bromine adds to 1,4-dimethylbenzene to produce bromo-1,4-dimethylbenzene, how many different compounds can form?
    A) zero   B) one   C) two   D) three   E) four

16. The correct name for $CH_3CH(OH)CH(CH_3)CH_3$ is
    A) 2-pentanol   B) 2-methyl-3-pentanol   C) 3-methyl-2-pentanol   D) 2-methyl-3-butanol
    E) 3-methyl-2-butanol

17. The main organic product obtained from the reaction

$$CH_3CH_2CH_2OH \;+\; \text{alkaline } KMnO_4$$

is

A) $CH_3\underset{\underset{O}{\|}}{C}CH_3$ B) $CH_3CH_2\overset{\overset{O}{\|}}{C}\!-\!H$ C) $CH_3CH_2C\!\!\diagdown^{\displaystyle O}_{\displaystyle O}$

D) $CH_3CH = CH_2$ E) $CH_3CH_2CH_2OCH_2CH_2CH_3$

18. The main organic product obtained from the reaction

$$CH_3CH(OH)C(CH_3)_2CH_3 \;+\; \overset{\text{conc.}}{H_2SO_4} \;+\; \text{heat}$$

is
A) $CH_2\!=\!CHC(CH_3)_2CH_3$ B) $CH_3C(CH_3)\!=\!C(CH_3)CH_3$
C) $CH_3CH\!=\!C(CH_3)_2CH_3$ D) $CH_3CH_2C(CH_3)_2\!=\!CH_2$
E) $CH_3CH\!=\!C(CH_3)CH_3$

19. Which of the following would have the higher boiling point?

A) $CH_3CH_2CH_2CH_3$ B) $CH_3CH_2CH_2C\!\!\diagup^{\displaystyle O}_{\displaystyle H}$

C) $CH_3CH_2CH_2CH_2OH$ D) $CH_3CH=CHCH_3$

E) $CH_3-C-CH_2CH_3$
$\qquad\quad \underset{O}{\overset{\|}{}}$

20. What is the name of $CH_3CH_2C \underset{H}{\overset{O}{\diagup\!\!\!\backslash}}$?

A) 1-propanol   B) propanal   C) propanoic acid   D) propanone   E) n-propyl ether

21. The organic product obtained from the reaction

$$CH_3CH_2CCH_3 + HCN$$
$$\underset{O}{\overset{\|}{}}$$

is

A) $CH_3CH_2C(CN)CH_3$
$\qquad\quad \underset{OH}{|}$

B) $CH_3CH_2CHCH_3$
$\qquad\quad \underset{OH}{|}$

C) $CH_3CH_2CHCH_3$
$\qquad\quad \underset{C\equiv N}{|}$

D) $CH_3CH_2C \underset{OCH_3}{\overset{CN}{\diagup\!\!\!\backslash}}$

E) $CH_3CH_2C \underset{NH_2}{\overset{O}{\diagup\!\!\!\backslash}}$

22. What is the main organic product obtained from the following reaction?

$$CH_3CH_2CH_3 \xrightarrow[\text{ether}]{CH_3Mg_3Br} \xrightarrow{H_2O}$$
$$\qquad\quad \underset{O}{\overset{\|}{}}$$

A) $CH_3CA_2C \underset{BrCH_3}{\overset{O}{\diagup\!\!\!\backslash}}$

B) $CH_3CH_2CHCH_3$
$\qquad\quad \underset{OCH_3}{|}$

C) $CH_3CH_2CHCH_3$
$\qquad\quad \underset{MgX}{|}$

D) $CH_3CH_2O^+-O-CHCH_2CH_3$
$\qquad\quad\quad \underset{CH_3}{|} \quad \underset{CH_3}{|}$

E) $CH_3CH_2CHCH_3$
$\qquad\quad\quad \underset{OH}{|}$

23. NaOH would react more readily with a hydrogen in which of the following compounds?

A) CH_3CCH_3
$\qquad \underset{O}{\overset{\|}{}}$

B) 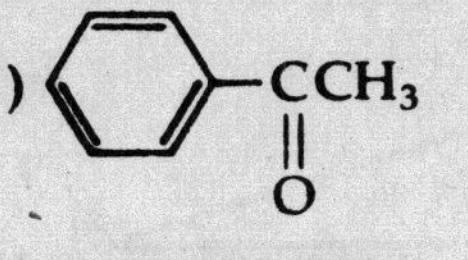 $\langle\!\!\!\bigcirc\!\!\!\rangle\!-CCH_3$
$\qquad\qquad \underset{O}{\overset{\|}{}}$

C) $CH_3CH=CHCH_3$

D) CH_3OCH_3

E) $CH_3CCH_2CCH_3$
$\qquad \underset{O}{\overset{\|}{}} \quad \underset{O}{\overset{\|}{}}$

24. The best name for the compound 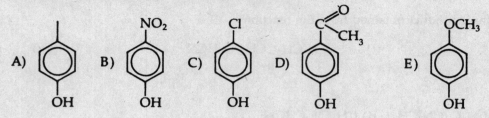 is

   A) m-isopropylphenol   B) p-t-butylphenol
   C) 1-t-butyl-3-hydroxybenzene   D) 3-t-butylphenol
   E) trimethylphenyl alcohol

25. Which of the following phenols is more acidic?

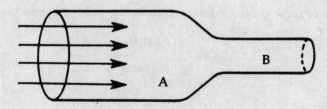

PHYSICS

time—50 minutes

1. Which of the following changes results from the emission of a beta particle from the nucleus of an atom?
   A) the atomic number decreases by 1   C) the atomic number increases by 1
   B) the mass number decreases by 1   D) the mass number increases by 1

2.

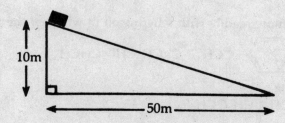

   In the figure above, a pipe narrows as shown. If a fluid is flowing through the pipe and the velocity of the fluid is the same at points A and B, then
   A) Bernoulli's Equation does not apply
   B) the pressure at A is greater than at B
   C) the pressure at B is greater than at A
   D) the pressure at A is equal to the pressure at B.

3.

A block of mass 10 kg slides down the inclined plane shown in the figure at the bottom of page 224. If the block starts from rest and its final speed is 5 m/sec, how much energy was converted to heat?
A) 50 joules   B) 250 joules   C) 855 joules   D) 980 joules

4. If an object is thrown upward with an initial velocity of 96 ft/sec, it will return to the original height from which it was thrown in
A) 3 seconds   B) 6 seconds   C) 9 seconds   D) 12 seconds

5.

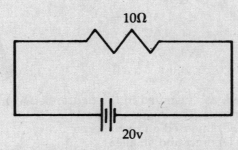

A 10-ohm resistor is connected as shown in the figure above. If additional resistors were connected in parallel with the one shown
A) the current would increase
B) the voltage drop across the original resistor would be less
C) the voltage would decrease
D) the total resistance would increase

6.

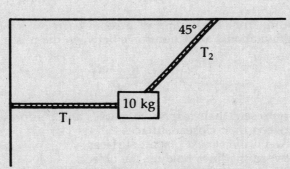

The figure shows a 10-kg object supported by two cords. What is the tension (T_1) on the horizontal cord?
A) 10 n   B) 10 $\sqrt{2}$ n   C) 98 n   D) 98 $\sqrt{2}$ n

7.

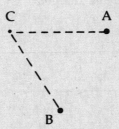

Two charged particles, A and B, are located each 1 meter away from point C. If each of the two particles is removed an additional 2 feet further from point C along their same directions, the ratio of the new to the original electrical force between them is
A) 1:9   B) 1:4   C) 1:3   D) 1:2   E) cannot be determined from the information given

8.

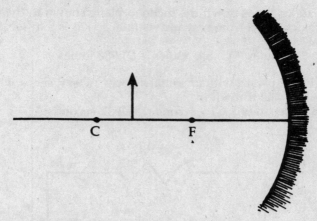

An object has been placed, as illustrated in the figure, between the focus and the center of curvature of a concave mirror. The image will be
A) erect and larger   C) inverted and smaller
B) inverted and larger   D) erect and smaller

9. A bullet is fired from a gun aimed 45° above the horizontal. Neglecting air friction, which of the following statements is true?
A) the acceleration of the bullet is greater when it is going up.
B) the acceleration of the bullet is greater when it is going down
C) the acceleration depends on the gun's muzzle velocity
D) none of these

10. Two objects are hung from the ceiling of a room each by a very thin plastic line. The magnitude of the gravitational attraction force between them is given by

$$F = G \frac{m_1 \cdot m_2}{r^2}$$

where m_1 and m_2 represent their respective masses and r^2 represents
A) the distance between their closest surfaces
B) the distance between their most distant surfaces
C) the distance between the lines holding the objects
D) the sum of the distances from the floor of the two objects

11. A positive-charge body is brought near an uncharged electroscope. The electroscope is grounded for a moment and later the charged body is removed. The electroscope is now
A) negatively charged   B) positively charged   C) uncharged

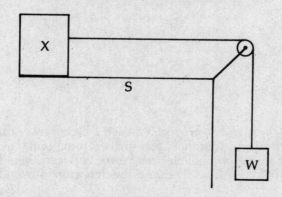

12. A body, X, is drawn across a surface, S, by tension on a cord as shown in the figure above. If the mass of X is 20 kg and the coefficient of kinetic friction between X and S is .5, what mass of W will produce an acceleration of 2 m/sec on X?
   A) 15 kg   B) 24 kg   C) 30 kg   D) 36 kg

13. A rock weighs 43 newtons in air. When submerged in water it weighs 21.5 newtons. What is the specific gravity of this rock?
   A) .5   B) 1.0   C) 2.0   D) 21.5

14. In order to shield experimenters from a type of radiation, a 1-foot-thick wall is built. If this wall stops 50% of the radiation, a similar 4-foot-thick wall would stop what part of the original radiation?
   A) 75%   B) 93.75%   C) 100%   D) 200%

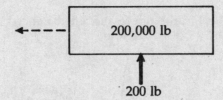

15. A 200-pound force is applied on 200,000-pound object as shown in the figure above. If the object moves 10 feet in the direction shown by the broken line, the amount of work done by the 200-pound force is
   A) 0   B) 2000 ft-lbs   C) 2×10^6 ft-lbs   D) 4×10^8 ft-lbs

16. An object is dropped (from rest) from the top of a tower. Which of the following is needed in order to determine the height of the tower?
   A) the time the object takes to fall   C) both A and B
   B) the mass of the object   D) none of these

17. Three resistances of 6 Ω, 6 Ω, and 3 Ω are wired so that their equivalent resistance is 6 Ω. Which of the following will result in the correct equivalent resistance?

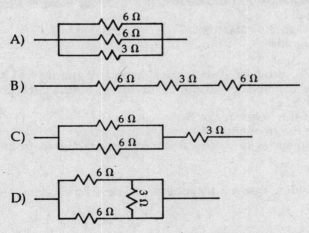

18. An object is falling starting from rest. How far does the object travel during the 2nd second of its fall?
   A) 16 ft   B) 32 ft   C) 48 ft   D) 64 ft   E) 80 ft

19. Isotopes of a given element have
   A) different atomic numbers   C) different number of electrons
   B) different mass numbers   D) different nuclear charges

20. A moving object is acted upon by a constant force. The object is moving
    A) with constant velocity   C) with a jerking motion
    B) with constant displacement   D) with constant acceleration

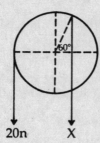

20n   X

21. If the freely revolving wheel in the figure above is balanced, find the value of X.
    A) 20 n   B) $20\sqrt{2}$ n   C) $20\sqrt{3}$ n   D) 40 n

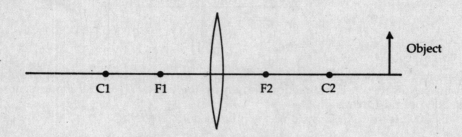

C1   F1   F2   C2

Object

22. If F_1 and F_2 represent the two foci of the thin lens in the figure above, the image of the object shown will be
    A) to the left of F_1 C) between the lens and F_2
    B) between F_1 and the lens   D) to the right of F_2

23. A parallel-plate capacitor has a capacitance of 3 picofarads. If a sheet of glass is slipped between the plates, its capacitance will be
    A) 0 picofarads   C) more than 3 picofarads
    B) less than 3 picofarads   D) 3 picofarads

24. Two vibrating tuning forks, A and B, produce 10 beats per second. If tuning fork C is substituted for tuning fork A, the new combination (B and C) produces 15 beats per second. Which of the following statements is true?
    A) the frequency of A is greater than the frequency of B
    B) the frequency of B is greater than the frequency of A
    C) the relationship between the frequencies of A and B cannot be established from the information given

25. Two blocks of different masses are sliding down a frictionless incline. The acceleration on the heavier one is
    A) greater than on the lighter one
    B) less than on the lighter one
    C) equal to the acceleration on the lighter one

26.

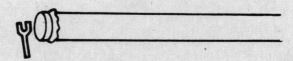

A tuning fork (page 228) is used to drive a membrane which in turn produces waves traveling through a tube. While the tuning fork makes one vibration, the wave travels
A) about 1100 feet   C) the full length of the tube
B) one wavelength   D) half of the length of the tube

27. Sound travels at different speeds through different substances. Through which of the following can sound *not* be transmitted?
A) gas   C) crystal solid
B) supercooled liquid   D) vacuum

28. At a certain temperature, more heat added to a liquid does not increase the temperature of the liquid. This heat is the
A) heat of sublimation of the liquid
B) heat of vaporization of the liquid
C) specific heat of the liquid
D) molar heat of fusion of the liquid

29. For our convenience, we have developed conversion factors interrelating different units, such as 1 yard = 36 inches, or even different systems of measurement, such as 1 inch = 2.54 centimeters. These conversion factors are based upon the units converted and are independent of external factors. One "weird" conversion factor is 1 kg = 2.2 lbs; it establishes an equality between a quantity of mass (kg) and a quantity of force (lbs). This conversion
A) holds true only if the gravitational acceleration is 9.8 m/sec
B) holds true everywhere
C) holds true only in Europe
D) holds true only in America

30. A planet of equal density but half the radius of Earth would have what fraction of the gravity of Earth?
A) 1/8   B) 1/6   C) 1/4   D) 1/2

31. Emission of successive alpha and beta particles will transform $_{94}Pu^{244}$ into
A) $_{90}Th^{232}$ B) $_{92}U^{240}$ C) $_{93}Np^{240}$ D) $_{95}Am^{244}$

32. Which of the following is an accurate description of simple harmonic motion?
A) the object is always accelerating
B) the object is moving with constant velocity
C) the object moves on a circular path
D) the object is acted upon by a force proportional to but opposite in direction to its displacement.

33. The siren of an approaching ambulance has a pitch higher than· when the ambulance is getting farther and farther away. This phenomenon is known as the Doppler effect and may also be used to determine
A) the location of black holes
B) whether a particular star is getting closer or farther from us
C) the density of stars
D) the distance to a particular star

34. The magnifying power of a thin lens is 10 diopters. If an object is placed 10 centimeters outside the focus, its image will be
A) 10 centimeters from the lens   C) 40 centimeters from the lens
B) 20 centimeters from the lens   D) nonexistent

35. A spring resting on a frictionless surface and tied on one end is suddenly compressed and released. The wave described by the end of the spring is
A) transverse   B) bias   C) longitudinal   D) none of these

36.

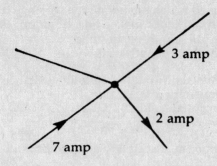

Four wires are brought together at a point. If three of the wires carry the indicated current, the fourth wire carries
A) no current   B) 12 amp   C) 6 amp   D) 8 amp

37.

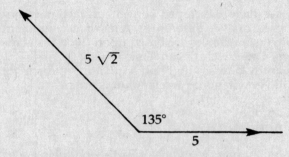

What is the magnitude of the resultant vector above?
A) 5   B) $5\sqrt{2}$ C) $5\sqrt{3}$ D) 10

38. If light passes obliquely from one medium to another of lower refractive index
A) the light ray will be refracted toward the normal
B) the light ray will be refracted away from the normal
C) the angle of refraction will equal the angle of incidence
D) the ray will be reflected

Science Problems

The following questions are in groups of three, with each group preceded by descriptive material. First study the material; then select the one best answer to each question in the group.

time—85 minutes

A printed circuit board is made according to the schematic at right. Either resistors or wire connectors may be plugged in at positions A through H.

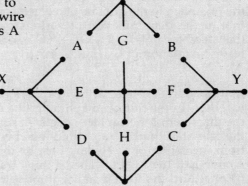

1. If 10-ohm resistors are plugged in at positions A, B, C, and D, and wire connectors (no resistance) are plugged in at the remaining positions, the equivalent resistance across X-Y is, in ohms,
   A) 0   B) 10   C) 20   D) 40

2. If 20-ohm resistors are plugged in at positions A, B, C, D, E, and F, and the remaining positions are left open, the equivalent resistance across X-Y is, in ohms,
   A) 10   B) 20   C) 30   D) none of these

3. If an 80-v dc source is connected across X-Y, the current in the circuit described in the preceding problem is
   A) 3 amps   B) 4 amps   C) 6 amps   D) 12 amps

   Some muscles are not attached from bone to bone, but from bone to skin and, in some cases, even from one part of the skin to another. In man, the latter muscles appear mainly in the face, where they are employed in speech and facial expression.

4. Scientific observation of facial muscles shows that when they are stimulated repeatedly in the absence of free oxygen, they fatigue more rapidly than when an abundance of free oxygen is present. Also, when the drug monoiodoacetic acid—a citric acid inhibitor—is applied to a muscle, the muscle contracts in the typical manner. This suggests that
   A) oxidation is the immediate source of energy for muscle contraction
   B) glycolysis is the immediate source of energy for muscle contraction
   C) neither oxidation nor glycolysis is the immediate source of energy for muscle contraction
   D) accelerated oxidation inhibits glycolysis under anaerobic conditions in muscle contraction

5. Paralysis of the muscles involved in speech and facial expression would involve damage to what division of the nervous system?
   A) the cervical spinal ganglia, one through seven
   B) the sympathetic nerve fibers of the neck and face
   C) the afferent nerve trunks within the face and tongue
   D) the seventh and twelfth cranial nerves, derived from the brain

6. Considering the manner in which facial muscles are attached to the body, which of the following terms would *not* apply directly to the anatomical and physiological description of these muscles?
   A) point of origin   C) point of articulation
   B) mode of action   D) point of insertion

   The cells of higher animals obtain their energy from the burning of foods in a process called "respiration." The end products of the process of respiration are carbon dioxide, water, and energy.

7. The respiratory quotient (R.Q.) is the ratio of the volume of carbon dioxide produced by the organism to the volume of oxygen consumed ($CO_2:O_2$). The R.Q. is a valuable diagnostic tool in the determination of various pathological conditions. In the oxidation of glucose (balanced formula: $C_6H_{12}O_6 + 6O_2 \rightarrow 6H_2O + 6CO_2$) the R.Q. is exactly 1. Find the R.Q. for the oxidation of $C_{51}H_{98}O_6$, a fat.
   A) .02   B) .70   C) 1.35   D) 2.8

8. In most active tissues, where respiration occurs at a rapid rate, the capillaries are very close together. In the human diaphragm, the distance between adjacent capillaries is about twice the diameter of the capillary itself. Assuming that all capillaries are the same diameter, and the cells are situated exactly midpoint between the capillaries, a molecule of oxygen diffusing from the center of a capillary has, by the time it reaches the cell wall, already gone.
   A) one-half the total distance it must travel in order to reach the cells at midpoint
   B) one-third the total distance it must travel in order to reach the cells at midpoint
   C) one-fourth the total distance it must travel in order to reach the midpoint
   D) one-fourth the total distance it must travel in order to reach the other capillary

9. To determine the R.Q. for the brain, a dye visible when mixed with blood (such as methylene blue) is injected into the jugular vein and the time elapsed between injection and the appearance of the dye in the carotid artery is noted. During that interval the dye has traveled through all of the following vessels *except*
   A) the pulmonary vein   C) the superior vena cava
   B) the left ventricle   D) the inferior vena cava

A rock weighing 42 lbs is suspended from a cable and completely submerged in a tank of water in such a way that it touches neither the side nor the bottom of the tank. Water weighs 62.4 lbs per cubic foot

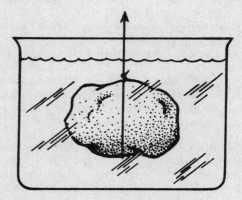

10. The tension in the cable holding the rock is 20 lbs. Find the volume of the rock in cubic feet.
    A) .25   B) .35   C) .75   D) 1.0

11. If the tank is filled to the brim with water it weighs 2 tons before putting the rock in it. When the rock is immersed in the water some water spills; the cable is then released so that it no longer supports the rock and the rock is allowed to rest on the bottom of the tank. Find the combined weight of the tank, the water in the tank, and the rock in the water.
    A) 2022 lbs   B) 4020 lbs   C) 4022 lbs   D) 4042 lbs

12. Suppose a piece of wood weighing 10 lbs is allowed to float on the tank filled with water described in the preceding problem (some water still spills over). The weight of the tank with its content is affected in the following manner by the presence of the wood
A) increased by 10 lbs
B) increased, but by less than 10 lbs
C) decreased
D) unchanged

The graph at right shows the results of an experiment on the growth of Salmonella typhi in closed containers under two different temperatures. The containers were exposed and then closed and placed at the required temperatures. The number of colonies in the containers were counted at periodic intervals and the average number of colonies per container for each of the two temperature groups were plotted on the graph. The continuous lines on the graphs are the "least squares" curves best fit to the data thus obtained.

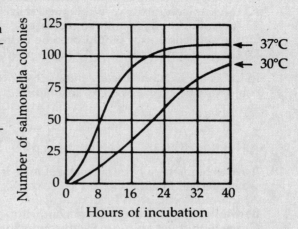

13. The statement "differences in the rate of increase at the two temperatures are due to differences in the rates of reproduction" is
A) a fact
B) contradicted by the evidence on the graph
C) a conclusion
D) a conjecture

14. The 37°C curve appears almost flat in the region from 28 to 40 hours. One possible explanation for this is that the death rate
A) is decreasing
B) is constant
C) is increasing
D) equals the reproductive rate

15. The number of colonies of salmonella which could be expected to be found at 32 hours in a culture grown at 34°C is
A) 80
B) 100
C) 110
D) impossible to predict

Pure silicon or germanium crystals are not conductors of electricity. All of the electrons present in each atom's valence shell are involved in forming covalent bonds with neighboring atoms in the diamond-type crystal lattice. If an arsenic atom is inserted in the lattice replacing either a silicon or germanium atom, it uses four of its five valence shell electrons in forming bonds to its four neighbors. With its valence shell thus filled, the extra electron is promoted out of the valence shell and into one of the higher orbitals. In this higher-energy orbital the electron is not held very strongly by the arsenic and is more or less free to travel about in the lattice in a network of overlapping vacant orbitals surrounding the silicon or germanium atoms. Under the influence of an electric field in the solid, the electron will migrate toward the positive pole. Any Group IV element can thus be "doped" with a Group V element—this combination is called an *n-type semiconductor* to indicate that a negative charge moves in the lattice.

A *p-type semiconductor* is produced by "doping" a Group IV element lattice with a small amount of a Group III element. The Group III element is short one valence electron for bonding to the four neighboring Group IV atoms. This creates a "hole" in the valence electron distribution where there should be, but is not, a bonding electron. If a bonding electron from a nearby bond jumps into the hole it will leave a hole behind. Under the influence of an electric field, the electrons move toward the positive pole by jumping from hole to hole and the holes thus seems to move toward the negative pole. N-type and p-type semi-conductors can be combined in various ways to produce diodes and transistors.

16. What would be the effect of doping with indium (Group III) an n-type semiconductor consisting of germanium doped with arsenic?
A) the semiconductor would be neutralized
B) the conductivity would be increased
C) the semiconductor would become more selective of the paths of electrons
D) the semiconductor would remain unaffected

17. InAs, as a stoichiometrically pure substance, would be an insulator. Which of the following could also be classified as an insulator?

    I—Si
    II—Ge

A) I only B) II only C) both I and II D) neither I nor II

18. If a stoichiometrically pure crystal of InAs is doped with additional In, which of the following would be the result?
A) it would remain an insulator
B) we would get a p-type semiconductor
C) we would get an n-type semiconductor
D) the behavior would be totally unpredictable

One equivalent of a substance is the weight which

1.   as an acid, contains 1 gram atom of replaceable hydrogen; or

2.   as a base, reacts with 1 gram atom of hydrogen; or

3.   as a salt, is produced in a reaction involving 1 gram atom of hydrogen

A solution containing one equivalent of a solute in 1 liter of solution is a 1 N (normal) solution. 100 ml of a .5 N aqueous solution of the acid HA is mixed with 200 ml of a .25 N aqueous solution of the base BOH.

19. The pH of the solution is approximately
A) 2 B) 5 C) 7 D) it cannot be predicted

20. If the formula for the base is $B(OH)_3$ instead of BOH, the pH of the mixed solution can now be predicted to be
A) 2 B) 5 C) 7 D) it cannot be predicted

21. If we add an additional 100 ml of .5 N aqueous solution to the mixed solution of the preceding problem, we can expect the pH of the new solution to be
A) less than 2   C) 7
B) between 2 and 7   D) it cannot be predicted

The Wheatstone bridge circuit is a device widely used for measuring an unknown resistance rapidly and precisely. R_1, R_2, and R_3 are known resistances and X represents the unknown resistance. To use the bridge, the switches are closed and the resistance of R_3 is adjusted until the galvanometer, G, shows no deflection. When this happens, points b and c are at the same potential, the current I_1 through R_1 equals the current through R_2, and the current I_2 through R_3 equals the current through X.

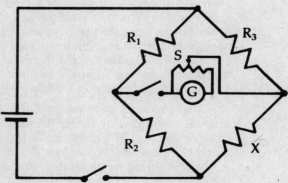

Since $V_{ab} = V_{ac}$, it follows that $I_1R_1 = I_2R_3$, and since $B_{bd} = V_{cd}$,

$$I_1R_2 = I_2X.$$

Dividing one equation into another, we get

$$X = \frac{R_2 R_3}{R_1}$$

22. What is the value (approx.) of the current passing through R_1 in the preceding problem if V_{ac} is 20 v?   A) 5   B) 25   C) 50   D) 250

23. What is the value of the current passing through R_1 in the preceding problem if V_{ac} is 20 v (approx.)?
    A) .02 amps   B) .2 amps   C) 2 amps   D) 20 amps

24. What is the purpose of the shunt resistor, S?
    A) fine adjustment
    B) protection of the galvanometer
    C) elimination of the error caused by the internal resistance of the galvanometer
    D) none of the above

> Blood is chemically different in various people. Early this century Dr. Karl Landsteiner discovered the reason that blood transfusions from one person to another sometimes resulted in the death of the recipient. He discovered that some red blood cells contain agglutinogens that react with agglutinins in the plasma of other people to produce agglutination or clumping of the blood. Based on the differences he found, he classified people into four blood types, A, B, AB, and O.
>
> Inheritance of blood type is predictable and based on the action of multiple alleles. There are three alleles involved: the allele for type A, I_a; the allele for type B, I_b; and the allele i. The first two alleles are dominant over the third but are not dominant over each other. When the two alleles for type A and type B appear, blood will be type AB; when they are both absent, type O results. The possible genotypes for each of the blood types are summarized in the table below.

BLOOD GROUP	GENOTYPE
A	I_aI_a or $I_a i$
B	I_bI_b or $I_b i$
AB	I_aI_b
O	ii

25. What is a patient's blood type if it clumps with both anti-A and anti-B serum?
    A) A   B) B   C) AB   D) O

26. Based on the assumption that all three alleles occur with equal frequency, what percent of the population can be expected to have type O blood?
    A) 3%   B) 9%   C) 11%   D) 33^1/3%

27. The approximate rates of occurrence for the blood types are: O (47%), A (41%), B (9%), and AB (3%). From this data we may conclude that allele i occurs _____ % of the time.
    A) 47   B) 50   C) 60   D) 69

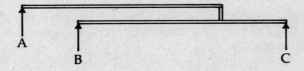

A   B   C

Two 10-ft-long beams are placed as shown in the figure above in such a manner that they overlap by 7 feet. Each beam weighs 100 lbs and is supported at both ends.

28. Find the magnitude of the supporting force at A.
   A) 50 lbs   B) 30 lbs   C) 15 lbs   D) 0 lbs

29. Find the magnitude of the supporting force at B.
   A) 50   B) 65 lbs   C) 75 lbs   D) 85 lbs

30. Find the magnitude of the supporting force at C.
   A) 50 lbs   B) 65 lbs   C) 75 lbs   D) 85 lbs

Specific heats of solids are generally much lower than those of liquids. This is apparently caused by a much smaller mass motion factor per degree Celsius change in the solid state than in the liquid state. While the specific heats of solids vary considerably with temperature, the specific heats of all solids approach zero as the temperatures approach absolute zero.

31. The law of DuLong and Petit, an experimental finding of many years ago, states that "the atomic weight of a metal multiplied by its specific heat approximates the constant 6.4." Using this law, approximate the specific heat of tin (atomic weight 118.7).
   A) .54   B) .23   C) .054   D) .023

32. Determine the heat required (approximately) to raise the temperature of 60 g of lead from 30°C to 400°C, given that the atomic weight of lead is 207.2 and its specific heat as a liquid is .0375. The heat of fusion of lead is 5.86 cal/g and its melting point is 327°C.
   A) 1066.5 cal   B) 990 cal   C) 947.4 cal   D) 850.6 cal

33. Given the table of atomic weights and specific heats below, determine which of the four elements listed most closely follows the prediction of the law of Dulong and Petit.

ELEMENT	ATOMIC WEIGHT	SPECIFIC HEAT
Magnesium	24.32	.246
Iron	55.85	.12
Copper	63.5	.092
Mercury	200.6	.03325

A) magnesium   B) iron   C) copper   D) mercury

The E° values of a table of oxidation potentials are relative values, with the E° for the standard hydrogen half-cell taken as zero. An E° value in the table of oxidation potentials represents the voltage of a cell composed of the single electrode in question and the standard hydrogen electrode.

The dependence of E upon the concentrations of the species involved in a half-reaction is given by the Nernst Equation,

$$E = E° + \frac{.0591}{n} \log\frac{Q_{ox.}}{Q_{red.}}$$

E is the single-electrode potential of the system. The larger E is, the greater the oxidizing power is. E° is the standard single-electrode potential of the system. The Q's are the mass-action expressions for the oxidizing and the reducing sides of the half-reaction, respectively.

The voltage generated by a cell is the difference between the E's of the two systems constituting the cell. The electrode with the higher E is positive and reduction occurs there.

$$E_{Zn}^{\circ} = -.763 \text{ v} \qquad E_{Ag}^{\circ} = .799 \text{ v}$$

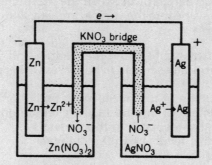

34. Find the single-electrode potential for zinc in the cell above if the concentration of Zn (NO₃)₂ is .05 M and the concentration of AgNO₃ is .09 M.
    A) $-.763$ v   B) $-.801$ v   C) $-.737$ v   D) $-.799$ v

35. Find the single-electrode potential for silver in the cell above under the conditions previously described.
    A) $+.763$ v   B) $+.801$ v   C) $+.737$ v   D) $+.799$ v

36. Find the voltage generated by the cell above.
    A) 1.562 v   B) 1.600 v   C) 1.500 v   D) 1.538 v

   For a body in the form of a rod or a cable, we are often interested in the change of length with temperature. If L is the length, we define a coefficient of linear expansion, α, by

$$\alpha = \frac{1}{L} \frac{dL}{dT}$$

   Over a moderate temperature range we may take $\dfrac{dL}{dT} = \dfrac{\Delta L}{\Delta T}$ so that

$$\Delta L = L_o \cdot \alpha \cdot \Delta T$$

37. As the temperature of a bar doubles, its length
    A) doubles   B) quadruples   C) increases   D) is multiplied by a factor of $\sqrt{2}$

38. Thin strips of two different metals are joined as shown in the figure below. A temperature increase will

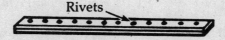

Rivets

   A) increase the length of the joined strip in a straight line
   B) bend the joined strip toward the side of the metal with the smaller value of α
   C) bend the joined strip toward the side of the metal with the greater value of α
   D) increase the length of the joined strip only by the amount it would increase the length of the strip of the metal with the smaller α

39. The coefficient of linear expansion of brass is 2×10^{-5} per degree C. Find the length of a brass rod (original length 1 meter) which has been heated from 35°C to 105°C.
    A) 1000.4 mm   B) 1001.4 mm   C) 1004 mm   D) 1014 mm

A fistula, or false passage, is sometimes formed between the bladder and uterus, between the bladder and vagina, or between the urethra and vagina. This passage allows the urine to escape into the vagina, and is a source of great annoyance and suffering.

40. In order to correct a fistula situated between the bladder and vagina, a woman's parasympathetic nerve fibers were surgically severed in both areas. This procedure would be expected to cause
A) decreased pain and inhibition of urinary bladder excitation
B) decreased pain and inhibition of urinary bladder relaxation
C) decreased pain and negative feedback to the adrenals
D) decreased pain and positive feedback to the kidneys

41. The pain caused by a fistula during urination can be somewhat alleviated by reducing the solute concentration of urine. The result is a more dilute excretion and less pain. A possible method for bringing this about would be
A) injection of ACTH into the patient
B) injection of ACTH-inhibitor into the patient
C) injection of ADH into the patient
D) injection of ADH-inhibitor into the patient

42. The reason why urine does *not* escape into the vagina of this woman when a fistula is *not* present is due to
A) the presence of cilia rhythmically controlling its descent through the vaginal tube
B) the involuntary contractions of the bladder's smooth muscle fibers inhibiting its movement downward
C) the contraction of a sphincter by the autonomic nerves innervating the area
D) the presence of ADH within the collecting tubules affecting water retention

A new technique to prevent tooth decay has been developed by a private medical research laboratory. It involves a simple technique whereby a transparent "sealant" is brushed onto the tooth—literally painting it—after which the coating is exposed to ultraviolet rays. The procedure is painless and quick.

43. Which of the following would *not* be a contributing factor in tooth decay prevention?
A) the use of the new transparent sealant
B) the fluoridation of drinking water
C) motivating people to keep teeth free of food debris
D) avoiding the tiny pits and fissures on the tooth's surface which a toothbrush rarely gets into

44. When tooth-decaying oral bacteria, believed to be mainly streptococcus mutants, are exposed to fermentable carbohydrates (particularly refined sugar), the carbohydrates are metabolized to produce acid. Isolation of these bacteria would most *likely* reveal any of the following genetic variations *except*
A) deletion   B) deficiency   C) duplication   D) replication

45. Research in tooth decay has resulted in the use of a new enzyme, dextranase, which breaks down dextran, a sticky constituent that permits colonies of bacteria to cling to the teeth. The enzyme can either be directly applied to the enamel as a coating or suspended in isotonic solution and injected intravenously. Oral ingestion of dextranase would most likely
A) prevent tooth decay by breaking down dextran
B) prevent tooth decay by inhibiting bacterial growth
C) not prevent tooth decay because the molecule is too large to be absorbed by the intestinal villi
D) not prevent tooth decay due to the action of pepsin and chymotrypsin

A 200-lb man is standing in an elevator. The upward push of the elevator on the man is indicated by F.

F

46. Determine the force F exerted by the elevator floor on the man when the elevator is going up with a constant velocity of 4 ft/sec.
    A) 200 lbs   B) 220 lbs   C) 225 lbs   D) 240 lbs

47. Determine the force F_1 exerted by the man on the elevator floor when the elevator is going down with constant velocity of 4 ft/sec.
    A) 175 lbs   B) 180 lbs   C) 192 lbs   D) 200 lbs

48. If the cable snaps and the elevator is falling freely, what is the force exerted by the man on the elevator floor (before it stops)?
    A) 0 lbs   B) 20 lbs
    C) 32 lbs   D) 200 lbs

The diagram at right shows the radioactive decay series for U-238. The numbers on the lines represent the half-lives of the different isotopes formed during the decomposition of U-238

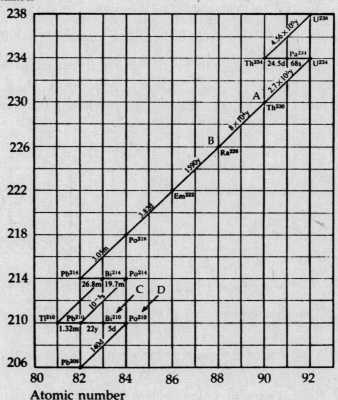

Mass number

Atomic number

49. Of all the isotopes formed, the most unstable is
    A) Bi^{210} B) Pb^{210} C) Po^{218} D) Po^{214}

50. In going from Th^{230} (A) to Ra^{226} (B), which of the following particles is emitted?
    A) α B) β C) γ D) deuterium

51. If we start out with 10 kg of Bi^{210}, how much of it will remain after 10 days?
    A) 5 kg   B) 2.5 kg   C) 1.25 kg   D) none

A diagram of a hydraulic press is shown at right, with A and a representing the respective areas of pistons 1 and 2. The following questions pertain to the given diagram.

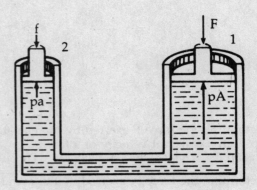

52. If the diameters of the acting areas of pistons 1 and 2 are on a 3:1 ratio, and forces F and f are balanced in the press, what is the ratio f:F?
    A) 3:1   B) 1:9   C) 9:1   D) none of these

53. The radius of piston 1 is 2 inches while the radius of piston 2 is 1 inch. If the magnitude of force f is 2 lbs, the magnitude of force F needed to balance it is
    A) 1 lb   B) 2 lbs   C) 4 lbs   D) 8 lbs

54. In the previous problem, if piston 1 moves 1 inch, the corresponding movement in piston 2 should be
    A) ½ inch   B) ¼ inch   C) 8 inches   D) none of these

A body weighing 20,000 dynes is attached to a spring of constant 10 d/cm. The spring is attached to the wall and the body rests on a surface with which it has

$$\mu_{static} = .002$$
$$\mu_{kinetic} = .001$$

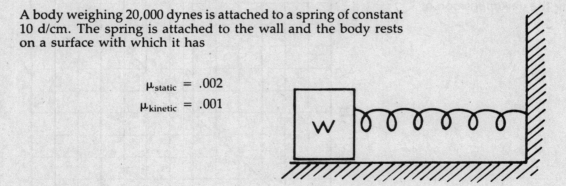

The spring at equilibrium is compressed a distance of 10 cm and released.

55. The acceleration of the mass at the time of release is (in cm/sec²)
    A) 0   B) 1   C) 3   D) 5

56. The force of the spring at the moment of release is
    A) 10   B) 50   C) 60   D) 100

57. The acceleration of the body at the equilibrium point of the spring is
    A) 0   B) 32.2 ft/sec²   C) 980 cm/sec²   D) 60 cm/sec²

Much has been written about collisions between particles and between particles and walls. One very interesting and special case is that in which two particles moving on a common straight path collide.

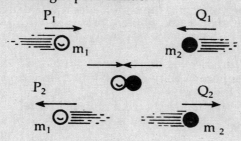

58. If the masses m_1 and m_2 are equal, then the molecules simply exchange velocities ($Q_2 = P_1$, $P_2 = Q_1$). If the masses are different, then which of the following relations hold?
 A) $P_2 = Q_2$ B) $P_1Q_1 = P_2Q_2$ C) $P_1m_1 = Q_2m_2$ D) $P_2m_1 = Q_2m_2$

59. If $Q_1 = 0$ and $m_2 > m_1$, then which of the following will result after collision?
 A) $P_2 = 0$, $Q_2 > P_1$ B) $Q_2 = 0$, $P_2 < P_1$ C) $P_2 = 0$, $Q_2 < P_1$ D) $Q_2 = 0$, $P_2 > P_1$

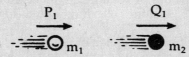

60. Suppose the two particles have equal mass, are moving in the same direction, and $P_1 > Q_2$. Which of the following is correct?

A) $P_2 = Q_1$, $Q_2 = P_1$

B) $P_2 = 0$, $Q_2 = P_1 + Q_1$

C) $P_2 = Q_2 = P_1 + Q_1$

D) $P_2 = P_1 - Q_1$, $Q_2 = P_1 + Q_1$

It has been established that the most important components of tissue culture media are the large molecules—that is, the proteins and protein-bound materials. Only a very few human cell strains will grow in completely defined media (whereby all the constituents are known and in their precise amounts). However, most will grow in defined media supplemented with dialyzed serum.

61. To prepare dialyzed serum, its volume is first measured and it is then dialyzed against distilled water for 48 hours (V_1). At the end of this time it is diluted three times (V_2) its volume with standard balanced salt solution, after which the volume (V_3) is then made up

with distilled water to twice the (V_2) volume. After filtration through a Millipore filter this material constitutes 50% dialyzed serum. If a laboratory technician begins with 45 cc blood serum, and finally winds up with 180 cc dialyzed serum (which is *ready-to-use*, 100%-dialyzed serum), then what was the volume of the serum *after* it was dialyzed against distilled water for 48 hours—that is, just *before* it was diluted 3 times with salt solution?
A) 5 cc   B) 15 cc   C) 30 cc   D) 50 cc   E) 100 cc

62. The permeability of a cultured cell is dependent on the quality of the culture medium. To experimentally *decrease* the permeability of a cell grown in vitro you would *exclude* from the culture medium which of the following?
A) balanced salt solution   B) dialyzed serum   C) pH buffer
D) distilled water   E) defined serum

63. In most of the capillaries throughout the body, pressure is about 25 millimeters of mercury, but within the glomerulus of the kidney it rises to between 60 and 70 millimeters. As a result of this high pressure, blood fluids are filtered through the capillary walls and pass into the Bowman's capsule. By this mechanism, whole blood is partially dialyzed as it flows through the millions of glomeruli within the kidney. The remaining blood fluids within the collecting tubules are *further* dialyzed due to
A) the decreased concentration of solutes in the distal convoluted tubules compared with the higher concentration in the proximal convoluted tubules
B) the stimulating affect of ADH on the collecting tubules to reabsorb water from the efferent vessels
C) the excess concentration of blood colloids in the efferent vessels, and their high colloidal osmotic pull on the fluids within the convoluted tubules
D) the presence of glucose in the urine increasing the ability of the tubules to reabsorb blood proteins
E) the retention of lower-molecular-weight materials by the efferent vessels as they ramify (branch) through the collecting tubules

The effects of parasitism on a human host are intimately related to the effects of the host on the parasite. The two organisms involved in the partnership react on each other. Some of these reactions, such as special growth, are easily seen, but most of them induce only slight changes in body form or behavior—or they are of a purely biochemical nature.

64. Phagocytosis is limited to the macrophages (any of various phagocytic cells in connective tissue, lymphatic tissue, bone marrow, etc.) in human malarial infections. Phagocytosis by these macrophages occurs as early as four hours following infection. Thereafter, it occurs constantly during the entire acute period. The height of this activation is coincident with the crisis of infection. An antimalarial drug that is eventually incorporated into the infected cells at the crisis of infection, would *most likely* be detected in which of the following organs?
A) lungs and bronchi
B) dermis and epidermis
C) liver and spleen
D) bone marrow and heart
E) tonsils and larynx

65. Suppose a research investigator finds that the diet of an animal is of major importance in determining the kinds and numbers of its worm parasites. The investigator proceeds to starve a perch infected with tapeworms and, curiously enough, finds that an increase in the ability of the parasites to utilize glucose has occurred. However, when an infected dogfish shark is starved, the worms lose weight, and this loss can only be prevented by the administration of starch to the shark's diet. From these results we may conclude that
A) fish which feed on animal plankton have entirely different parasites than those fish whose diet consists of algae
B) the effect of starvation on intestinal tapeworms would hardly justify starving a man in an effort to rid him of the worms

C) the bacterial flora of the gut of both types of fishes are biochemically dissimilar enough to cause a difference in availability of nutrients to the worm parasites

D) starvation of a hamster would *probably* cause a reduction in the weight of its tapeworms, but would not increase the worm's ability to utilize glucose

E) the nature and quantity of the host's dietary carbohydrate has a definite effect on the growth and production of eggs by worm parasites

66. A doctor discovers, during a routine physical checkup, the presence of tiny ciliates living within the mucous lining of the coil-shaped cochlea of a patient's left inner ear only. These organisms appear to obtain their nutrients by filtration of the endolymph bathing the inner ear canal, and the breakdown of bacteria from the filtrate. Microscopic examination of the surrounding cochlear cells shows an immunity reaction of the same order and magnitude as those cells in the right cochlea. From this information we may *deduce* that the ciliates are

A) commensal parasites   C) host-specific parasites
B) saprophytic parasites   D) nonparasitic

Skills Analysis: Reading

The following questions are in groups, with each group preceded by descriptive material. First study the material; then select the one best answer to each question in the group.

---

time—85 minutes

Reading

The history of electrical research in the first half of the 18th century provides a concrete and well-known example of the way a science develops before it acquires its first universally received paradigm. During that period there were almost as many views about the nature of electricity as there were important electrical experimenters (men like Hauksbee, Gray, Desaguliers, Du Fay, Nollett, Watson, Franklin, and others). All their numerous concepts of electricity had something in common: they were partially derived from one or another version of the mechanico-corpuscular philosophy that guided all scientific research of the day. In addition, all were components of real scientific theories, of theories that had been drawn in part from experiment and observation and that partially determined the choice and interpretation of additional problems undertaken in research. Yet though all the experiments were electrical and though most of the experimenters read each others' works, their theories had no more than a family resemblance.

One early group of theories, following 17th-century practice, regarded attraction and frictional generation as the fundamental electrical phenomena. This group tended to treat repulsion as a secondary effect due to some sort of mechanical rebounding and also to postpone for as long as possible both discussion and systematic research on Gray's newly discovered effect, electrical conduction. Other "electricians" (the term is their own) took attraction and repulsion to be equally elementary manifestations of electricity and modified their theories and research accordingly. (Actually, this group is remarkably small—even Franklin's theory never quite accounted for the mutual repulsion of two negatively charged bodies.) But they had as much difficulty as the first group in accounting simultaneously for any but the simplest conduction effects. Those effects, however, provided the starting point for a third group, one which tended to speak of electricity as a "fluid" that could run through conductors rather than as a "effluvium" that emanated from nonconductors. This group, in its turn, had difficulty reconciling its theory with a number of attractive and repulsive effects. Only through the work of Franklin and his immediate successors did a theory arise that could account for very nearly all these effects with something like equal facility, and that therefore could and did provide a subsequent generation of "electricians" with a common paradigm for its research.

1. As used in the preceding selection, the term "paradigm" means
   A) a contradiction to established beliefs
   B) a pattern

C) a set of two or more mutually contradictory observations
D) a theorem
E) an experiment

2. According to the passage, the effect discovered by Gray is
   A) repulsion   B) frictional generation   C) effluvium   D) attraction
   E) conduction

3. The author feels that there were many views on the nature of electricity because
   A) all researchers wanted to have their "own" views
   B) experiment design and interpretation of results were biased by the experimenters' beliefs
   C) no real experiments were being performed
   D) experimenters interpreted the same results in different ways
   E) an effluvium was hard to control and study

4. The author would agree with which of the following statements?
   A) there was no communication among experimenters and so they did not know of each others' work
   B) experimenters were in agreement on the relative importance of different electrical phenomena; they only disagreed on their views on the nature of electricity
   C) a paradigm does not have to be correct, it just has to work
   D) many contradicting views must be expressed before a paradigm can develop
   E) the most important electrical researcher was Franklin, because he came closest to a working theory of electricity

5. Which of the following men is not referred to as an "electrician" in the preceding passage?
   A) Faraday   B) Hauksbee   C) Du Fay   D) Watson   E) none of these

Reading

Radar was predicted by Marconi, who stated in a speech in New York on June 20, 1922,

> In some of my tests I have noticed the effects of reflection and deflection of electric waves by metallic objects miles away. It seems to me that it should be possible to design an apparatus by means of which a ship could radiate or project a divergent beam of these rays in any desired direction, which rays, if coming across a metallic object, such as another steamer or ship, would be reflected back to a receiver screened from the local transmitter on the sending ship, and thereby immediately revealing the presence and bearing of the other ship in fog or thick weather.

Shortly thereafter, while performing basic research on radio-wave propagation, A. H. Taylor and L. C. Young of the Naval Research Laboratory obtained experimental confirmation of these speculations by detecting a ship moving down the Potomac River. Little was accomplished over the next few years, but interest in radio detection was renewed in 1930 at the Naval Research Laboratory when L. A. Hyland, during the course of experiments in radio direction-finding, noted that radio waves were reflected from aircraft that accidentally came within range.

The idea that finally sparked the initiation of a radar project occurred to Young sometime in 1930. At that time, while studying transmitter key clicks, he made observations that led him to suggest that the pulse method of echo ranging (used in underwater depth finding) with radio frequency be applied to the detection of aircraft. After much preliminary thinking and calculating, a project was finally initiated March 14, 1934.

By 1939, the U.S. Navy had thoroughly developed sample radar sets for use on ships, and in cooperation with the Navy, the Army Signal Corps had developed aircraft-locating systems for use at short and long distances. Just before World War II, the United States used a small number of these radar sets to build a warning ring around the coastline, at the Panama Canal, and in Hawaii. Indeed, the Japanese planes that attacked Pearl Harbor on December 7, 1941, were discovered by radar when they were still 130 miles away. It was only due to unskilled use of this discovery that American forces on the Hawaiian Islands were so devastatingly surprised.

6. A major defect of the "radar" predicted by Marconi and made by Taylor and Young was that
A) it was too slow in receiving the signal
B) without "clicking" an operator should not know if he had found a new object
C) its direction-finding ability was questioned because a divergent beam of rays was used
D) it did not have range-finding capabilities
E) aircraft within range would reflect waves, thus creating interference

7. Which of the following contributed the *least* to the invention and development of radar?
A) radio   B) telephone   C) cathode-ray tube   D) sonar   E) none of these

8. Who suggested that the receiver should be screened from the transmitter?
A) Taylor   B) Hyland   C) Marconi   D) Young   E) Morse

9. When radar was fully developed, the Navy's first use was in
A) coastline protection   C) detection of other ships in the fog
B) submarine range-finding   D) airplane detection

Reading

Tic douloureux or trigeminal neuralgia is one of the more common neuralgias or paroxysmal pains, usually beginning in the middle life and occurring more frequently in women. It is characterized by an intense stabbing pain which strikes one or a combination of three facial branches supplied by the trigeminal (fifth cranial) nerve.

The attacks occur without warning, in violent, knife-like darts of pain. The face is twisted in spasms and there is a free flow of tears and saliva. The seizure lasts only a few seconds and may clear up spontaneously, with varying periods of relief. The pain may involve the first or ophthalmic division, which includes the forehead and eye, the second division around the nose, or the third or side of the mouth. The second and third branches seem to be more frequently affected. The pain does not spread to the back of the head or across to the other side of the face. The attacks tend to increase in acuteness and extent, and as the condition becomes worse the periods of freedom from pain become shorter. The seizures often are influenced by seasonal changes and occur more frequently in spring and fall. Pain may be prompted by touching the affected side of the face, exposure to cold, washing, eating, drinking, or talking, and emotional tension or fatigue intensify the attack.

10. Tic douloureux
A) attacks both sides of the face
B) frequently spreads to the back of the head
C) attacks the area around the eye and forehead more frequently than the area around the nose and mouth

D) is unaffected by temperature variation
E) occurs more frequently in women

11. Neuralgia is
A) an emotional condition
B) a pain
C) a nerve blockage
D) a connection between neurons
E) a cranial nerve

12. The usual warning signal before the onset of an attack is
A) a knifelike pain   B) crying   C) facial spasms   D) fatigue   E) none

13. The name "trigeminal" refers to the _____ of the nerve.
A) size   B) branches   C) location   D) importance   E) cranial quality

Reading

A disturbance of the action of the diaphragm due to injury to the nerves may have serious effects. Inflammation or infection of the diaphragm causes shortness of breath, soreness, and a sense of pressure in the lower chest region. Spasm of the diaphragm may be either hiccups—the more common form known as clonic spasm—or a constant tension of the muscle called tonic spasm. The tonic spasm is the more severe form and results from such diseases as tetanus, rabies, or epilepsy. Tonic spasm of long duration may cause exhaustion and, ultimately, death by asphyxiation. Sometimes vigorous rubbing around the chest walls, the back, and the region over the stomach will relieve the spasm.

Hernia or rupture of the diaphragm may be caused by an injury, by a deformity before birth, or by a part of the stomach passing upward through the opening of the diaphragm at the esophagus. When a rupture occurs suddenly, symptoms of shock with severe pain in the lower part of the chest, hiccups, shortness of breath, and vomiting may be present. The most prominent symptoms of a hernia of long duration are shortness of breath and cyanosis. This is due to the possible displacement of the heart and to interference with the movement of the lungs. A child born with a large diaphragmatic hernia may also have what has been called an "upside-down stomach." Unless this condition is detected promptly and corrected surgically, the infant may not survive.

14. Hiccups are usually
A) clonic spasms
B) tonic spasms
C) ruptures of the diaphragm
D) chronic spasms
E) phonic spasms

15. Tonic spasms of long duration may cause death by
A) dehydration   B) regurgitation   C) heart displacement   D) asphyxiation   E) exhaustion

16. Which of the following may cause a hernia?
A) rabies
B) inflammation of the diaphragm
C) part of the stomach passing up through the opening at the esophagus
D) epilepsy
E) a tonic spasm of long duration

Reading

Zinc is an essential trace mineral. Only tiny amounts are needed: a daily intake of 15 milligrams and a total of about two grams in the body. It was not until the 1960s that we learned just how essential this mineral is to human health. Zinc is required to transport carbon dioxide in the blood and to eliminate it from the lungs. It is necessary for the proper utilization of alcohol, and also for getting rid of the lactic acid that accumulates in the blood during exercise.

Zinc is also a part of insulin and enhances the action of other hormones. It is a component of some enzymes and activates others. It is important in the digestion of protein and essential to the formation of nucleic acids.

A number of disorders (including tuberculosis and other chronic infections, alcoholism, thyroid and liver diseases, malabsorption syndromes, and others) can lead to zinc deficiency. Certain types of cancer also sequester zinc, leading to a deficiency in the rest of the body. In some cases an inadequate diet can produce serious symptoms of zinc deficiency; a few years ago, a combination of dwarfing, lack of sexual development, severe anemia, enlarged spleens and livers, and strange aberrations of appetites in groups of poverty-level young Iranian and Egyptian boys was traced to a lack of zinc in their diets.

Later, pediatricians in Denver found milder growth retardation among young patients from middle- and upper-income families. Measuring the level of zinc in their hair, investigators found it to be very low. After several months on zinc supplements, the children's growth accelerated.

The following statements are related to the preceding passage. Based on the information given, select

A—if the statement is *supported* by the information in the passage

B—if the statement is *contradicted* by the information in the passage.

C—if the statement is *neither supported nor contradicted* by the information in the passage

17. Many midgets have been found to have no serious zinc deficiency.

18. Cancer cells removed from some patients have been found to have an unusually high concentration of zinc.

19. Zinc deficiency may lead to tuberculosis.

20. Zinc deficiency may lead to diabetes.

21. The normal total amount of zinc in a human body is about 15 milligrams.

Reading

The thyroid gland, one of the most significant of the endocrine glands which produce secretions that regulate many basic processes of the body, lies in the front part of the throat along the windpipe.

The thyroid secretion, thyroxin, is involved in the process of oxidation which occurs within the cells and by which the tissues generate the energy they require. Its importance is indicated by the serious consequences of excessive or deficient amounts of it in the body. A child born with insufficient thyroid activity becomes a cretin, physically undergrown, and mentally an idiot. Thyroid deficiency in later life causes physical and mental coarsening and dulling. Excessive thyroid produces general restlessness, speeds up the heart, and may have other untoward effects. Both hyperthyroidism (too much thyroid) and hypothyroidism (too little) can be successfully treated.

The thyroid is susceptible to a variety of diseases, the most common being simple goiter, usually due to a lack of iodine. In Graves' disease (exophthalmic goiter), overactivity of the thyroid causes a popeyed appearance and other serious symptoms. Tumors of lesser or greater malignancy may affect the thyroid. Surgical removal is indicated for most types of thyroid cancer. X-ray and radium treatment and radioactive iodine have also been beneficial in certain cases. A number of infectious and noninfectious diseases of the thyroid also respond well to treatment.

The following statements are related to the preceding passage. Based on the information given, select

A—if the statement is *supported* by the information in the passage
B—if the statement is *contradicted* by the information in the passage
C—if the statement is *neither supported nor contradicted* by the information in the passage

22. Some mongolian idiots have perfectly normal thyroid functions.

23. Hyperthyroidism may cause a speeding up of the pulse rate.

24. Common goiter is usually caused by a minor tumor in the thyroid.

25. Insulin is also secreted in the thyroid.

Reading

Diabetes insipidus is a disorder of the urinary system in which larger amounts of urine are excreted. The urine is itself normal and sugar is not present as in diabetes mellitus. The origin of diabetes insipidus is not yet definitely established. In a specific case, damage to the pituitary gland because of hemorrhage, infection, or a tumor, may be responsible. A disorder of the pituitary is probably accountable.

As much as 4 to 10 quarts of urine may be excreted daily, as contrasted with 1½ to 2 quarts normally. One report describes the case of a 16-year-old boy who excreted 33 quarts of urine every 24 hours, and the equivalent of his own body weight in 40 hours. Intense and practically uninterrupted thirst is another symptom, and sleep is disturbed frequently because of the urge to urinate. The abnormal excretions caused by the disease result in weakness and emaciation. If a tumor or serious abscess in the pituitary region is not present, the person may get along satisfactorily; but if one of these conditions is found, fatality usually insues. Death then is the result of the original disorder and not of the diabetes insipidus caused by it.

The following statements are related to the preceding passage. Based on the information given, select

A—if the statement is *supported* by the information in the passage
B—if the statement is *contradicted* by the information in the passage
C—if the statement is *neither supported nor contradicted* by the information in the passage

26. In diabetes insipidus, sugar is present in the urine.

27. Diabetes insipidus is characterized by excretion of a great amount of urine.

28. Emaciation is a hazard of diabetes mellitus.

29. Diabetes insipidus is usually caused by a tumor on the pituitary.

30. Diabetes insipidus is a later disease stage of diabetes mellitus.

Reading

Ancient science failed to develop not because of its immanent shortcomings but because those who did scientific work did not see themselves, nor were they seen by others, as scientists, but primarily as philosophers, medical practitioners, or astrologers. Only this can explain why the appearance of Galileo had to wait for some 1,800 years after Archimedes, or the even longer gap between Aristotle's and Theophrastus' systematizations of living and growing things and those of Linnaeus and Cuvier. Had there existed among the Greeks several generations of intellectuals conceiving of themselves as scientists—with the motivations and obligations entailed in that—they could undoubtedly have applied themselves to the discovery of a less cumbersome method of mathematical notation and have made many of the scientific advances accomplished in the 16th and 17th centuries and subsequently. It is true that much of the Greek tradition was lost in the Middle Ages as a result of catastrophes, but the stagnation and deterioration of the tradition had started earlier. Furthermore, had there been a group of persons who inherited the Greek scientific tradition and who regarded themselves as scientists anywhere in the Christian or the Moslem world or among the Jews, the Greek achievements might have been rediscovered in the Middle Ages or, at any rate, much more efficient use would have been made of them in the 15th century.

The question, therefore, is what made certain men in 17th-century Europe, and nowhere before, view themselves as scientists and see the scientific role as one with unique and special obligations and possibilities. The general conditions necessary for this occurrence were: either there had to be some striking scientific discoveries of practical value convincing people that the practice of science was an economically worthwhile occupation; or there had to be a group of persons who believed in science as an intrinsically valuable preoccupation and who had a reasonable prospect of making their belief generally accepted, even before science proved its economic worth.

The following statements are related to the preceding passage. Based on the information given, select

A—if the statement is *supported* by the information in the passage
B—if the statement is *contradicted* by the information in the passage
C—if the statement is *neither supported nor contradicted* by the information in the passage

31. Galileo saw himself primarily as a philosopher.

32. Descartes contributed to the simplification of mathematical notation in the 17th century.

33. Archimedes is accredited with a systematization of living organisms.

34. The most important scientific achievement of the 16th and 17th centuries was the rediscovery of Greek achievements.

Reading

Arterial hypertension is a condition of sustained elevated systemic arterial blood pressure. Since arterial pressure is influenced by many factors, including age, sex, body type, race, body temperature, and emotional state, the participation of these factors must be discounted before the diagnosis of hypertension can be made. The minimum level of systemic arterial pressure considered to be hypertensive has been arbitrarily set at 140/90 mm Hg. While hypertension usually involves elevations in mean and pulse pressures, the rise in diastolic pressure is clinically regarded as the critical criterion, suggesting that hypertension is due primarily to an increased peripheral resistance.

Hypertension is a serious cardiovascular disease. It is responsible for approximately 15% of the deaths in people over 50 years of age. However, many of the people in this age group may have blood pressures as high as 170/90 without displaying any symptoms of hypertension, and approximately 75% of these individuals die of diseases unrelated to hypertension.

In approximately 10% of the cases of hypertension, the elevated blood pressure is a clinical symptom of a specific disease (e.g., renal disease), and not a disease entity in itself. Such conditions of elevated blood pressures are referred to as *secondary hypertension.* In the remaining 90%, the development of hypertension cannot be attributed to any known origin and probably represents a specific disease state. This form of hypertension is called *primary* or *essential hypertension.*

Hypertension is an important clinical disorder because it leads to organic alterations of the heart, brain, kidneys, and arterial vasculature. In hypertension, the heart must pump blood into the arterial system against a higher-than-normal level of pressure. Consequently, the heart must perform additional work, and therefore, it hypertrophies. Hypertrophy may eventually lead to myocardial failure. The cerebral vasculature does not possess the tissue support found in other regions of the body, and cerebral hemorrhages in hypertensives are not uncommon. Renal insufficiency, which results from altered renal hemodynamics, is a frequent complication of hypertension. The continuous added stress placed upon the arterial system in hypertension ultimately leads to sclerosis of the arterial wall. This alteration of the vascular system may modify tissue blood flow and thereby cause disruption of tissue function.

35. A diagnosis of hypertension is primarily based on the
   A) pulse
   B) proper metabolic rate for the patient's age, sex, race, body type, temperature, and emotional state
   C) systolic pressure
   D) associated malfunctions (e.g., renal failure)
   E) diastolic pressure

36. Cerebral hemorrhages are not uncommon in hypertensives because
   A) cerebral tissue support in these patients is defective
   B) the higher pressure at which the blood is pumped cannot be withstood by the relatively weak cerebral vasculature, and leakage occurs
   C) the heart hypertrophies
   D) the brain can withstand considerably less variation in blood pressure than the other parts of the body
   E) hypertension alters the brain

37. The percentage of people over 50 who display blood pressure as high as 170/90 without symptoms of hypertension is
   A) 25%   B) 75%   C) 15%   D) 90%   E) not indicated

38. Sclerosis of the arterial walls disrupts tissue function because
   A) too much blood enters the tissue, "drowning" it
   B) larger-than-usual blood cells enter the tissue, clogging it
   C) permeability of the arterial wall is decreased
   D) permeability of the arterial wall is increased
   E) too little blood enters the tissue, starving it

Reading

Central American countries burdened by the high cost of imported oil are poking into a volcanic region known as the "Belt of Fire" in search of what could be an inexhaustible source of geothermal energy.

El Salvador and Mexico already operate electrical plants using steam from the earth's interior to power giant turbines. Nicaragua, Guatemala, Costa Rica, and Panama are all exploring their volcanic regions and expect to be in production by the early 1980s.

The steam lies beneath the surface, constantly replenished by rainwater filtering down to the hot earth near a string of volcanoes stretching from northern Mexico to Panama. "Drilling for steam is similar to exploring for oil. The vapor is right there, it's a matter of drilling in the right spot," said Hugo Rolando Betancourt of the Guatemalan National Electrification Institute (INGE).

He estimates that Guatemala's first geothermal plant, at Moyuta volcano, would produce about 30,000 kilowatts of power.

Betancourt said geothermal energy has several advantages over hydroelectric facilities and oil-burning generating plants. Most important, he said, is the constant supply. The heat has been there for millions of years and is not going to cool down fast. The plants are small and the theory simple: the steam is under natural pressure and moves directly through pipes from the well to the turbines.

Furthermore, geothermal energy is clean. Since there is no burning, there are no polluting fumes. The minerals and gases found in the vapor are easily removed.

The following statements are related to the preceding passage. Based on the information given, select

A—if the statement is *supported* by the information in the passage
B—if the statement is *contradicted* by the information in the passage
C—if the statement is *neither supported nor contradicted* by the information in the passage.

39. Iceland is rich in geothermal springs; however, Icelanders have suffered problems because of damage caused to the equipment by sulfur-rich steam, which has contributed to their disillusionment with this form of energy.

40. Hydroelectric power is also clean, since there is no burning. Geothermal plants, however, are small and simple to build.

41. The cost of establishing a geothermal plant is greater than that of a conventional oil-burning plant but the operation costs are less in the case of a geothermal plant.

42. One risk particular to geothermal generating plants is that areas rich in geothermal energy are also areas of high seismic activity, which can cause damage or even destroy the wells.

43. Transmission of electricity is cheaper with geothermal power plants, since the latter are usually located in more remote places.

Reading

Fats and oils are the most abundant lipids in nature. They are organic esters (sometimes called triglycerides) formed by the reaction between glycerol (a trihydroxy alcohol) and a variety of carboxylic acids called fatty acids.

Because each fat or oil contains glycerol, any differences between them are probably due to differences in the fatty acid components. Naturally occurring fatty acids usually have an even number of carbon atoms. Solid fats, such as lard, are esters of glycerol and saturated fatty acids. Liquid fats are called oils. Structurally, these oils are glyceryl esters of unsaturated fatty acids. Corn, peanut, linseed, and olive oils are familiar liquid fats.

When esterification occurs between fatty acids (such as myristic, palmitic, and cerotic acids) and high-molecular-weight alcohols (such as cetylalcohol,

$CH_3(CH_2)_{15}OH$, and myrcyl alcohol, $CH_3(CH_2)_{29}OH$), the lipids formed are called waxes. Lipid waxes are not to be confused with paraffin wax, which is merely a mixture of hydrocarbons. Examples of common, naturally occurring waxes are beeswax (found in honeycomb), lanolin (obtained from wool), spermaceti (obtained from the sperm whale), and carnauba wax (obtained from palm leaves). Lanolin finds wide use as a base for many ointments, salves, and creams; spermaceti is used in cosmetics, pharmaceuticals, and in the manufacture of candles; and carnauba is used in floor waxes and in furniture and automobile polishes.

The reactions of fats and oils are of commercial importance. Hydrolysis, the reverse of the esterification reaction that produces the fat or oil, is an important reaction. The product of hydrolysis in the presence of a mineral acid, such as hydrochloric acid, is a fatty acid or a mixture of fatty acids. However when hydrolysis is carried out in the presence of strong alkalis such as sodium hydroxide, the process is called saponification and the product is soap. Soaps are the sodium or potassium salts of fatty acids and find wide application as cleansing agents. Another important reaction, mainly of oils, is hydrogenation in which the degree of unsaturation is reduced by the addition of hydrogen at the double bonds of fatty acids. The reaction is most often employed in the production of solid cooking shortenings or margarines from liquid vegetable or animal oils. A metal catalyst (finely divided nickel) is used to speed up the reaction.

Fats and oils play an important role as sources of energy in humans. Some fats are burned as fuel, some are used to build important constituents of the body cells, and still others are stored in the body to serve as a source of energy in times of prolonged hunger. Fat also serves to insulate the body against loss of heat and to protect vital organs from injury.

The following statements are related to the preceding passage. Based on the information given, select
A—if true of X, but not of Y
B—if true of Y, but not of X
C—if true of both X and Y
D—if true of neither X nor Y

44. The substance is the result of the esterification of glycerol and fatty acids.
    X) oils   Y) waxes

45. The result of hydrolysis of a fatty acid and a high-molecular-weight alcohol.
    X) waxes   Y) solid fats

46. The pair of processes listed are mutually opposite. That is, they are the reverse of one another.
    X) esterification and hydrolysis
    Y) esterification and saponification

47. Nickel is used as a catalyst to speed up the following reaction.
    X) hydrogenation
    Y) esterification of fatty acids and high-molecular-weight alcohols into waxes

Reading

The compound formed when one hydrogen atom from a saturated hydrocarbon is replaced by a halogen is known as an alkyl halide. To name a few typical alkyl halides we may mention methyl chloride (CH_3Cl), methyl bromide (CH_3Br), and ethyl chloride (C_2H_5Cl). They are made by direct substitution of halogen into an alkane in the presence of ultraviolet light. The reaction is hard to control and tends to give a mixture of products. Because the alkyl halides are very active, they are used for the synthesis of many other compounds. Methyl bromide is used as a fumigant, ethyl chloride as a local anesthetic for minor surgery, and the higher alkyl halides are useful as good solvents.

Many polyhalogen compounds of the hydrocarbons are equally interesting and useful. A group of compounds, known as freons, contain fluorine as well as chlorine.

Freon-11   Freon-12   Freon-22   Freon-114

They are used as refrigerants and also as dispersing gases in aerosol cans. Ethylene dibromide ($C_2H_4Br_2$) is used as a constituent of the antiknock additive for motor gasoline (it produces volatile lead compounds that prevent engine deposits from tetraethyllead, $Pb(C_2H_5)_4$, in the fuel; however, the vapors thus produced contribute significantly to air pollution). The analogous chlorine compound, ethylene dichloride, is an excellent solvent for some plastics and an ingredient in the manufacture of synthetic rubber. Tetrafluoroethene (C_2F_4) on polymerization yields Teflon, one of the newer plastics widely used because of its high stability and excellent resistance to chemical attack.

Aryl (aromatic) halides are equally important. Chlorobenzene (C_6H_5Cl) and its relatives are widely used in the synthesis of other organic compounds. The polychlorinated hydrocarbon dichlorodiphenyltrichloroethane, known as DDT, first saw extensive application as a delouser among the troops in World War II. It was also used to kill typhus-bearing lice and malaria-bearing mosquitoes, often being sprayed from airplanes.

DDT

The following statements are related to the preceding passage. Based on the information given, select

A—if true of only one of the given choices
B—if true of only two of the given choices
C—if true of all three of the given choices
D—if true of none of the given choices

48. The following *freons* are used as refrigerants and as dispersant agents for pressurized aerosol cans.
    1) CH_3Cl 2) CCl_3F 3) C_2F_4

49. The following are *alkyl halides*.
    1) freon-11   2) ethyl bromide   3) paradichlorobenzene

50. The following substances are considered excellent solvents for some plastics and are also used as ingredients in the manufacture of synthetic rubber.
    1) C_6H_5Cl 2) $C_2H_4Br_2$ 3) $Pb(C_2H_5)_4$

51. The following substances contain a ring structure in their molecular configuration.
    1) Teflon   2) chlorobenzene   3) DDT

Reading

The following statements represent several viewpoints about social class determination and class mobility in the United States.

Speaker 1
A person's social class is still determined by inheritance in modern societies. Aristocratic families continue being aristocratic regardless of their actions. In the United States the lower classes can improve their lot in many ways, but even then most people will never feel the class gap has been bridged.

Speaker 2
Happily, an individual in the United States today can, with ability and drive, advance to any class status. The vehicle for class mobility is competition and the major field of competition has switched from physical to mental labor. Economists, for example, are considered higher-class than plumbers, although the latter may earn more at times. Wealth only plays a part in the determination of status if the individual earned it competitively or uses it to enhance his or her competitive position.

Speaker 3
Flexibility is the characteristic of the class structure in the United States today. Differences between classes are becoming smaller and smaller, although there will probably never be a true classless society in America. Class standing depends on both heredity and individual effort, but life style is becoming increasingly more important as a class determiner.

Speaker 4
There are basically two social classes—the oppressed (who must sell their labor) and the oppressors (who control the production means). Some members of the latter class manage and exploit the laborers although they themselves do not own property; they are "administrators." The two classes have completely different interests, which only accentuates their interdependency.

Speaker 5
Traditional social structure survives in the United States. Social level is usually determined by racial or ethnic origin and thus, every person born into a particular class is destined to remain there. We have no religious or legal restrictions on class mobility, yet we keep groups in place by allowing people only the type of treatment and the opportunities appropriate to their social status.

Speaker 6
Social class in the United States is determined primarily on wealth. This is in contrast to many other modern societies. Wealth is usually measured by income in the case of working-class people and by bank account size in the case of members of the leisure class. Accumulation of material goods and consumption are occasionally used as class criteria, but money is still the most commonly used yardstick.

52. Which speakers would agree on considering the intellectual elite a social class in the United States?
    A) 1 and 2   B) 2 and 3   C) 4 and 5   D) 3 and 5

53. Occasionally some skilled workers earn more than college professors. Which speaker(s) would rate them higher than the professors on a social-class scale?
    A) 6 only
    B) 1 and 6 only
    C) 1, 2, and 6 only
    D) 1, 2, 3, and 6 only
    E)) some other combination

54. If the terms "open" and "closed" are used to classify societies in terms of their ease of class mobility, which of the speakers would claim that the United States has a closed society?
    A) 4 only   B) 5 only   C) 1 and 4 only   D) 1 and 5 only   E) 1, 4, and 5

Reading

The following speakers discuss state legislatures and ways to make them function more effectively and be more responsive to the will of the people.

Speaker 1
Cumbersome procedures for adopting legislation and short sessions often hamper state legislators. Frequently, these restrictions cause lack of action or deadlocks. The majority of legislators, including many who are well qualified, do not understand the many complex problems facing the states today. All these and other difficulties must be remedied if state legislatures are going to function effectively.

Speaker 2
The majority party controls the legislature to such an extent that good government becomes endangered. The Speaker of the House, for instance, has full power to decide procedural questions, recognition, and committee appointments. This situation could be easily remedied by each district electing one Democratic and one Republican legislator, and each by committee being composed of equal numbers of Democratic and Republican members.

Speaker 3
The Supreme Court has recently forced representation by population on state legislatures and now we can concern ourselves with seeing that each district's minority is represented. We can accomplish this most effectively by recombining the districts so that each new district has three representatives instead of one; voters who have a maximum of three votes, may influence the election by voting for fewer if they want to do so, voting only for those who represent their interests.

Speaker 4
The bicameral legislature has become obsolete; the two houses should be replaced by a single legislative body. Membership in a unicameral legislature would not only be more prestigious, drawing more able people to seek public office, but it would also result in a streamlined operation which would save time, reduce costs, eliminate stalemates, and pinpoint responsibilities for unpopular actions or for inaction.

Speaker 5
The average citizen is too little involved in state government—he has too little voice in it and too little information about it. If the number of legislators per unit area is increased so that minorities and the majority are all represented, they would be more accountable to the public for their actions and much more likely to seek their constituents' opinions. Another vehicle for involving the general public more in state government could be the more frequent use of direct-legislation instruments, such as referendums.

55. If a person is planning to run for public office as an independent, he or she would be most opposed to which speaker's suggestions?
    A) 1   B) 2   C) 3   D) 4   E) 5

56. Which speaker would most likely accept the suspension of legislative rules near the end of the session in order to complete important legislation?
    A) 1   B) 2   C) 3   D) 4   E) 5

57. Which of the following does not seem to be a concern of speakers 1 and 4?
    A) legislative structure
    B) ability of elected public officials
    C) efficiency of legislative process
    D) minority representation
    E) 1 and 4 seem to be concerned about all of these topics

58. Which of the speakers suggests that he fought against the practice of having legislative districts coincide with the county boundaries?
    A) 1   B) 2   C) 3   D) 4   E) 5

59. For which of the following reasons would speaker 1 most likely oppose speaker 2's plan?
    A) increased number of stalemates
    B) slower legislative process (since Speaker of the House would be weaker)
    C) inadequate minority representation
    D) decreased ability of legislators to understand state's problems
    E) speaker 1 would probably agree with speaker 2's plan

Reading

Two billion tons of animal waste are produced in the United States each year. That is equivalent to about 10 tons per person per year (enough to cover the Chicago metropolitan area to a depth of 10 feet! This amount is substantially greater than the 250 million tons of household, commercial, and municipal solid wastes generated yearly.

Manure is no longer valuable as a fertilizer because it is difficult or unpleasant to handle and spread and may have an undesirable composition. The amount of potassium and other minerals available in 1 ton of manure can be obtained in a 100-lb bag of fertilizer. Grain farmers prefer fertilizers with a lower nitrogen content than that found in manure because they help keep the grain stalk from growing too high. Chicken manure can no longer be used for many crops because chicken feed contains many antibiotics that are passed into feces. What can be done with this abundant natural resource?

The U.S. Bureau of Mines has recently discovered that if you heat manure in a reaction vessel with carbon monoxide at 1200 pounds per square inch pressure at 380°C for 20 minutes, oil is produced. The oil can be used for fuel. Manure will not solve the energy problem, but using it for energy could solve the manure problem.

The following statements are related to the passage above. Based on the information given, select
A—if the statement is *confirmed* by the article
B—if the statement is *indirectly implied* by the article
C—if the statement is *neither confirmed nor contradicted* by the article
D—if the statement is *indirectly contradicted* by the article
E—if the statement is *contradicted* by the article

60. Manure + $CO_2 \xrightarrow[\text{1200 psi}]{\text{380°C}}$ oil.

61. Manure of chicken origin has too high a nitrogen content to be used as a fertilizer.

62. Manure contains aldehydes and ketones.

63. The percentage of K in manure is 10 times as concentrated as in commercial fertilizers.

64. Contaminated water from feed-lot runoff can enter municipal waterways and over 100 animal diseases can be passed on to humans.

Reading

Monosodium glutamate is a flavor enhancer; with liberal use it produces profuse sweating, a condition called Kivok's disease.

$$\left[\begin{array}{c} \overset{\displaystyle O}{\overset{\|}{\text{HO—C—CH—CH}_2\text{—Ch}_2\text{—C—O}}} \\ \underset{\|}{\text{NH}_2} \end{array} \right]^{-} \quad (Na^+)$$

Monosodium Glutamate   (MSG)

Determination of a safe level of consumption for a drug requires getting a considerable amount of information about the drug's fate in the body: whether it is metabolized or excreted, the site or sites it acts upon, and the biological response it initiates. This is just a portion of the information that should be available before a safe dosage can be prescribed. Unfortunately, answers to these questions are not generally known and the mode of action of most chemicals in the body is not well understood. To circumvent this problem, compound testing is carried out on a more empirical basis. In the case of new food additives and drugs, for example, animals are fed large doses of the prospective additives for consecutive generations and the effects of the drug are noted. The dosage may be 10 to 100 times the amount designed to be used for human consumption. Thorough efforts are made to determine what happens to the additive after it is ingested and to determine the effects of this additive in combination with other frequently used additives. After some further testing, safe dosage is estimated and the substance is released for its final test by the public.

The following statements are related to the preceding passage. Based on the information given, select

A—if the statement is *supported* by the information in the passage
B—if the statement is *contradicted* by the information in the passage
C—if the statement is *neither supported nor contradicted* by the information in the passage

65. MSG is the salt of an acidic amino acid.

66. It is a simple scientific procedure to establish safe dosages for food additives.

67. MSG is safer to use than salt for people on a salt-restricted diet.

68. It is invalid to test drugs or additives to dosages 10 to 100 times human use.

Skills Analysis: Quantitative

The following questions are in groups, with each group preceded or accompanied by descriptive material. First study the material; then select the one best answer to each question in the group.

time—85 minutes

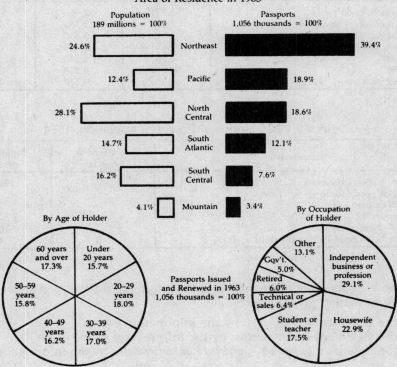

PROFILE OF U.S. TRAVELERS OVERSEAS

Based Upon Passports (Issued and Renewed) in 1963

Area of Residence in 1963

1. How many persons receiving a passport in 1963 lived in the Northeast Area?
   A) 400,000   B) 427,000   C) 416,000
   D) 394,000   E) 246,000

2. How many more passports were issued to persons in the North Central Area than to persons in the South Central Area in 1963?
   A) 491,000   B) 116,000   C) 272,000
   D) 303,000   E) none of these

3. For what area is the ratio $\dfrac{\text{passports}}{\text{population}}$ greatest?

   A) Northeast   B) Pacific   C) North Central
   D) South Central   E) South Atlantic

4. Approximately how many passports issued in 1963 were for persons over 60 years old?
   A) 160,000   B) 173,000   C) 49,000
   D) 183,000   E) none of these

5. How many passports were issued in 1963 to government employees?
   A) 30,000   B) 5,000   C) 9,450,000
   D) 94,500   E) none of these

POVERTY
Estimated Average Poverty Thresholds, 1976

Size of Family	Total	Non-Farm	Farm
1 person, under 65 years	$2,950	$2,960	$2,530
1 person, 65 years and over	2,720	2,730	2,320
2 persons, head under 65 years	3,810	3,830	3,260
2 persons, head 65+	3,420	3,440	2,930
3 persons	4,520	4,540	3,850
5 persons	6,840	6,870	5,870
7 or more persons	9,450	9,540	8,080

Selected Characteristics: Poverty Population, 1974

Characteristic	Household heads	Number of persons
Number of poor (millions)	8.7	24.2
Number of poor (millions) who are		
Age 55 or over	3.9	5.1
Age under 17	—	10.0
Age 17–21 in school	—	0.6
Female household head with child under 6	1.0	1.0

The following statements are related to the information presented above. Based on the information given, select

A—if the statement is *supported* by the information given
B—if the statement is *contradicted* by the information given
C—if the statement is *neither supported nor contradicted* by the information given

6. There were 24.2 million people with income under $3,000 in 1974.

7. In 1974 there were 1.2 million other family members whose head of household was 55 years old or more and whose income was considered to be at the poverty level.

8. The poverty threshold in 1976 was $1,460 lower for families with 7 or more persons living on farms than for families of the same size not living on farms.

9. In 1976 there were 3.8 million households classified as "poor" whose household head was younger than 55.

10. There were more non-farm poor 3-person families than farm families of the same size.

11. According to the figure, what percentage of the male population had between a 5th- and 8th-grade education?
   A) 9%   B) 18%   C) 27%
   D) 70%   E) 84%

12. According to the figure, what is the percentage of women who have completed high school?
   A) 32%   B) 50%   C) 35%
   D) 53%   E) none of these

13. If the male population of the United States was 80 million, approximately what number of males had an 8th-grade education or less?
   A) 30 million   B) 20 million   C) 24 million
   D) 15 million   E) 32 million

EDUCATION IN THE U.S.

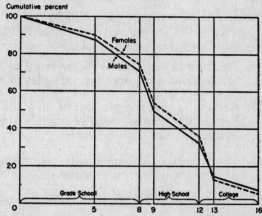

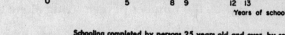

Schooling completed by persons 25 years old and over, by sex, 1950.

(Percent completing various numbers of years or more.)

14. Which of the following statements is the information contained in the figure?
   A) there were more women than men in the United States in 1950
   B) there were more men than women with a college education in the United States in 1950
   C) on the average, women had a higher educational level than men in the United States in 1950
   D) all of the above
   E) none of the above

15. The percentage of U.S. citizens in graduate schools in 1950 was
   A) less than 10%   B) between 10% and 20%   C) 0%   D) none of these

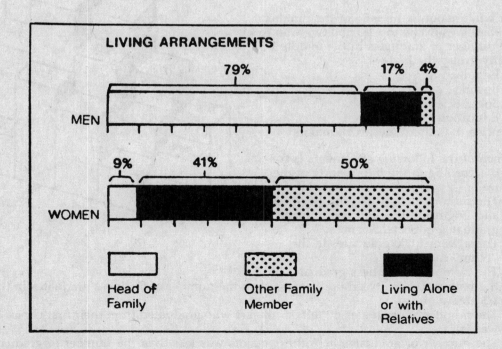

The following statements are related to the information contained in the figure at the bottom of page 261. Based on the information, select

A—if the statement is *supported* by the information given
B—if the statement is *contradicted* by the information given
C—if the statement is *neither supported nor contradicted* by the information given

16. The number of men who are head of a family is 70% greater than the number of women in the same category, assuming there are about as many men as there are women.

17. Assuming that the number of men and the number of women are about equal, if there are 5.4 million women head of families, then there are about 10.2 million men who are either living alone or with relatives.

18. The number of women who are "other family member" is about 22% greater than the number of women who either live alone or with relatives.

19. The number of women classified under the heading "other family member" is three times as large as the number of men living alone or with relatives.

20. There are about 20 times as many men who are classified as "head of family" as there are men classified as "other family member."

21. According to the figure at right, how many seniors graduated with majors in education?
    A) 325   B) 500   C) 765
    D) 975   E) 1500

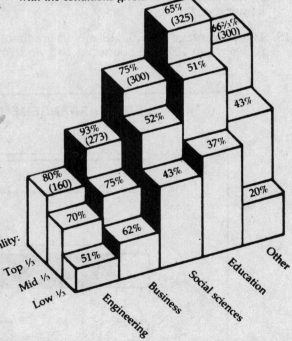

PERCENT OF COLLEGE SENIORS GRADUATING FROM THEIR FIRST-CHOICE MAJOR AT XYZ UNIVERSITY

NOTE: Figures in parentheses are the actual number of students for that ability level and major who graduated with the conditions given.

22. How many more seniors in the upper ability group graduated in their first-choice major in Business than seniors in the middle ability group in Social Sciences?
    A) 65   B) 18   C) 73   D) 70   E) 48

23. For what major is the ratio of the number of graduates in the top 1/3 ability group to the number of graduates in the middle 1/3 ability group the highest?
    A) Engineering
    B) Business
    C) Social Sciences
    D) Education
    E) none, it is the same for all majors

24. Which of the following statements is correct, according to the information in the figure?
    A) The number of graduates in Business and Engineering equals the number of graduates in Social Sciences.
    B) There were 1,000 graduates in the "other" majors.
    C) The number of Business graduates in the bottom 1/3 ability group was less than the number of Business graduates in the top 1/3 ability group.
    D) The number of graduates in "other" majors who graduated from their first-choice major was 90.
    E) The number of graduates in "other" majors was less than the number of graduates in Social Sciences

25. What is the number of Education majors who graduated from their first-choice major?
A) 325   B) 500   C) 765
D) 975   E) 1500

Health Care Expenditures Per Person, 1976

Type of expenditure	Total	Direct payments	Third-party payments			
			Total	Private health insurance	Government	Philanthropy and Industry
Hospital care	$253.70	$ 22.48	$231.22	$ 89.04	$139.20	$2.98
Physicians' services	120.67	46.70	73.97	43.51	30.37	.08
Dentists' services	39.38	31.92	7.46	5.31	2.15	....
Other professional services	10.99	5.27	5.72	1.87	3.63	.22
Drugs and drug sundries . .	51.14	43.15	7.99	3.30	4.69	....
Eyeglasses and appliances .	9.07	8.40	.66	.14	.52	....
Nursing-home care	48.54	21.12	27.42	.43	26.82	.18
Other health services	18.01	....	18.01	....	14.35	3.66
Total per person	551.50	179.05	372.46	143.61	221.72	7.13

The following statements are related to the information presented on the table above. Based on the information given, select

A—if the statement is *supported* by the information given
B—if the statement is *contradicted* by the information given
C—if the statement is *neither supported nor contradicted* by the information given

26. Private health insurance payments for hospital care covered approximately 38½% of the total cost for this category.

27. The individual, through direct payment, pays a higher percent of the cost of nursing home care than of hospital care.

28. Third-party payments account for more than 2/3 of the coverage for health care expenditures.

29. The government coverage of eyeglasses and appliances accounted for a greater percentage of the total than any other source.

30. Private health insurance is the second largest source of health care expense payment, second to the government and much ahead of philanthropy and industry.

31. According to the figure at right, approximately what percent of executives work for small and medium-sized corporations?

A) 16%   B) 20%   C) 18% D) 36%   E) 57%

32. What fraction of the executives aged 40–50 work for large corporations?
A) 1/7   B) 2/5   C) 5/9   D) 1/2   E) 3/7

33. How many more executives aged 20–25 work in large corporations than in small corporations?
A) 70,000   B) 214,000   C) 144,000
D) 87,000   E) 106,000

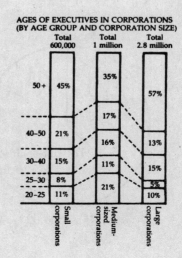

AGES OF EXECUTIVES IN CORPORATIONS
(BY AGE GROUP AND CORPORATION SIZE)

34. Which of the following statements is correct according to the information in the figure?
    1. There are more executives in the age group 20–25 working for medium-sized corporations than for large corporations.
    2. There are more executives in age group 50+ working for large corporations than all other executives combined.
    A) 1 only   B) 2 only   C) both 1 and 2   D) neither 1 nor 2

35. How many more executives are there in the 50+ age group working in large corporations than in the next-most-numerous category?
    A) 1,246,000   B) 1,232,000   C) 1,456,000
    D) 1,378,000   E) 1,204,000

The following statements are related to the information presented in the figure at right. Based on the information given, select

A—if the statement is *supported* by the information given
B—if the statement is *contradicted* by the information given
C—if the statement is *neither supported nor contradicted* by the information given

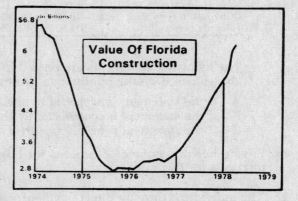

36. The value of all construction done in Florida during the year 1975 was about $4 billion.

37. Construction in Florida hit its lowest point ever around August 1975.

38. All construction done in Florida during the calendar year 1977 had an aggregate value of approximately $50 billion.

39. The value of construction in Florida during the year 1977 was more than twice the value of Florida construction during the year 1976.

40. February 1974 has the highest value for the period shown in the graph above.

Dade County

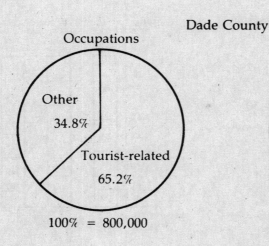

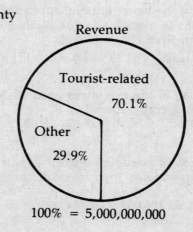

41. According to the chart at the bottom of page 264, what is the per capita revenue generated by tourist-related occupations?
   A) $8,280   B) $10,910   C) $5,720
   D) $6,730   E) $11,020

42. What is the per capita revenue generated by other occupations?
   A) $7,020   B) $5,350   C) $5,720
   D) $2,090   E) $9,220

43. What is the approximate number of degrees in the central angle of the sector for other occupations?
   A) 125°   B) 135°   C) 100°
   D) 110°   E) 160°

44. What is the approximate number of degrees in the central angle of the sector for tourist-related revenue?
   A) 180°   B) 252°   C) 270°
   D) 240°   E) 300°

45. Approximately what percent of the per capita revenue generated by tourist-related occupations is the per capita income generated by other occupations?
   A) 52.75%   B) 37.5%   C) 87.5%
   D) 62.5%   E) 79.5%

Speed of Animals

Most of the following measurements are for maximum speeds over approximate quarter-mile distances. Exceptions—which are included to give a wide range of animals—are the lion and elephant, whose speeds were clocked in the act of charging; the whippet, which was timed over a 200-yard course; the cheetah over a 100-yard distance; man for a 15-yard segment of a 100-yard run; and the black mamba, six-lined race runner, spider, giant tortoise, three-toed sloth, and garden snail, which were measured over various small distances.

Animal	Speed mph	Animal	Speed mph	Animal	Speed mph
Cheetah	70	Mongolian wild ass	40	Man	27.89
Pronghorn antelope	61	Greyhound	39.35	Elephant	25
Wildebeest	50	Whippet	35.5	Black mamba snake	20
Lion	50	Rabbit (domestic)	35	Six-line race runner	18
Thomson's gazelle	50	Mule deer	35	Squirrel	12
Quarter horse	47.5	Jackal	35	Pig (domestic)	11
Elk	45	Reindeer	32	Chicken	9
Cape hunting dog	45	Giraffe	32	Spider (Tegenearia atrica)	1.17
Coyote	43	White-tailed deer	30	Giant Tortoise	0.17
Gray fox	42	Wart hog	30	Three-toed sloth	0.15
Hyena	40	Grizzly bear	30	Garden snail	0.03
Zebra	40	Cat (domestic)	30		

The following statements are related to the information presented above. Based on the information given, select

A—if the statement is *supported* by the information given
B—if the statement is *contradicted* by the information given
C—if the statement is *neither supported nor contradicted* by the information given

46. The cheetah can run a fourth of a mile in less than 13 seconds, while the pronghorn antelope would take about 15 seconds to run the same distance.

47. A lion can beat a quarterhorse in a quarter-mile race.

48. Since T = D/R, we may conclude that an elephant can run a mile in 2 minutes.

49. Thompson's gazelles have been clocked at 50 mph over a quarter-mile distance, as have wildebeests and lions.

50. Zebras can run 40 miles in 1 hour.

Public School Attendance, Teachers, Expenditures
Source: U.S. Office of Education; Salaries cover supervisors, principals, and teachers

School Year	Pop. 5 to 17 yrs.	Pupils Enrolled	Av. daily attend.	Teachers[1] Male	Female	Total	Salary[2]	Total Expenditures
1900	21,404,322	15,503,110	10,632,772	126,588	296,474	423,062	$ 325	$ 214,964,618
1910	24,239,948	17,813,852	12,827,307	110,481	412,729	523,210	485	426,250,434
1920	27,728,788	21,578,316	16,150,035	95,654	583,648	679,302	871	1,036,151,209
1930	31,571,322	25,678,015	21,264,886	141,771	712,492	854,263	1,420	2,316,790,384
1940	29,805,259	25,433,542	22,042,151	194,725	680,752	875,477	1,441	2,344,048,027
1950	30,788,000	25,111,427	22,283,845	194,968	718,703	913,671	3,010	5,837,643,000
1960	43,881,000	36,086,771	32,477,440	392,700	962,300	1,355,000	5,174	15,613,255,000
1968 (Fall)...	52,288,000	44,961,662	41,157,000	617,805	1,324,980	1,942,785	8,200	35,511,170,000
1969 (Fall)...	52,799,000	45,618,578	42,283,000	634,358	1,379,478	2,013,836	8,840	40,561,997,000
1970 (Fall)...	52,435,000	45,909,088	42,495,346	649,250	1,411,865	2,061,115	9,570	44,423,865,000
1971 (Fall)(P)	52,133,000	46,221,000	42,800,000	682,000	1,379,000	2,061,000	10,100	47,652,000,000

(1) Prior to 1954 includes other nonsupervisory instructional staff (librarians and guidance and psychological personnel)
(2) Average annual salary per member of instruction staff, (P) Preliminary.

51. What was the expenditure (to the nearest dollar) per student in average daily attendance for the year 1960?
A) $481   B) $702   C) $20   D) $200   E) $903

52. How much was spent (to the nearest million) for expenses other than teacher salaries in 1950?
A) $3,127,000,000
B) $5,838,000,000
C) $2,710,000,000
D) none of these
E) it cannot be determined

53. The expenditure for teacher salaries was what percent of the total for the year 1940?
A) 53%   B) 97%   C) 72%   D) 47%   E) none of these

54. What percent of the population age 5–17 was enrolled in public schools in 1970?
A) 91%   B) 73%   C) 57%   D) 88%   E) none of these

55. What was the expenditure on teacher salary per pupil enrolled for the year 1970?
A) $450   B) $730   C) $670   D) $900   E) $980

Expectation of Life by Age and Sex for Selected Countries

Country	Period	Average future lifetime in years at stated age											
		Males						Females					
		0	1	10	20	40	60	0	1	10	20	40	60
North America													
United States........	1974	68.2	68.5	59.8	50.4	32.2	16.5	75.9	76.0	67.3	57.5	38.5	21.3
Canada	1970–72	69.3	69.8	61.2	51.7	33.2	17.0	76.4	76.6	67.9	58.2	39.0	21.4
Mexico.............	1975	62.8	68.0	59.2	49.9	32.7	17.9	66.6	69.3	62.6	53.1	35.3	19.1
Puerto Rico.........	1971–73	68.9	70.1	61.4	51.9	34.2	18.6	76.1	76.9	68.2	58.0	39.0	21.5
South America													
Bolivia	1949–51	49.7	56.1	54.8	46.9	33.4	20.4	49.7	55.9	54.8	47.2	32.9	19.2
Brazil	1960–70	57.6	....	56.2	47.0	30.0	15.0	61.1	....	58.9	49.7	32.5	16.6
Chile	1969–70	60.5	64.9	56.7	47.3	29.9	15.5	66.0	70.0	62.2	52.7	34.5	18.0
Colombia	1950–52	44.2	50.4	48.2	39.6	24.8	11.8	45.9	51.1	49.4	40.9	26.6	12.8
Uruguay	1963–64	65.5	68.0	59.5	50.0	31.7	15.9	71.6	73.7	65.2	55.5	36.7	19.5
Venezuela..........	1961	66.4	68.8	61.8	52.4	34.6	18.9	....	....	....	....	....	....
Europe													
Austria	1974	67.4	....	59.7	50.2	31.8	15.7	74.7	....	66.5	56.7	37.5	19.8
Belgium............	1968–72	67.8	68.4	59.9	50.3	31.6	15.2	74.2	74.5	65.9	56.1	36.9	19.2
Czechoslovakia	1970	66.2	67.0	58.4	49.9	30.6	14.6	72.9	72.6	64.9	55.2	35.9	18.3
Denmark...........	1972–73	70.8	70.8	62.2	52.6	33.7	17.0	76.3	76.1	67.4	57.6	38.3	20.8
England and Wales ..	1970–72	68.9	69.3	60.6	52.0	31.9	15.3	75.1	75.3	66.6	56.8	37.4	19.9
Finland	1972	66.6	66.5	57.9	48.4	30.1	14.9	74.9	74.6	65.9	56.1	36.8	18.8
France	1972	68.6	68.6	60.0	51.0	32.2	16.3	76.4	76.3	67.6	57.9	38.7	21.1
Germany (West)	1971–73	67.6	68.4	59.8	50.4	31.9	15.4	74.1	74.6	65.9	56.2	37.0	19.3
Germany (East)......	1969–70	68.9	69.3	60.8	51.2	32.7	16.1	74.2	74.4	65.8	56.1	36.9	19.3
Greece.............	1960–62	67.5	70.5	62.5	52.9	34.0	17.0	70.7	73.5	65.5	55.8	36.7	18.9
Hungary	1972	66.9	68.4	59.8	50.1	31.8	15.6	72.6	73.8	65.1	55.3	36.1	18.6
Iceland............	1966–70	70.7	70.9	62.4	48.4	34.6	18.0	76.3	76.0	67.3	57.5	38.2	20.5
Ireland.............	1965–67	68.6	69.5	60.8	51.2	32.2	15.6	72.9	73.4	64.8	54.9	35.7	18.4
Italy	1970–72	69.0	70.1	61.6	52.0	33.2	16.7	74.9	75.8	67.1	57.3	38.1	20.2
Netherlands.........	1973	71.2	71.2	62.6	53.0	34.0	17.0	77.2	77.0	68.2	58.4	39.1	21.1
Norway............	1972–73	71.3	71.3	62.7	53.1	34.3	17.4	77.6	77.4	68.7	58.8	39.3	21.1
Poland.............	1970–72	66.8	68.0	59.4	49.8	31.6	15.5	73.8	74.6	66.0	56.2	37.0	19.3
Portugal	1974	65.3	67.2	59.0	49.6	31.5	15.4	72.0	73.5	65.3	55.6	36.5	18.7
Scotland	1971–73	67.2	67.8	59.2	49.8	31.3	15.0	73.6	74.1	65.4	55.6	36.3	18.9
Spain	1970	69.7	....	62.0	52.4	33.7	17.0	75.0	....	66.9	57.1	38.0	20.1
Sweden............	1970–74	72.1	72.0	63.3	53.6	34.8	17.7	77.5	77.2	68.4	58.6	39.3	21.2
Switzerland	1969–72	70.2	70.4	61.9	52.3	33.6	16.7	76.2	76.2	67.5	57.7	38.4	20.4
U.S.S.R.	1971–72	64.0	....	....	....	....	....	74.0	....	....	....	....	....
Asia													
Burma	1954	40.8	49.8	45.5	36.8	21.1	10.6	43.8	51.6	47.0	38.3	23.7	12.4
India	1951–60	41.9	48.4	45.2	36.9	22.1	11.8	40.6	46.0	43.8	35.6	22.4	12.9
Israel	1974	70.1	71.1	62.5	53.0	34.1	17.4	73.3	73.8	65.2	55.5	36.1	18.3
Japan..............	1974	71.2	71.0	62.5	52.8	33.0	17.0	76.3	76.0	67.4	57.5	38.3	20.3
Jordan	1959–63	52.6	58.2	52.7	44.1	28.6	14.4	52.0	58.2	54.4	46.0	30.7	15.7
Korea..............	1970	63.0	66.0	58.0	49.0	31.0	16.0	67.0	69.0	61.0	52.0	34.0	17.0
Sri Lanka	1967	64.8	67.4	60.5	51.2	33.2	17.0	66.9	68.9	62.4	53.0	35.0	17.8
Syria..............	1970	54.5	60.7	56.4	47.4	30.5	15.2	58.7	64.1	59.5	50.5	33.3	17.3
Africa													
Egypt.............	1960	51.6	56.2	56.6	47.7	30.5	15.1	53.8	59.9	62.0	52.9	35.0	18.0
Kenya	1969	49.6	52.6	51.0	43.0	28.3	14.5	51.2	56.6	54.1	45.7	30.3	15.7
South Africa......... (white population)	1959–61	64.7	65.9	57.5	48.0	30.2	15.0	71.7	72.5	64.1	54.4	35.5	18.6
Oceania													
Australia...........	1965–67	67.6	68.1	59.5	50.0	31.4	15.8	74.2	74.4	65.8	56.0	36.9	19.5
New Zealand........	1960–62	68.4	69.2	60.7	51.2	32.5	16.0	73.8	74.2	65.6	55.9	36.7	19.3

The following statements are related to the information presented in the chart. Based on the information given, select

A—if the statement is *supported* by the information given
B—if the statement is *contradicted* by the information given
C—if the statement is *neither supported nor contradicted* by the information given

56. A 21-year-old Canadian male can expect to live to a greater age than a 1-year-old Canadian male

57. There is a higher rate of newborn mortality among Mexican males than among Danish females.

58. A 40-year-old Spaniard can expect to live until age 73.

59. A person in a category with a life expectancy of 46 can reasonably expect to live to a greater age than a person in a category with a life expectancy of 20.

60. Males of every age group in every country have a lower life expectancy than the females of the same age group of the same country.

Consumer Price Index by Groups (1967 = 100)
Source: Department of Labor, Bureau of Labor Statistics.

Items	1977	1976	1975	1974	1970	1959	1945
All items.................	181.8	170.5	161.2	147.7	116.3	87.3	53.9
Food total..................	193.6	180.8	175.4	161.7	114.9	87.1	50.7
Apparel and upkeep	153.9	147.6	142.3	136.2	116.1	88.2	61.5
Housing total..............	189.0	177.2	166.8	150.6	118.9	88.6	59.1
Rent.....................	152.9	144.7	137.3	130.6	110.1	90.4	58.8
Gas and electricity	213.0	188.8	169.6	145.8	107.3	94.7	79.6
Fuel oil and coal	283.1	250.8	235.3	214.6	110.1	89.8	48.0
House operation..........	177.1	168.5	158.1	140.5	113.4	93.1	....
House furnishings	154.7	150.7	144.4	130.8	111.4	99.0	73.3
Transportation..............	179.2	165.5	150.6	137.7	112.7	89.6	47.8
Medical care................	201.8	184.7	168.6	150.5	120.6	76.4	42.1
Personal care	170.6	160.5	150.7	137.3	113.2	88.7	55.1
Reading and recreation	157.6	151.2	144.4	133.8	113.4	85.3	62.4

The following statements are related to the information presented in the table above. Based on the information given, select

A—if the statement is *supported* by the information given
B—if the statement is *contradicted* by the information given
C—if the statement is *neither supported nor contradicted* by the information given

61. The category which showed the most marked increase from 1959 to 1967 in the table above is medical care.

62. The cost of food almost doubled between 1945 and 1967, and almost doubled again by 1977.

63. The cost of personal care was 10.1% higher in 1977 than it was in 1976.

64. The percentage change in the Consumer Price Index from 1970 to 1974 was greater than the percentage change from 1976 to 1977.

The following questions refer to the hypothetical reaction

$$2A + 3B + C \longrightarrow D + 2E$$

and the data in the table on page 269.

EXPERIMENT	INITIAL MOLAR CONC. $\times 10^2$			INITIAL RATE OF FORMATION OF D (moles/min.)
	A	B	C	
1	1.0	1.0	1.0	3.0
2	1.0	2.0	2.0	6.0
3	1.0	2.0	3.0	6.0
4	1.0	3.0	4.0	9.0
5	2.0	3.0	5.0	36.0
6	3.0	3.0	6.0	81.0

65. Doubling the concentration of A causes what percent increase in the reaction rate?
   A) 100   B) 300   C) 400   D) 800

66. Tripling the concentration of B
   A) doubles the rate
   B) triples the rate
   C) increases the rate to 9 times its value
   D) has no effect on the rate

67. Tripling the concentration of C
   A) doubles the rate
   B) triples the rate
   C) increases the rate to 9 times its value
   D) has no effect on the rate

68. What should the reaction rate be for an experiment with the following molar concentrations ($\times$ 100): A (3), B (2), and C (1)?
   A) 54   B) 18   C) 180   D) 48

SAMPLE TEST ANSWER KEY

Science Knowledge

Biology

1. B	11. D	21. A	31. B
2. D	12. C	22. C	32. C
3. A	13. D	23. A	33. D
4. B	14. B	24. B	34. B
5. C	15. A	25. B	35. C
6. C	16. B	26. D	36. A
7. A	17. C	27. C	37. C
8. D	18. C	28. A	38. C
9. B	19. D	29. D	
10. A	20. B	30. D	

Inorganic Chemistry

1. B	7. C	13. D	19. B
2. C	8. C	14. D	20. C
3. A	9. B	15. A	21. A
4. A	10. C	16. B	22. D
5. D	11. D	17. C	23. C
6. A	12. E	18. D	24. C

Organic Chemistry

1. B	8. C	15. B	22. E
2. D	9. A	16. C	23. E
3. B	10. C	17. C	24. D
4. D	11. E	18. B	25. B
5. B	12. E	19. C	
6. D	13. A	20. B	
7. B	14. B	21. A	

Physics

1. C	11. A	21. D	31. C
2. D	12. B	22. A	32. D
3. C	13. C	23. C	33. B
4. B	14. B	24. C	34. B
5. A	15. A	25. C	35. C
6. C	16. A	26. B	36. D
7. A	17. C	27. D	37. A
8. B	18. C	28. B	38. 8
9. D	19. B	29. A	
10. C	20. D	30. A	

Science Problems

1. A	6. C	11. C	16. A
2. D	7. B	12. D	17. C
3. B	8. B	13. D	18. B
4. C	9. D	14. D	19. A
5. D	10. B	15. D	20. A

21. B	33. D	45. D	57. A
22. D	34. B	46. A	58. C
23. D	35. C	47. D	59. C
24. D	36. D	48. A	60. A
25. C	37. C	49. D	61. B
26. C	38. B	50. A	62. B
27. D	39. B	51. B	63. C
28. A	40. A	52. B	64. C
29. B	41. D	53. D	65. C
30. D	42. C	54. D	66. A
31. C	43. D	55. C	
32. A	44. D	56. D	

Skills Analysis

Reading

1. B	18. A	35. E	52. B
2. E	19. C	36. B	53. A
3. B	20. A	37. E	54. E
4. C	21. B	38. E	55. B
5. A	22. C	39. C	56. A
6. D	23. A	40. A	57. D
7. B	24. B	41. B	58. C
8. C	25. C	42. C	59. A
9. D	26. B	43. C	60. D
10. E	27. A	44. C	61. D
11. B	28. C	45. D	62. C
12. E	29. B	46. C	63. E
13. B	30. B	47. A	64. C
14. A	31. B	48. A	65. A
15. D	32. A	49. A	66. B
16. C	33. B	50. D	67. C
17. C	34. C	51. B	68. C

Quantitative

1. C	18. A	35. B	52. C
2. B	19. C	36. B	53. A
3. A	20. A	37. C	54. D
4. D	21. E	38. A	55. A
5. E	22. A	39. B	56. A
6. C	23. E	40. A	57. A
7. A	24. D	41. D	58. A
8. A	25. C	42. B	59. B
9. B	26. B	43. A	60. C
10. A	27. A	44. B	61. A
11. B	28. A	45. E	62. A
12. C	29. B	46. C	63. B
13. C	30. B	47. C	64. A
14. C	31. D	48. B	65. B
15. A	32. C	49. B	66. B
16. B	33. B	50. C	67. D
17. A	34. D	51. A	68. A